MANAGING THE DOLLAR: FROM THE PLAZA TO THE LOUVRE

Managing the Dollar:

YOICHI FUNABASHI

From the
Plaza to the Louvre

INSTITUTE FOR INTERNATIONAL ECONOMICS
Washington, DC 1988

Yoichi Funabashi, a Visiting Fellow at the Institute in 1987, is the Deputy Editor for Economic Affairs for the Japanese newspaper Asahi Shimbun. *He has covered politics and economics in Japan for 20 years and was formerly* Asahi's *correspondent in Washington and Beijing and a Neiman Fellow at Harvard University. He is the author of several books, including* Theory of Economic Security *(1978),* Neibu-Inside China *(winner of the Suntory Humanities Award of 1983), and* The U.S.–Japan Economic Entanglement—The Inside Story *(1987). He was also awarded the 1985 Vaughn–Uyeda Prize—often called Japan's Pulitzer Prize—for his coverage of US–Japan economic frictions.*

INSTITUTE FOR INTERNATIONAL
ECONOMICS
11 Dupont Circle, NW
Washington, DC 20036
(202) 328-9000 Telex: 261271 IIEUR
FAX: (202) 328-5432

C. Fred Bergsten, *Director*
Ann L. Beasley, *Director of Publications*

The Institute for International Economics was created, and is principally funded, by the German Marshall Fund of the United States.

The views expressed in this publication are those of the authors. This publication is part of the overall program of the Institute, as endorsed by its Board of Directors, but does not necessarily reflect the views of individual members of the Board or the Advisory Committee.

Printed in the United States of America
92 91 90 89 88   5 4 3 2 1

Library of Congress Cataloging-in-Publication Data

Managing the Dollar: From the Plaza to the Louvre/Yoichi Funabashi

Funabashi, Yoichi, 1944-
    1. International finance.   2. Monetary policy.   3. Dollar, American.
4. Balance of payments.   5. Free trade and protection.   I. Institute for International Economics (U.S.)   II. Title.
HG3881.F847   1988
332.4'560973–dc 19   88-9239
                                                           CIP

ISBN 0–88132–071–4

Contents

Foreword

The research program of the Institute has devoted considerable attention to the functioning and possible reform of the international monetary system, on the view that effective global financial arrangements are of critical importance to the smooth operation of the world economy and to the maintenance of open trading arrangements. Our work has attempted to analyze the operation and shortcomings of the present regime of flexible exchange rates and how it might be improved in the future.

This volume is not another analytical study of international money. Rather it is a unique, fascinating, behind-the-scenes account of how the present system (or nonsystem) works in practice—and how the officials of the leading industrial countries have been trying to make it work better. It is a journalistic rendition, based on interviews with most of the leading participants, of the momentous international monetary events of the mid-1980s dating from the Plaza Agreement of September 1985 through the Louvre Accord of February 1987 and, to some extent, beyond. In its basic approach, the book parallels *The Mexican Debt Rescue* by the late Joseph Kraft, a journalistic account of the onset of the Third World debt crisis published by the Group of Thirty in 1984.

The book tells the story of two major policy initiatives. First, it traces the decision by the United States and the rest of the Group of Five to reverse their policies of the early 1980s in order to actively seek a decline in the value of the dollar, to attack the massive international payments imbalances which had emerged by 1985 and the trade protectionism which they had spawned, and the effort to implement that decision effectively. Second, it details the subsequent program, launched 17 months later at the Louvre, to try to stabilize the dollar—and why it failed to replicate the success of the Plaza. In doing so, the volume includes scores of detailed revelations of the international monetary diplomacy of the mid-1980s and its domestic political underpinnings in the major countries, as well as a coherent story of how the process came together from the Plaza to the Louvre.

The volume was written by Yoichi Funabashi, a veteran economics correspondent of the *Asahi Shimbun* and one of the leading journalists in Japan. One of Funabashi's earlier works, an in-depth study of China, won the prestigious Suntory Humanities Award of 1983 and a series of articles written during his years as Washington correspondent received a national award that is the Japanese equivalent of the Pulitzer Prize. A collection of his essays on the United States–Japan economic relationship hit the best seller list in Tokyo for a number of weeks in late 1987 and has sold well over 100,000 copies.

This book was written while Funabashi was a Visiting Fellow at the Institute during 1987. After serving for three years as the *Asahi*'s senior correspondent in Washington, Funabashi came to the Institute as the first Ushiba Fellow chosen and largely supported by the new Ushiba Foundation in Tokyo—which was created in 1986 to honor the late Nobushiko Ushiba, one of Japan's leading international statesmen and former Ambassador to the United States. Funabashi is now Deputy Editor of Economic Affairs at the *Asahi*'s head office in Tokyo.

The Institute for International Economics is a private nonprofit research institution for the study and discussion of international economic policy. Its purpose is to analyze important issues in that area and to develop and communicate practical new approaches for dealing with them. The Institute is completely nonpartisan.

The Institute was created by a generous commitment of funds from the German Marshall Fund of the United States in 1981, and continues to receive substantial support from that source. In addition, major institutional grants are now being received from the Ford Foundation, the William and Flora Hewlett Foundation, and the Alfred P. Sloan Foundation. A number of other foundations and private corporations are contributing to the increasing diversification of the Institute's financial resources.

The Board of Directors bears overall responsibility for the Institute and gives general guidance and approval to its research program—including identification of topics that are likely to become important to international economic policymakers over the medium run (generally, one to three years) and which thus should be addressed by the Institute. The Director, working closely with the staff and outside Advisory Committee, is responsible for the development of particular projects and makes the final decision to publish an individual study.

The Institute hopes that its studies and other activities will contribute to building a stronger foundation for international economic policy around the world. Comments as to how it can best do so are invited from readers of these publications.

C. FRED BERGSTEN
Director
March 1988

Preface

I would be remiss if I did not express at the outset my gratitude for the assistance received during the writing of this book. First and foremost the names of C. Fred Bergsten, Director of the Institute for International Economics in Washington, DC, and Tadashi Yamamoto, President of the Japan Center for International Exchange (JCIE) and also the Executive Director of the Ushiba Memorial Foundation, must be mentioned.

Both of them made this endeavor possible, intellectually and financially. The grant for nine months' stay in the United States and two trips to Europe and to Japan to conduct research was given by the Ushiba Memorial Foundation, a newly established, nonprofit organization in commemoration of the late Nobuhiko Ushiba, a former Japanese Ambassador to the United States. The Institute for International Economics welcomed me as a Visiting Fellow, and provided an office and solid secretarial support.

I was extremely fortunate to work with two highly competent and professional research assistants during the period of my affiliation with the Institute, first, Will Winkelstein, and later, Donna Grebe. It is no exaggeration to say that their support was indispensable.

The Institute's specialists were the best resources for my intellectual training. C. Fred Bergsten provided encouragement and stimulation to my work throughout the period. His keen sense of the news often challenged me and motivated me to probe further the Plaza strategy material. I sometimes wondered whether I had been rewarded or punished with such a tough editor in my year off from journalism.

My special thanks are also due to Thomas O. Bayard, William R. Cline, I. Mac Destler, David Finch, C. Randall Henning, Stephen Marris, Marcus H. Miller, and John Williamson, who read the entire initial draft of my manuscript and provided numerous suggestions. My special gratitude is extended to C. Randall Henning, who, from the angle of a trained political scientist, helped me to clarify vital political issues and put them into the proper context. Robert D. Putnam, a professor at Harvard University with whom I have shared a special interest in the G-7 economic summitry since the late 1970s, again encouraged and facilitated my intellectual training. I am also grateful for five senior government officials in the G-5 countries who read the manuscript. All opinions and errors, needless to say, are the sole responsibility of the author.

This book includes interviews with over one hundred government and central bank officials. All of the comments quoted, unless otherwise cited, are from my interviews with the officials on the interviews list (page 254). In most cases, I requested that the interviews be "on the record" but had to compromise that they be on a background (or deep-background) basis. Some officials gave me permission to cite them directly. With gratitude, I acknowledge the invaluable information and insight they all have provided.

YOICHI FUNABASHI
Visiting Fellow
December 1987

to Ken

Introduction

"Mr. President, I would like to tell you something very important today," Japanese Prime Minister Yasuhiro Nakasone said to President Ronald Reagan during their bilateral meeting before the Venice Summit Conference in June 1987. "Please cut the budget deficit, in serious and significant ways. Otherwise, the world economy will be in a serious situation. I think the other heads of state think the same way. Do you know why others do not ask you bluntly?"

With a smile, Nakasone looked into the twinkling eyes of Reagan.

Well, three reasons:

First, we're all protected by US defense forces; therefore, it's difficult for us to ask to cut the US defense budget.

Second, drastic budget cuts may cause a worldwide recession and create unemployment.

Third, your personal charm. We just don't dare to say to you those kinds of things before your charm. But, I have to tell you now.

Reagan did not utter a word. He just listened quietly.

Nakasone confided later that he had made up his mind that his personal mission at the Venice Summit would be to convey his grave concern about the destructive consequences of the US budget deficit. He was confident that the 6 trillion yen stimulus package had strengthened his hand sufficiently to make this special plea to Reagan.[1]

From the outset, the Plaza strategy, the economic policy coordination process initiated at the Plaza meeting by the Group of Five (G-5) countries, had as an Achilles heel its inability to effect a significant reduction in the US budget deficit. Thus, Nakasone's critical advice struck to the core of the

---

1. Interview of Prime Minister Yasuhiro Nakasone with the author.

problem—the administration's fiscal policy—but fell short of a solution for correcting it. It took the New York stock market meltdown later in October 1987 to convince the administration of the gravity of the problem.

The US administration's continued reliance on devaluation of the dollar after the crash called into question the validity of the Louvre Accord, the pact to stabilize currencies agreed upon at the Louvre meeting in February 1987. Some observers declared hastily that "the Louvre pact is dead." Others pronounced "the end of policy coordination." By the end of the year, the G-5 could not even hold a meeting for fear that the unrealistic expectations it would create would lead to a subsequent market reaction.

One G-5 central banker observed that the monetary system now operates on a "meeting standard" as opposed to a formal regime, meaning that the G-5 meetings themselves are used to maintain the momentum of cooperation and induce good behavior in the absence of systemic rules. Even this "meeting standard" now appears to be under considerable stress.

The Plaza strategy gives rise to several questions. What were its real goals? What are the long-term implications? Do the results justify efforts to build on the process initiated during the period from Plaza to Louvre? Or, should we, as some argue, abandon policy coordination? And if so, what is the alternative? A return to freely floating exchange rates? But, was the Plaza strategy not essentially a response to the anarchy of floating exchange rates?

In this book I shall try to answer these questions, appraising the Plaza strategy from the standpoint of the ideal type of policy coordination. I shall focus on the activities of the Group of Five and the Group of Seven (G-7) summits, which were the vehicles through which the Plaza strategy was promoted. The principal actors consisted of finance ministers, their deputies, and central bankers.

Each had his own political battles to fight. US Treasury Secretary James A. Baker III waged a four-front war: with President Reagan on fiscal policy; with Paul A. Volcker, Chairman of the Federal Reserve Board, on interest rates; with the Congress on protectionism; and with foreigners on growth. Finance Minister Kiichi Miyazawa's adversaries included Prime Minister Yasuhiro Nakasone and officials of the Ministry of Finance over fiscal policy; Noboru Takeshita in a factional struggle within the Liberal Democratic Party (LDP); and Baker on exchange rates. Gerhard Stoltenberg, German Finance Minister, faced formidable institutional obstacles: the proud and independent Bundesbank; the Free Democratic Party (FDP), the powerful swing party; and the European Monetary System (EMS).

Their conversations sometimes turned tense and even emotional, but on more than one occasion, potentially embarrassing scenes were avoided through humor, particularly that of British Chancellor of the Exchequer Nigel Lawson. To explain why he was late arriving at the Louvre meeting, for example, Lawson declared upon entering the room, "I'm sorry, gentlemen, for being late, but I had to take an Air France flight!"

Sometimes the G-5 was joined by representatives of two other countries, Italy and Canada, to form the Group of Seven. The Managing Director of the International Monetary Fund (IMF) also joined the group to give an evaluation of each country's economic performance in conjunction with IMF multilateral surveillance.

Meetings of the G-5 provided an opportunity for frank and spontaneous discussion of sensitive economic issues, such as exchange and interest rates. The markets, now genuinely global ones, watched vigilantly to determine what they were trying to do and gave an instant judgment whenever the G-5 or the G-7 made a statement. Yet in reality, neither the market nor the rest of us know very much about how the G-5 works. International currency diplomacy among the great powers, like issues of national security, is a sensitive and secretive area, which creates obstacles for journalists as well as scholars. After all, the Plaza strategy is still in process and most of the original participants are actively involved.

This book is a case study in the policy coordination involved in the G-5 Plaza strategy, focusing primarily on its central protagonists, the United States, Japan, and West Germany. The time frame is roughly the period from the Plaza Agreement, in September 1985, to the Louvre Accord, in February 1987. The book has three objectives. The first is to present, through original reporting and interviews with the leading actors, a comprehensive account of the Plaza strategy as it has evolved since September 1985. The second is to explain these events in the context of both domestic and international politics. This will include an examination of the roles and initiatives of the actors in relation to the economic institutions in which they operate. The final task is to analyze the Plaza strategy in terms of its implications for international economic policy coordination and regime building. I shall attempt to highlight the successes and failures of the Plaza strategy, and finally, to draw useful lessons.

To write about policy coordination among nations is to write about the entanglement of policy formulation with both politics and markets. This book is not meant primarily to analyze the economics of policy coordination but to explore the political and institutional interests that influence policy development.

The interaction between politics and the markets is a focal point of the study. From the beginning of the Plaza strategy, the actors were aware that they had to heed the hidden protagonist—the one absent from the meeting room—which was the market, particularly the currency market.

It is difficult to remember just how heated the relationships between the United States and its trading partners were in the spring and summer of 1985, especially those with Japan and West Germany. At that time, the trade-weighted exchange rate of the dollar became overvalued by about 30–35 percent. Had the prevailing exchange rate continued, the current account deficit of the United States was predicted to reach $300 billion by 1990.[2] In 1985, the United States became a debtor nation for the first time since the end of World War I. The US Congress grew annoyed with the inaction of the administration on the trade deficit and trade disputes. Likewise, the inability of the Congress to do anything about the swollen budget deficit frustrated the administration. There loomed foreboding signs of slower growth. Furthermore, thoughts of midterm elections in 1986 had an unsettling effect on the politicians. Protectionist forces raged throughout Congress, as well as through business and labor. "Smoot-Hawley would have been passed overwhelmingly in the fall of 1985," Congressman Bill Frenzel of Minnesota, a Republican free trader, later remarked.

US trading partners were utterly exasperated by the hands-off approach of the Reagan administration. They had pleaded for three years for a reduction of the budget deficit and a decrease in the value of the dollar, but their requests had fallen on deaf ears. Currency relationships oscillated wildly, straining the world trading system. Trade wars, both between the United States and Japan and between the United States and Western Europe, seemed ready to erupt. Something needed to be done. This was the environment that gave rise to the Plaza strategy.

The Plaza strategy was the political manifestation of the Reagan administration's decision to succumb to reality. It was designed and promoted by the new Baker Treasury to fulfill three main objectives—first, to combat protectionism in the Congress (short-term strategy); second, to maintain world economic growth by stimulating domestic demand in Japan and West Germany (medium-term strategy); and third, to ease the burden of debt service of the United States (long-term strategy).

The rest of the G-5 participants supported the new policy initiative primarily out of fear of the destructive effects of protectionism and of recession caused by unsustainable imbalances. Beyond their mutual concerns, each brought his own domestic concerns to the policy coordination process. The powerful Ministry of Finance in Japan sought to deflect pressure for fiscal stimulus through realignments of the yen and dollar. West German officials feared that a free fall of the dollar would sabotage arrangements in the EMS and hence pushed for a "soft-landing" scenario. The French recognized an opportunity to use policy coordination to put pressure on West Germany for more growth and a stronger commitment to intervention in currency markets. They were also eager to promote the idea

---

2. C. Fred Bergsten, statement before the Subcommittee on International Economic Policy and Trade, US House Foreign Affairs Committee, 5 March 1985.

of target zones. The British Treasury, through new efforts to manage currency relationships, wanted to link the pound sterling with the deutsche mark and later found virtue in pursuing a reference range strategy to strengthen monetary relations with EMS countries in preparation for future entry into the EMS.

The strategy was presented as a comprehensive package that included fiscal, monetary, and exchange rate policies. As a matter of fact, the finance ministers focused excessively on realignment of exchange rates because they failed to produce a means for fiscal policy adjustment. They could only agree on depreciation of the dollar, which was the sine qua non of the blitz operation to lower the dollar.

The depreciation of the dollar, however, was meant to be a long-term strategy—to be conducted on an orderly basis to avoid a "hard-landing" scenario in favor of a "soft landing." Throughout the new coordination process, relations between the two institutions responsible for economic policy making, the finance ministry and the central bank, were not always smooth.

Central bankers were cautious in employing monetary policy for the purpose of coordination, as called for in the case of the Plaza exchange rate realignment and the creation of reference ranges at the Louvre. At the root of central bank resistance to coordination was a desire to maintain institutional independence, which was sometimes given priority over price stability and economic growth. Notwithstanding the resistance of the central bankers, the finance ministers, in general, gained most of what they wanted from the central banks during the period from the Plaza to the Louvre, including a series of coordinated reductions in interest rates. It was the failure of the finance ministers to achieve serious fiscal policy coordination that led them to focus excessively on the exchange rates.

By early 1987, US interest rates started to increase sharply. Concern that the flow of foreign capital into the United States was drying up, evidenced by higher yields in US Treasury auctions, persuaded the Baker Treasury to focus on currency stability and led to the Louvre Accord. The Louvre Accord, however, heralded a fragile ad hoc process. Fiscal policy adjustment was mobilized in Japan with a 6 trillion yen stimulus package but was practically ignored in the United States and never pursued vigorously in West Germany. Monetary policy was not activated or even designed to defend the ranges for exchange rates agreed at the Louvre meeting.

The Plaza strategy produced a finance ministers' G-7 and an indicator mechanism for strengthening the monitoring of economic policy adjustments. By imposing disciplinary restrictions on Japan and West Germany through the use of indicators, the United States hoped to induce faster growth and to stimulate domestic demand. Japan and West Germany, on the other hand, resisted this "robotization" of economic policy making.[3] They recognized that an indicator system could become an instrument by which the deficit country, the United States, would be able to push more of the adjustment burden on the surplus countries, Japan and West Germany. The American design to infuse more political authority into the G-5 process of policy coordination by linking the G-5 with the G-7 Summit did not develop according to Baker's expectations. Baker had hoped that the addition of the heads of state—the highest national authorities—would expand the decision-making power of the G-5. One of the principal obstacles was the hesitancy of the heads of state to throw their political weight behind the policy coordination process.

Some might be tempted to draw hasty conclusions from the results of the Plaza strategy to date, such as, that the United States will renege on international agreements whenever it appears to be in its interest to do so. A recent example is the ignoring of the Louvre Accord by US policymakers immediately after the October crash. It is likely, moreover, that US officials can and will lower the value of the dollar further. Second, macroeconomic policy adjustment has proven ineffective against the problems of external imbalances and currency instability. It is now high time to focus more closely on microeconomic policy adjustment. Third, the failure of attempts to manage exchange rates warrants the return of floating rates.

The above conclusions can be argued forcefully, and I suspect they will attract more followers in the future. Unilateral machismo may resurface with the arrival of a new administration, and the problems of productivity and competitiveness in the United States are likely to be focal points of policy debate beyond the immediate task of budget deficit reduction. Nonetheless, based on the results of this study, I will question the validity of these conclusions. US policymakers are sure to become sensitized to international implications when formulating macroeconomic policy in the coming years. Although the possibility of destructive unilateral depreciation of the dollar cannot be ruled out, policymakers will inevitably find their options narrowed as they are forced to ensure a steady flow of financing from foreign countries. The G-7 announcement on 23 December 1987, which did not reject the Louvre reference range mechanism, amplifies more than ever before the counterproductive aspects of further depreciation of the dollar. The Louvre Accord can still be used as the foundation on which to build a more stable regime. With regard to the second conclusion above, I would point out that the lesson ought to be that macroeconomic policy adjustment did not go far enough. Considerable impediments prevented fuller activation. My conclu-

---

3. Karl Otto Pöhl, "You Can't Robotize Policy Making," *The International Economy* (Washington), October/November 1987: 20–26.

sion, instead, is that the Plaza strategy of policy coordination must be maintained and strengthened. The problem with coordination is not that it has not worked but that it has not been *made* to work fully.

Efforts to regulate the international economy are valuable and urgently needed given the increasing instability of international monetary and trade relations. System building merely for its own sake, however, does not equip countries to redress underlying imbalance and instability. To do this, there must be systematic incorporation of external considerations into domestic economic policy making.

The real test of the Plaza strategy lies in its ability to tilt national policies toward stronger international cooperation. Whether it will pass this test is, of course, part of the unfinished story.

■ *Plaza*

The Plaza Hotel meeting on 22 September 1985 of the Group of Five economic powers (G-5) has been hailed as a major initiative in international economic policy coordination. The meeting marked a reversal of the Reagan administration's hands-off approach to international economic policy— exchange rate policy, in particular—and set the stage for subsequent policy coordination among the G-5 countries.

When the finance ministers and central bank governors from the United States, Great Britain, West Germany, France, and Japan sat down at the negotiating table in New York, their immediate concerns were protectionism and the overvalued US dollar. By September 1985, four years of the Reagan administration's "benign neglect" international economic policy had resulted in a soaring dollar, high interest rates, a bloated current account deficit, raging protectionism in the US Congress, and exasperation on the part of America's trading partners.

The Plaza communiqué declared that in the present situation "some further orderly appreciation of the main non-dollar currencies is desirable" and that exchange rate policy "should play a role" in the adjustment process. The G-5 representatives stated that they "stand ready to cooperate more closely to encourage this when to do so would be helpful"—an unequivocal signal of intention to intervene in the markets.

US trading partners in the G-5 praised what they interpreted as a new American attitude toward exchange rates. "The Administration has conceded that its stance of 'benign neglect' was wrong," said a Bundesbank official . . . [and] has joined the rest of the world in saying that intervention can be helpful.[1] A Bank of France official also noted the abrupt shift in administration policy: "Suddenly Reagan's men are thinking that maybe the market isn't the best way to solve this problem."

---

1. *Business Week*, 17 October 1985.

Some US officials played down the shift in policy. One Treasury Department official said that the administration's change was "more of a rhetorical shift that hopefully will have some impact on the markets than it is a policy shift toward intervention."[2] Another added that the administration continued to reject the use of "currency intervention to buck a trend in the market."[3] But at least one Treasury official acknowledged "a major change taking place in [US intervention] policy." Whether through intervention or jawboning, President Reagan, who, according to Senator Lloyd Bentsen (D-TX), "just a couple of weeks ago was saying how a strong dollar showed how strong our nation was,"[4] clearly now wanted the dollar down.

Although the word *intervention* was absent from the communiqué the message was clear and the markets responded accordingly. After massive joint intervention on the Monday following the Sunday meeting, the dollar fell 4.29 percent against foreign currencies, the largest single-day drop in the history of the London and New York currency markets.

The details of the behind-the-scenes maneuvering before and during the Plaza meeting have never been fully disclosed. The participants often worked from secret documents, many of which had been negotiated during the preceding months both at the G-5 deputy level (G-5D) and at the bilateral level, mostly between the United States and Japan, and to a lesser extent between the United States and West Germany.

The process that culminated in the Plaza Agreement originated from exploratory talks between the United States and Japan to address the huge trade imbalances between them. Since his installation as Secretary of the Treasury in early 1985, James A. Baker III and his deputy, Richard G. Darman, discussed the necessity of reformulating US international economic policy. The first signal of a departure from the hands-off policy of their predecessors was intervention in the currency markets, which was the result of an agreement produced at the first G-5 meeting they attended on 17 January 1985. The frequency of intervention, although modest in volume, became apparent in February 1985, as the dollar became stronger. At that time, when asked whether the United States had moderated its resistance to intervention in currency markets since the January G-5 meeting, Baker said: "I think that's true, and I think that occurred as a result of the meeting."[5]

Serious efforts to manage international economic policy accelerated after

---

2. *New York Times*, 23 September 1985.

3. Ibid.

4. Ibid.

5. Tom Redburn, "U.S. Moves to Slow Rise of the Dollar," *Los Angeles Times*, 16 February 1985.

April 1985. Darman attempted to institutionalize the new approach to currency stabilization and coordination of economic policies for US trading partners, beginning with the Japanese.

In Japan, Prime Minister Yasuhiro Nakasone had directed Finance Minister Noboru Takeshita and Tomomitsu Oba, Vice Minister of Finance for International Affairs, to look into the possibility of a comprehensive strategy, including realignment, to cope with the imbalance problem that threatened the US–Japan partnership. The Japanese decided to use bilateral meetings between Baker and Takeshita to persuade the Reagan administration to move toward intervention. At a Group of Ten meeting on 22 June 1985, the finance ministers of both countries met for the first in a series of exploratory talks.

Leaning with the Wind

Japanese hopes had been kindled when David C. Mulford, Assistant Secretary of the Treasury for International Affairs, told Oba in a preparatory meeting on June 19 that Baker might propose a realignment between the dollar and the yen and that the Europeans would be asked to assist. In a discussion with Baker on June 21, the day before the G-10 meeting, Takeshita reacted favorably to Baker's proposal for a realignment and suggested following a "leaning with the wind" intervention strategy.[6]

According to Takeshita, Baker responded cautiously to the idea and stressed that macroeconomic policy coordination, not market intervention, was the key to currency realignment. Baker, showing no signs of bending on this point, instead asked Takeshita what he could do on the macroeconomic front if the United States agreed on a realignment. Would Japan boost its domestic demand? At the conclusion of the meeting, Takeshita proposed further discussion of macroeconomic problems. He said that the United States and Japan, as the two largest economic powers, should take the lead in initiating coordinated macroeconomic policy adjustment.

Although Japanese officials were disappointed by Baker's lack of commitment to intervention, some, including Takeshita, saw signs that the United States might reconsider its laissez-faire policy on exchange rates. One participant in the meeting noticed how Baker took notes while listening intently to Takeshita. "What a difference from the table-pounding Regan!"

---

6. "Leaning with the wind" intervention strategy had been advocated by C. Fred Bergsten since the fall of 1984. Its aim was gradual depreciation of the dollar in line with the perceived downward trend through mutual intervention in major currencies. See C. Fred Bergsten, "The Case for Leaning with the Wind," *Financial Times*, 24 October 1984.

he said, referring to former Treasury Secretary Donald Regan's not-so-subtle manner during discussions with Takeshita over Japan's capital market liberalization talks.

The first follow-up meeting to the Baker-Takeshita discussion was held in Paris on July 23 between Mulford and Oba at a Working Party 3 (WP-3) meeting of the Organization for Economic Cooperation and Development (OECD). Mulford informed Oba of the administration's plan for a counter-offensive aimed against congressional protectionism some time in mid-September, after Congress reconvened. He stressed the need for effective timing, explaining that a joint initiative on monetary policy could be coordinated with the proposal on trade policy. They agreed that any measures should be presented as policy packages with provisions for revised policies in each country.

They did not agree, however, on specific macroeconomic policies. The Treasury had already concluded that global demand management was needed urgently. Since the US trade deficit would force the United States to cut back its imports—not only from advanced trading partners, but also from the debt-ridden developing countries—Japan and West Germany would have to increase domestic demand to pick up the resultant slack in world demand. Mulford therefore insisted that Japan stimulate its economy, arguing that Japan needed to reform its tax structure. He stated that the Japanese government could determine the specific measures used to boost domestic demand, either through an increase in government expenditures, or by stimulating private investment. On specific issues, the Japanese side made no commitments, however, offering the excuse that, since tax reform provisions were in the process of being drafted by the Government Tax Commission, the government was not in a position to comment. Under these circumstances, fiscal policy adjustment would not be ruled out, although Baker avoided any appearance of proposing a "locomotive" strategy.* Baker's growth strategy was set.

Baker was not satisfied with the results of the July Mulford-Oba meeting and wrote to Takeshita urging that Japan take more drastic measures to boost domestic demand and lower taxes. Oba and Mulford met again in Hawaii on August 21 to refine specific measures to be included in the policy package. For the United States, the package included tax reform. For the Japanese, it included deregulation and liberalization of Japanese capital markets and flexible implementation of monetary policy. Again, Mulford attempted, unsuccessfully, to persuade the Japanese to lower their tax rates.

---

* locomotive strategy—Plan for coordination of fiscal policies created by Japan, the United States, and West Germany at the 1978 Bonn Summit. It was designed to stimulate economic growth in the three countries through measures including tax reductions and increased government expenditures.

After the Hawaii meeting, Mulford needed European support for an effective realignment, so he set off to meet his counterparts in London, Paris, and Bonn. The Europeans at first gave a lukewarm response, sensing that the administration's approach was in fact derived from a "G-2" (United States–Japan) strategy. The Germans, in particular, had ample reason for skepticism. They felt that since global external imbalances were essentially due to US intransigence on the budget deficit and to the severely strained United States–Japan relationship, there was no justification for asking the Germans or other Europeans to share the burden of correcting it. Besides that, previous attempts on the part of the Europeans to realign currencies with the Regan Treasury had met with resistance from Washington.

Yet the Europeans finally went along with the United States and Japan in preparing the package deal, after the rise of the dollar in midsummer revived concern throughout the G-5 capitals. By the time the G-5 deputies met in London in late August, their bosses were committed to the strategy ultimately launched at the Plaza.[7]

London G-5D

In a preparatory meeting in London on September 15, one week before the Plaza meeting, the G-5D (G-5 deputies) negotiated the principal points of the agreement. It was a long meeting, lasting from 8:30 in the morning until 6:00 in the evening. They hammered out differences, word by word and line by line, throughout the nine-page communiqué. German unwillingness to be treated the same as the Japanese was quite visible. German Deputy Minister of Finance Hans Tietmeyer at first strongly objected to Germany's inclusion as a "surplus country," while Mulford insisted that West Germany's surplus was a problem that should be acknowledged. Oba feared political damage at home if Japan were named as the sole offending surplus country. Finally, West Germany retreated from its opposition and settled for being named a "surplus country to a lesser extent."

The deputies had left some key points unresolved, however. The first problem concerned the language used to discuss the dollar. In short, which currency was to be named the culprit? Was the communiqué to read "the depreciation of the dollar is desirable," or instead, "the appreciation of the main nondollar currencies against the dollar is desirable"? All the deputies except Mulford maintained that the overvalued dollar was the problem, not the undervaluation of their currencies.

---

7. On the preparatory discussions see Art Pine, "To Avert a Trade War, U.S. Sets Major Push to Drive Down Dollar," *Wall Street Journal*, 23 September 1985.

The second unresolved matter hinged on the intervention. The deputies could not agree whether the decision to intervene in the currency markets should be stated explicitly or merely implied. Mulford was strongly against including the word *intervention*. He reasoned that deliberate ambiguity in the communiqué would arouse nervousness in the markets and create too strong an effect. The other deputies, while aware of the powerful groups in the US administration and the Congress opposed to an intervention policy, nevertheless wanted explicit reassurance that the United States backed the new policy. To them, any change in policy should be spelled out in the language of the communiqué. Therefore, they adopted the phrase "They stand ready to cooperate more closely," with the intention that it would be clarified later by the ministers and central bank governors.

The unclear attitude of the Treasury toward intervention added to the nervousness of US trading partners up to the very day of the Plaza meeting and prompted the three European countries to hold secret discussions on the two days preceding it, seizing the opportunity of a ministerial conference of the European Community (EC) in Luxembourg on September 20 and 21 for this purpose.

The nine participants at this meeting included Finance Minister Gerhard Stoltenberg, Bundesbank President Karl Otto Pöhl, and Vice Minister of Finance Hans Tietmeyer from West Germany; Finance Minister Pierre Bérégovoy, Bank of France President Michel Camdessus, and Vice Minister of Finance Daniel Lebegue from France; Chancellor of the Exchequer Nigel Lawson, Governor of the Bank of England Robin Leigh-Pemberton, and Vice Minister of Finance Geoffrey Littler from Great Britain. They met for two hours on Friday afternoon to assess the US move and explore the implications of the new strategy for the European Monetary System (EMS).[8] They foresaw that depreciation of the dollar might be accompanied by increased speculation in the deutsche mark, thereby straining currency rates within the EMS. In addition, they were as yet unsure whether US monetary

---

8. The European Monetary System was formed in 1979 to promote coordination of economic and monetary policies within the European Community (EC) and eliminate the use of the exchange rate as a competitive weapon. Greece and Great Britain do not participate in the support mechanism. Italy is allowed a 6 percent, rather than a 2.25 percent divergence. When in the late 1970s, as Europe once again experienced the destabilizing effects of large speculative capital movements that accompanied a falling dollar, eight EC countries created the EMS. The system is a binary one in which a country's exchange rate is defined both by the value of the Euro currency unit (ECU) in that country's currency and the bilateral rates that are calculated using the central rate (the value of the ECU in a country's currency). Whenever a currency diverges up to 2.25 percent above or below its central rate, central banks will intervene to support the currency. This is called intramarginal intervention and is not obligatory. However, beyond the margins intervention is compulsory.

authorities would really relinquish their former hands-off policy to launch into a joint intervention.

Similarly, the Japanese tried hard to guess what the Treasury had in mind as far as intervention strategy went until the last moment. In a strategy session in Takeshita's suite the morning before the meeting, Japanese Ministry of Finance (MOF) officials expressed bafflement at the US position. Was the Treasury really changing its intervention policy? Were they determined to intervene forcefully, or would they back out? Toyoo Gyoten, Director of International Finance at the MOF and noninterventionist himself, doubted the US administration's commitment. Makoto Utsumi, Minister at the Embassy of Japan in Washington, argued that the shift was real and that the United States was indeed embarking on a new course.

On Sunday 22 September 1985, at 11:30 A.M., the finance ministers and central bank governors convened for five hours in the White and Gold Room of the Plaza Hotel to forge an agreement.

Having consented to much of the Accord as fashioned by the deputies, they turned to the language snags. On the issues of how to describe the realignment and intervention, the United States prevailed. The document called for the appreciation of the yen and the deutsche mark, instead of the depreciation of the dollar. The word *intervention* was not mentioned directly.

Negotiations over one word in the communiqué proved critical. Paul A. Volcker, Chairman of the US Federal Reserve Board, insisted that the word *orderly* be inserted before the word *appreciation* to hedge against a possible free fall of the dollar. Karl Otto Pöhl and Nigel Lawson supported Volcker. In its final form, the text read, "Some further orderly appreciation of the main nondollar currencies against the dollar is desirable."

US Protectionism

One extremely important part of the announcement was the mutual pledge to fight protectionist pressures, although its importance was overshadowed by the more dramatic provisions for intervention.

To a great degree, the Plaza strategy was a response to the threat of protectionism rampant in the US Congress—a threat that would take more than a G-5 meeting to dampen. For a variety of reasons, but primarily because of the high dollar and slower growth abroad, US exports were floundering and imports were soaring. As the US trade deficit swelled during the summer of 1985, protectionism gained momentum. One bill, introduced by Senator Lloyd Bentsen (D-TX), and Representatives Dan Rostenkowski (D-IL) and Richard A. Gephardt (D-MO), would have slapped import surcharges on countries with large trade surpluses with the United States. The Reagan administration's decision in the summer not to give relief to the US footwear industry in the form of a higher protective tariff infuriated some members of Congress, including Senator John C. Danforth (R-MO), Chairman of the Subcommittee on International Trade of the Finance Committee. "There's a prairie fire burning out there," said Baker. "It's going to take considerable energy on our part to fight this."[9] With such threats to the world trading system in mind, the G-5 drew a dreary portrait of a world beset by closed markets.

During the preparatory London G-5D meeting, Mulford had proposed that the mutual pledge to fight protectionism should be assigned a high priority and be expressed in an independent section of the announcement. Section 11 warned, therefore, that "protectionist pressures, if not resisted, could lead to mutually destructive retaliation with serious damage to the world economy: world trade would shrink, real growth rates could even turn negative, unemployment would rise higher, and debt-burdened developing countries would be unable to secure the export earnings they vitally need." At the behest of the US team, each country declared its determination to resist protectionism at home. The ministers threw their weight behind the pledge.

To supplement the Plaza's macroeconomic assault on protectionism, President Reagan unveiled a carefully timed trade policy the day after the meeting. The President's "Trade Policy Action Plan" included measures to intensify unfair trade proceedings under the Office of the US Trade Representative (USTR), establish a $300 million "war chest" for the Export-Import Bank to counter foreign subsidies, tighten copyright laws, and push for a new round of GATT negotiations. The US side had hoped to hold the G-5 meeting before Labor Day, as an early assault on protectionist legislation when the Congress reconvened. The meeting was scheduled for several weeks later, however, because planning took longer than expected, and many of the ministers and governors had prior engagements. Nevertheless, the President's trade plan, coupled with the G-5's assault on exchange rates, took Washington by surprise.

The Nonpaper

For three hours in the afternoon of September 22, the ministers at the Plaza grappled with the issue of intervention strategy. How far would the realignment go? How much foreign exchange reserves would each country permit to be used for intervention? For how long would intervention continue? These questions required the most delicate negotiations because they spelled out specific actions each country would take.

---

9. *Business Week,* 7 October 1985.

Though the participants delved into nearly all aspects of intervention, they omitted details of the intervention from the communiqué, and they refused to disclose any specific information about the plan in the briefings following the meeting. Although they had agreed on an intervention strategy, they kept it secret to prevent wild speculation in the markets.

Prepared initially by the G-5D at the secret London meeting on September 15, the statement of intervention policy, dubbed the "nonpaper" because of its sensitivity, has never been made public. The original draft of the nonpaper was prepared by Mulford and distributed to the other deputies during the preparatory stage. It was so sensitive that Mulford collected the drafts when the meeting ended. According to US participants, the ministers and central bankers agreed to its basic points at the Plaza, which were incorporated in, with some modifications, the three-page nonpaper drafted by the G-5D, entitled "Points for Discussion on Intervention." This document covered a wide range of issues including rates, strategy, total scale, currency of operation, and country shares, as elaborated below.

Rates

On rates, the paper stated "a 10–12 percent downward adjustment of the dollar from present levels would be manageable over the near term," which meant a drop to 214–218 from the current yen–dollar rate of 240, and a drop to 2.54–2.59 from the current deutsche mark–dollar rate of 2.85. The moment they started to discuss the issues contained in the nonpaper, the Germans questioned the advisability of specifying targets of 10–12 percent. The French defended the targets, as did the Americans, but both Stoltenberg and Pöhl stuck to their position. Somebody resolved the stalemate by proposing to add the words *aiming at* in front of the sentence. After such movement, countries would be relieved of obligations to intervene, although a collective decision to continue could follow, as could voluntary individual operations. Although the basic thrust of the strategy was short-term, it was also agreed that "further downward adjustment would be desirable over the long term." Sharp downward movement should be avoided, they stressed. In sum, they agreed on the "desirability of a lower dollar in both short and longer term without losing control of the market."

The discussions at the Plaza included conjectures as to probable reactions of the markets. Some participants expressed anxieties about the possibility of a free fall of the dollar in the future, while others feared a dollar rebound. In general, the main concern, especially among central bankers like Volcker and Pöhl, was the possibility of the free fall of the dollar. References to specific exchange rate goals at the Plaza meeting revealed the positions of the monetary authorities. An exchange rate of 2.10–2.20 dollars to the deutsche mark was mentioned by the Germans. Takeshita at one point expressed strong support for a realignment of "at least 10 percent" between the dollar and the yen. Then he mentioned 200 yen to the dollar—about a 17 percent revaluation of the yen and equivalent to the realignment at the Smithsonian conference in 1971. "Six years ago on the very day that I was first assigned to the Finance Ministry in Masayoshi Ohira's Cabinet, the yen stood at 242. It appreciated to 219 on the day that I resigned. Thereafter I was called Minister '*Endaka*' (high yen) in Japan," Takeshita related. "This time, I will not leave office before the yen revalues up to 200," he declared.[10] One European participant contended that a rate of 200 yen to the dollar was still not enough for the yen. "I had 190 in mind as well," recalled another European participant who pointed out that the Europeans had tried to differentiate the rate of dollar realignment with the yen from the rate of dollar realignment with the European currencies.

Takeshita may have tried to forestall European interference by mentioning 200 yen. From the start, the Europeans did not hide their lack of enthusiasm for the Plaza strategy, for they thought that the "problem of the overvalued dollar" was between Japan and the United States. They had argued even in preparatory meetings that the yen and European currencies should appreciate differentially against the dollar. Within the US administration, some likewise voiced a preference for a differential realignment of the yen and the deutsche mark. A range of 10–12 percent was proposed by the United States for the first time at the Plaza. In the nonpaper discussed in London a week before, the figure had been left out deliberately. This range was regarded as an American effort to accommodate the Europeans who sought differentiated realignment between European currencies and the dollar on the one hand and the yen and the dollar on the other hand. In fact, the primary motivation was to blur the figure to make it more acceptable to those participants with a known aversion to anything resembling fixed targets. Thus, the G-5 nonpaper stated that it would be desirable to avoid major distortions in yen–European currency relationships, although some changes in the current crossrates might be unavoidable. At the Plaza, the Europeans once again reminded Japan of their concerns.

Strategy

The basic strategy was to resist appreciation of the dollar, recognizing that resistance to its rise could lead in time to a decline of the dollar. Maximum

---

10. Three participants, in the United States and Europe, confirmed Takeshita's remarks on the 200 rate. One Japanese participant denied the episode.

intervention would take place when the dollar showed strength, with less aggressive operations contemplated at progressively lower dollar levels.

In the interest of preventing a reversal of the direction of currency realignment, it was agreed that decisions on intervention would be made from day to day. Monetary authorities would manage currency realignment with the use of ratchet-like adjustments based on daily market conditions to maintain a steady course of realignment. Expressing concern that the dollar might decline too fast and too far, however, they declared themselves "prepared to support the dollar if necessary stemming from excessive dollar decline or disorderly markets." During the meeting, it was Pöhl who insisted that the central banks should be allowed to intervene should the dollar decline too fast, and so it was agreed.

Total Scale

The intervention period was established at six weeks with the total amount of the intervention set at $18 billion. Maximum daily operations in each participant market were envisaged "on the order of $300–400 million." The participants were mindful of the different market conditions each would have to face, however, causing maximum levels to be exceeded on some days in individual markets or even in the total of all markets. It was not expected that maximums could be reached each day to carry out the agreed-upon strategy. Each central bank would be allowed to intervene in other markets subject to prior consultation. This provision formed part of the plan for intervention in currency markets to cope with the globalization of markets, now open 24 hours a day.

Currency of Operation

The document recognized that the basic currencies used for operations should be the dollar, the yen, and the deutsche mark, although, on occasion, the United States would be prepared to purchase pounds sterling and French francs if others were prepared to do the same; the Bundesbank and the Bank of England could purchase French francs. The United States made it clear, however, that it would not be prepared to purchase non-G-5 currencies, thus revealing its refusal to commit itself to defense of the parity band of the EMS currencies, especially weaker ones such as the Italian lira, if the operation should cause pressure on the EMS mechanism. In this connection, the document specified that EMS participants—that is, West Germany and France—should avoid purchasing dollars for EMS-related interventions. Furthermore, the G-5 was discouraged from purchasing dollars—a warning against the temptation to replenish dollar reserves when the value of the dollar went down.

Proportion of Action

In the prepared nonpaper, intervention shares were assigned in the following way:

United States	25 %
Germany	25 %
Japan	25 %
United Kingdom	12.5%
France	12.5%

Nonetheless, the participants recognized that although these proportions should represent a broad objective over time, it might not be possible or appropriate to achieve them if the strategy were to be maintained. If the "actual shares depart from agreed shares over time," then "consideration should be given to a sharing arrangement."

The Europeans contended that the United States and Japan should share more of the burden. They also held that a depreciating dollar would create tensions within the EMS, forcing the deutsche mark to the top of its band and pushing the French franc to the bottom. Furthermore, from practical considerations of the way the EMS works, they argued that European intervention should be treated collectively instead of individually. In this way, Great Britain could "do" some of the German intervention as long as the total amount of European intervention was equal to the three individual shares.

The United States offered the following compromise plan:

United States	30%
Germany	25%
Japan	30%
United Kingdom	5%
France	10%

The Europeans, however—especially the Germans—were opposed. They proposed an alternative formula in which the United States and Japan would have a share of 30 percent each, and EMS 35 percent, collectively, with the United Kingdom having 5 percent.

The nonpaper also dealt with relations between the finance ministries and central banks—a delicate problem for all monetary authorities. "The central bank should have flexibility of operations consistent with internal relationships between central banks and ministries," it said, clearly indicating the expectation of the finance ministry officials that the central banks would cooperate fully with them on the intervention and the monetary policy front. To facilitate closer contact, they also stressed the need to strengthen interfinance-ministry consultations and consultations between finance ministries and central banks, although they made no specific recommendations for how this was to take place. The sensitivity of the matter was also illustrated in the way monetary policy was described in the paper. The section entitled "Implications for Interest Rates" omitted any mention of the subject except for one notation in parentheses that it was to be discussed.

As will be elaborated in later chapters, the central bank governors did not discuss the implications for interest rates and monetary policy coordination at the Plaza. They considered it too sensitive a topic to be discussed in the presence of politicians. They endorsed the basic principles of flexible response under various conditions and a commitment for close contact, however. Almost two months after the Plaza meeting, central bank currency specialists of the principal countries met secretly in Basel to discuss the more technical matters of exchange rate and monetary policy with regard to the Plaza strategy. A byproduct of this cross-agency consultation was more direct contact between the Bundesbank and the US Treasury and continuing discussion between the Japanese Ministry of Finance and the Federal Reserve Board.

Finally the Plaza participants confirmed that they must not reveal any indication of amounts or other details to the media and that they needed to adopt a consistent approach to answering questions concerning the intervention strategy. The deputies had drafted anticipated "questions and answers" before the Plaza meeting on which they agreed.

Following their discussion of intervention strategy, the Plaza participants returned to drafting the statements setting out each country's commitments and responsibilities. The United States pledged to continue its efforts to reduce the fiscal deficit by 1 percent of GNP for fiscal 1986 and to make "further significant reductions in subsequent years." Japan agreed to stimulate domestic demand by increasing private consumption and investment, to be accomplished through enlarged consumer and credit markets. Japan's fiscal policy was to focus on reducing the central government budget deficit and providing a positive-growth environment for the private sector. West Germany committed itself to reducing the role of the public sector in the economy through tighter spending and affirmed its planned 1986 and 1988 tax cuts.

The Politics of Intervention

As previously mentioned, the G-5 announcement sent the dollar sharply downward in world currency markets. In New Zealand's Wellington market, the first to open on Monday September 23, the dollar fell from its pre-Plaza level of 239 yen to the dollar to 234 to the dollar. With Tokyo closed for a holiday, the first central bank operations took place in Europe. The dollar had fallen against major foreign currencies (around 230 yen to the dollar) by the time the Bundesbank stepped in to sell dollars that afternoon in Frankfurt for the first time in more than six months. By the time the New York market opened, the yen was trading at 231 yen to the dollar—a sign that it was rebounding from its lowest level. The US authorities conducted the first operation, selling dollars for yen and deutsche marks, and the dollar closed at 225.5 yen to the dollar—a clear manifestation of the tremendous impact of US intervention on the markets.

During the next few days, the market eyed the dollar's drop skeptically, questioning its permanence. The phenomenon was most dramatic in the Tokyo market, which opened on Tuesday, September 24, after a three-day weekend, with strong dollar demand from corporations and investors spurring the largest turnover on record for spot dollar–yen trading. The Bank of Japan (BOJ) responded with massive dollar sales. "The climax came between 10:30 and 11:00 in the morning. I was almost about to give up the defense line. But I stuck to intervention and told the MOF desk to sell dollars as much as possible," recalled Mitsuhide Yamaguchi, Vice Minister of Finance for Domestic Affairs. Japan's published foreign exchange reserves dropped by nearly $1 billion during the month of September.

During the last week of September and the first week of October, US authorities sold a total of $199 million against the deutsche mark and $262 million against the yen. In the two weeks beginning October 7 the dollar came under heavier upward pressure. The demand for dollars accelerated when the annual World Bank–IMF meetings in Seoul, Korea, concluded without any announcement of additional policy coordination. The G-5 ministers and central bank governors merely reaffirmed their earlier strategy, and some statements attributed to monetary officials in European countries were interpreted as expressing satisfaction with the extent of depreciation of the dollar, suggesting that it would not go much farther.

Both the Federal Reserve Board and the Bank of Japan continued to intervene forcefully. The Fed went so far as to make its first direct intervention in the Tokyo market, in accordance with the new intervention scheme agreed on at the Plaza. A Bank of Japan official immediately leaked the information to the Japanese press in Seoul in an effort to combat upward pressure on the dollar in the Tokyo market by demonstrating the solidarity of central banks. The dollar rebounded persistently, however, first against the deutsche mark in mid-October, then against the yen in late October.

On October 16, as the dollar staged its strongest rebound since the Plaza, the US monetary authorities sold $797 million against the deutsche mark. During the last two weeks of October, upward pressure on the dollar against the deutsche mark abated, but pressure against the yen was slower to subside, despite the announcement by the Japanese government on October 15 of a stimulus package to increase domestic demand. The United States had sold $483 million against the yen during the six weeks following the Plaza.[11]

The central banks had ended their intervention mission by the end of October. The only operation the US monetary authorities conducted during the next three months, from November to January, was on November 7, when the dollar rose significantly against both the yen and deutsche mark.[12] On that day Japanese authorities made a final stand in the market by selling dollars. "The dollar was about to rebound from 205. So we hit the move. That was the last operation to appreciate the yen. Afterward, the prospect of the oil price decline lowering the interest rate pushed the dollar downward," recalled a Japanese Ministry of Finance official.

The dollar ended October some 13 percent down from the level at which it had traded during the week before the G-5 meeting in relation to the yen, 10.5 percent down in relation to the deutsche mark, and 8 percent down in relation to the pound sterling. The initial goal of 10 to 12 percent realignment had already been accomplished.

The magnitude of collective intervention was impressive, although the $18 billion "war chest" was not completely expended. The impact of intervention exceeded the expectations of the Plaza participants. With unconventional openness, Sam Cross, Director of the Operations Desk of the New York Federal Reserve Bank, boasted of the success of mutual intervention and revealed specific figures on the amount of intervention of other countries between the Plaza meeting and the end of October: total intervention sales of dollars by the United States came to $3.2 billion; those by the central banks of Japan, West Germany, France, and Great Britain amounted to $5 billion; and those by the central banks of the remaining G-10 countries exceeded $2 billion.[13]

Although the *Federal Reserve Board of New York Quarterly Review* did not specify individual contributions by US trading partners in the G-5, Kiichi

---

11. *Federal Reserve Bank of New York Quarterly Review* 10 (Winter 1985–86): 47.

12. *Japan Economic Institute Report* (Washington), 13 December 1985.

13. *Federal Reserve Bank of New York Quarterly Review* 10 (Winter 1985–86): 47.

Miyazawa, then Chairman of the Liberal Democratic Party's Executive Council, said Japan had spent $3 billion through late September to early November.[14] Evidently, the monetary authorities had meant what they said this time.

The immediate effect of the G-5 announcement at the Plaza on dollar exchange rates, in part, reflected the fact that the announcement was unexpected. More importantly, market participants noted that the initiative had come from the United States and saw it as a change in the US government's strong-dollar policy. Furthermore, the agreement was interpreted as having eliminated the likelihood that the Federal Reserve Board would tighten reserve conditions in response to rapid monetary growth.[15]

Despite what appeared to be a highly coordinated plan of action, the ministers and governors left three crucial issues of intervention strategy unresolved when they left the Plaza Hotel. First, they had not agreed to the pace or extent of dollar depreciation beyond the 10 to 12 percent target set for the initial six-week phase. Second, they failed to formulate a plan to divide the costs of European intervention among the G-5 members of the EMS, part of the broader unresolved issue of how EMS currencies should be related to the dollar and the yen for international monetary stability. Third, the group had not specified how the exchange rate realignment would interact with monetary policy.

Pace

While the Plaza participants had broadly agreed to "aim at" lowering the dollar by about 10–12 percent over six weeks, they did not decide how far and how fast it needed to drop beyond that, although they envisaged the need for general depreciation over the long run. At the US Treasury, some supported a final goal of 165–170 yen to the dollar. However, the American negotiating team—Baker, Darman, and Mulford—were careful to avoid any mention of a target for fear of alienating top officials in the administration who regarded dollar targets with suspicion and ideological disdain. Japanese officials considered levels of, first 210, and then 200 yen to the dollar in a two-stage approach, an appropriate goal after the initial shift of 10 percent, but they kept their wishes to themselves.

German officials were reluctant to commit themselves to any further target for depreciation of the dollar. Nevertheless, they did have figures in mind,

---

14. Ibid., 46.

15. Ibid., 46.

which they did not disclose to the others. Their first line was 2.60–2.65 deutsche marks to the dollar, with a second of 2.10–2.20 deutsche marks to the dollar. After barely two weeks had passed, the dollar had dropped 7 percent to 2.65 deutsche marks to the dollar, and Bundesbank President Pöhl declared that the dollar had fallen to a level "acceptable to us."[16] The apparent resistance of Germany to the currency plan displeased US Treasury officials. Assistant Secretary Mulford complained that Germany had been the "least responsive" of the five to the Plaza strategy and had "not satisfied" the administration. Pöhl contended that "too much is now being interpreted into the agreement" and tried to remind US officials that the G-5 had made "no commitments or agreements of any sort" toward target zones.

Volcker and Pöhl had both expressed their concern about the possible free fall of the dollar during the Plaza meeting. They both felt that dramatizing the Plaza Agreement might spark panic in the markets. Pöhl had warned Stoltenberg on numerous occasions to be careful. "It is very hard to trigger an avalanche, but once it starts, it is much harder to stop."[17] According to a participant in the meeting, Pöhl urged that the five countries "move [the dollar] down step by step."

Volcker also showed the same concern. Volcker believed that "self-reinforcing, cascading depreciation of a nation's currency, undermining confidence and carrying values below equilibrium levels, is not in that nation's interest or that of its trading partners."[18] He was particularly anxious that dollar depreciation would reduce capital inflows, requiring a rise in interest rates as a result. He was constantly aware of the ominous implications of US debtor status for monetary and overall economic policy.

"The fact that we had a large current account deficit and that we had to finance a debtor position was a matter of concern to Volcker at the Plaza," said a senior Treasury official later. The Treasury, however, took a different view. The same official explained, "[These factors] were never a concern to me because in my view, we could depreciate the currency without the threat of raising interest rates and without scaring away investors because the fundamentals in the United States were still very strong, very sound. . . . I thought the market was . . . with us."[19]

Both Volcker and Pöhl had personally seen the dangers of the strategy of depreciation of key currency in the early 1970s. Long experience as international money men made them cautious. A confidante of Pöhl testified that

---

16. *Wall Street Journal*, 9 October 1985.

17. Interview of a Bundesbank official with the author.

18. Paul A. Volcker, testimony before the US Senate Banking Committee, 23 July 1986.

19. Personal interview.

the Bundesbank president had a highly developed instinct for danger—perhaps the most valuable trait for a good central banker.[20] Volcker had long ago earned a reputation for his intuition. Both men felt that the newcomers on the scene were too inexperienced to be playing this dangerous game. Both hesitated to endorse the down-with-the-dollar fanfare at the Plaza, though they were not opposed to realignment to avoid the hard landing of the dollar. To be sure, they preferred a gradual approach to realignment. Volcker had argued for the need to correct the overvalued dollar since early 1985. In late 1984 the Federal Reserve Board staff had already concluded, internally, that the United States should move toward the weaker dollar because the current account deficit could not be sustained. Pöhl was of the same view, and he took the lead in promoting intervention both in the fall of 1984 and early 1985.

Eventually the two central bankers went along with the finance ministers' proposal, perhaps feeling that a soft landing could be engineered more effectively if political will and authority were linked to macroeconomic policy changes than if depreciation were left completely to the vicissitudes of the market. The finance ministers also supported the soft-landing strategy, as illustrated in the nonpaper, which emphasized "manageable downward adjustment of the dollar."

At the same time, most of the finance ministers and their deputies were more concerned about a dollar rebound than a free fall. US trading partners remained unconvinced that the United States was committed to intervention. At the Treasury Department fears lingered that a failure to depreciate the dollar would exacerbate the congressional protectionist fever in the US Congress. The concern over a possible dollar rebound and the failure of the realignment should not be underestimated. "With hindsight, you can easily argue that the dollar decline was doomed to proceed steadily since February 1985, therefore market forces dictated the whole thing. But, we were genuinely worried about the dollar's rise at the time," confided a senior State Department official. The rebound of the dollar in midsummer of that year heightened their worry.

The 10–12 percent depreciation target for the dollar was another source of uncertainty during the negotiations. Although the figure was seen neither as a "mathematical figure" nor as the "final target but the first stage," as a French official put it, the Germans were reluctant to endorse it. "It's all nonsense," confided one German participant later. After all, some even questioned the legitimacy of the nonpaper. The Germans considered the nonpaper an agenda for discussion, but did not endorse it formally. "Comments were made on each point by all of them. . . . Some parts were

---

20. Interview of a Bundesbank official with the author.

agreed, but others were not," explained a German official later. The British position was similar. One British official characterized it simply as "a sketchy summary." A Japanese official bemoaned its lack of procedure and later admitted that because of German opposition, he was uncertain how binding the intervention agreement really was. On the other hand, the US participants emphasized that the nonpaper had been accepted at the meeting, even though one US official admitted that they had agreed on everything in the nonpaper except for the *rates*, which was why the expression "aiming at" was added.[21]

Cost

During the G-5 meeting, the question of how much each country would contribute toward intervention became a major source of contention, each country seeking to avoid bearing more than its fair share of the burden. Although the five agreed to distribute the "cost" of intervention roughly by thirds among the United States, Japan and Europe, the timing and amount of intervention proved a politically delicate operation.

The Germans failed to intervene to Washington's satisfaction after the Plaza meeting. Part of their distrust dated from January 1985, when the G-5 agreed in Washington to attack "disorder" in the markets, a statement that Bonn interpreted as a pledge to bring down the soaring dollar. The Germans had proceeded to conduct a massive intervention operation, only to find their allies conspicuously absent from exchange markets. From the end of the G-5 meeting in January until March 1, US monetary authorities had in fact intervened in the market—on two occasions in late January and three times in February—selling a total of $659 million against foreign currencies,[22] but although such intervention could be seen as a stepping stone to the Plaza strategy, the Germans did not regard it as satisfactory because of what they perceived as a half-hearted US position. Furthermore, since the Japanese authorities generally kept completely out of sight, Bonn felt betrayed.

At the Plaza, Oba responded to German criticism by pointing out that the yen had stabilized during the winter of 1985 and that the situation was not, in the expression of the Washington G-5 agreement, "disorderly." He then reminded Pöhl that in the case of the current agreement, he should remember that Monday, September 23 was a Japanese holiday (celebrating the vernal

---

21. Personal interview.

22. *Federal Reserve Bank of New York Quarterly Review* 10 (Spring 1985):60; and 10 (Autumn 1985):52.

equinox) and that the Japanese markets would be closed. (In his hotel room on the previous night, Oba had consulted a Japanese-English dictionary to make sure that he used the right word for vernal equinox.) "Now you have another excuse," Pöhl shot back, provoking a rare burst of laughter in the otherwise tense meeting. The Germans contended that the Bundesbank had already assumed a disproportionate share of the intervention burden before the Plaza, a share that should be factored into the new strategy. German officials later said that their intervention in February and March of 1985 triggered the long decline of the dollar. One official said that the German operations altered market sentiment fundamentally and marked "the beginning of the turnaround."

Indeed, as their skepticism at the Plaza seemed to predict, the Germans did not intervene after the Plaza as heavily as did the United States or Japan. For one thing, they did not consider the agreement compulsory. "We never never believed in [setting] an amount," a German participant said later. Instead, the Germans saw the agreement on intervention as a mere "signal" of intentions and that intervening with a set amount for the sake of an agreement would be imprudent. "You have to look at market development," continued the German official. West Germany was also constrained by its responsibility as the de facto leader of the European Monetary System.[23] As will be seen in chapter 3, it is essential to appreciate West Germany's position within the context of the EMS to understand the German Plaza strategy. To the Germans, it was as important to minimize the effect of depreciation of the dollar on the EMS as it was to realign the currencies to prevent the import of inflation that would occur with a weak deutsche mark. That is the reason Pöhl insisted so passionately on gradual and orderly dollar depreciation, or a "soft-landing strategy." A rapid appreciation of the deutsche mark would drive all the EMS currencies upward in relation to non-EMS currencies unless EMS countries simultaneously sold deutsche marks. If they did not, the band within which each currency is fixed would be strained. The weakest currency with a higher domestic inflationary rate would be sold because the markets would anticipate the realignment. Both the Germans and the French were deeply worried about the downward pressure on the French franc and the upward pressure on the deutsche mark created by its realignment with the dollar. It was, in fact, the main point of discussion in the secret meeting of West Germany, France, and Great Britain in Luxembourg immediately before the Plaza.

Exchange rates among EMS currencies respond unevenly to fluctuations

---

23. Niels Thygessen, Minutes of Evidence before the Subcommittee on the European Communities, UK House of Lords, 3 May 1983, 152.

of the dollar. The deutsche mark tends to move either upward or downward more sharply than the other EMS currencies because it is a substitute for the dollar as an international store of value. The growing international importance of the deutsche mark poses a dilemma for the Bundesbank, which refuses to lend deutsche marks to finance intramarginal intervention. Since a central bank that wants to intervene "intramarginally cannot have easy access to other EMS currencies because of the Bundesbank's refusal to let the deutsche mark be used," the dollar has become the natural vehicle for intervention within the EMS. On the other hand, the United States has not shown the slightest interest in diversifying its own interventions in such a way as to enhance the cohesiveness of the EMS—by buying the weakest EMS currency and selling the strongest, as was recommended in the nonpaper.[24] The refusal of the Bundesbank to allow the use of the deutsche mark for intramarginal intervention means that other EMS members do not hold deutsche marks in their official portfolios. These countries therefore have an incentive to accumulate dollar reserves with which to purchase deutsche marks that will be used subsequently to defend EMS margins. The first reaction of the other members of EMS after the Plaza meeting would logically have been to buy dollars so as to enhance their dollar reserve position.

This type of action could counteract mutual efforts of the G-5 to devalue the dollar and could, furthermore, destabilize the EMS if the Bundesbank were selling dollars and buying deutsche marks at the same time that other EMS members were buying dollars and selling deutsche marks, because this would accelerate the upward pressure on the deutsche mark in relation to the other EMS currencies. One of the solutions to this dilemma is the "Intervention Redistribution Plan," an internal bilateral swap line in the EMS, by which West Germany can lend dollars that such countries can sell in order to buy their own currencies aiming at softening the upward drive of the deutsche mark relative to those currencies when the dollar is depreciating. This was the solution adopted.

In effect, the EMS countries outside the G-5—such as Italy, Belgium, the Netherlands, Denmark, and Ireland—would bear the burden of an agreed-on intervention plan they had no part in fashioning. Faced with an appreciating currency in their midst, they could be expected to sell that currency to prevent their own from appreciating concurrently. Mindful that such actions, particularly from such a player as Italy, would defeat the purpose of the Plaza exercise, Pöhl and French central banker Michel Camdessus agreed to share responsibility for notifying the EMS partners of the currency plan.

---

24. Personal interview.

Pöhl telephoned Governor of the Bank of Italy Carlo Ciampi on the morning of September 24 to inform him of the G-5 decision, telling him "it would be absolutely counterproductive" to the Plaza strategy if Italy sold deutsche marks to maintain EMS parity levels. In addition, Pöhl warned, selling deutsche marks and buying dollars would weaken the lira because Italy's foreign reserves, held largely in dollars, would depreciate. According to a Bundesbank official, Italy was "very cooperative" and sold $2 billion in dollar reserves, $500 million of which was lent from the Bundesbank under the bilateral intervention redistribution plan.

Lamberto Dini, Deputy Governor of the Bank of Italy, later confirmed the swap-line operation and made it clear that Italy had sold one-half of the $6 billion total European intervention—equal to that of the US Federal Reserve. "So we did play, in this regard, a very important role in the strategy," he said.[25]

The friction between the United States and West Germany concerning intervention carried over to the Paris G-5D meeting on 13 November 1985. At that meeting Mulford criticized Tietmeyer for not honoring the agreement to intervene made at the Plaza. Tietmeyer responded that Europe's intervention should be counted collectively, not country by country. As exemplified by Italy's intervention, Europe as a whole had lived up to the pledge, said Tietmeyer. Later a Bundesbank official complained bitterly that West Germany was in no position to sell dollars on a large scale because it would have strengthened the deutsche mark within the EMS, putting pressure on the other EMS members. The official said that the other Europeans "had to sell dollars instead of us" and complained that the Americans "never understood" the mechanism of the EMS. On this basis, Pöhl and Stoltenberg agreed that American criticism of West Germany for insufficient intervention was unwarranted. As a matter of fact, US monetary authorities were fully aware of the EMS mechanism. Yet they were not convinced of the German argument claiming EMS intervention as part of the Plaza Agreement. A Treasury official later expressed his views on the issue as follows:

We would have preferred that the Germans had engaged in more direct deutsche mark–dollar exchange. We were well aware that the Bundesbank was financing a substantial part and that exchange to us is an EMS problem. That is not the EMS versus the other two currencies (the dollar and the yen). That is an intra-EMS financing problem that does not count in a sense as moving the EMS against the other two currencies.[26]

---

25. Personal interview.
26. Personal interview.

The skeptical attitude of the United States regarding the EMS is rooted in the origins of that body. During the late 1970s, when Chancellor Helmut Schmidt proposed its creation, the EMS was perceived in some quarters in Washington as having a distinctly anti-American thrust. Some of its proponents had criticized the Carter administration's neglect of exchange rate policy and had portrayed the EMS as a defensive system. Although there was considerable sentiment in the Treasury against the formation of the EMS, neither Anthony M. Solomon, Under Secretary of the Treasury, nor C. Fred Bergsten, Assistant Secretary of the Treasury, wanted to oppose it. Interference by the State Department—urging the Treasury not to oppose the EMS publicly—also influenced the Treasury's decision to take a neutral stance. The coolness of the Treasury toward the EMS, however, lingered after the Reagan administration had taken over in Washington. "After all, the EMS is irrelevant to the dollar and the yen," asserted a senior US official.[27]

While arguing that it was not bound by the intervention strategy, West Germany hastened to criticize the United Kingdom for its neglect of the agreement. At the Plaza, the United Kingdom's delegation had made clear its reluctance to endorse the intervention strategy. The British pound, not an EMS currency, had grown stronger during the summer of 1985 from its low ebb earlier in the year. Indeed, Lawson asserted that Britain took note of, but did not agree to, the terms of the nonpaper. In the eyes of the German officials, however, the British operation "was not consistent with the spirit of the agreement." They claimed that the British, on some occasions, were busily purchasing dollars to replenish reserves depleted by heavy support of the pound in early 1985 in spite of the pledges to avoid doing so.

While the Americans may have been disappointed with West Germany's contribution to the realignment, they were wholly satisfied, at least initially, with Japanese efforts. Indeed, Takeshita, at Kennedy Airport in New York on his way back to Japan, instructed the Japanese delegation to tell Mitsuhide Yamaguchi to intervene on the 24th "as decisively as possible." The following day, Yamaguchi called an emergency meeting at the MOF headquarters with the aim of selling enough dollars to make the yen appreciate from 240 to the dollar to 230 to the dollar as soon as possible. The Japanese were determined to fight the buying drive for the dollar in the Tokyo market.

"Since we initiated the Plaza strategy with Baker, we thought we would lose face if the dollar rebounded in the Tokyo market," a top MOF official said later.[28] When Yamaguchi was in command of an intervention operation

---

27. Personal interview.

28. Personal interview.

during the crucial hours of the morning of September 24, all the members who attended the Plaza meeting were still on the plane. Before he ordered the MOF desk to intervene "as decisively as possible," he sought approval for the intervention from Yoshihiko Yoshino, Director of the Budget Bureau at the MOF, explaining that the government would lose about 20 yen per dollar whenever the Bank of Japan intervened in the market and the whole operation might amount to a loss of tens of billions of yen. Yoshino approved. On the plane back to Japan, Takeshita and Oba wagered on how much the yen had appreciated in the Tokyo market. Just before they got on board, the yen registered 225 in the New York market. Both of them bet that the yen would have appreciated to a little above 225. Upon arriving in Tokyo, both were disappointed to find the yen hovering around 230. The Japanese authorities continued to intervene on a grand scale throughout October.

A top BOJ official later explained that Pöhl's skepticism of Japan's pledges, European insistence on driving the yen farther upward in relation to the European currencies, and the agreement on a ratchet intervention policy were three major factors behind Japan's decisive market operations.[29]

Monetary Policy

It is interesting to note that for all the talk at the Plaza about intervention, the participants did not fully discuss monetary policy coordination. The G-5D had broached the idea of coordinated interest rate reductions in preparatory meetings before the Plaza, but the September meeting yielded no specific arrangements. "There was discussion of interest rates, but there was not an agreement reached in the Plaza to have a coordinated interest rate reduction," said one US Treasury official.[30] In the preparatory stage, officials of the MOF appeared willing to commit themselves to the rate cut, but only on the condition that the other countries would go along with it. After learning that the Germans showed no interest in the measure, they, therefore, toned down their commitment noticeably.

Some Japanese newspapers speculated after the meeting that the BOJ would soon lower the discount rate as part of its commitment to "flexible management of monetary policy."[31] Contradictory reports also surfaced in Japan that the BOJ would maintain the discount rate to help devalue the

---

29. Personal interview.

30. Personal interview.

31. "Tax cut and reduction of interest rate surfaces as next issues," *Mainichi Shimbun,* 25 September 1985.

dollar.[32] The vagueness with which the G-5 had handled monetary policy became all too apparent when, to the dismay of Volcker, the BOJ suddenly raised the short-term interest rate in late October. This action, which was considered equivalent to a one-percent increase in the discount rate, was designed by the Business Bureau of the BOJ to cool bond markets and, secondarily, to strengthen the yen. Volcker, fearful lest a higher Japanese interest rate send the dollar plunging and hamper Japanese growth, conveyed to the BOJ that its policy was "unnecessary and unwise."

The G-5 deputies had questioned Oba about the higher Japanese interest rates during the November preparatory meeting in Paris. On the defensive, Oba justified the action by arguing that, as a first objective, Japan must reduce the external imbalance through appreciation of the yen. Only then could Japan initiate a domestic stimulus by lowering interest rates. Thus, the increase in interest rates was meant to be temporary in an effort to reinforce currency realignment. Oba added that it was a BOJ decision and that the MOF had not been consulted. On the surface, Oba's explanation was intended to defend the BOJ policy; in fact, it was an effort to distance the MOF from the BOJ. In the light of Japan's awkward position, Oba felt obliged to offer new pledges to boost Japan's domestic demand. He later admitted that his explanation must have been "hard to accept."

The Bank of Japan's abrupt decision to raise the short-term interest rate illustrated the unpreparedness and unwillingness among the central bankers to coordinate monetary policy. The Federal Reserve Board was not inclined to lower the discount rate to depreciate the dollar and decided to maintain a cautious stance on monetary policy after the Plaza. The Bundesbank was troubled over the increase in the money supply and did not indicate willingness to ease its grip on money reserves.

Although various aspects of monetary policy coordination will be examined in more detail in the next chapter, it is necessary first to shed more light on the tricky nature of the intervention process and its implications for monetary policy—that is, the issue of sterilization* versus nonsterilization. At the Versailles Summit in 1982, the participants had initiated a study of the effects of intervention on exchange markets, including the issue of sterilization. The result of that effort, the "Report of the Working Group on Exchange Market Intervention," better known as the "Jurgensen Report,"[33]

---

* sterilization—The purchase or sale of securities to offset the effects of exchange market intervention on the domestic money supply.

32. "Bank of Japan decides not to lower the discount rate for a while," *Nihom Keizai Shimbun,* 26 September 1985.

33. The Jurgensen Report was named after the chairman of the committee, Philippe Jurgensen, Deputy Director of the Treasury for International Affairs, French Ministry of Economics and Finance.

was presented the next year at the Williamsburg Summit. Basing its findings on previous intervention operations and econometric modeling, the group concluded that sterilized intervention alone "did not appear to have constituted an effective instrument in the face of persistent market pressures." Further, the group's models led to the conclusion that the effect of sterilized intervention on exchange markets was "much smaller" than the effect of unsterilized intervention, which directly affected a country's monetary base.

Despite this conclusion in the Jurgensen report on sterilization, it does not seem to have been discussed.[34] Indeed, the Plaza Agreement contained no recommendations at all for desirable monetary policy action to go along with exchange rate realignment. According to a German official, sterilization was not discussed because, "the whole argument was too academic."[35] In Japan, Yamaguchi felt obliged to heed the Jurgensen report's counsel. Directed by Takeshita to intervene decisively, Yamaguchi stressed to BOJ officials the need for unsterilized intervention operations to maximize their effectiveness. A Bank of Japan official who received this unusual instruction from the top level of the Ministry of Finance was puzzled and asked whether the Ministry would not be concerned about higher interest rates due to unsterilized operations. Although he did not receive a clear answer, senior officials at the Bank of Japan did not in fact pursue nonsterilization tactics.

Like the other central banks, the Bank of Japan regarded the sterilization issue as largely academic, pointing out that the exchange rate desk's daily operations were carried out independently of the daily open-market operations of the Business Bureau people. "The basic stance of monetary policy was the vital issue, and we maintained that at least we should not move into a higher interest rate at that point given the perceived slow growth during the period." Yet when the BOJ raised short-term interest rates in late October, partly to combat the rebounding dollar, it was justified as proof of Japan's adherence to a policy of unsterilized intervention by some who wanted to dodge criticism, both from the MOF and from foreign monetary authorities.

The Germans felt that the signal of intervention was more important than the actual amount of intervention or any offsetting shifts in monetary policy. According to a Bundesbank official, they felt that sterilization is effective only in altering conditions in the money market—that does not affect the monetary aggregates; thus "the whole sterilization question was not so

---

34. The Jurgensen Report's conclusion has been disputed increasingly by economists and, more importantly, it was viewed by some as a cover for Sprinkel's nonintervention strategy.

35. Personal interview.

important [at the Plaza]."[36] Yet the Germans did not believe that intervention could be divorced from domestic monetary policy in general. "You have to accompany intervention with appropriate monetary and fiscal policy," explained one German official, adding that monetary policy should be one part of a "whole strategy."

The United States did not elaborate on the sterilization question, either. At the Treasury it was understood that intervention needed to be nonsterilized. The question was not discussed between the Treasury and the Federal Reserve Board, because it was believed to be up to the discretion of the central bank.

Intervention by the Federal Reserve Board was generally considered to be sterilized. The Federal Reserve Board basically maintained the same stance on monetary policy until the end of the year. "Well, all intervention, I mean essentially all Federal Reserve intervention is sterilized. I think it's easier to think of it that way. And that certainly was true at the time of the Plaza Agreement. We did not nonsterilize," testified a US central banker.[37] Nonetheless, the conclusion should not be drawn automatically that the Fed sterilized the whole intervention. Although most of the staff at the central bank believed in sterilizing the effects of foreign exchange market operations on the domestic money supply, Volcker was inclined not to separate the sterilization issue from the context of domestic monetary policy, in line with his use of monetary policy to keep the markets guessing at the next move of the Federal Reserve. The same official elaborated further:

The real question you have is whether when we're trying to get the dollar down we want an easier monetary policy or whether when we're trying to get the dollar up we want a tighter monetary policy. But that might be going regardless of whether there is intervention or not. And it's important to separate those two . . . I know my friend Mr. Volcker doesn't always like to think about it that way.[38]

The Treasury—at least at this point—did not regard monetary policy as a policy instrument for dollar devaluation but did consider its implication for the domestic economy. The issue, whether or not to sterilize the effects of intervention, was never fully clarified.

The different stance of central bankers in the United States, Japan, and West Germany with respect to the sterilization and, more broadly, the

---

36. Personal interview.

37. Personal interview.

38. Personal interview.

relationship between intervention and monetary policy, reflected the political, institutional, and operational considerations in each country. The Bank of Japan was confident that its open-market operations could effectively counter the effect of intervention on the money supply, while the Bundesbank believed it lacked the tools to do so. The flexibility of the Bank of Japan, therefore, was a matter of skepticism to the Bundesbank. A top Bundesbank official confided:

The question is, are the Japanese authorities able to avoid the consequences of increases of liquidity into the banking system and the nonbanks? Are they able to compensate it, neutralize it, or sterilize it? And my answer is yes. They have *some* instruments which are helpful for them but in the end the results are of the same direction. . . . Nobody is really able to have a *complete* sterilization of . . . intervention. That is not true even for Japan.[39]

Compared to the rather clear-cut policy of the Bank of Japan and the Bundesbank, the Federal Reserve Board's position on the question was murky. The Fed's policy is conditioned on a political factor not present to the same degree in Germany and Japan. The US central bank must report its monetary targets to the Congress twice a year. Once this has been done, the Fed is kept from deviating officially from the target, knowing that any change must be justified or explained—a justification that itself will perhaps affect the markets. The requirement to report offical targets and to justify deviations becomes in itself a tool of monetary policy since it can precipitate changes in the markets. This requirement doubtless led the Fed to claim that its basic policy was sterilized intervention.

The Process

In the minds of its framers, the Plaza strategy was meant to achieve meaningful coordination of economic policies, and not just a realignment of exchange rates. About one year later after the Plaza meeting, a US administration official elucidated its significance as follows when asked the difference between the Plaza strategy and previous currency realignment operations undertaken in 1971, 1973, and 1978.

To me the big difference is that the Plaza was not just a currency exercise. If you remember, the adjustment in currencies began at the Plaza. It did not begin and end at the Plaza. It just began there. The more important thing, perhaps, is the reaffirmation of that group to pursue a closer economic policy coordination effort. I think the other level of interest

---

39. Personal interview.

which may prove to be more important in the long run was the fact that for the first time there was a substantial agreement reached about policy intentions.[40]

It is debatable whether the former realignments, especially the one in 1978, were "just currency exercises," for realignment was also a part of the broad policy coordination of the Bonn Summit of 1978.

Currency intervention was the most dramatic part of the Plaza strategy, but it was not supposed to stop there. Fiscal policy and monetary policy were seen as integral elements of the coordination process, but there were strong obstacles to macroeconomic policy coordination among the G-5. In the case of the United States, the ideological and political resistance to relating the overvalued dollar to misalignments of the fundamentals—that is, the budget deficit and the high interest rate—remained strong in the administration. The explicit avowal of this relationship would have contradicted the Treasury's previous position and would have hindered fuller policy coordination, since the coordination, if it was to be effective, by definition presupposed interrelated performance for adjustments. In this respect, the Plaza was significant because it legitimized the treatment of domestic economic conditions in connection with exchange rate considerations.

To Baker and Darman, the Plaza strategy needed to operate within political constraints and still be comprehensive enough to address a range of macroeconomic policy aspects, including assignments of specific contributions to each country. But how were the countries to implement the pledges and how would others check them? The fundamental problem was to create a credible process of surveillance. A European official later commented, "Surveillance was already there. Surveillance goes back to Group of Ten discussions, and earlier G-5 meetings had already implemented surveillance. The novelty of the Plaza was that we actually took an exchange market position."[41] On this point, the Plaza G-5 announcement declared that the participants "agreed that exchange rates should play a role in adjusting external imbalances." By recognizing the need for systemic government intervention, the G-5 effectively repudiated the conclusions of the G-10 Report of June 1985, which rejected target zones or any other monetary reform. This statement set the stage for both economic indicators and the Louvre reference range mechanism. The idea of surveillance based on economic indicators was introduced later. The same European official explained:

---

40. Personal interview.

41. Personal interview.

In the run-up period of the preparations there was talk about the rate of growth of the United States and German and Japanese economies particularly, and the beginning of the argument that the German and the Japanese must have higher domestic demand growth than they have had, and the United States lower. But there was an awful lot of muddle—I remember having an argument in which I kept saying that it was domestic demand that you wanted to talk about and David Mulford was talking about GNP. We were much less accustomed to talking in terms of world economic forecasts or putting our national forecasts together. That developed afterwards.[42]

The Plaza process set a precedent for political bargaining over the ingredients of macroeconomic policy—exchange rates, monetary policy and fiscal policy. For example, Baker's stance of noncommitment to the intervention strategy, even after he had decided to support it, was at least partly due to the desire to use his support for it as a bargaining chip to get stimulative fiscal policies from Japan and West Germany. Mulford's refusal to commit to intervention until the last moment at the Plaza can be explained the same way.

Legitimization of the package deal was contingent upon gaining the sanction of the institutions involved, which in turn necessitated an alliance between finance ministry and central bank. Thus, to argue that a change in fiscal policy should be made in conjunction with exchange rate realignment was to say that the task of adjustment should be shouldered by both finance ministers and central bankers. "That is why, contrary to what my good friend Paul Volcker has thought at times, . . . finance ministers have to be involved. The central bankers do not have authority to speak on the questions that are on the list, with the exception of monetary policy,"[43] said a senior administration official.

Shadows

The ministers and central bankers left the Plaza Hotel with vague targets for their plan. There was little talk of the specific effect of realignment on trade and current account imbalances, of the J-curve effect of exchange rate shifts, of the possible implications for capital flows into the United States, or of monetary policy coordination.[44] Some of these issues, notably the J-curve effect and monetary policy coordination, had been discussed at the

---

42. Personal interview.

43. Personal interview.

44. Interview of a Reagan administration official with the author.

G-5D level. The J-curve effect refers to the way currency depreciation basically improves the current account balance only with a lag. This lag is caused by both a price effect and a volume effect. The depreciation of the dollar causes consumers in both US and foreign markets to respond to price differentials by increasing consumption of US products, which are cheaper in relation to foreign products. US imports will fall and US exports will rise as a consequence. But the improvement in the trade balance will not come immediately because the rise in the dollar price of US imports relative to the price of US exports reduces the dollar's value of the trade balance. The improvement in the dollar value of the trade balance only comes later when the volume effects of higher exports and lower imports more than makes up for the deterioration in the terms of trade.[45]

A Treasury official involved in the negotiations said that the J curve "was not considered a major consideration why one might not wish to move" toward a devaluation strategy and that in terms the actual effect of the strategy on prices, the participants may not have had a "clear vision of how things may have turned out." In the United States, the Federal Reserve Board staff provided to the Treasury staff a skeptical analysis of the prospect of reducing the trade deficit through the dollar devaluation. The Treasury staff reached similar conclusions. "But the politicians clung to a too rosy scenario," said a US official. Indeed, the picture that emerges from these discussions is one in which many of the theoretical and policy implications of the coordinated action were not given close attention. Obviously, there was no ultimate goal or "equilibrium levels" set, although the Baker Treasury later found it necessary to depreciate the dollar to manage the accumulated current account deficit.

Another factor acting on the process was the preference of Japan—and to a lesser extent West Germany's for exchange rate realignment over fiscal policy as a strategy for attacking economic imbalances. Both countries abhorred a return to the "locomotive" fiscal strategy of the 1970s, and each found in realignment a means of deflecting foreign pressure away from the fiscal approach. At the Plaza, Japanese participants made it clear that they would continue to focus on the twin goals of reducing the central government deficit and providing a pro-growth environment for the private sector. As an "offering," they agreed to increase investment by local governments, conditional on "the individual circumstances of the region."

Faced with the choice between realigning the yen or stimulating the economy through fiscal policy, MOF officials preferred realignment simply

---

45. For further explanation of the J-curve effect, see Stephen Marris, *Deficits and the Dollar: The World Economy at Risk*, rev. ed. (Washington: Institute for International Economics, 1987), 108.

as the lesser of two evils. In large part it was a matter of which should come first. Takeshita felt strongly that realignment must come first; otherwise, undertaking policy adjustments to correct the imbalance would be "like filling a bamboo basket without a bottom." Takeshita often said that the misalignment of the yen–dollar exchange rate was "sort of a subsidy to Japan's exports to the United States and an import surcharge on US exports to Japan." Yet, he did not envision a new direction for fiscal strategy *after* the realignment, because at the time no one expected that realignment would continue beyond a level of 200 yen to the dollar so quickly.

On many occasions, Yamaguchi reminded Oba that Japanese strategy at the Plaza should be first to realign the currencies, and second, to reduce interest rates jointly, stressing the need to leave the "main castle [fiscal policy] free from attack." Takeshita initially considered that *endaka* (high yen) was to be tolerated as long as Japan's fiscal policies were left alone.[46]

At the Plaza meeting, both Stoltenberg and Pöhl were opposed to a coordinated fiscal policy strategy. In the domestic context, however, their viewpoints diverged since Pöhl was relatively more supportive of tax reform.

In the United States, the new strategy invigorated the debate over fiscal versus monetary solutions to America's deficits. According to senior administration officials, Volcker was concerned that realignment might divert attention from the urgent task of balancing the federal budget.[47] The United States agreed to "implement fully the deficit reduction package for fiscal year 1986." This package, passed by Congress and approved by the President would, as they assured their trading partners, not only reduce the budget deficit by more than 1 percent of GNP for fiscal 1986, but would lay the foundation for further significant reductions in the deficit for the years to come.

The US Treasury Department did not have any hidden agenda to avoid fiscal policy coordination. It had already set the agenda to reduce the budget deficit. Baker and Darman anticipated that fiscal policy coordination—namely, greater stimulus of domestic demand by Japan and West Germany—would help the United States pursue more vigorous measures to reduce the budget deficit. When asked to what extent Baker thought of using foreign pressure to include cutting the budget deficit in the Plaza strategy, a senior US administration official replied, "To some degree, we thought of it that way. That wasn't the main reason to it but we did think that there would be such pressures and that wouldn't be a bad thing." The United States did not try to use foreign pressure more skillfully and forcefully, because, in the words of the same official, "foreign pressure on the United States, generally

---

46. Interview of Noboru Takeshita with the author.

47. *Business Week*, 7 October 1985.

speaking ... doesn't make that much difference and sometimes it's counterproductive."[48]

One sure US objective was to exact firmer commitments from Japan and West Germany to stimulate domestic demand. They also had political and psychological constraints to mobilize the fiscal policy coordination, and the US Treasury took care not to make the stimulation it was pushing on them look like a "locomotive" strategy. The US budget deficit reduction was to follow the Gramm-Rudman-Hollings scheme, which the Treasury hoped would assure US trading partners of the seriousness of the US administration.

In retrospect, the blitz intervention, which deterred the rush of congressional protectionist bills, nonetheless seems to have foreclosed serious effort by the US government to reduce its budget deficit. A strengthening of political will and the pledge to reduce the budget deficit could have put more pressure on, or given more incentive to, Japan and West Germany to come up with additional measures for their respective fiscal policies. The President's campaign pledge not to raise taxes clearly tied the hands of Baker, although with the existing political and ideological constraints on the intervention strategy itself, it might have been implausible for Baker to initiate action on two fronts—exchange rate and fiscal policy—at the same time. Thus, a genuine call for fiscal policy coordination was left unanswered, and announcement of the the ministers and governors at the Plaza glossed over its need:

After the particularly rapid U.S. growth of 1983–1984, there is now increased evidence of internal growth in the other countries. In particular, private investment has picked up strength. The current expansion is occurring in a context of fiscal consolidation. It is not dependent on short-lived fiscal stimulus.[49]

---

48. Personal interview.

49. Announcement of the Ministers of Finance and Central Bank Governors of France, Germany, Japan, the United Kingdom, and the United States, 22 September 1985.

■ *Bankers*

In January 1986 the Group of Five (G-5) convened in London. Finance ministers and central bank governors conducted the first session over dinner on Saturday, January 18 and then met for a second session the next morning at 11 Downing Street, the residence of Britain's Chancellor of the Exchequer, Nigel Lawson. The G-5 issued only a three-sentence statement after the meeting:

The meeting was an informal one to take stock of developments since the meeting in New York on 22 September. The finance ministers and central bank governors were satisfied with the progress made so far. They agreed that their cooperation should continue and that the progress which has been made so far should not be reversed.

Comments made by officials after the meeting suggested that important differences on exchange rates and monetary policy had emerged among the G-5. Treasury Secretary James A. Baker III, for instance, was concerned that the dollar's fall had not had sufficient impact on the US trade deficit. One high Treasury official is reported to have said that while the G-5 welcomed the decline of the dollar "to date," the Reagan administration would like to see the dollar decline more than the approximately 25 percent it had fallen since its peak in 1985. "Although we don't have a target" for the dollar, he is reported to have said, "if over time, it finds its way to a lower level, we won't write letters to the editor."[1] Japan and West Germany, on the other hand, contended that there was no immediate need for any further realignment and suggested that the US administration be patient, since the benefits of currency changes take 15 months to manifest themselves completely.

---

1. *New York Times*, 20 January 1986.

Much of the discussion at the London G-5 meeting focused on interest rates. The participants had agreed that lower inflation worldwide and lower oil prices had created conditions for lower interest rates and that the central banks should "study the possibility of lowering rates when appropriate."[2] It is important, however, that none of the G-5 countries wanted to lower its discount rate unilaterally. A Japanese official admitted to Japan's willingness to lower rates, but added, "America must do so also." A West German official added that "the United States has to take the lead in any reduction in interest rates."[3]

Other topics of discussion included fiscal policy and internationalizing the yen. Both Germany and Japan rejected US suggestions that they stimulate their domestic economies, claiming that their respective growth rates were sufficient. Japanese Finance Minister Takeshita forecast Japanese growth of 4 percent in FY 1986. As for the US budget deficit, Secretary Baker was optimistic that Congress would observe the Gramm-Rudman-Hollings Amendment and asserted that questions about its constitutionality were only technical and temporary.[4] Finally, Takeshita reported that the Japanese government was adopting a three-pronged approach to internationalization of the yen: first, development of an offshore market in yen investments; second, issuance of more short-term government bonds; and third, promotion of the use of the yen in trade. Traders were unimpressed. "Given the fact that the G-5 meeting was such a yawn, a lot of currency traders who had been prepared to come to work decided to take the holiday," said Richard B. Dickson Jr., a vice president in the foreign exchange department at Salomon Brothers. "The G-5 is not likely to be a factor unless the dollar moves up or down more than 5 percent," he added. Many traders were disappointed that there was no commitment on interest rates. "The market had been hoping for near-term good news on interest rates from the G-5. . . . I think attention will now shift to the uncertainty about the future of Gramm-Rudman," said A. Marshall Acuff of Smith Barney, Harris, Upham & Company.[5]

At the Plaza, the G-5 members had agreed to move toward greater coordination of policies at the next meeting. During the London meetings, Japan and France led the push for joint interest rate reductions. French Finance Minister Pierre Bérégovoy saw the London meeting as possibly his last chance to preside over a coordinated reduction since the French elections in May were threatening to shake Mitterrand's Socialist government.

---

2. Ibid.

3. Ibid.

4. *Financial Times*, 20 January 1986.

5. Ibid., 21 January 1986.

Japan also sought lower rates in large part to dispel misgivings by other G-5 members over the Bank of Japan (BOJ) rate hike in October. Japanese Finance Minister Noboru Takeshita, seeking to reconcile his support of a coordinated rate cut in London with the BOJ's action, said that issues of timing and amount should be "left to the central bankers." Takeshita was pressured to support a cut by Prime Minister Yasuhiro Nakasone, who had called for a joint interest rate reduction by Japan and the United States in a speech on 18 December 1985 to the Economic Policy Council, an advisory body to the Prime Minister. Nakasone's eagerness for a coordinated rate cut—at one point, he declared that if interest rates were cut all at once, "Bang! Bang!", the world would be better off—caused some alarm among central bankers abroad.

Treasury Secretary Baker was driven even more by political necessity than the other G-5 ministers to nurture the embryonic coordination process he had launched at the Plaza. With currency adjustment under way, the next logical step for him was adjustment of monetary policy. Lower interest rates would ease the payment burden on the LDC debtors facilitating the so-called Baker plan outlined during the IMF-World Bank meeting in Seoul in September 1985. Lower US growth estimates for 1986 also suggested an impending need for lower interest rates to maintain domestic growth. Baker had made it known in the preparatory meetings that he wanted monetary cooperation, and beginning in early 1986 he launched a campaign to bring interest rates down among the G-5. He warned that unless the others cooperated the dollar would fall further—a pressure tactic he would use throughout the period of rate cuts. Conditions in the global economy gave justification to Baker's campaign. The collapse in the world oil prices, very low inflation in West Germany, bond and stock market rallies, and a considerable easing of LDC debt overall presented to the G-5 an opportunity to pursue noninflationary growth and a reduction of external imbalances with some impunity. The same task would appear much more daunting in a negative economic environment characterized by inflation, threats of recession, high energy prices, and a burgeoning of developing-country debt.

The central bankers were reluctant to support any interest rate reductions dictated by finance ministers. Federal Reserve Board Chairman Paul A. Volcker, concerned since the Plaza about a possible free fall of the dollar, opposed any US rate cuts unaccompanied by similar moves in Germany and Japan, and in the United Kingdom. He was unconvinced that Germany and Japan would go along and he also disliked the idea of finance ministers meddling in monetary policy. Bundesbank President Karl Otto Pöhl, like Volcker, was suspicious of the G-5 ministers' dictating monetary policy. "Both Volcker and I refused any commitments [on monetary policy] at the London meeting," Pöhl said later. Protective of their independence in conducting monetary policy, Volcker and Pöhl sought to dispel any ideas that interest rate decisions were taking place in the G-5 meeting. BOJ Governor Satoshi Sumita was also wary of any unilateral action on interest rates, partly because he feared a dollar rebound if the Bank of Japan were alone to cut its rate. Upon returning to Japan after the London meetings, Sumita told reporters that Volcker gave him the impression that the Fed would not be reducing its discount rate in the near future.

The delicate balance of power between finance ministers and central bankers over the control of monetary policy often resembled a tug-of-war: finance ministers promoted monetary policy coordination and central bankers resisted. In the end, finance ministers obtained what they wanted from their central banks, and the Plaza Agreement and the subsequent coordination process helped them to get it.

At the root of central bank resistance to coordination was a desire to maintain institutional independence, a priority placed ahead of price stability and economic growth. Had the alternative existed, central bankers would have preferred using fiscal policy to monetary policy to correct current account imbalances without risking inflation. However, the political obstacles to changing fiscal policy, combined with forecasts for slow growth, put pressure on the central banks to loosen monetary policy. Currency appreciation further narrowed the ability of the Japanese and German central bankers to resist the interest rate cuts that their finance ministers wanted.

Monetary Policy in Action: Coordination

In London, Takeshita had been put on the defensive. His peers were skeptical of the Japanese government's forecast for 1986 of 4 percent growth and asked why he had failed to come up with a fiscal stimulus package. Takeshita's only response—a reassertion that Japanese growth would exceed 4 percent in fiscal 1986—was designed to temporize with the trading partners. In fact, Takeshita realized the official government forecast was unrealistic.

The Japanese economy had been steadily weakened by the higher yen, and the Ministry of Finance (MOF) came under attack from domestic interests to do something. The dollar's depreciation had brought scant improvement in the trade imbalance between Japan and the United States. Indeed, Commerce Department trade figures released on January 30 showed that the American deficit with Japan in 1985 had reached a whopping $50 billion. Takeshita feared that if currency adjustment was not reducing that figure, Japan would come under increasing pressure from foreigners to undertake domestic economic adjustment to correct the external imbalance.

In response to pressure from trading partners, particularly the United States, and in anticipation of increased pressure from domestic industry,

Takeshita urged Sumita to lower the discount rate to stimulate the economy. MOF officials expected that Sumita, former Vice Minister of Finance, would understand the difficulties in his position. Sumita complied by cutting the discount rate from 5 percent to 4.5 percent on January 30. The reduction made little impact, however, perhaps because the markets expected the BOJ to cut the rate again in the near future as part of an international effort.

G-3 Coordinated Reduction (March 1986)

The first coordinated interest rate reductions came on March 6 and 7. On March 6, Germany cut its discount rate from 4 percent to 3.5 percent, followed by France, which cut its rate the next day from 8.5 percent to 8.25 percent. Japan further reduced its discount rate from 4.5 percent to 4 percent on March 7, followed by a US cut later that morning from 7.5 percent to 7 percent—its lowest rate in eight years. Coordination and timing were given high priority. Indeed, the Federal Reserve Board announced its cut in the morning of March 7, instead of in the afternoon as is usually done, to stress the coordination.

There has been some dispute about the influence of the G-5 meeting in instigating the coordinated reductions. While the finance ministers hastened to take credit, the central bankers played down any connection between interest rate reductions and the London talks. "This has no direct relationship with any G-5 meeting or discussion, although it is obviously not inconsistent with the spirit of consultations among the G-5 countries," said Fed spokesman Joseph Coyne. "Consultation has been entirely among the central banks," he added.[6]

In fact, the real breakthrough occurred in February during the monthly Bank for International Settlements (BIS) meeting in Basel of central bankers representing 11 industrial countries. At a secret meeting Volcker and Pöhl agreed to lower their discount rates in tandem, according to a Bundesbank official, without telling their peers at the meeting. Volcker did not even report the decision to the other governors at the Fed. As one of them complained later: "Very typically, he did not share with us the Pöhl conversation."

Volcker was already under pressure from domestic sources to ease monetary policy. The White House, expressing concern over the sluggish US economy, reminded Volcker that 1986 was an election year. Reagan appointees to the Federal Reserve Board, particularly Vice Chairman Preston Martin and Governor Martha Seger, had advocated easing monetary policy

---

6. *Wall Street Journal,* 10 March 1986.

since late 1985; they were now supported by two new Reagan appointees, Manuel H. Johnson, former Assistant Secretary of the Treasury, and Wayne D. Angell, a former banker from Kansas.

By March, decreasing oil prices had eased German fears of inflation, while the mark had appreciated from 2.49 to 2.24 to the dollar and the yen had appreciated 12 percent to 176 yen to the dollar since December 1985. Baker continued to press US trading partners to stimulate their domestic economies, threatening further depreciation of the dollar if they did not.

Chairman Volcker, however, was genuinely concerned about the possibility of a free fall of the dollar, particularly after it dropped below 180 yen. He testified to the House Banking Committee on February 19 that "a sharp depreciation in the external value of a currency carries pervasive inflationary threats. . . . We have to recognize that depreciation of our currency does not in itself provide a fundamental solution, and is in fact a two-edged sword." Already fearing the inflationary effects of dollar depreciation, Volcker was unwilling to take any additional risks by lowering interest rates unilaterally. After the secret meeting with Pöhl, Volcker sought to delay any US action until after the March 6 meeting of the Bundesbank Council, which was the next opportunity for Pöhl to propose a reduction of the German discount rate. Volcker therefore opposed a motion for a unilateral discount rate reduction during the meeting of the Board of Governors on February 24, but was outvoted 4 to 3 by the other governors.

Palace Coup

The other governors disagreed with Volcker chiefly over the probability of recession in 1986. Angell cautioned that without interest rate cuts the world might be in a deflationary cycle. Another governor argued that conditions in the financial sector called for lower interest rates and faster economic growth. Martin, Johnson, and Angell advised Volcker to counsel his counterparts at the Japanese and the German central banks to engineer a joint interest rate reduction. They insisted also that they preferred a joint action to a unilateral one.

Volcker, however, refused to entertain their requests. Shortly after the vote for a discount-rate reduction on February 24, Volcker excused himself, leaving the other governors in the room. Later in the day, Volcker invited Martin and Angell to his office and said, "You both know that I cannot remain chairman if the votes go against me—do you want me to continue?" He then proposed that if they would delay implementation of the vote, he would get in touch with the other central bankers. Martin and Angell accepted, and Volcker called for another governors' meeting.

During the second meeting, Volcker "came around to a compromise . . .

[and] agreed to contact Pöhl and Sumita . . . and assur[ed] us that we could get a coordinated interest rate move within the next two weeks."[7] After the others agreed to defer implementing the cut until after the Bundesbank meeting, the vote to lower the rate was unanimous. Volcker later telephoned Pöhl for assurance of the Bundesbank's similar intentions.

The so-called palace coup nearly led to Volcker's resignation, since as spokesperson he no longer represented the majority opinion of the Board. Some observers have played down the dispute over policy. One Federal Reserve Board official later emphasized the personality conflict between Volcker and Martin.[8] Some speculate that in spearheading the opposition, Preston Martin was angling for the chairmanship and that the palace coup was staged as a test.

The divergence over policy reflected the difference in political priority between the "internationalists" and the "domesticists" or "unilateralists." Volcker, an internationalist, fully perceived that a unilateral discount-rate cut would lead to further depreciation of the dollar. The domesticists, led by Preston Martin, were preoccupied with the domestic economy and gave less consideration than Volcker to the international repercussions of monetary policy. This is not to say that they were unaware of the repercussions; indeed, assigning domesticist and internationalistic labels exaggerate the reality of the situation. Martin had at one point advised that the Japanese discount rate should be reduced before the US rate to avoid the possibility of the precipitous decline in the dollar that might occur as a result of a unilateral US action.[9] Angell, stressing his loyalty to Volcker, later said that he, too, regarded coordination as necessary. He was sure to mention that Volcker inscribed "To The Defender of the Faith" on the photograph he gave him upon his departure from the Fed.

The difference lay more precisely in conflicting analyses of the effects of depreciation. Volcker warned of an inflationary surge that would result from a free fall, while Martin considered the likelihood of either event very low. Martin had in occasional event meetings of the board argued that depreciation would cause foreign exporters to lower prices and maintain volume to defend market shares, thereby avoiding inflation. Volcker was no doubt more concerned than Martin about international status of the dollar. His experience as Under Secretary of the Treasury during the early 1970s and his personal dedication to low inflation also shaped his thinking about the dollar.

---

7. Interview with the author of a governor who opposed Volcker.

8. Personal interview.

9. *Asahi Shimbun,* 25 January 1986, evening edition.

G-2 Coordinated Reduction (April 1986)

By April 1986 both Takeshita and Sumita were worried about a rapid appreciation of the yen and the gloomy economic forecasts for Japan and the United States. They were willing to lower the discount rate in Japan if it would encourage the Fed to do the same. Takeshita and Nakasone calculated, furthermore, that a strong show of policy coordination between Japan and the United States would also boost Japan politically before the economic summit to be held in Japan in May.

On April 21, three weeks before the Tokyo Summit, the United States and Japan harmonized a discount-rate cut. The Japanese rate now stood at 3.5 percent, the lowest it had been since World War II. According to Takeshita, the decision for a coordinated reduction emerged from meetings with Secretary Baker in Washington on April 8. Perhaps more crucial was an urgent conversation on April 10 between Volcker and Sumita in Washington. Volcker expressed concern over the prospects for US economic growth in the second quarter (April–June). He also indicated that the Fed was inclined to cut the discount rate again, and appealed to Sumita to cut the Japanese discount rate simultaneously to maintain the exchange rate. Sumita responded "in positive terms" but did not make a firm commitment during the conversation.[10]

The Fed announced the discount-rate reduction on April 18, to be effective on April 21. Japanese authorities smoothed the way for the Fed rate cut by purchasing $200 million in the New York foreign currency market on the day of the announcement.[11]

Analysts noted that the low-key tone of the announcement suggested a lack of enthusiasm and predicted that no further cuts would be likely to follow.[12] Volcker stated before a House subcommittee on April 23 that interest rates in the United States had fallen far enough and that he would not favor another cut in the near future. Volcker added that he saw "no reason why [stimulus] measures in Europe and Japan await comparable action by the United States."[13]

---

10. "Volcker expresses strong expectation about Japan's rate cut," *Asahi Shimbun*, 12 April 1987, evening edition.

11. *Asahi Shimbun*, 19 April 1986, evening edition.

12. The announcement stated: "The action taken is a technical change designed to place the discount rate in a more appropriate alignment with the prevailing level of market rates." Reported in the *New York Times*, 19 April 1986.

13. Paul A. Volcker, testimony before the Subcommittee on Telecommunications and Finance, US House Committee on Energy and Commerce, 23 April 1986.

Monetary Policy in Action: US Unilateral Cuts

During the summer of 1986, the Fed lowered the discount rate two more times, on July 10 and August 21, each time by half a percentage point. The July cut came during a period of perceived weakness in the economy and frustration with the reluctance of US allies—especially West Germany—to stimulate their domestic economies.

After the Tokyo Summit in early May, Baker and Volcker resumed pressure on Japan and West Germany to stimulate domestic demand, which the Bank of Japan and the Bundesbank resisted. In Japan, the Ministry of Finance wanted the BOJ to lower the discount rate again, preferably in conjunction with a US rate cut. Another cut would have helped Liberal Democratic Party (LDP) leaders who were preparing for a general election in early July. The Japanese central bank deflected steady political pressure by arguing that the independence of the central bank and monetary policy in general should not be compromised by election considerations. Takeshita later admitted that the timing was poor for a discount-rate cut because "the BOJ united against rate cuts near election time traditionally and single-mindedly."[14] The main election issue, the sales tax proposal, drew attention from broader economic and monetary policy, effectively strengthening the position of the BOJ. The real danger to the BOJ was the undeterred appreciation of the yen, although public preoccupation with the sales tax issue probably prevented any stronger pressure for lower interest rates.

The MOF instead used an indirect means to provoke the BOJ rate cut. Aware that the BOJ feared the Fed's unilateral action would cause further appreciation of the yen, the MOF refused the Bank's request for additional intervention reserves following the US announcement. Through its inability to support the yen–dollar exchange rate with intervention, the Bank was forced to lower the Japanese discount rate to prevent increased speculation in the yen. Commenting later on the MOF's maneuverings, a BOJ official ruefully said, "It was a cheap bluff. Regardless of their manipulation, the yen would have appreciated at that stage anyway. They just hurled away their responsibility [for fiscal policy] and made us look bad."[15]

The solo action by the Fed "appeared appropriate in the context of relatively slow growth, comfortably within capacity constraints, in the United States and in the industrialized world generally." But aside from the main objective of "forcing the Japanese and the Germans to follow the US

---

14. Personal interview.
15. Personal interview.

rate cut," the administration may have also wanted to stimulate the economy in anticipation of November congressional elections.[16]

Neither Japan nor West Germany immediately copied the US move: in Japan, a post-election political vacuum was responsible for BOJ inactivity; in Germany this was due to bullish forecasts for the German economy. In the United States, Baker described as "regrettable" the unwillingness of West Germany and Japan to follow the Fed's discount-rate reduction. During a television interview he stated, "With respect to Germany in particular you are looking at unemployment of around 9 percent, you are looking at negative inflation and negative growth. We need some help. We have carried to a large degree the world economy for the last 42 or 43 months. . . . We would like to see some help from over there."[17]

Following Nakasone's landslide victory in the general election, Kiichi Miyazawa replaced Takeshita (who had left to become general secretary of the LDP) as Finance Minister. Miyazawa had long advocated expansionist economic policies, criticizing the Nakasone cabinet for "mishandling the exchange-rate policy" and for its austere fiscal policies.

Takeshita's replacement gave US monetary authorities an opportunity to renew policy coordination efforts, which by this time had gone stale. The very next day, July 22, after the formation of the new cabinet, a high-ranking US official expressed a desire to see Japan lower its discount rate as part of the stimulus package scheduled for the fall.[18] Miyazawa did not comply immediately, retreating instead to Karuizawa, a posh summer resort, with the statement, "Monetary policy should be left to the central bankers."

The resistance of the Bundesbank proved even stronger than that of the BOJ. Although Bonn favored a more accommodating monetary posture than the Bundesbank, Finance Minister Gerhard Stoltenberg and Vice Finance Minister Hans Tietmeyer refrained from directly pressuring Bundesbank officials until mid-August, when the dollar fell to two deutsche marks and the Kohl government's economic policy came under increasing attack from abroad and at home.

The funeral of Otmar Emminger, former President of the Bundesbank, provided the occasion for an exchange between Volcker and Pöhl, which they continued at Pöhl's home the following afternoon, joined by Bundesbank Vice President Helmut Schlesinger. To Volcker's anxiety over the prospects for growth in the German economy, Pöhl responded that it was indeed expanding and that economic reports for the second quarter were expected to be positive.

---

16. *Wall Street Journal,* 11 July 1986.

17. *Wall Street Journal,* 13 July 1986.

18. *Asahi Shimbun,* 23 July 1985, evening edition.

Still unconvinced, Volcker insisted that the Bundesbank lower its discount rate. Pöhl responded that he and his colleagues would consider a rate cut, but only with the stipulation that Baker announce publicly after the next G-5 meeting that the United States was prepared to stabilize the dollar. Volcker promised to discuss the proposal with Baker.

Shortly thereafter, Pöhl received a negative response from Baker, who cited pressure from Congress as his excuse.[19] Thus the first attempt to link currency stability with stimulus measures failed. In the ensuing months, the domesticists at the Bundesbank refused to be swayed by what they considered high-handed attempts by top Treasury officials to pressure them into lowering the discount rate.

Bundesbank resistance notwithstanding, the Fed unilaterally lowered its discount rate again on August 21 to stimulate a languishing US economy and avoid a recession. At 5.5 percent, the discount rate stood at its lowest level in nearly nine years. The Fed announced that "the action appears consistent with the objective of sustaining orderly growth within a framework of greater price stability."

Monetary Policy in Action: Japan's Move, Germany's Move

Japan was the next major country to reduce its discount rate, cutting it to 3 percent, another postwar low. The reduction came during a period of continued sluggishness in the Japanese economy and the result was in part from the so-called Baker-Miyazawa Accord of 31 October 1986, which traded assurances by Japan to cut the discount rate and initiate tax reform for those by the United States to stop depreciating the dollar.

This Accord grew out of a meeting between the two finance ministers in San Francisco on 6 September 1986, in which Baker expressed anxiety that policy coordination might fail if West Germany refused to lower the discount rate. He pressed Miyazawa to cut the Japanese rate, arguing that Japan's action would induce West Germany to do the same. Miyazawa was reluctant to commit himself to a rate cut, responding that "it is not the best timing now." He added that Japan was experiencing extraordinary growth in its money supply and spiraling real estate prices in the Tokyo metropolitan area, "as if he represented the governor of the Bank of Japan," related a senior MOF official. Yet he did not hide his willingness to stimulate domestic demand and went so far as to say, "If the coordinated action of interest-rate reduction would be such an important matter, you might tell the Germans that Japan would be ready to lower the rate."[20]

---

19. Interviews of US and West German monetary authorities with the author.

20. Interview of American and Japanese officials with the author.

It is interesting to note the manipulative tactics used to further the coordination of monetary policy between the United States, Japan, and West Germany. Here was Miyazawa supplying verbal ammunition to Baker, who could then use it to assault West German policy. For his own part, Miyazawa refused to commit himself to a rate reduction, bucking pressure from the United States and his domestic bureaucracy as well. He anticipated that a strategy of inaction—that is, no cut in the discount rate—would prompt the reluctant MOF to propose a stimulative fiscal package in the fall. After the San Francisco meeting, Miyazawa continued to push for a more flexible *fiscal* policy instead of a more flexible *monetary* policy.

On September 26, the day of the G-5 meeting, Volcker met with Sumita over breakfast. As his part of a campaign orchestrated with Baker, he tried to convince Sumita of the necessity of a discount-rate cut. Sumita's reservations prompted Baker to make the same request to Miyazawa later that day. Baker was told of the Japanese government's decision to enact a supplementary budget as a domestic stimulus measure. Although he received only a lukewarm response to his own proposal, Baker was reluctant to give up the "Japan card."

Three days after the meeting, Miyazawa was handed a note from the Office of the US Executive Director of the IMF at a meeting of the Interim Committee of the IMF, which read, "I would like to meet you privately. I will wait in Room 320 on the 13th floor. Jim Baker." In this meeting, Baker criticized the "uncooperative attitude of West Germany" and said that the United States and Japan should proceed with policy coordination, again urging a Japanese discount-rate cut as a necessary step in the process. Miyazawa, after reiterating the importance of yen–dollar exchange rate stability, promised that he would discuss the idea with Sumita and have him meet with Volcker.

By October 2, when Sumita came to Volcker's office, US monetary authorities were on the defensive. It was generally believed that there was no room for the Fed to lower the discount rate in the near future. The reduction in the discount rate a month earlier had not influenced the direction of long-term interest rates, which were climbing higher. The August cut was then made to look like a political ploy and a monetary failure. Even strong advocates of relaxed monetary policy, such as Manuel H. Johnson, were suggesting that the eased monetary posture had gone far enough.[21] Sumita, well aware of the situation, did not question Volcker about his plans for US monetary policy. When asked why he did not, he replied, "It is an act of chivalry not to ask an embarrassing question."[22]

---

21. *Asahi Shimbun,* 28 September 1986.

22. Interview of Sumita with the author.

Instead, sharing concern over a further depreciation of the dollar, Sumita promised Volcker that he would consider reducing the discount rate in Japan. Whereas Sumita himself may have supported a discount-rate reduction, he could not alone have persuaded the BOJ bureaucracy without the insistence of the Ministry of Finance. Miyazawa considered a reduction crucial in halting the yen appreciation. Both he and Yoshihiko Yoshino, Vice Minister of Finance, conveyed in no uncertain terms the ministry's position to key members of the BOJ bureaucracy, and succeeded in convincing Vice Governor Yasushi Mieno.[23]

One week before the Baker-Miyazawa announcement, Mieno telephoned Sumita, who happened to be in China, to ask him whether the decision had been made. At the same time, a story leaked to the press indicated that the BOJ, not the MOF, was responsible for the decision. In fact, the MOF was responsible, and it was up to the BOJ simply to accept the MOF argument that a cut in the discount rate was the only way to stop appreciation of the yen.

Following Japan's unilateral rate cut in October, US pressure shifted to West Germany. On 23 January 1987, just before German parliamentary elections, the Bundesbank ostensibly eased monetary policy by cutting the discount rate but simultaneously moved to tighten the money supply and raised the reserve requirement to 10 percent. US officials protested that the cut, from 3.5 to 3 percent, would contribute only marginally to the stimulation of the German economy or the stabilization of currency markets. According to one Fed source the counterbalancing actions produced a "sterilized effect" on the markets. "This leaves us in the same position we were in before," he added.[24] A Treasury official later remarked:

We did not believe that any discount-rate cut without a fiscal policy would be sufficient to get that economy stable. We also had a couple of experiences where the discount rate cuts had not been transposed into reductions of market rates. The Bundesbank became very astute at moving the discount rate one way and changing the reserve requirement intervention points the other way—which is a bit much the second or third time through. . . . You can fool us once, sometimes twice, but the third time we catch on.[25]

The German action came amid a slide in the value of the dollar, then at 151.93 yen and 1.8390 deutsche marks. Pöhl alleged that by talking down

---

23. Interview of Japanese monetary authorities with the author.

24. *Wall Street Journal*, 23 January 1987.

25. Personal interview.

the dollar, "anonymous US officials" were "playing with fire." He then recalled the troubles that accompanied the falling dollar during the late 1970s.

Finally, as a sort of pre-Louvre gesture, the Bank of Japan lowered its discount rate on February 20 for the fifth time since January 1986. Sumita asserted that it was designed to help stabilize the yen and "promote steady expansion of domestic demand."[26] The move originated from Miyazawa's hurried visit to Washington in January 1987, when he sought Baker's assurance on the viability of the bilateral agreement made between the two in October 1986.

Miyazawa got only about half of what he wanted from Baker. Although he agreed in principle to intervene in the market when the yen appreciated above 150, Baker declined to commit to automatic and obligatory intervention. During the meeting, furthermore, Darman suggested that Miyazawa save the rate cut for the next G-5 meeting, when it could be coordinated with action by other countries to exercise a stronger effect.[27]

The Politics of Monetary Policy Coordination

The process of monetary policy coordination, activated by Japan, the United States, and West Germany, was shaped by institutional arrangements and political considerations. First, the relative roles of the finance ministers and the central bank governors in the policy coordination effort must be noted. Here the degree of cooperation among finance ministers and central banks varied among countries. The Bank of Japan was strongly influenced by the Ministry of Finance throughout the entire period, except for one brief stand during the summer of 1986. The Federal Reserve Board cooperated with the Treasury Department, in particular by allowing a series of discount-rate cuts during the summer of 1986. A top Fed official recalled that "every step of the way in which we eased [monetary] policy in 1986 was to be coordinated as much as possible in order to avoid sharp dollar depreciation, and if that could be through coordinated intervention or simultaneous interest rate changes, that was our preference." The Bundesbank demonstrated its traditional independence by consistently resisting political pressure from the German finance ministry.

Second, policymakers focused increasingly on the effect that domestic monetary policy would have on exchange rates, although to varying degrees.

---

26. *Wall Street Journal,* 25 February 1987.

27. Yoichi Funabashi, "The myth and reality of G-2," *Nichibei Keizai Masatsu—Sono Butaiura* (The US-Japan economic entanglement—The inside story) (Tokyo: Iwanani Paperbacks, June 1987), 215–16.

The Bank of Japan was most sensitive to exchange rate implications. The Bundesbank was equally concerned with domestic policy as it affected currency realignments within the EMS. The Federal Reserve Board, although also sensitive to the exchange rate issue, was more directly concerned with domestic policy considerations in the face of the coming election and the perceived weakness of the American economy. The Fed used monetary policy to stimulate the US economy or at least to keep it buoyant, but it did not burden domestic monetary policy with exchange-rate management. Instead, it used *coordination* of monetary policies—more accurately, the monetary policies of others—to keep the dollar from dropping precipitously.

The Role of Monetary Policy

Throughout this period, central bank officials were unenthusiastic about coordinating monetary policy with finance ministers. The intrusion of finance ministers into territory occupied traditionally by central bankers left the latter suspicious and anxious that "monetary sovereignty" would be threatened by the politicization of monetary and exchange rate policies.

In some cases, central bankers valued institutional interests higher than what the politicians perceived as "national interests" and found that they had more in common with their counterparts in foreign central banks than with their native finance ministries. Central bankers attended confidential meetings and met for unofficial dinners in Basel. So secretive were they that some ministry of finance officials in G-5 countries long suspected that central bankers had held their own separate G-5 meetings, although this was in fact not the case. There have been meetings of what is known as the "Gang of Four" (G-4), however, consisting of central bank officials, governors, and other BIS regulars from the United States, Japan, West Germany, and Switzerland. The group usually dines together the night before a formal BIS meeting. Some suggest that the history of the G-4 dates from the mid-1970s, roughly paralleling the evolution of the G-5.

While in the process of formulating the Plaza strategy, the US Treasury realized that co-opting the Bundesbank was the key to any coordination process. According to one official, the Treasury appreciated the Bundesbank's independence in formulating monetary policy and the fact that the German Ministry of Finance backed the authority to commit the government to any change in monetary policy. Treasury officials remembered their frustration during the coordination process of the 1978 Bonn Summit, when their counterparts at the German Ministry of Finance were unable to follow what the Bundesbank was doing. "That's the backdrop of the finance ministry-central bank consultation agreement at the Plaza," he said.[28]

---

28. Personal interview.

In spite of the resistance of the central banks to the policy coordination efforts of the finance ministers, the ironic result of the process was a series of concessions by the central banks to the political demands of the finance ministers. Central bankers throughout the G-5 were aware of the political needs of finance ministers. Even Volcker, imposing central banker that he was, proved no exception. Baker's strategy to use exchange rate policy as the lever by which the executive branch could influence monetary policy represented a reversal from the hands-off policy of his predecessor. It also gave no choice to Volcker but to create a united front with Baker.

Later, Volcker's doubts about the wisdom of rapid depreciation of the dollar were easily overridden by the Baker Treasury. Furthermore, Volcker's constant efforts to brake the slide of the dollar were offset by the Treasury's practice of "talking down the dollar." One top Japanese central bank official later confided that Volcker, too, appeared to have been persuaded to lower the discount rate. The Fed rate cuts in July and August 1986 in particular seemed to have been pushed on Volcker, he added. Finally, the palace coup undermined Volcker's once unquestionable authority and reputation.

Exchange Rates

The second aspect of monetary policy coordination during this period was that policy was "totally swayed by exchange rate considerations," in the phrase of a Bank of Japan official. This was particularly significant in Japan, where the specter of yen appreciation constantly threatened to send shock waves through the political system.

The March and April 1986 joint discount-rate reductions were carefully designed not to upset the exchange rate. The Bank of Japan intervened heavily in the market to maintain the value of the dollar and ensure that the Fed cut would go off smoothly. Perhaps most illustrative, however, was Japan's fifth and final discount-rate reduction in February 1987. Even before his January trip to Washington, Miyazawa had decided with Sumita to lower the rate in what was "none other than an effort to stop yen appreciation. Nothing else," according to BOJ officials. Further, in an effort to control as many variables as possible to prevent miscalculation, the BOJ wanted the Fed's assurance it would not lower its discount rate.

While the Japanese monetary authorities focused obsessively on the yen–dollar relationship, the main concern of Bundesbank officials was to safeguard the domestic currency and the currency relationships within the European Monetary System (EMS). West Germany's compliance under EMS pressure—mainly from the French—to revalue the deutsche mark and its subsequent willingness to subordinate the goals of domestic policy for harmony among the EMS countries demonstrate a priority given to maintenance of EMS arrangements. In the rate cuts of both March 1986 and January 1987, it was pressure from other EMS countries rather than from the United States that most directly compelled Bundesbank action. The January 1987 cut came ten days after a realignment of six EMS currencies. Despite Germany's deep abhorrence of inflation and its related insistence on the constitutional independence of the Bundesbank, which otherwise limits the extent of German commitment to international coordination, the Bundesbank sacrificed a degree of independence in order to prevent further speculation and destabilization in the EMS.

The Bundesbank's monetary policy was not swayed by dollar exchange-rate considerations to the extent that the BOJ's policy was. A high-ranking official at the German central bank later stressed:

[T]he exchange rate is a variable that enters into the consideration, but it is not a target or an instrument in any sense. . . . On the whole, the exchange rate was to us much less of a concern, relatively speaking, than perhaps to the Japanese. You see, we have never allowed industry to believe that the government or the Bundesbank can do much about the exchange rate. It is different in Japan.[29]

To a greater degree than the Bank of Japan and the Bundesbank, the Federal Reserve Board held that US monetary policy primarily served the needs of the domestic economy. This philosophy was demonstrated by the series of rate cuts in the summer of 1986, which were made in reaction to perceived weaknesses of the economy and in anticipation of the midterm elections. Yet even here, considerations of the relation of exchange rates to the performance of monetary policy were given high priority. A senior Federal Reserve Board official concluded later, "In that period of time, the exchange rate was an important variable among several in framing the monetary policy. It is not to say that it was the only, most important thing. But, the exchange rate was more important than it had been in the past."[30]

From the beginning of the process the Fed and the Treasury approached monetary policy with different objectives. In shaping the Plaza strategy, the Treasury had expected the Fed to lower the discount rate as part of an overall US package. The latter meanwhile was apprehensive over the rapid decline of the dollar and the possible negative effect a rate cut would have on foreign capital inflows, a vital concern since the United States had become the world's largest debtor nation. The Treasury analyzed the picture differently, "We were aware that we were a debtor. Paul [Volcker] was

---

29. Personal interview.

30. Personal interview.

worried about it a day after Plaza, but we at the Treasury assessed it differently. We did not think that market issues would cause problems."[31]

With the decline in oil prices, the Treasury's optimism was borne out, at least until the end of 1986. In the spring of 1987, however, "a change took place ... [and] the direct linkage between exchange rates, interest rate expectations, and inflation rate expectations appeared every day. That was when I became fearful of the confidence of world markets."[32] According to a senior administration official, US monetary authorities were then forced to raise the short-term interest rate in April while Baker pressed Japan to lower its short-term interest rate once again. Before Prime Minister Nakasone's visit to Washington in late April, President Reagan sent him a personal letter urging him to consider lowering the rate to "stabilize the currency." In the United States, too, monetary authorities focused increasingly on the exchange rate during the period from the Plaza to the Louvre, and even more so afterward.

The International Politics of Central Banking

Coordination of policy suffered from two sets of conflicts. First were divergent conceptions of the respective roles of monetary policy and fiscal policy, a conflict that cut across national boundaries, producing international solidarity between finance ministers on the one hand and central bankers on the other. At the Plaza meeting itself, finance ministers committed themselves to pursue fiscal policy coordination and then deftly sidestepped the task, leaving any coordination efforts to the central bankers. On an international level, each nation blamed the inappropriate mix of policies on other nations.

Second was a conflict over the lines of authority in setting monetary and exchange rate policy, which occurred between the central bankers and finance ministers in each country. These conflicts complicated the overall process of monetary policy coordination. The inherent institutional tension between finance ministries and central banks does not necessarily translate into actual, constant conflict between the two groups. The institutional footing of each central bank in the G-5 varied so that it often made a united approach difficult. One of the G-5 deputies commented:

What is very striking is the differences in the underlying relationships in the different G-5 or G-7 countries. At one extreme, you have the Bundes-

---

31. Interview of a senior Treasury official with the author.

32. Interview of a senior Treasury official with the author.

bank, immensely independent, having indeed its own constitutional objectives to which it is accountable, and, at the other extreme, you probably have the Banque de France and the Bank of England, both of which are innocent agents for the government. . . . Japan is rather nearer to France and Britain. The Fed is perhaps a little bit between these banks, but in the last resort it can't be as independent as the Bundesbank and particularly in foreign exchange because that is an area in which the US Treasury is formally in charge. So you have this discordant pattern in relationships.[33]

As a result, "what did happen was that the Bundesbank took a particular position and sometimes got some support from the other bankers." In each country, central bankers were mindful of the political needs of the finance ministers at the same time as they sought to protect the institutional interests they shared with other central bankers.

At the London G-5 the Japanese Ministry of Finance revealed its priority in a strategy it would use again and again. Takeshita sought to maintain autonomy in his own domain, fiscal policy, by evading international coordination. He therefore directed attention on monetary policy and, specifically, on coordinated discount-rate cuts to relieve the pressure on him to stimulate the economy with fiscal tools.

The German Bundesbank refused to be dictated to like the Bank of Japan and instead adhered faithfully to the "Bundesbank Doctrine," whereby the Bundesbank allowed the mark to revalue when market pressure forced it in an upward direction rather than adjusting domestic monetary policy— that is, lowering the discount rate. Especially on the EMS matter, German central bankers tried to shift the decision-making burden from the central bank to the ministry of finance, a move to be envied by BOJ officials. A top Bundesbank official said of the EMS currency realignment in January 1987, "Well, I was very grateful to Stoltenberg to make the politically painful decision to revalue the D-mark."[34] The contrast between the Bundesbank's ability to deflect political pressure while maintaining its independence and the BOJ's inability to withstand pressure from the MOF reflects organizational differences between the two countries' central banks. Whereas the Bundesbank is free from supervision by any other government body, the BOJ is subject to MOF supervision that includes the right to issue general directives, dismiss BOJ officials, and permit or approve almost all activities of the BOJ.[35]

---

33. Personal interview.

34. Personal interview.

35. Bank of Japan Economic Research Department, *Money and Banking in Japan* (New York: St. Martin's Press, 1973), 228.

The institutional differences among the players directly affected the negotiating process. The constitutionally guaranteed independence of the Bundesbank clearly enhanced the bargaining power of West Germany, allowing Bonn to block any move that threatened to undermine its authority. At the same time, the constitutional constraint may have tied otherwise more flexible hands and led to intransigence on the part of Bonn. Furthermore, once the other players perceive this intransigence, they are discouraged from making strong commitments if they feel that the burden will not be shared equally. For example, the Bundesbank's neglect of US requests to lower its discount rate during the summer of 1986, enabled the BOJ to resist US appeals also. According to a BOJ official, Sumita was encouraged to learn from Pöhl at a BIS meeting in Basel in early July that the Bundesbank would resist US pressure. This emboldened resistance was a departure from usual BOJ practice; some bank officials expressed it as the "heroic solidarity of the central bankers."

From the perspective of the Bundesbank, its anti-inflationary policy acts as an anchor in the world monetary system. German central bank officials believe that they carry perhaps the heaviest burden since they must uphold responsible economic policy "amid all the political nonsense apparent in international policy coordination efforts."[36] These officials regard the BOJ as a "free rider" within the group and disapprove of its willingness to accommodate political interests and bow to pressures.

The US Federal Reserve Board also enjoys considerable independence from the administration. The administration has no explicit channel through which it can influence Fed policy. The Federal Reserve Board was created as an instrument of Congress, to which it reports. The personal authority of the officials concerned, moreover, has in practice shaped the nature of interinstitutional relations between the Federal Reserve Board and other government bodies.[37] As chairman of the Federal Reserve, Paul Volcker exemplified the strong central banker. His fight against inflation during the early 1980s evoked respect and even awe among central bankers throughout the world. A high-ranking Bundesbank official said admiringly, "Folcker, I suppose, is a German deep in his bones. That's why he is so anti-inflation."[38] Volcker was able to resist administration pressure from then Under Secretary of the Treasury Beryl Sprinkel when he attempted to increase his influence on monetary policy during the first Reagan administration.

Volcker's strong plea for Japan and West Germany to stimulate their

---

36. Interview of a German monetary official with the author.

37. Fred Hirsch, *Money International* (New York: Doubleday & Company, 1969), 206.

38. Personal interview.

economies, particularly since spring 1986, therefore puzzled fellow central bankers, as did the palace coup incident. Volcker's unchallenged authority and power eroded perceptibly once Baker had initiated the Plaza strategy and forced Volcker to become another one of the players in the round of policy coordination. The Bundesbank reacted by establishing direct contacts at the Treasury after opening a representative office in New York in October 1986. This effort to keep close watch on the epicenter of policy coordination preceded a series of discussions between Pöhl and Mulford.

In the United States, the constitutional separation of the legislative branch from the executive branch provides the administration with a scapegoat, the Congress, upon which any blame can be dumped. A current and notable example is the administration's assertion that Congress is to blame for not reducing the budget deficit. For US trading partners, this translates into a problem of credibility: once the ability of the US administration to deliver on any commitment is put in question, the credibility of US diplomacy in general is undermined.

In this sense, the Plaza strategy was propelled forward by the Gramm-Rudman-Hollings Amendment because the administration gained some credibility from its pledge to reduce the budget deficit. According to one governor, the legislation also persuaded some governors at the Federal Reserve Board to take a more positive look at lowering the discount rate in the United States.

■ The End of Unilateralism: The United States

Somehow, a *strong* dollar was transformed overnight into an *overvalued* dollar. Surely this was Baker magic. After all, Baker was working with firmly entrenched policy and rhetoric. To President Ronald Reagan, the Plaza Agreement demonstrated continuity in policy, not change. Certainly "the President supported the Plaza strategy" and "was very pleased with the reaction around the world, and the aftermath of the Plaza," a Reagan administration official later remarked. But a new strategy had to be depicted as an extension, not as a departure from or an alternative to the formal policy. One month after the Plaza meeting, the Subcommittee on International Finance and Monetary Policy of the Senate Banking Committee met to examine "the causes and effects of the overvalued dollar and, more importantly, what can and should be done to correct the imbalance." During the hearing, Senator William Proxmire (D-WI) launched the discussion:

In February of this year [1985], when asked about the overvalued dollar at a press conference, the President said, "It really wasn't a problem, it was a blessing." Well, farmers and laborers who have lost their farms and jobs because of the loss of our overseas markets don't see the John Wayne dollar as a blessing. I think most Americans would prefer a Woody Allen wimp dollar, or maybe a Rodney Dangerfield dollar that wasn't beating their brains out.[1]

Congressional attention to the value of the dollar increased in the spring of 1985. Although many members of Congress wanted the depreciation of the dollar, there was a considerable psychological block against currency depreciation, especially after years of the Reagan administration's preaching that a strong dollar represented a strong America. The inconclusive discussion

---

1. Hearings before the Subcommittee on International Finance and Monetary Policy, US Senate Committee on Banking, Housing, and Urban Affairs, 23 October 1985.

of the Senate committee illustrated the uncertainty over which level of the dollar actually did reflect a strong America.

According to the Reagan administration's "capitalism in one country" approach to world economic problems, a thriving American economy would automatically lead to growth and the maximization of welfare in the rest of the world. Already in the early 1980s, some critics had expressed apprehension over the danger and costs of such a unilateral approach. The administration gave international economic consideration a lower priority than had any other administration in the postwar period and has formulated its domestic economic policies "in almost total disregard for the outside world."[2]

Recovery of the US economy since late 1982, however, gave credence to the "America First" approach and confidence to its proponents. Intellectual reinforcement for economic unilateralism was provided by Henry R. Nau, a professor at George Washington University. He argued that:

[T]he domesticist perspective offers better prospects for the 1980s. The Reagan administration has rightfully reasserted US power to lead the world back to the domesticist triad of world economic rearmament, low inflation, market incentives, and freer trade. . . . The domesticist perspective offers a useful and long-overdue intellectual template both for appreciating the fundamentally correct international economic policy course charted by the Reagan administration and for appealing to the administration to follow through on its own domesticist priorities.[3]

The new administration was staffed with people of all ideological types, although most were true believers in the market mechanism. To the free floaters, either "fixing" exchange rates or devaluing the dollar was anathema. Reaganites, opposed to the weak dollar bequeathed by the Carter administration, were pressuring instead for a stronger dollar. A former senior Treasury official explained:

Carter people at the Treasury had tried to talk the dollar down and they did it so effectively that it collapsed and everybody was really panicking over the weak dollar. . . . The dollar was the world reserve currency and no one wanted it.[4]

---

2. Benjamin J. Cohen, "An Explosion in the Kitchen? Economic Relations with Other Advanced Industrial States," in *Eagle Defiant: United States Foreign Policy in the 1980s*, ed. Kenneth A. Oye, Robert J. Lieber, and Donald Rothchild (Boston: Little, Brown, 1983), 116.

3. Henry R. Nau, "Where Reaganomics Works," *Foreign Policy*, no. 57 (Winter 1984–85): 14–37.

4. Personal interview.

Furthermore, they were tired of the never-ending stream of complaints from trading partners, especially the Europeans, about the level of the dollar whichever direction it happened to take. The same official noted:

I remember being in Italy in 1982, late 1982, when the dollar started to get stronger. A deputy of the Italian Finance Minister started to complain that the dollar was too strong. So I pointed out to him, "Well, I heard the last time you complained to my predecessor about the weak dollar." He said, "Well, that's the problem with the dollar. It's strong when it shouldn't be strong, and it's weak when it shouldn't be weak." You know, there wasn't any level that was going to please everybody. You see, they were unhappy with the weak dollar because it made us that much more competitive, they were unhappy with the strong dollar because it made oil costs that much higher.[5]

Exasperation over the weak dollar and the practical difficulty of setting the right value for the dollar contributed to the Reagan administration's unilateral, strong-dollar approach.

The free market philosophy of the US Treasury headed by Donald T. Regan, which stressed noninterference in the markets, was endorsed by the "Chicago" economists in the administration, such as Beryl Sprinkel, then Under Secretary of the Treasury, and bolstered by the ideological and political demands imposed by the conservatives. For example, conservatives like Senator Jesse Helms (R-NC), and Representative Jack Kemp (R-NY) put pressure on the administration to adopt a new gold standard. To this end, the Treasury conducted a study for Congress on the desirability and feasibility of going back to a gold standard. As expected, negative conclusions were drawn; out of the process, however, emerged one important by-product. The Treasury was forced "to be rather vociferous in defending the current floating exchange rate system vis-à-vis the gold standard. That, and the fact that we couldn't find a better alternative perhaps caused us to have a more market-oriented rhetoric [and] made us sound more committed than in fact we were," recalled former Deputy Secretary of the Treasury, Tim McNamar.[6]

The administration's laissez-faire attitude toward burgeoning budget deficits, high interest rates, and a strong dollar eventually alienated its trading partners. At the Versailles Economic Summit in 1982, President Reagan was isolated on the question of the dollar and macroeconomic policies. At the Williamsburg Summit the following year, Reagan's policies were "clearly opposed by everyone else from the Japanese to the Canadians to us Europeans," according to Chancellor Helmut Kohl.[7]

---

5. Personal interview.

6. Personal interview.

7. *New York Times,* 31 May 1983.

The most bitter dispute between the United States and its trading partners concerned exchange rate policy. In response to repeated requests to intervene jointly to realign the exchange rate, the Regan Treasury promulgated a doctrine of "convergence." The reasoning was that exchange rates were determined by fundamentals and fluctuate only if the fundamentals diverge conspicuously between nations. In April 1981, Regan announced that the United States would not intervene in the foreign exchange markets except in extraordinary cases. Reflecting the new nonintervention policy, the Federal Reserve Bank of New York publicly announced in December of the same year that it had not bought or sold any foreign currencies during the May–October period. It was the first six-month period in almost a decade that monetary authorities had not conducted exchange market intervention. Thus, according to Regan, the American goal at the Versailles Summit was "a convergence of our economies with each more stable and with less inflation," which would ostensibly "stabilize exchange rates."[8]

Nonintervention in the currency markets, like nothing else, brought home the true message of Reaganomics. Pressure on the Treasury to arrest dollar appreciation through intervention in the market during the first term of the Reagan administration came not only from foreign countries but also from the Federal Reserve System, particularly the New York Federal Reserve Bank. Anthony Solomon, then President of the New York Federal Reserve Bank, argued internally that it was a good time for US monetary authorities to build foreign currency reserves, with the aim of creating a $9 billion "war chest." The Treasury promptly dismissed the idea.

The relationship between the Treasury and the Federal Reserve Board, taking the cue from chiefs Regan and Volcker, respectively, remained an uneasy one. McNamar recalls:

One morning [Regan] had an attack in the office. Volcker knew he was in town. Volcker knew he was in the office. And Regan's secretary . . . because Regan was sick, wouldn't return Volcker's phone calls. So he said, "Let me talk to Tim!" He was agitated about something—I don't remember what the event was—the markets were jumping around, something had happened. Volcker told me, "Tell him to return my goddam phone calls!"

When I called Volcker back to tell him [Regan] was tied up with something else, he said, "Well, you have the authority to make the decisions. How much are we going to go in for?" I answered that we should watch it for a half an hour. "Half an hour!" Volcker screamed.[9]

---

8. Quoted in C. Randall Henning, "Macroeconomic Diplomacy in the 1980s," *Atlantic Paper No. 65* (Paris: Atlantic Institute for International Affairs, March 1987), 18.

9. Personal interview.

Pressures

During the first half of the 1980s, the strong dollar caused the manufacturing and agricultural sectors of the US economy to fall under severe competition in world markets. Although it enumerated the benefits of the strong dollar, the Annual Report of the Council of Economic Advisors admitted the negative side, too:

As the dollar has risen, some US industries that compete in international markets have experienced difficulties. Many of these problems are concentrated in the manufacturing sector, where declines in trade balances across the industries have been widespread. . . . The traditional US surplus in agricultural products has contracted by about $8.5 billion from its level of three years ago as dollar appreciation and slower demand growth have kept dollar prices and export volumes down. Declines have also occurred in US exports of raw materials.[10]

The manufacturing and agricultural sectors were the most visible victims of the strong dollar, although they did not voice concerted grievances until 1985. Even Walter Mondale, contender in the 1984 presidential race, was not able to use the strong dollar effectively as an issue, focusing instead, to the demise of his presidential aspirations, on tax policy.

Clearly, the political clout of these sectors had eroded significantly. Producers of automobiles, steel, machine tools, and other internationally competitive goods, management and labor union alike, could not change the strong-dollar policy of the administration. Ideology aside, the fundamental transformation of the American industrial structure explained the long duration of the overvalued dollar to a considerable degree. The comments of a Washington representative of an automobile maker were telling:

We still think of manufacturing as the "big mule" in politics, but it's not true. The financial sector, the service sector, are all so much bigger. The strong dollar was good for them and it was good for consumers. It kept prices down and guaranteed cheap goods, while the tax cuts and deficits meant there was plenty of money to spend. It was anti-manufacturing, anti-labor—but it was pro-consumption, pro-services.[11]

The service sector is extensive and ever growing: health services, banking and finance, insurance, real estate, retailing, hotels and restaurants, travel

---

10. *Economic Report of the President, February 1985* (Washington: US Government Printing Office), 106.

11. Cited by William Greider, *Secrets of the Temple: How the Federal Reserve Runs the Country* (New York: Simon and Schuster, 1987), 600.

and transport, the legal and technical professions, and the media and communications. In terms of political and electoral constituencies, the strong-dollar policy, roughly speaking, suited the "white collar" Republican voters while hurting the "blue collar" Democratic supporters. The dollar policy was not affecting Republican voters directly, except for the farmers. As a former senior Treasury official said, "there was no Wall Street pressure to drive the dollar downward," because money men on Wall Street cared less about the strong dollar than about budget deficits since their primary concerns are controlling inflation and promoting investment. Another ally of the strong-dollar policy was the powerful defense contractors, shielded from international competition and boosted by the Reagan administration's huge increase in the defense budget.[12]

By late 1984, however, the wind had changed subtly. The National Association of Manufacturers (NAM), the Chamber of Commerce, and farm lobbies began to cry out. Cabinet members such as Secretary of Commerce Malcolm Baldridge, United States Trade Representative William E. Brock, and Secretary of Agriculture John R. Block began arguing in favor of dollar depreciation. But the Reagan White House and the Regan-Sprinkel Treasury refused to be persuaded. He felt so helpless with the inaction at the Treasury that Block privately asked Bob Dole (R-KS), the Senate majority leader and friend of the American farmer, to try to persuade the President to change exchange rate policy.[13]

Protests emerged from various interest groups in business and industry. Here, two examples of lobbying are illustrative. One was the Lee Morgan campaign. Another was Lee Iacocca's "lone ranger" battle.

Lee Morgan, Chairman of Caterpillar Tractor and Chairman of the Business Roundtable Task Force, spearheaded a campaign to sensitize Congress and the administration to the effects of the exchange rate on business. As early as December 1981, Lee Morgan began what was to be a long campaign to urge economic policymakers to stabilize the exchange rates of major currencies.[14] On 11 December 1981 Morgan stated before the House Ways and Means Subcommittee on Trade that unstable exchange rates were beginning

---

12. Ibid., 600–601.

13. Based on information provided by a congressional source.

14. Concerns over the impact of the exchange rate of the dollar on American competitiveness and the trade balance were expressed as early as 1981 by C. Fred Bergsten and his colleagues at the new Institute for International Economics, and repeated frequently in public presentations and congressional testimony before being picked up politically by these groups when the forecasts turned out to be accurate. Among the most important of Bergsten's early statements were "The Costs of Reaganomics," in *Foreign Policy*, no. 44 (Fall 1981), 24–36; and "What to Do About the United States–Japan Economic Problem," in *Foreign Affairs* 60 (Summer 1982), 1059–1075.

to hurt American business. He gave no specific recommendations for the problem, just that "high interest rates and unstable exchange rates are complicating the financial management of multinational corporations and depressing international trade and investment."

One year later, Morgan and the Business Roundtable decided that "more stability" increasingly meant a realignment of the dollar against the yen. "The problem facing American business today as a result of the misalignment in the exchange rate between the dollar and the yen is the single most important trade issue facing the US today," Morgan told the Congress. He added that many of his colleagues in the business community held this view. "What we want as a long-term goal is a freely traded international yen." He testified that a joint US–Japan initiative on the yen should include: (1) Japanese measures to encourage capital inflows and stimulate foreign investment in yen instruments in Japan, (2) a surcharge on Japanese manufactured goods, (3) foreign exchange intervention by US and other central banks, and (4) measures to lower US interest rates further. In April 1983 Morgan testified before the Senate Foreign Relations Committee on the problem of the undervalued yen, then at 235 yen to the dollar. He again cited industry analysts' views that 200 yen to the dollar represented "basic structural equilibrium."

In the fall of 1983, Morgan continued to press for an appreciation of the yen, this time before the House Banking Committee. On October 27 Morgan focused on the "exchange rate advantage" that "alone is sufficient to impair the competitiveness of US firms and workers. . . . Even highly efficient firms like Caterpillar find it difficult to compete effectively in such a distorted climate." He blamed interest rate differentials and one-sided capital flows for the weakness of the yen.

Throughout 1984, Morgan continued his assaults on prevailing exchange rates and claimed that present "exchange rate relationships are wreaking havoc on our international competitiveness," noting that Caterpillar had sold $3.5 billion in exports in 1981, but only $1.6 billion in 1983. This had caused the company to trim 15,000 jobs in just two years.

Although Lee Morgan channeled much of his lobbying effort toward the Congress, this was ancillary to his assault on the administration. He and other members of the Business Roundtable met first with top Treasury officials in what proved to be a frustrating encounter. "Treasury people, especially Beryl Sprinkel were 100 percent free market believers. They just kept saying, 'Markets determine values of currency,' " recalled one business executive who attended that meeting. Afterward Morgan switched tactics and aimed directly at the White House. Republican congressmen from Illinois, where Caterpillar is headquartered, helped to open the door to the Oval Office. Representative Robert Michel (R-IL), House Minority Leader, and Senator Charles H. Percy (R-IL), Chairman of the Foreign Relations

Committee, in particular, helped to arrange three meetings between Morgan and other business executives and the President during 1983 and 1984.

The first meeting was set just before Reagan's visit to Japan in November 1983. Representatives of the business community included James F. Beré, Chairman of Borg-Warner; Philip Caldwell, Chairman of Ford Motor Company; and John Roderick, Chairman of US Steel (now USX). From the administration, Reagan, Regan, Shultz, Brock, Baldridge, and Martin Feldstein attended. While Regan maintained support for free reign of the market and refused to make any commitments, other cabinet members seemed more concerned. Shultz, in particular, expressed support for the position of business.

A second meeting, held before the London Economic Summit in 1984, was attended by Morgan and David Packard, Chairman of Hewlett-Packard. President Reagan, Vice President George Bush, and Regan were present. The third meeting was held soon after Reagan's landslide victory in the 1984 election. Representative Bob Michel accompanied both Lee Morgan and Ed Spencer, Chairman of Honeywell Corporation and successor to Morgan for the chairmanship of the Task Force of the Business Roundtable. The discussion focused mainly on the exchange rate. Morgan stressed the negative consequences of the overvalued dollar for the US economy. Once again, the President made no commitment, although this time, he appeared to perceive that a problem did exist.[15]

Initially, Morgan focused on the alleged manipulations of the yen by the Japanese Ministry of Finance. In addition to his plea that the Treasury Department look into the matter, he asked Senator Charles H. Percy to request that the General Accounting Office (GAO) conduct a study on whether the Japanese government had manipulated exchange rates to force the yen lower, to which Percy agreed. The results were inconclusive and gave no evidence of Morgan's contention of Japanese yen-rigging.

Morgan then decided to take a different tack. He asked David C. Murchison, a Washington attorney, and Ezra Solomon, a Stanford University economist, to examine the misalignment of the dollar and the yen. The report was submitted on September 19, in time for Morgan to press the White House to place currency realignment on the agenda for the Nakasone-Reagan meeting in November. By this time, the trade deficit problem had surfaced as a presidential campaign issue. On October 17 Reagan formally appointed a re-election committee, thereby confirming his intention of seeking a second term. Reagan's campaign strategists found it expedient to attribute the trade deficit to the yen. It was not the dollar that was too strong, but the yen that was too weak.

---

15. Interview with the author of one participant in the meeting.

While Lee Morgan's campaign was part of a well-organized business lobbying effort, Lee Iacocca waged a lonely battle against the undervalued yen, albeit with much greater headline coverage. On 27 June 1983 Iacocca stated that even if American quality, performance, and productivity were equal to that of the Japanese, they still had a "$2,000 per car advantage" because of taxes and currency. Yet, he also recognized the root of the dollar problem. To the American Chamber of Commerce in Tokyo in April 1985, Iacocca focused more on "our half" of the trade problem. "Let's face it, the high dollar is a bastard child of our own scandalous budget deficit in the United States and only we can fix that."

Iacocca did not forget to cite trade barriers and closed markets as being "Japan's half":

By not opening its markets as widely as ours are, Japan is really letting us off the hook. The focus right now is on Japan's protectionism, not on the high dollar. . . . People don't get excited about the high dollar. Not on Main Street USA, they don't: that's economics . . . the old dismal science. . . . People don't really understand it. So nobody's going to get up in arms over the high dollar.[16]

By the time Iacocca addressed the Financial Analysts Meeting in Savannah, Georgia, 18 February 1986, the trade deficit had reached $150 billion and the dollar had depreciated to 181 yen to the dollar. Iacocca quoted Regan as saying for four years that "absolutely nothing could be done about the currency gap." He then referred to him as:

The guy who invented Acne Economics, remember? Whatever the problem, the answer was always, "Don't worry, we'll grow out of it." Well, we got a new Treasury Secretary last year, and one who apparently wasn't about to be laughed at. He simply called a weekend meeting at the Plaza in New York with four other guys, and by magic (I guess) the currency gap has been getting smaller and smaller ever since.[17]

Meanwhile, congressional reaction to the trade problems caused by the strong dollar had started to erupt in the spring of 1985. Newborn concern over the dollar exchange rate arose out of various considerations. In April, the Senate unanimously passed the "anti-Japan" resolution. In the ensuing months a rash of trade bills poured out of the Congress, one of which was the Democrats' highly protectionist trade bill cosponsored by Lloyd Bentsen (D-TX), Richard A. Gephardt (D-MO), and Dan Rostenkowski (D-IL).

---

16. Lee Iacocca, address to the American Chamber of Commerce, Tokyo, April 1985.

17. Lee Iacocca, address to the Financial Analysts Meeting, Savannah, Ga., 18 February 1986.

In the April 5 announcement of a hearing to be held on the impact of floating exchange rates on international trading, Senate Finance Committee Chairman Bob Packwood (R-OR) raised the question of "the viability of the international trading system in an era of floating exchange rates." He went on to say:

Those who believed that a floating exchange rate system would operate to restore equilibrium in our international payments should re-examine their thesis in light of modern movements of capital which overwhelm the effects of surpluses and deficits in the trade account.[18]

Packwood's fundamental question, "whether an open market for dollars, free of government intervention, to moderate the movements in exchange rates, is compatible with free and open markets for traded goods," was important, coming from a moderate Republican free trader. In order to resist protectionist trade legislation, Packwood sought an alternative in some set of practical policies that could correct the external imbalance.

The Democrats pursued a similar line of questioning but focused more directly on intervention. A thirteen-member Senate Democratic Working Group on Trade Policy called on the Reagan administration to adopt a more interventionist exchange rate policy by coordinating efforts with trading partners to set up what could be a system of target zones for currencies. Senator Lloyd Bentsen, who chaired the group said: "We have to find something between the excess rigidity of the Bretton Woods system and the excess gyrations we're seeing now." Bentsen criticized the administration for "blatant disregard" of exchange rate gyrations, noting that this had caused US companies to relocate overseas.[19]

The linkage between monetary and trade issues was reinforced by the formation of an agenda for the new General Agreement on Tariffs and Trade (GATT) round. Senators John C. Danforth (R-MO) and Bentsen conditioned their approval of a new GATT on the inclusion of monetary issues. Danforth said: "Congress should insist on clear plans for rectifying the exchange rate problem. . . . as conditions for granting the President . . . authority for implementing a new negotiating round. . . . No trade policy can work if the exchange rate problem is not resolved."[20]

Some congressmen tried to incorporate congressional oversight of the exchange rate into trade legislation. One of those bills, the Competitive

---

18. Announcement for hearing on "The Impact of Floating Exchange Rates on International Trading," US Senate Finance Committee, 5 April 1985.

19. Clyde H. Farnsworth, "Democrats Seek Currency Intervention," *New York Times*, 25 April 1985.

20. *Wall Street Journal*, 26 April 1986.

Exchange Rate Act of 1985, would have reduced the discretionary power of the Federal Reserve Board and the Treasury in international monetary policy, requiring the US administration to intervene in the foreign exchange markets when the current account balance was in substantial deficit.[21] Another bill, introduced by Senators Max Baucus (D-MT) and Daniel Patrick Moynihan (D-NY) required the Secretary of the Treasury and the Chairman of the Federal Reserve Board to develop a Strategic Foreign Currency Reserve to "resist and moderate any increase in the dollar; to try to bring down the dollar in a steady way to a so-called soft landing; and to counteract wild fluctuations such as possible free fall of the dollar." On August 1, Senator Bill Bradley (D-NJ) introduced the Strategic Capital Reserve Act, which called for essentially the same thing, except that it would not have allowed sterilized intervention.

It would overstate the case to claim that the Congress became preoccupied with currency matters. In fact, the Congress was deeply concerned with trade issues but did not focus on currency matters per se. Packwood later said that the Congress did not put pressure on Baker to realign currencies, and there were no demands from his colleagues in the Senate to do so:

I don't think the Senate was thinking so much of the overvalued dollar as they were of the trade deficit and what they regarded as unfair practices by some of our trading competitors. Congress regards itself as in a position to pass trade legislation, good or bad, and taxes, up or down. But we don't think of ourselves often as the group that should try to realign world currencies.[22]

Baker's move, therefore, was not a direct reaction to congressional pressure for dollar depreciation: it was more a preemptive action to stave off the protectionist forces in the Congress by attacking the trade problem through an alternate route.

The Art of the Possible

When Baker came to the Treasury, by way of a much publicized swap with Regan, he arrived without a set of policies on the dollar and the nation's steep imbalances.[23] As one ranking cabinet official later observed, "Baker

---

21. As proposed by C. Fred Bergsten in "Correcting the Dollar and Reforming the International Monetary System," statement before the Subcommittee on International Finance, Trade, and Monetary Policy of the US House Banking Committee, 19 November 1985, especially 12-13.

22. Personal interview of Senator Bob Packwood with the author.

23. For a thorough account of the job swap, see Jeffrey H. Birnbaum and Alan S. Murray, *Showdown at Gucci Gulch: Lawmakers, Lobbyists, and the Unlikely Triumph of Tax Reform* (New York: Random House 1987), 66-67.

has very few economic convictions other than a Texan's aversion to high interest rates and a politician's indifference to long-term effects."[24] Baker's deputy, Richard G. Darman, was also new to international currency diplomacy. Inexperience in the field inhibited neither from formulating plans for systemic change. In April, Darman drafted a paper outlining the desired changes in the international economic system. Baker and Darman sought to change the system on an orderly basis. From their outlook, the pressure from business, the Congress, and foreign countries necessitated some kind of action with regard to the dollar, "but it was also a good excuse to start changing the system, for those who were interested in changing the system independently [of these immediate considerations]."[25]

Their mutual agreement to change the system in no way diminished the obstacles that had to be overcome. Baker waged battle on many fronts and against formidable opponents. First, the President would not like the idea of dollar depreciation. Second, Regan might resist the immediate reversal of his policies by his successor. Third, Baker threatened to upset the comfortable officialdom at the Treasury. Fourth, as an economist and himself one of the creators of floating rates in 1973, George P. Shultz might interpret the "new system" as a step toward a managed floating system. Fifth, Beryl Sprinkel would assuredly protest any attempt to disturb the natural movement of the market. Sixth, Volcker, as chief of the nation's central bank, might feel that his independence in conducting monetary policy would be compromised. Finally, foreigners would be reluctant to endorse any departure from the status quo.

Of these potential opponents to the new approach designed by Baker and Darman, Volcker and Shultz would be handled most carefully. Before both the Plaza meeting and the Tokyo Summit, Baker showed his proposals to Volcker and Shultz before presenting them to the foreign participants.

Baker had held regular breakfast meetings with Shultz since June 1985, which Darman and Deputy Secretary of State John C. Whitehead usually joined. Baker asked Shultz's views on almost all vital questions of international economic policy. "We exchanged some papers, very sensitive ones, between the Treasury and State, and it formed the basis for the event of the fall [the Plaza]," related a senior administration official later. Shultz warned Baker not to make public statements on the exchange rate and expressed reservations over the intervention tactics, telling him that "intervention is not a panacea." He was so concerned that at one point he told Whitehead to caution Darman directly on the use of intervention.

Another heavyweight whom Baker and Darman could not afford to ignore

---

24. Personal interview.

25. Comment by a senior US administration official to the author.

was Paul Volcker. Shortly after he became Deputy Secretary of the Treasury, Darman had lunch with Volcker and explained his ideas for a new international economic policy—policy coordination and intervention tactics. "My gosh, it is a big change," growled Volcker. Volcker led Darman to think, however, that he was not against a new policy. Baker and Darman realized the importance of aligning themselves with Volcker. They decided not to repeat the Fed-bashing tactics of their predecessors but instead sought the same objective by circumventing the Fed through use of the exchange rate, the policy instrument that the Treasury holds over it. Volcker thus had no choice but to get along with the new team.

In the end, Shultz, who favored a freely floating system, was persuaded to sanction Baker's new approach and Volcker proved not to be a problem. Other potential obstacles were also dealt with. A senior official later remarked:

You've got all different points of view, you see. The President favors a gold standard, so he is for very strict exchange rates. Regan had favored very much a floating system, but at another time, he had said that he wanted to have an international monetary conference, so he had been in a couple of different positions. . . . Beryl Sprinkel totally favored a floating system. Al Kingon, who was Regan's principal substantive advisor, favored a stable system, so we had people from all lots.[26]

The same official went on to explain how the Baker-Darman strategy avoided opposition from Sprinkel or, more important, any joint attack from Sprinkel and Shultz: "Sprinkel, generally speaking, didn't know what was happening. In the first step, at the OECD [Organization for Economic Cooperation and Development] meeting, he learned about it [the plan to hold an international monetary conference] by reading it in the newspapers."[27]

In fact, Sprinkel was not the only one who "didn't know what was happening." One element of the Baker-Darman strategy was surprise. "I think that we informed most of the key people in the US government within 24 hours of [the Plaza], so there wasn't a lot of time to organize opposition." Baker mentioned the Plaza plans briefly to the President "right before Plaza, within a couple of days."[28] Darman informed both Robert McFarlane, National Security Advisor to the President, and Alfred Kingon, Assistant to the President, in the afternoon of the day before the Plaza meeting.

The tactics they used did not stop with the blitz operation. They manipulated the White House speechwriting process to their advantage when they

---

26. Personal interview.

27. Personal interview.

28. Comment by a senior US administration official to the author.

inserted into the State of the Union Message of 1985 a hint of a plan to hold an international monetary conference. "We put it in [the State of the Union] in a rather late draft, we didn't put it in an early draft that was circulated. We had the support on it of the key speech writers."[29]

It remains somewhat of a mystery why Shultz, an advocate of floating exchange rates in the early 1970s, endorsed the Plaza strategy. There are several possibilities. First, Shultz, truly a Washington inside player, knew when to move and on what. Therefore, he was cautious in becoming involved in economic matters, although he maintained an interest in the issues, especially those concerning international economic policy. Shultz recognized the Treasury's jurisdiction over currency policy, as one of his aides emphasized, "Remember, he was the former Secretary of the Treasury. He knows the rules of the game." Besides that, the other issues on Shultz's agenda—arms talks, Nicaragua, the Middle East—occupied his time and energy. He delegated much of the international economic policy making to Allen W. Wallis, Under Secretary of State for Economic and Agricultural Affairs. Wallis was generally not kept informed by the Treasury, and whenever endorsement from the State Department was needed, the Treasury chief contacted Shultz directly.

Second, Shultz, unlike Sprinkel, was never an ideologue on the issue of floating exchange rates. He was more pragmatic, owing perhaps to his experience as the Chairman of the Bechtel Corporation before he joined the Reagan team in 1982. His experience as chief of America's largest construction service industry, might have sensitized him to the danger of an overvalued dollar.

Lee Morgan remembers Shultz's support on the position of business in realigning the yen–dollar exchange rate: "He was an early sympathizer; he kept the subject alive. . . . It was Shultz who said to Regan, 'Don, the business community here is in trouble.' " Shultz demonstrated his sympathy for business interests when he abruptly proposed to discuss the "yen-dollar problem" during a meeting with Japanese Foreign Minister Shintaro Abe in September 1983. It shook the Ministry of Finance back in Japan, which could not fathom what Shultz aimed for and grew concerned that its turf would be invaded by the Ministry of Foreign Affairs. In November 1983, Shultz again brought up the issue with Abe, specifically reminding him that it was advisable for both the State Department and the Ministry of Foreign Affairs to stimulate the monetary authorities in both countries to

---

29. Interview of a senior US administration official with the author.

cope with the issue, since both appeared reluctant to delve into the serious problem of currency misalignment.[30]

Shultz shook the US Treasury, too. Regan "went off like a rocket on that," recalled McNamar, adding:

I recall that we came down pretty hard on that. I went and had a talk with Ken Dam [then Deputy Secretary of the State Department] and he agreed that his bureaucracy was not going to do anything and that George was simply expressing our interest in seeing if we could do something about the problems and recognize that Gaimusho [Ministry of Foreign Affairs] and State were not really the places to do them.[31]

Shultz's aggressive stance prompted monetary authorities in both countries to take the issue more seriously and was "a major contributing factor" in pushing them in the direction of a yen–dollar accord.

Finally, the position from which Shultz acted was critical. As Secretary of State he was in a position to listen to the requests and complaints of foreign countries, especially principal trading partners. Their message was unanimous: do something about the strong dollar. Thus, Shultz was duty-bound to heed that message when Baker began to "do something."

It is fair to say that Shultz's endorsement and Volcker's support proved to be invaluable to Baker. Shultz, though usually behind the scenes, did much toward catalyzing the new strategy by advocating yen–dollar realignment. Even though he was unsure about the Baker-Darman approach to constructing a new system, Volcker's support was indispensable. This kind of backing enabled Baker to act on the proposal drafted by Darman.

President Reagan might have changed the course of US economic policy making had he chosen to become more involved. Instead, when Baker informed him of the Plaza plan only a few days before the Plaza meeting, the President "supported it and had no problems with it," recalled a Reagan administration official. Thereafter his involvement was minimal. Perhaps it is a question of which system that Reagan believed to be more conservative, fixed or floating exchange rates. Publicly, of course, his position was unambiguously in favor of leaving adjustment to the marketplace, as he affirmed in response to the challenge posed by French President François Mitterrand's proposal for a target zone system before the Williamsburg Economic Summit in 1983. Other evidence suggests that Reagan was attracted to the idea of fixed exchange rates—along the order of the good

---

30. On the Shultz-Abe meeting, see Michihiko Kunihiro, *Taikenteki Keizai Masatsu Ron* (On the personal observation of the economic entanglement) (Tokyo: Sekaino Ugoki Sha, 1987), 89-93.

31. Personal interview.

old days of Bretton Woods in the 1950s or even the gold standard. Martin Feldstein recalls:

[Reagan] has ambiguous views about exchange rates. On one hand he liked the idea of fixed exchange rates. He knew them as a young man. That was one of the solid things. But, at the same time, he realized that the exchange rate is a relevant price and that's part of believing in the market in general: to believe the exchange rate should be set by the market rather than government intervention.[32]

It was said among the White House staff later that, in a conversation with Milton Friedman, the President argued for greater management of exchange rates as an alternative to instability, which reportedly displeased Friedman.

Thus, given Reagan's explicit and unyielding position against tax increases, his more ambivalent position on exchange rates left Baker with room to maneuver in the area of currency intervention.

In most matters of currency diplomacy, the Treasury Department traditionally holds a monopoly and dictates the terms of negotiations to the Federal Reserve Board. As was the case with John B. Connally's Smithsonian Agreement of 1971 and W. Michael Blumenthal's dollar defense package of 1978, Baker's Plaza strategy was, first and foremost, a solo performed exclusively by the Treasury.[33] As Treasury Secretary, Baker served as Chairman of the President's Economic Policy Council (EPC), a position that helped him to launch the Plaza strategy and manage it from a domestic point of view. The EPC itself did not play a decisive role in shaping the Plaza strategy, which never made it onto its agenda.

Treasury officialdom was at first hesitant to sanction the reversal in intervention policy. Although the Treasury Department was filled with an able and dedicated army of civil servants, it did not have a reputation for initiating progressive measures. Instead, it usually found itself mired in day-to-day details, at one point drawing the assessment that it was "an agency that couldn't see the Bretton Woods for the Bretton trees."[34] Initial reluctance gradually gave way when Treasury officials realized they had to "play safe" with the high-powered political appointees at the top of the department.[35]

---

32. Personal interview.

33. John B. Connally was Secretary of the US Treasury in the Nixon administration from 11 February 1971 to 12 June 1972. W. Michael Blumenthal held the post in the Carter administration from 23 January 1977 to 4 August 1979.

34. Hendriks Houthakker, quoted in Joanne Gowa, *Closing the Gold Window: Domestic Politics and the End of Bretton Woods* (Ithaca, NY: Cornell University Press, 1983), 111.

35. *Wall Street Journal,* 9 October 1986.

Pressure from Congress represented a significant incentive for the Treasury to act. Congressional intrusion into the jurisdiction of the Treasury seemed likely if the Treasury were to balk on the exchange rate problem. Several bills were aimed at reducing the discretionary power of the monetary authorities, requiring them to intervene in the markets. The Treasury, therefore, had to demonstrate its willingness to take action.

The incoming Baker-Darman team, in stark contrast to its predecessors, was sensitive, and even receptive to the needs of Congress. Conditions were ripe for steering US policy in new directions. Baker, ever the pragmatic politician, was less concerned with Wall Street than Regan had been and more sensitive to business interests and public opinion. Furthermore, by the spring of 1985, it was becoming difficult to ignore the cacophony of voices raised in Congress over trade issues. In the end, the pressures facing Baker and Darman mounted to a level that the Regan-Sprinkel team had never experienced.

Engaged in the reformulation of trade policy since late August 1985, the Reagan administration had, by the time of the Plaza, finally admitted that "it must recognize the adverse impact of excessive government spending and budget deficits, [and] the recent strength of the dollar" and that it would "encourage its trading partners to adopt policies that will accelerate their economic growth by urging Bonn Summit participants to act on their commitments to remove rigidities and imbalances in their economies." The administration hoped that a new strategy "would contribute to a gradual strengthening of their currencies and will enhance US exports."[36]

Two problems were still unresolved. First was the question of whether the United States should sponsor a high-level meeting of the larger industrial countries to review the issues and possibly implement reforms or to continue to rely on the Interim Committee to follow up on G-10 studies. The Treasury did not divulge any details of its plan to the other departments or agencies. The consensus of the other cabinet secretaries was that the Treasury, by itself, was not likely to hold a high-level meeting of the industrial countries. On this point, it was perhaps Shultz's support that convinced Baker to use the G-5 as a vehicle for policy coordination.

The second question concerned the debt issue. Again the Treasury Secretary played his cards close to his chest. Even in the EPC meeting right before the Plaza, Baker told the other secretaries in vague terms that they could leave the dollar problem and the LDC debt issue for him to solve,

36. "International Trade and Economic Policy Initiative" (United States administration internal document). Reported by Yoichi Funabashi, "The US will ask trading partners to revalue their currencies," *Asahi Shimbun,* 18 September 1985; and "The US administration's internal document shows tougher trade and vigorous international economic policy emerging," ibid., 19 September 1985.

although there was already broad agreement that "adverse impact of the budget deficits and the strong dollar" were the loci of the problem. With regard to the debt issue, Baker, Shultz, and Volcker started to devise a new growth-oriented strategy in June. Whitehead, Wallis, and Douglas McMinn from the State Department, and Darman and Mulford from the Treasury Department, joined in the meetings to discuss LDC debt. The so-called Baker Plan, which was announced in October 1985, was an amalgamation of the proposals from various members of this group.

Disparate views within the administration with regard to the dollar problem helped to strengthen Baker's hand. The "traders" in the administration, especially the US Trade Representative and the Department of Commerce, favored dollar depreciation. In an end-of-tour report as head of the International Trade Administration, Under Secretary of Commerce Lionel H. Olmer argued in June 1985 that a decline in the value of the dollar "requiring a major reduction in federal budget deficits" was essential for US manufacturing to survive in the global economy.[37] Even the Pentagon worried about over-dependence on imports caused by the high dollar. Nonetheless, as a senior Treasury official later pointed out, Shultz's support was decisive because "with that, we silenced the White House."[38] The gathering force of the argument in favor of currency realignment started to eclipse the ruling free market philosophy.

Baker and Darman's cautious introduction of the new policy and its incremental application prevented an explosion of ideologically motivated attacks on it. They carefully avoided the appearance of a radical departure from the strategy of their predecessors. Once the devaluation of the dollar was under way, the next step was the mobilization of fiscal policy, which proved much more difficult. With regard to fiscal policy, the usually like-minded Baker and Darman seemed to hold slightly different views. Darman, on some occasions, expressed his skepticism about the effectiveness of a policy that depended on Japanese and German fiscal stimulus to solve the imbalance problem. While he recognized that their domestic growth was important to avoid world recession, he did not consider it an effective solution to the trade problem. To some extent, his well-reported barrage against the bloated bureaucracy and the poor quality of the education system reflected his interest in microeconomic solutions. Baker, on the other hand, placed a high value on the growth of Japanese and German domestic demand from the start.

---

37. Lionel H. Olmer, *U.S. Manufacturing at a Crossroads* (Washington: US Department of Commerce International Trade Administration, 14 June 1985). Although his views did "not necessarily reflect the official position of the Department of Commerce," they did indicate clearly which side Commerce was on.

38. Personal interview.

A breakthrough for the growth strategy came from Shultz in April 1985. In what one senior State Department official called "one of the most important economic speeches of the Reagan Administration," Shultz bridged the gap between Regan's convergence strategy and potential fiscal policy coordination. Shultz proposed to restructure the relationship between consumption and savings in both the United States and Japan. The structural imbalance between the two countries, he argued, was largely due to oversaving in Japan and undersaving in the United States, causing massive capital inflows in the United States from Japan in response to interest rate differential and hence, the overvalued dollar. Instead of currency intervention, which he did not mention, he proposed that Japan should dismantle structural obstacles to increased investment and consumption.[39]

Although Baker agreed with Shultz's diagnosis, he was not drawn to his prescription—restructuring—on the basis that it took too long to implement fundamental reform and thus, to achieve concrete results.

Shultz's speech helped to reduce deep-rooted sentiment against locomotive strategies in the administration, thereby paving the way for the Plaza strategy, Shultz's original intention to avoid both currency intervention and locomotive strategy notwithstanding.

Baker and Darman applied a gradualistic approach knowing that the Reagan administration suffered from an overdose of ideology and that some Republican heavyweights, Representative Jack Kemp (R-NY) for one, were keeping a vigilant eye on the course of economic policy making. After all, as late as the summer of 1984, the Republican presidential platform included a gold standard, while other conservatives clung zealously to floating exchange rates and nonintervention. Moreover, the President himself had put his political prestige on the "strong dollar means a strong America" bandwagon. One senior administration official said, "We did not say that it was a radical departure, in fact, within the administration, we took pains to say that it was really just a modest change, that it was not all that significant a change."

The extent to which the Baker-Regan job switch caused the change in policies is debatable. For one thing, Regan was not as dogmatic as Sprinkel. Regan's lieutenant, Alfred Kingon, recommended to Regan that he consider sponsoring an international monetary conference early in the second term of the Reagan presidency, a suggestion to which Regan was favorably disposed. With the dollar decline beginning in February, Regan might have reacted to incentives similar to those faced by Baker. In fact, as White House

---

39. George P. Shultz, "National Policies and Global Prosperity," address at the Woodrow Wilson School of Public and International Affairs, Princeton, NJ, 11 April 1985.

Chief of Staff, Regan did not object to Baker's strategy. According to a Regan aide at the White House, Regan was "supportive" of the new policy for it was within "Baker's responsibility."[40] Feldstein concluded that "anybody who was a spokesman for [the falling dollar] had to deal with the reality of the dollar coming down. I think as far as Plaza is concerned, who knows what Regan would have said. He couldn't continue to maintain that the dollar was a measure of the success of administration policy."[41] It should also be noted that the tax reform legislation of 1986, proposed by Baker and Darman, would not have been possible without Regan's support of the original blueprint for tax reform drafted by Treasury tax professionals. How far Regan would have committed himself to the policy coordination that developed, such as the plan for economic indicators and the Louvre Accord reference range mechanism remains in question, particularly given the fact that had Regan stayed at the Treasury Department, Sprinkel would have also.

Most probably, the main influence of the Baker-Regan job change was its timing. Soon after Baker's installation at Treasury, the dollar began to fall and "around mid-March a more pessimistic reassessment of the outlook for the US economy and a shift of view about interest rates began to weigh on the currency. At the same time, signs of strain in US financial markets became more prominent, raising the risk that financial as well as economic dislocations would intensify."[42]

An immediate and effective jolt to the system occurred with the failure of three secondary government securities dealers. A number of customers sustained losses, including local governments and thrift institutions, which led to large deposit outflows from state-insured thrifts, particularly in Ohio. The markets had expected the Federal Reserve to provide assistance to the domestic financial institutions. When it did not, the dollar moved lower rather quickly.

The depreciation of the dollar presented Baker with a propitious opportunity to "lean with the wind" to further the currency realignment. From its peak in late February until the middle of April, the dollar had dropped 20 percent against the pound sterling, 15 percent against the other European currencies, and 6.5 percent against the yen.[43] Strong protectionist sentiment in Congress increased the probability of strong legislative actions on monetary policy and gave Baker the grounds from which to launch his new policy. The Reagan administration set out to counter the protectionist

---

40. Personal interview.

41. Personal interview.

42. *Federal Reserve Bank of New York Quarterly Review* 10 (Autumn 1985): 52.

43. Ibid., 53.

legislation, especially in the fall when Congress reconvened. Some bold new measures were a political necessity. Currency realignment seemed all the more appealing with the activation of protectionist measures such as Section 301 of the 1974 Trade Act, which requires the President to take action against "unfair" trade practices.

At a chance meeting in the Washington, DC, National Airport immediately after the conclusion of the Plaza meeting, Darman is said to have quipped to Senator Bill Bradley, the author of the Strategic Capital Reserve bill, "Now you can take your bill out of the hopper."[44] This comment revealed the close link between congressional action and the administration's preemptive action. Timely congressional pressure helped to make the Baker strategy possible.

Baker's "art of the possible" also owed something to the strong Republican presidency. Following the landslide victory in the 1984 presidential election, the perceived strength of the Reagan presidency reached its zenith in 1985. The strategy to depreciate the dollar and abandon the splendid isolation of domesticist economic policy would have assumed greater political risk had the executive appeared weak. On this point Robert Kuttner's argument hits the mark:

> If, say, Walter Mondale had proposed this scheme, it would have been dismissed as a naive call for global planning. . . . Like Eisenhower's pull-out from Korea, de Gaulle's accord with Algeria, or Nixon's embrace of China, it could have been done only by a conservative administration.[45]

To conclude, the abandonment of unilateral economic policies, symbolized by the Plaza Accord, was the product of a realignment of domestic political forces in the United States and the heightened saliency of trade issues in the face of rising protectionism. By the summer of 1985, pressure on the administration to alter its stance on exchange rates was exerted by domestic business interests, foreign countries, and both parties in the Congress. Baker's ability to launch a complete reversal in policy and Reaganomic rhetoric should be attributed not so much to magic as to the strategy used and the institutional position of the Treasury Department, with endorsement from heavyweights like Shultz and Volcker. The Baker-Darman strategy was incremental, designed in part to disguise the change taking place. In addition, because of the institutional arrangements in the United States, responsibility for exchange rate policy fell to the Treasury Department, so the tools were already there for Baker to use. Furthermore, the credibility of the strategy was enhanced by the very strength of the Reagan presidency.

---

44. *Wall Street Journal,* 9 October 1986.

45. Robert Kuttner, "Jim Baker Remakes the World," *The New Republic,* 21 April 1986.

In the process of formulating the new trade initiative, the administration, with Baker and Darman in the vanguard, came to the conclusion that huge budget deficits were the cause of the high interest rate and overvalued dollar and therefore needed to be reduced. They had found the root but were prevented by the very strength of the Reagan presidency and the robustness of the economy from recognizing the urgency of the problem.

With regard to domestic fiscal policy, the administration did not depart from previous fiscal policy. Baker's tax reform was merely a restatement of the Reaganomic formula. As far as the budget was concerned, the administration chose to focus on the Gramm-Rudman-Hollings legislation, portraying it as the panacea of the global imbalance problem.[46] Nevertheless, tax reform, Gramm-Rudman-Hollings, and antiprotectionism were the three contributions that the United States had to offer to its partners in the G-5.

46. During an interview with the author, Senator Bob Packwood emphasized the intractable dilemma Baker faced with regard to the fiscal strategy laid down by President Reagan's opposition to tax increases.

He explained:

If we had tried to narrow the budget deficit by increased taxes at the time of the tax reform bill, we would have lost both tax reform and the increased taxes. The only way tax reform could be passed is if it was revenue neutral. So, while many of us had a great concern about the deficit, and we tried to raise taxes at the time, the President would have vetoed it and we would have had no tax reform bill and a big deficit.

We [Baker and Packwood] talked about it [the way to cut the budget deficit], but he is pretty much, of course, stuck with the budget that the President presents and he's not really in a position to go outside the budget. And the President's budget had not realistically been [made] to cut the deficit much. I don't think Jim Baker is in a position to say, "I don't care what the President's budget says, pay no attention to it." He can't say that.

■ *The Political Economy of the Yen: Japan*

Japanese leaders played an active role in formulating the Plaza strategy. As described in chapter 1, the Plaza meeting itself was a product of the personal initiatives of Baker and Takeshita and foreshadowed the emergence of a Group of Two (G-2).

In Japan, the Prime Minister's office was a source of constant pressure. At one point the office suggested a capital control plan to be applied to capital flows from Japan to the United States, which the Ministry of Finance rejected. The proposal was leaked to the press and immediately alarmed US monetary authorities. A high-ranking official of the Federal Reserve Board told a Japanese visitor, "You terrorized us!" Another source of pressure was the leadership of the Liberal Democratic Party (LDP), particularly from statesmen such as Susumu Nikaido. Ministry of International Trade and Industry (MITI) officials also persistently complained to the Ministry of Finance (MOF) that currency misalignment exacerbated the existing bilateral trade crisis, which relegated to MITI the unwelcome responsibility of mitigating disputes.

The Plaza strategy of yen appreciation was made possible by the severity of the strain on the US–Japan relationship by the middle of 1985. By then, various domestic interest groups had increased pressure on the government to cope with the trade imbalance. Prior to that time, no Japanese government would have dared to lead a campaign for yen appreciation against the opposition of the Japanese business community—exporters in particular. In the spring of 1985, both houses of Congress passed almost unanimously a resolution attacking Japan for unfair trade practices. Concern over protectionist legislation in the United States and the growing realization that the Market Oriented Sector Selective (MOSS) talks were not likely to yield far-reaching results compelled Japanese leaders to take action.[1]

---

1. The MOSS talks were sector-by-sector trade liberalization negotiations.

The Japanese Plaza strategy was motivated by a combination of domestic and external factors. As in the preceding rounds of currency realignment in 1971–73 and 1978–79, foreign pressure was critical to Japanese decision making, and, in fact, became more deeply entrenched in the political system. From within the ambit of domestic politics, the Plaza strategy was influenced by the public's heightened aspirations for a higher profile in international diplomacy and its desire for a more open economy, reflected in a growing emphasis on the leadership qualities of its politicians. Additionally, the role of politicians in economic policy making had been expanding as a result of their role in the liberalization of Japanese financial markets and in the resolution of trade disputes, which involved negotiation with foreigners and domestic legislation.

Nakasone Politics

Shortly after he stepped down from the premiership in the fall of 1987, Yasuhiro Nakasone told how he had engineered Japan's Plaza strategy:

In the first half of 1985, we tried very hard to solve Japan's surplus problem. We initiated MOSS talks with the US administration to open Japan's markets. And we decided on action programs to liberalize further. We were thinking of another liberalization plan some time for September. But by June it became more evident that those specific trade liberalization negotiations simply were not enough to cope with the imbalance problem. Therefore, I made up my mind to launch a comprehensive scheme to tackle the issue with US support. It, of course, included yen–dollar currency realignment. I told my idea to Takeshita and Oba. They both agreed.[2]

Nakasone indicated his intentions to Baker in late June when Baker was in Tokyo attending the Group of Ten ministerial meeting. According to Nakasone, the plan had to be comprehensive "because that was the only way to get the US administration to commit to reducing the budget deficit and lowering the interest rate. To facilitate the process, I thought we should accept the political risk of a higher yen."

In formulating the Japanese Plaza strategy, Nakasone did not dream of the runaway yen appreciation that occurred after the Tokyo Summit and just before the Japanese elections of 1986, at which time he referred to it as reaching the "maximum threshold of pain." At the Plaza, his target for the yen–dollar exchange rate had been about 210 to begin with, later reduced to about 200.[3]

---

2. Personal interview.

3. Personal interviews.

Nakasone did not single-handedly engineer Japan's Plaza strategy, however. Although his motivations were not identical to Nakasone's, Takeshita also was drawn to the yen–dollar realignment and directed the Ministry of Finance to study the possibilities. Nakasone, unlike Reagan and Kohl who did not show much interest in macroeconomic policy making, was keenly interested in the decision making of the Plaza strategy from the outset. His strong-yen policy formed part of his overall message, which reflected the Japanese public's demands for political leadership during the first half of the 1980s. Widely noticeable were a heightened consciousness of the political and socioeconomic position of Japan in the world and, concomitantly, growing demands by the public that policy agendas be adapted to meet new international and domestic imperatives. The rise of Nakasone in Japanese politics symbolized the "new Japan." Without Nakasone's politics, Japan's Plaza strategy would have taken a much different shape.

Unlike his peers in the LDP, Nakasone had fervently supported a strong yen since his entry into politics. About a quarter of a century ago, he had preached a foreign policy based on "yen in the right hand and Zen in the left." Coming at a time when Japan was still struggling out of the ruins of war, the idea of an aggressive exchange rate policy elicited derision from seasoned politicians who considered it silly talk from a callow political novice.[4] Yet to a nationalist such as he was, a strong yen was a symbol of a strong Japan, to which the young Nakasone aspired.

Since he had become Prime Minister in 1982, Nakasone had been informed daily of the yen–deutsche mark exchange rates of the dollar at the opening and closing of each session. At a press conference in late 1982 soon after taking office, he made it clear that he would manage the Japanese economy in a way compatible with yen appreciation.[5]

Nakasone's push for a higher yen was part of a broader objective to translate Japan's newly acquired economic wealth into international prestige. During the early 1980s, the overvalued dollar prevented him from realizing his hopes to strengthen the yen, but Nakasone persisted. The Advisory Friends Group, an informal circle of Nakasone's long-time friends, including bankers, businessmen, and former officials, strongly recommended that he pursue the high-yen strategy. Prominent among them was Goro Koyama, senior banker at Mitsui, who provided consistent support for appreciation of the yen and liberalization of Japanese capital markets.

Nakasone commissioned one of the members of the group, Takashi

---

4. Yoichi Funabashi, "It's time to switch locomotives on the economic train," *Asahi Evening News* (Tokyo), 20 January 1983.

5. Yoichi Funabashi, "Nakasone's economic credo," *Asahi Evening News* (Tokyo), 9 December 1982.

Hosomi, former Vice Minister of Finance for International Affairs, to map out the "process for appreciating the yen." In his private recommendation to the Prime Minister, known among the group as the Hosomi Memorandum, Hosomi proposed a gradual revaluation of the yen to 170–180 yen to the dollar and, afterward, a structural reform of Japan's economy from export-led growth to growth from within. Furthermore, he called for joint intervention by the United States and Japan to realign the currency rates.

As Nakasone testified later, he was inclined to endorse a "managed float" or a "controlled float," often expressing skepticism for the theoretical arguments for free-floating exchange rates. He also demonstrated interest in a trilateral approach for coping with the currency problem, saying that:

Only a tripod framework can work and therefore, Germany's participation in a new system is indispensable. . . . I thought that the floating exchange rate was not desirable but the French-type target zone was not feasible. I thought we should aim at broader zones and try to manage the exchange rate in cooperation among the United States, Japan, and Western Europe. The basic premise of the zone strategy was the erosion of US economic power and the limitation of Japanese influence. The US economy is worn out temporarily, therefore, the Number Two economy should shoulder more burden. The yen, however, is still a virgin in the international monetary arena. Japan also needs help from Europe. Currency stability cannot be maintained without three poles of cooperation since the volatility of the D-mark inevitably spills over into the stability of the yen and vice versa.[6]

In late 1985, on Hosomi's recommendations, Nakasone requested the MOF to study the possibility of forming an international monetary regime based on a "snake" arrangement—a flexible and broad exchange rate range—among the three poles, establishing a large-scale strategic reserve fund for mutual intervention, and holding a Bretton Woods style international monetary conference in 1987.[7]

Nakasone's desire for high-yen diplomacy and a new international monetary regime did not crystallize into any solid strategy or set of policies, mostly resulting from the resistance exerted by the Ministry of Finance. The Ministry remained an apostle of floating exchange rates, after having experienced the attempt at trilateral management in early 1973, when the United States and Western Europe had forced an asymmetric appreciation of the yen.[8]

---

6. Personal interview.

7. *Mainichi Shimbun,* 5 November 1985.

8. Takashi Hosomi, *Gekidosuru Tsuka Gaiko* (Turbulent currency diplomacy), (Tokyo: Jiji Tsushin Sha, 1982), 28–38.

What finally enabled Nakasone to overcome the intransigence of the MOF were gradual but profound changes in political perceptions and objectives, for which he was personally responsible. Since assuming power in 1982, Nakasone had altered the fabric of Japanese politics in three important ways. First, he redefined the function of leadership in Japan. Second, he fostered public aspirations to a higher profile of Japan in the world. Third, he offered new social and economic directions to match his vision of Japan's emerging world role.

The political system in Japan has traditionally restrained the powers of the Prime Minister to a far greater degree than the US Constitution limits the power of the American President. Always conscious of factional politics, the Prime Minister must answer to "policy tribes," which are groups of politicians committed to one-dimensional special interests. The Prime Minister must also placate vast armies of bureaucrats, not always from a position of strength. In Japan, it has often been said, politicians reign, but bureaucrats rule. Nakasone challenged these traditional restraints on the power of the premiership, circumventing factional politics by using professionals and academics outside the bureaucracy to formulate policy agendas and carry them out. The Maekawa Reports, which recommended sweeping changes in the Japanese economy and were written by a Nakasone-appointed commission, stand out as an example of the way Nakasone tapped new modalities to get around the system.

Within Japan, Nakasone inspired an awareness of Japan's image in the international arena and in so doing raised public expectations of leadership. He exploited the G-7 summit institution for this purpose, demonstrating that an assured presence and a leading role in the G-7 paid off both internationally and domestically. Nakasone thus set an example for prospective new leaders of Japan and provided the training grounds for those like Shintaro Abe, Foreign Minister, and Noboru Takeshita, Finance Minister, who attended four summit meetings with Nakasone. With Nakasone, "Japan was coming of age in international politics."[9]

In sum, although Nakasone's high-profile diplomacy involved a more openly trilateralist position than had those of his predecessors, its foundation was nonetheless firmly grounded in the US–Japan bilateral relationship. His untiring efforts at projecting a new image for Japan were always directed primarily towards the United States and included building a strong personal relationship with the American president, ergo the "Ron–Yasu relationship."

Nakasone's astute manipulation of political symbolism was illustrated by his visit to Theodore Roosevelt's residence on Long Island after a UN General

9. Robert D. Putnam and Nicholas Bayne, *Hanging Together: The Seven-Power Summits* (Cambridge: Harvard University Press, 1984), 190.

Assembly meeting in the fall of 1985. With his own similar global aspirations, he could identify with Roosevelt, a reform conservative in the age of America's rapid rise to world power, as noted by one State Department official. Teddy Roosevelt's inaugural address on 4 March 1905 seemed to describe the Japan of 1985: "We have become a great nation, forced by the fact of its greatness into relations with the other nations of the earth, and we must behave as befits a people with such responsibilities."[10]

The foundation of Nakasone's vigorous thrust into foreign affairs had been laid since the 1970s with Japan's economic and social transformation. Nakasone's politics deliberately targeted the more affluent, metropolitan middle class as an untapped source of support for his policies and the LDP in general. While well integrated into "corporate Japan," this segment of the population was underrepresented in the political process. It recognized increasing threats to its economic welfare posed by protectionism abroad and, more generally, the failure of the Japanese economy to keep pace with international developments. For this reason it found itself in direct confrontation with deeply entrenched interests—landowners, realtors, rice farmers, mom and pop stores, and bureaucrats—which, in contrast, had benefitted from Japan's closed system and the pork barrel politics that had been a trademark of the LDP since the early 1960s.

Nakasone's high-yen strategy, beyond the symbolic "strong yen equals a strong Japan," was meant to accelerate the reform process, which included deregulation and liberalization of markets. It represented a severe setback for vested interests as a whole, first by throwing open overprotected markets to international competition and second, by threatening the pork barrel government expenditures that the "public works tribes" politicians had pushed. Nakasone's "small government" strategy had already made vulnerable those vested interests. Now the high-yen policy, as a solution to the external imbalance, would deprive them of the benefits that would have been forthcoming with a fiscal stimulus policy by way of increased funds for public investment. Nevertheless, the policy of gradual appreciation of the yen was maintained on the long-term agenda during the whole period from Plaza to Louvre. The Maekawa Report of April 1986 and its sequel, which appeared a year later, practically took for granted a sustained high-yen exchange rate as a prerequisite for pursuing economic restructuring.[11]

The Nakasone formula for politics—strong leadership, high profile in diplomacy, and realignment of the conservative supporters, with more

---

10. "Kironitatsu Nichibei" (United States and Japan at the crossroads), *Asahi Shimbun*, 18 September 1987.

11. The Maekawa Report addresses exchange rate policy as follows: "The government must work for the realization and stabilization of the exchange rate at an appropriate

emphasis on the liberal and internationally minded metropolitan constituents—produced new political dynamics that affected currency and fiscal policy. But in implementing his strategy, Nakasone had to face the mightiest of all bureaucratic foes—the Ministry of Finance.

The Ministry of Finance

Throughout the period from Plaza to Louvre, the Ministry of Finance found itself functioning as a reactor rather than an actor: as Nakasone said, "the MOF is an excellent engine of Japan's economic policy making, but after all, it is not the driver." Rather, it exercised "negative" power through its veto on budget and tax measures. At the same time, the MOF left undisturbed the basic economic precept of growth maximization with limited resources. In innovative policy formulation and achievement in modernization of the Japanese economy during the postwar era, the MITI was in the vanguard.

Following World War II, the principle of a balanced budget guided economic decision making in Japan, based on the professional assumptions of the Budget Bureau elites that it was the best way to guarantee economic stability and the maintenance of conditions necessary for economic development and independence. In 1965 the first issuance of public bonds initiated by Takeo Fukuda's new cabinet was to put an end to balanced budgets. Japanese economic policy was reoriented toward strengthening the welfare system and social infrastructure once the late Prime Minister Hayato Ikeda's high-growth strategy ("doubling income" plan) had been realized. Fiscal policy became the focus of greater attention as politicians discovered it as a means to carve out a piece of the pie—in the form of discretionary expenditures—for their own constituencies. The MOF was thus forced to abandon the strict "balanced budget" strategy for "sound fiscal policy."

Rather than restructuring the budget and establishing a set of policy priorities and guidelines, the Budget Bureau devised a Gramm-Rudman-Hollings type of mechanism that would ensure automatic restraint on expenditures. In effect, the resultant process represented a setback for the MOF, which was forced to undermine what had been enormous discretionary power over the politicians in the budget-making process and adopt a tiresome system of co-optation. Now the Ministry would have to co-opt

---

level and must further promote the liberalization and internationalization of the nation's financial and capital markets." *The report of the advisory group on economic structural adjustment for international harmony,* submitted to Prime Minister Yasuhiro Nakasone, 7 April 1987.

politicians by exploiting the competing forces among them and other government agencies, thereby dividing and thus neutralizing opposition.[12]

During the late 1970s, Prime Minister Masayoshi Ohira's cabinet began to promulgate a strategy of fiscal restructuring that rested on a general consumption tax. The Ministry used carrot-and-stick tactics that, on the one hand, put a low ceiling on expenditures to limit the politicians' flexibility in budgeting and, on the other hand, lured them into supporting the tax increase since this would mean that they could spend more overall. In 1979, however, the general consumption tax failed to pass through legislation. Consequently, the Ministry found that its power and influence over budgeting had gradually eroded because it, too, had to depend on the support of politicians in offsetting the pressures of the "policy tribes" around which each government agency built a coalition.

For the Ministry, increased spending without enlarging the tax base was considered a fatal blow to the integrity of the institution. The "fiscal mess" of the late 1970s, especially the widening of budget deficits caused by Japan's commitment to the "locomotive" strategy, was considered anathema to the MOF's credo of sound fiscal policy. Pledging never to repeat the situation, one MOF official and don of budget elites declared, "the era of overexpectation of the built-in stabilizing effect of fiscal policy ended in the 1970s. We got burned in the late 70s. That's the bottom line."[13]

The Ministry regarded favorably Nakasone's campaign pledge of "small government" administrative reform, recognizing its potential compatibility with a policy of fiscal austerity. The symbiosis of fiscal consolidation and administrative reform was thus born. The new Finance Minister, Takeshita, felt comfortable pursuing a tight fiscal policy with administrative reform and soon became one of the finest spokesmen for MOF officialdom.

The Ministry's neurotic obsession with sound fiscal policy was rooted in the perception of Japan's weakness and backwardness, on which the MOF had become fixated during the postwar years. Based on this perception, the Ministry rigidly maintained the yen–dollar rate at 360, which it equated with Japan's economic stability. The extended adherence to this strategy contributed to the serious external imbalances between the United States and Japan and to the collapse of the Bretton Woods system in the early 1970s. At that time, reflation was a major component of economic policy as a means of avoiding appreciation.

The oil crisis of 1973, however, tested the preference for fiscal stimulus

---

12. On the balance of power shift in the Japanese budget-making process see Jiro Yamaguchi, *Okura Kanryo Shihai No Shuen* (The end of Ministry of Finance bureaucratic supremacy), (Tokyo: Iwanami Shoten, 1987), 305–329.

13. Personal interview.

over yen appreciation that had prevailed under the influence of politicians like Kakuei Tanaka. The subsequent recession required more vigorous fiscal stimulus, resulting in larger government budget deficits. Accompanying the hike in oil prices was the realization of Japan's acute sensitivity to balance of payments constraints. As it became clearer that Japanese exporters had learned to live with the higher yen, the Ministry arrived at a position in support of exchange rate adjustment rather than a loosening of fiscal policy, at least as an initial step. Exchange rate adjustment featuring appreciation of the yen would ease the MOF's balance of payments constraints by making oil imports cheaper. In contrast, the Ministry's previous experience with fiscal stimulus measures, during the recession that followed the 1973 oil price hike, had caused the accumulation of budget deficits, making this approach undesirable as a means to correct the trade surplus. Since the introduction of floating exchange rates in 1973, the yen had gradually appreciated, to which the MOF responded periodically by trying to lower the yen artificially by means of the practice known as "dirty float" manipulation. This was how the Ministry first responded to the Carter administration's requests for macroeconomic policy coordination.[14]

Again in the spring of 1985, the Japanese responded to pressures for "coordination" with a willingness for exchange rate adjustment rather than fiscal policy change. The only difference, as perceived by the Ministry, was that the Reagan administration, unlike the Carter administration in 1977–79, did not openly advocate "locomotive" action as a means of stimulating the Japanese economy. Even so, the Ministry had cause for alarm, particularly when it learned that US Secretary of State George P. Shultz, in a speech at Princeton University in April 1985, had publicly called for Japan to stimulate its domestic economy. Shortly thereafter, Mitsuhide Yamaguchi, Vice Minister of Finance, started to explore intervention strategy in a more serious light. By that time the yen–dollar agreement had proved ineffective in realigning the currencies, at least in the short run. In fact, the Ministry and the US Treasury entertained divergent views concerning the impact of capital and financial liberalization for the currencies. Yamaguchi concluded that exchange rate adjustment was urgently needed. The top echelon of the MOF expected that a new team at the Treasury would be more receptive to intervention strategy.

The Bank of Japan was of the same view. Under the leadership of former governor Haruo Maekawa, the Bank of Japan had sought to revalue the yen in previous years and had been effectively blocked from lowering the discount rate on several occasions because of its effect on the exchange rate.

---

14. I. M. Destler and Hisao Mitsuyu, "Locomotives on Different Tracks: Macroeconomic Diplomacy 1977–1979," in *Coping with US–Japan Economic Conflicts,* ed. I. M. Destler and Hideo Sato (New York: Lexington Books, 1982), 151.

Like the US Treasury, the Ministry of Finance has traditionally had control over exchange rate policy, with virtually no room for other government agencies to influence it directly. The Diet [Japanese parliament] did not even try to interfere in the matter, although *endaka* (high yen) had been the subject of heated debate since the early 1970s. Until the Plaza meeting, the MOF had held exclusive and often unenviable rights over exchange rate policy with the Bank of Japan as a subordinate body. On numerous occasions the Bank of Japan had resisted attempts by the Ministry to dictate monetary policy. The BOJ, for example, did not consult the Ministry before raising the short-term interest rate only one month after the Plaza meeting. In the summer of 1986, the BOJ refused to comply with the Ministry's efforts to coordinate monetary policy internationally with a cut in the discount rate. Of course, the latter was made possible only by the political vacuum created by the general election, while the former occurred when the overwhelming consensus favored realignment of the currency anyway. Thus, although the BOJ attempted periodically to maintain credibility in its independence, it was in effect the Ministry of Finance that set the tone and pace of monetary and exchange policies. At most, the central bank exercised some degree of discretionary power over the timing of policy actions.

Floating exchange rates posed a real dilemma for the Ministry. The Ministry was freed of the pressure from those politicians who had previously attempted to dictate exchange rate policy. The Ministry could evade political demands by blaming the market for yen rises. On the other hand, the same argument could be used by the politicians, who could claim that fiscal discipline was unnecessary since market forces would eventually solve imbalance problems. Floating exchange rates, the MOF argued, were designed "to reward the micro interests [of individual politicians] at the expense of the macro interests [of the bureaucracy]."[15] It was under the floating exchange rate "regime" that the Ministry had to co-opt politicians in the budget process to exploit the built-in restraint effect on forces

---

15. Interview with Takashi Hosomi in a series of *Shogen* (testimony), (Tokyo: *Kinyu Zaisei Jijo* [Monetary and fiscal report], 16 September 1985), 35. During the interview, Hosomi pointed out that the main reason for the MOF's decision to embrace floating exchange rates was to avoid too frequent realignments with the dollar as well as to avoid upsetting the budget procedure during the Diet session, because changing the base rate was necessary for the proposal of the budget to the Diet. The real thrust of the MOF, however, was to obviate steep appreciation of the yen through realignment. A high-ranking official at the Bank of Japan put it simply: "The Ministry of Finance just politically could not revalue the yen. That is why they were swayed to the floating exchange rate. It was not an active decision, but merely a nonaction." The MOF was quite confident, at least around this period, that it could manipulate the exchange rate by its discretionary power under the floating exchange rate system, as Hosomi admitted in the same interview.

competing for government expenditures. In the process, the Ministry was forced to concede a share of its influence on the budget to the politicians.

It is difficult, however, to identify any conceptual framework behind the international monetary policies espoused by Japanese politicians, if indeed any existed. Inherently, they are pragmatists and rarely advocate an ideological preference, especially in matters of international economic policy. This is true particularly of conservative Japanese politicians whose ideological differences on international economic policy are minimal. In this respect Nakasone's managed float idea was more of a future vision than a concrete policy objective. By contrast, Takeshita did not have even a flash of vision on this issue; at least no MOF official interviewed could recall his having revealed any conception of a future international monetary regime.

Miyazawa, however, was different. He was much more receptive to the range idea embodied in the Louvre Accord than any other Japanese politician (besides Nakasone) because of his inclination toward greater management of currencies. It should be remembered that the meeting with Baker in September 1986 was the occasion of his first attempt to stabilize the yen–dollar rate at a particular level or range. Although Takeshita had also tried to "stabilize" the rate at around 180 yen to the dollar, he did not pursue the initiative in the same manner as Miyazawa, who explored various possible models for currency stability. This is not to imply that Miyazawa supported a reference-range mechanism or a target-zone system. Instead, like Takeshita, he also had above all to stop the yen from appreciating, for domestic reasons. Nevertheless, Miyazawa is remembered among the Kasumigaseki bureaucrats in Japan as inclined to accept a target-zone system.

As chief of the Economic Planning Agency (EPA) Miyazawa had expressed interest in Robert Roosa's target-zone proposal and had responded positively to the plea of Akio Morita, Chairman of the SONY Corporation, who had argued for currency stability while Miyazawa was Cabinet Secretary in the Suzuki Cabinet from 1980 to 1982. Miyazawa has not made explicit his stance on the target-zone issue since he became Finance Minister and has become more careful not to reveal his intentions since the Louvre Accord. Some of his confidants believe that he still favors some kind of a target-zone mechanism, perhaps one that is less rigid.

By outward appearances, it would seem that the power of the MOF bureaucracy eclipses that of the appointed politician at its head. In practice, the MOF bureaucracy treats its minister with cautious courtesy, particularly when that person is a leader in the LDP faction, as was Takeshita. The Ministry quickly recognized Takeshita's ability to maneuver around opposition party leaders. Takeshita was a pragmatist, well trained in political maneuvers and nurtured on Japan's consensus politics. He did not attempt grandiose programs, as Nakasone had, nor did he take an interest in discretionary policies over the banking and securities industries or the details of personnel management, as had Michio Watanabe, another influential member of Nakasone's faction.

Despite his shortcomings, Takeshita was master of his own game. He knew that as an aspirant to Nakasone's position, he needed international exposure. He was not well known abroad, being frequently kept in the background by Nakasone and by Foreign Minister Shintaro Abe, a political rival who was known to have a comfortable rapport with George P. Shultz. Takeshita therefore fostered a relationship with Baker, which he deemed politically useful and personally appealing after his experience with Don Regan, whose Wall Street executive style he had found somewhat uncongenial. Takeshita met with Baker in 1985 during the International Monetary Fund (IMF) Interim Committee meeting in April and the Bonn Summit in May. He proposed to Baker that they maintain a dialogue between politicians on any issue, not limited to financial matters—this as a signal to the "economic prime minister" of the Reagan administration from the Japanese politician most likely to succeed Nakasone.[16] It was not surprising, considering his objectives, that Takeshita suggested realignment of the currency through joint intervention in a meeting with Baker on June 21, anticipating that by launching a Baker-Takeshita G-2 strategy he would cast himself in the limelight internationally. By that time, Takeshita was fully cognizant of the need for yen–dollar realignment and therefore seized this opportunity to strike a bargain between the two countries.

Factional politics complicated the process of setting policy in Japan. One example was the friction that developed between Abe's Foreign Ministry and Takeshita's Finance Ministry. Takeshita was alarmed to learn that Abe had discussed the yen–dollar problem with George P. Shultz—albeit, at Shultz's request—in September 1983. Upon returning to Japan, Abe reported immediately to Takeshita that he had told Shultz, "I can't win this game since you are a professional economist," trying to erase unnecessary suspicion. Takeshita thanked Abe and insisted that "this type of issue should be left to the specialists and the MOF has already studied it."[17]

Takeshita's rivalry with Miyazawa was much more intense. As Chairman of the LDP Executive Council, Miyazawa openly criticized the austere fiscal policy of the Nakasone cabinet. The sharp appreciation of the yen in April 1986 put Takeshita on the defensive and gave Miyazawa the ammunition with which to attack the Nakasone cabinet's "do-nothing" policy. In a cabinet-LDP joint economic policy council in late April, Miyazawa bluntly

---

16. Personal interview.

17. Personal interview.

asked why the yen had again appreciated steeply after Nakasone's visit to Washington and wanted to know what Nakasone and Reagan had decided on the yen–dollar issue. The unusual criticism caught both Nakasone and Takeshita off guard.

In a speech made shortly after the incident, Miyazawa again pointed an accusing finger at the Nakasone cabinet, "Why did the cabinet not respond to the present plight more effectively? Everybody could foresee today's situation. Is Ron–Yasu after all the relationship of Japan's subordination to the United States?"[18] According to a confidant of Takeshita, upon hearing such harsh criticism directed at him, the Finance Minister exploded, "I won't forgive anyone who takes advantage of this kind of vitally important policy issue for his own political gain."

Controversy over the *endaka* policy has continued to simmer under the surface of Japanese politics since the spring of 1986. A letter to his constituency by Ganri Yamashita, a loyalist to former Prime Minister Kakuei Tanaka, illustrates its intensity. Yamashita and Susumu Nikaido, a former Vice Minister, were attempting to upset former Tanaka family member Takeshita by a vengeful sort of fratricide. In the letter, Yamashita charged, "Everybody is now enduring the hardship of the *endaka* depression. Who on earth was the culprit of this *endaka* mess?" in an obvious attempt to put Takeshita in the defendant's chair.[19]

Nakasone's decision to replace Takeshita with Miyazawa as Finance Minister after his landslide victory in the summer of 1986 was meant, in part, to contain further bitter factional struggles by having Miyazawa share the responsibility for decision making as a cabinet member. As it came to be known later, Takeshita's dilemma—that the successful Plaza campaign he had conducted had such a negative personal payoff—was mitigated in part later when Miyazawa, also, was unable to accomplish the "Mission Impossible"—controlling the runaway yen. By the rules of Japanese politics of consensus mongering and faction balancing, neither of the Finance Ministers was supposed to claim a victory, and in fact, neither had won.

On the fiscal policy front, political considerations lay behind the government's desire to avoid a clear victory of one policy over another. Nakasone therefore deftly accommodated Miyazawa's expansionist fiscal policy into the supplementary budget in the spring of 1987 while coopting Miyazawa by having him share the responsibility for maintaining the Nakasone cabinet's message of fiscal austerity.

---

18. Akio Kaminishi, "Seikyoku Yurugasu Ichi Doru Hyakurokujuen Dai" (The 160 yen unsettles the political scene), *Ekonomisuto* (Economist, Japan), 13 May 1986.

19. Ganri Yamashita, *Hozan* (Yamashita supporters' organization paper), 1 May 1987.

With Miyazawa's arrival at the Ministry, the chemistry that had developed between the Minister's office under Takeshita and the MOF bureaucracy was broken, even though Miyazawa was an MOF veteran. As soon as word reached the Ministry that Miyazawa would replace Takeshita, the warning spread not to harbor any illusions about Miyazawa simply because of his bureaucratic family ties. In particular, the MOF was alert to Miyazawa's unabashed sanction of loose fiscal policy and the fact that he was not "as good a listener as Takeshita." Furthermore, Miyazawa's numerous connections to "the Establishment" in Trilateral Commission countries and his intellectual sophistication were not necessarily welcome at the Ministry.

Despite intensive lobbying of the MOF bureaucracy against it, a stimulus package of six trillion yen was accepted during a summit meeting in late May 1987 of Miyazawa and Gotoda, the Cabinet Secretary, and Masayoshi Ito, Chairman of the Policy Research Council of the LDP. Frustration with Miyazawa grew among MOF officials, some of whom believed that he was not in their camp at all. They criticized him for his reluctance to "do the chores."[20]

In spite of its reservations about Miyazawa, it was impossible for the Ministry to ignore the weight he carried in political circles. MOF officialdom simply could not risk alienating such a powerful faction leader. Ironically, this very strength of Miyazawa debilitated the Ministry. In the fall of 1986, Miyazawa fought hard to include a heavy dose of fiscal stimulus in the supplementary budget. His involvement helped win LDP support for the more ambitious supplementary budget plan the following spring. In addition, the secret dialogue with Baker in San Francisco in October 1986, which produced the Baker-Miyazawa Accord, alarmed domesticist elites because of their exclusion from the plan but enhanced Miyazawa's own position, since he was able to exploit Baker's argument for a fiscal stimulus against strong bureaucratic resistance from the MOF.

The Ministry's resistance to a fiscal stimulus was also weakened by the divisions in Japan's economic policy-making community and the stagnation of domestic demand. During the "locomotive" period of 1977–79, MITI had supported stimulus measures, and MITI Minister Toshio Komoto, a Keynesian expansionist and faction leader, became more personally involved in the issue than would normally have occurred. MITI's campaign for a fiscal stimulus, at least until the spring of 1987, was not especially aggressive, although MITI had advocated it persistently since 1983. MITI's pursuit of appreciation of the yen concurrently with fiscal stimulus, however, was based on two concerns: first, the conflict-ridden trade situation with the

---

20. *Asahi Shimbun,* 30 May 1987.

United States; and second, the corrosive effects of volatile exchange rates on trade flows. Leading industrialists such as Akio Morita, Chairman of the SONY Corporation, had been arguing for the need to stabilize currencies since the late 1970s. Shoichi Akawaza, President of the Japan External Trade Organization (JETRO) and a former MITI official, suggested a target-zone system to Nakasone in his capacity as a close personal adviser. Generally speaking, exporters who had enjoyed almost five years of an undervalued yen were not strongly opposed to yen appreciation. By now, many of them had developed sophisticated currency-hedge techniques.

In general, the financial sector, backed by the increasing clout of the big securities houses, endorsed the yen-appreciation strategy. In the manufacturing sector, where financial experts gradually edged out the traditional corporate decisionmakers, the argument equating *endaka* with disaster was no longer persuasive. Perhaps most important, the rapid movement of production abroad in Japan's manufacturing sector dictated their emphasis on greater stability of the currencies. This real economic transformation gradually changed the perception of *endaka* in the Japanese business community, particularly as a result of the yen appreciation occurring after the Plaza meeting.

The turnaround of the yen–dollar relationship first hit the less competitive small- and medium-sized exporters. MITI hastily announced an emergency package of financial relief, which included 100 billion yen ($487.8 million at 205 yen = $1) of low-interest loans. The loans were to be offered from December through March by three quasi-governmental financial institutions. The proposal was based on MITI's survey, in which most industries reported that a yen–dollar rate of 220 to 250 was a break-even point for exports.

The Reagan administration and the Congress quickly protested this as "unfair government subsidies," clearly in violation of GATT rules. Administration officials recalled the similar forms of relief extended to this group of exporters after the 1978 appreciation of the yen—known as the high-yen law—which led to the initiation of countervailing duty cases in the United States against the manufacturers of five fabricated metal products. In short, the relief program was viewed as just a loophole that would sterilize the effects of yen appreciation. Such vehement criticism from the United States compelled MITI to administer relief funds solely toward restructuring the export-led small- and medium-sized industries into domestic demand oriented businesses.

International scrutiny of these traditional instruments of domestic economic policy—giving relief to industries hit by currency changes—limited MITI's range of action. Afterward, the Ministry kept to the sidelines, venturing only to encourage affected industries to move production abroad, especially to the United States. At the same time, the rapid fall of the dollar—with its potential for a free fall—provoked criticism from industry as it became convinced of the need for some stability in exchange rates. According to one top MITI official:

As the yen approached 180 yen to the dollar, the textile and steel industries started to scream. The shipbuilders came to ask for help. When it topped 170, electronics and even automobile people began to cry. However, interestingly, the thrust of the plea was more toward stabilizing the currencies rather than reversing the tide.[21]

It is reasonable to assume that throughout this period MITI was more sensitive to protectionist forces abroad, particularly in the United States, than to the negative impact of the high yen on Japanese industry. Perhaps for the first time ever, MITI was anxious that the worsening external imbalances between Japan and the United States would trigger a breakdown of the world trading system—the system that had been ideally suited to Japan's economic interests. Shinji Fukukawa, Vice Minister of MITI, expressed this concern in the fall of 1986:

Up until now Japan has tended simply to make use of the established international economic order, but I believe that we must change this attitude and that Japan must fulfill its share of the responsibility for maintaining the international economic system and should contribute to providing for the public good—internationally. From this standpoint we must also strive, in concert with our trading partners, to correct the problem of Japan's external imbalances.[22]

He also stressed MITI's distrust of the floating rate system, pointing out that the "floating system lacks the ability to control adequately the current account positions," although at the same time, he argued that "more comprehensive measures" than currency realignment "are necessary in order to eradicate the payments [imbalances] problem."[23] Significantly, at no time in this speech did he even allude to any policies to help battered industries.

As the yen continued to climb, MITI's campaign for a fiscal stimulus—the main pillar of what Fukukawa had called "comprehensive measures"—gained momentum. In this effort, MITI found surprisingly little support from the Keidanren (Federation of Economic Organizations), the main business lobby in Japan, although local business communities clamored for fiscal stimulus measures. Leaders of the Keidanren had backed Nakasone's administrative reform and fiscal austerity policy—to the extent that they

---

21. Personal interview.

22. Shinji Fukukawa, *A policy plan for restructuring industry—Focusing on MITI's policies for fiscal 1987*, 30 September 1986.

23. Ibid.

had put their personal reputations on the line, which precluded any rapid shifts to support looser fiscal policy. One business leader criticized the Keidanren leaders, "Nobody up there wants to upset Bunpei Otsuki, you know. He is now the Chairman of the Administration Reform Council. Even Eishiro Saito [Chairman of Keidanren] doesn't move!" Nakasone invited Bunpei Otsuki, former Chairman of Nikkeiren and one of Japan's most influential business leaders, to chair his commission to study the possibilities for further administrative reform.[24]

In the face of the inertia of the Keidanren, MITI even tried to sell the MOF on a deal: endorsement of the MOF-promoted sales tax in return for a commitment to spending. The Ministry of Finance remained unimpressed.

MITI's campaign accelerated after Hajime Tamura, a longtime member of the "public works tribe," was named Minister following the 1986 election. Tamura's intense lobbying of his colleagues among the "tribe" and direct pressure on the Budget Bureau of the MOF facilitated the adoption of new fiscal measures in the spring of 1987. It was probably his encounter with Baker on the occasion of the OECD ministerial meeting in Paris that most strongly impressed the MOF, which grew alarmed at this unorthodox coalition. The Ministry of Foreign Affairs (MFA) also had a role in pressuring the MOF for stimulus. In May, the MFA set up an ad hoc task force to review macroeconomic policy from the viewpoint of Japan's international responsibilities and the international implication of these policies for the domestic decision-making process. This action represented an unprecedented shift of the Ministry's focus on economic policy. Koji Watanabe, Director of the Economic Bureau of the MFA, approached the Baker Treasury and also put feelers out directly to the office of the Prime Minister and to the leaders of the LDP. The MFA's "macroeconomic diplomacy" at the time was also made necessary by the Ministry's status in G-7 summitry diplomacy, especially when Nakasone needed to strengthen his hand for the coming Venice Summit.

By the spring of 1987, the combined pressures of MITI and the MFA had succeeded in breaking down the MOF's resistance to fiscal stimulus. Yet, the crucial factor was the political weight of ruling LDP members, especially Masayoshi Ito. Ito, a veteran stalwart of Miyazawa faction and a respected elder statesman, advised Miyazawa to exploit this opportunity to implement his political platform of fiscal stimulus. It was reported that he told Miyazawa on the day before the decision on the six trillion yen package that it was a propitious moment for him to "imprint his own agenda on the package" since he might not remain finance minister and thus, in charge of drafting

---

24. Nikkeiren is the Japanese Federation of Employers' Associations.

the fiscal 1988 budget after Nakasone stepped down.[25] Another important factor that pushed both Nakasone and the MOF into accepting a fiscal stimulus package was their awareness of the unexpected increase in tax revenues by about 2.4 trillion yen for FY 1986, the data for which they kept confidential at that time. Nakasone later confided about the "trick": "Yukitsugu Nakagawa, [President] of Nomura Research Institute, informed me of the data much before the MOF reported it to me. The data secretly came from the Bank of Japan sources."[26] Nakasone then received endorsement from Keidanren leader Bumpei Otsuki of the new package for extraordinary measures to bypass limiting government expenditure.

Gaiatsu

The Ministry of Finance embraced realignment of the yen–dollar exchange rate as a means of obviating fiscal stimulus policies. To a considerable degree, this represented a departure from the kind of policy priorities determined in 1971. Yet it is fair to argue that the Ministry did not act, but reacted to the pressures emanating from various quarters.

In addition to pressures that originated within Japanese domestic politics, there was growing pressure from the outside. In response to the indictments directed against Japanese domestic policies by the United States, Takeshita's and Yamaguchi's initiatives were long overdue. In the final analysis, *gaiatsu* (foreign pressure) dealt the decisive blow to the resistance of the MOF.

Gaiatsu, in fact, became institutionalized in the Japanese decision-making process, the rigidity of Japan's economic policy-making process providing the environment in which it took root. Policymakers who needed to be constantly sensitive to interest groups could not ignore the infiltration of foreign interests into the domestic political arena.

The exploitation of foreign pressure to divert domestic attention away from unpopular policies is a strategy employed universally, and in this case, observers both in Japan and abroad recognized the crucial function of *gaiatsu* in overcoming the immobility of the Japanese system. This immobility is a product of institutional and cultural factors that include the bottom-to-top, consensus-oriented decision-making process, the supremacy of the domesticists over the internationalists, and the manner in which domestic political institutions must achieve mutual parity in burden sharing.

The potential losers from a proposed policy will try to mobilize all

---

25. *Asahi Shimbun,* 30 May 1987.

26. Personal interview.

resources to influence the "bottom" as well as the domesticists and will demand that other constituencies should also have to sacrifice something to even out the burden. The single-issue politics that emerge from the intrasectoral alliances among the "policy tribes" of the LDP, the bureaucracy, and the industry affected by the proposal strengthens the chances that the proposal is doomed to failure.

A candid essay written by an internationalist involved in Japan's Plaza strategy illuminates the complexity of Japan's decision-making process. The author, Shijuro Ogata, was Deputy Governor of the Bank of Japan throughout much of the period under review. The title of Ogata's essay, written for the Bank's in-house journal, was "Gaiyu Hyakkai" (one hundred reminders of going abroad). In it, he asks, "Why does Japan not play a leading role in international fora consummate with its economic power?" He enumerates the reasons as lack of linguistic ability and failure of the education system to promote the best and the brightest instead of encouraging the advancement of all students to average levels. Then he touches on a more delicate question:

Besides that, Japan's decision-making process was so structured in the consensus system that the Japanese representatives abroad would be easily coopted by the domestic crowds with the utmost effort to do *nemawashi* (consensus building) with them. However, if they did *nemawashi* too much, it would bind them too tightly and prevent them from responding flexibly to new developments.[27]

The domesticists always suspect the capacity and effectiveness of the internationalists to "explain fully" to foreigners the legitimate constraints on Japanese domestic policymakers that limit their ability to satisfy foreign requests. "I heard someone blame me saying, 'Does Volcker still talk about that crap? Gee, it must be due to the poor explanations of Ogata.' "[28]

Ogata points out that domesticists feel frustrated because they tend to believe that the internationalists, who indulge regularly in answering foreign criticism, are not forceful enough in counterarguing and criticizing the other countries' shortcomings. "It was more critical for us [internationalists] to dissipate the misunderstandings at home than abroad," he concluded. "One of the ways to cope with this sticky problem is to expose those domestic bullies directly to the foreign winds." He regretted not having accompanied those "bullies" to various international meetings.

---

27. Shijuro Ogata, "Gaiyu Hyakkai" (One hundred reminders of going abroad), *Koyu* (Tokyo), February 1987.

28. Personal interview.

When he abruptly resigned his post and was assigned to another, the London *Economist* mused over the possible implications:

He has many friends abroad, made on his frequent trips to meetings of the IMF and the Bank for International Settlements. More, it seems, than at home.

On September 25, Mr. Ogata started a new job, after a week's notice. Gone will be the silver-spooned whirl of central banking. He is being moved sideways to be Deputy Governor of the Japan Development Bank, a relic of the 1950s when Japan needed development. . . . Mr. Ogata is a sacrificial pawn in a political squabble. Normally, the Bank of Japan nominates senior appointments at the JDB. In August, it had pencilled in Mr. Yuichi Hirota, one of Mr. Ogata's juniors. But that proposal was apparently vetoed by the Prime Minister's office. It wanted somebody more senior, as the JDB's role is being enhanced.

Conspiracy theorists see other reasons: Was the Finance Ministry keen to reassert its influence over the central bank, which has squabbled about interest rates? Or had Mr. Ogata become too international for his own good?[29]

Actually, conspiracy theorists and even nonconspiracy theorists produced other reasons. Did the urbane Ogata foment institutional jealousy in the Ministry of Finance for his eminence in currency diplomacy and so make himself an easy target? His name had been mentioned as a possibility for President of the Asian Development Bank or even Managing Director of the IMF. Or perhaps he displeased the domesticists at the Bank of Japan, who resented his intimate chitchats with Volcker, which upset the Bank's traditional process of conducting monetary policy.

On his last day as a central banker, he received a visit from the Deputy Governor of the central bank of the Soviet Union. After Ogata explained that he would move to the Japan Development Bank and devote himself to domestic affairs from then on, the Soviet banker responded, "In light of Japan's importance in the world economy, the domestic problem of Japan *is* the international problem." Ogata agreed wholeheartedly.[30]

Gaiatsu, in effect, did "expose those domestic bullies directly to the foreign winds"; without *gaiatsu*, it is unlikely that radical changes in policy would have been made. In the spring of 1985, the winds of *gaiatsu* began to blow from the US Congress, where a protectionist storm raged. The new initiative, to realign the yen and dollar through joint intervention, was set in motion by Japan's exposure to this storm. Realignment itself was a direct outcome of the battle prevailing between the domesticists at the Budget Bureau and

---

29. *Economist,* 27 September 1986.

30. Shijuro Ogata, "Gaiyu Hyakkai" (One hundred reminders of going abroad).

the Tax Bureau of the Ministry of Finance, who insisted on leaving fiscal austerity intact at the sacrifice of exchange rates, and the internationalists at the International Finance Bureau, who argued that Japan should come up with some stimulus measures so as to persuade the United States to realign currencies through mutual intervention in the markets.

The patronizing manner in which the domesticists conceded to Oba the provision for additional investment by "local governments" in the Plaza communiqué illustrated the dynamics of the entanglement between the domesticists and the internationalists. The internationalists realized that they needed the US Treasury to commit to the intervention strategy; otherwise, progress on the fiscal policy front was inconceivable. On the other hand, the domesticists made a show of making the aforementioned "concession" as evidence of equal burden sharing—the third feature of *gaiatsu* politics.

As the Plaza strategy progressed, it tested the structural obstacles to decision making in Japan. Top-to-bottom and internationalist decision-making mechanisms involved in the coordination of economic policies shook the deeply entrenched structure of the Japanese political system. The sudden decision of the Bank of Japan's (domesticist) Business Bureau to raise the short-term interest rate was triggered in part by a sense of frustration with *gaiatsu*. A former senior official at the MOF described it as an action of "the macho . . . domestic bullies" at the Bank of Japan.[31] The strong resistance of junior Budget and Tax Bureau officials at the MOF to the indicator proposal at the Tokyo Summit put enormous constraints on Japan's international commitment.

Political oversensitivity to the "small guys" hurt by *endaka* sometimes forces a politician to behave differently from the way he or she actually feels. The reason for massive intervention by the Bank of Japan, for example, was largely a demonstration of the government's concern over the dangerous effects of *endaka* on the small guys. Miyazawa's calculated play-up of 160 yen to the dollar for the Baker-Miyazawa communiqué and his hurried visit to Washington to reaffirm the communiqué were also political exercises. His inability to defend the current ranges of exchange rates when confronted by the opposition party was tragicomic. Had he made his support clear, he would have been attacked instantly: "You can say that you want to stabilize currencies, but you cannot say that you want to stabilize them around the present levels. All you can do is to look very sad. Yes, I know, that's the way we are supposed to behave. But, it's a pity," confided one of the cabinet members.[32]

---

31. Personal interview.

32. Personal interview.

■ The Bundesbank Standard: West Germany

West Germany's Plaza strategy was influenced most strongly by Karl Otto Pöhl, President of the Bundesbank, and Gerhard Stoltenberg, Minister of Finance. Both had grown increasingly frustrated with the benign neglect policy of the United States over the dollar. The Bundesbank had tried to arrest the rise of the US currency through massive interventions in the fall of 1984 and again in February and March 1985. Lacking a firm commitment from US monetary authorities to realign currencies, however, the best that Bonn and Frankfurt could do was to complain about the inflationary impact of a weak deutsche mark on the German economy.

Bonn and Frankfurt

A senior German official said that the fear of inflation caused by undervaluation of the deutsche mark, at least at this point, was not the key factor in West Germany's Plaza strategy, although it was "a very important factor also."

The key factor was our deep fear of a hard landing of the US dollar. If unchecked, the dollar would have gone into a free fall. And we did not want to have its reverse consequences for the world economy. Yes, they were secondary effects. But, that's the key. We also had to think of its implication on the EMS. A hard landing of the dollar would cause serious difficulties in the EMS and the future of the EMS.[1]

The German Plaza strategy, in other words, was a search for a soft landing. The exchange rate realignment needed to go slowly and in an orderly

---

1. Personal interview.

fashion. "We had to buy time to correct the external imbalance as smoothly as possible," added the official.

Pöhl and Stoltenberg held nearly identical views on exchange rate policy. While continuing to support the EMS mechanism, they believed that the markets should determine the relationship of the deutsche mark to both the dollar and the yen—thereby preferring a combination of fixed exchange rates for Europe and floating rates outside of the EMS.

For both men, price stability was the primary objective of economic policy, although the degree to which each adhered to this precept varied. Furthermore, both the Central Bank Governor and the Finance Minister basically stood together on fiscal policy. As sherpa* for Chancellor Helmut Schmidt at the London Summit of 1977, Pöhl was responsible for attaching to the final communiqué a now famous phrase: "Inflation is not a cure for unemployment, on the contrary it is one of its basic causes." Similarly, Stoltenberg had improved his own political reputation as a deficit cutter and a strong advocate of "budget equilibrium." It was Stoltenberg who "perplexed Reagan" with his bluntness in asking the American President to cut the US budget deficit at the Williamsburg Summit in 1983.

The German diagnosis of external imbalances and currency misalignment boiled down to the mistakes of US macroeconomic policy and the trade problem between the United States and Japan. The Germans accepted no part of the blame. In a way, this denial of responsibility mirrored the hands-off policy the United States had espoused previously.

From the outset, the Germans participated only reluctantly in the Plaza strategy. From their point of view, the potential for inflation caused by a cheaper deutsche mark necessitated modest currency realignment, but they rejected out of hand the notion that coordination of macroeconomic policies beyond that extent was required.

Pöhl himself retained a valuable lesson on currency misalignment from his experience on the supervisory board of Volkswagen in the mid-1970s. He watched as a declining dollar put the firm in trouble. "Don't let us repeat this mistake of a misalignment of an exchange rate, leading to investment decisions that are not sustainable, and not profitable in the long run," he was known to say to his colleagues at the Bundesbank. Still, Pöhl was noticeably cautious throughout the Plaza meeting. Besides his distaste for such highly politicized fanfare, he found the proposal for currency realignment dangerous, because he predicted that it could too easily get out of hand.

---

* *sherpa*—Personal representative of the head of state, who collaborates with other sherpas on the preparation of the economic and political agenda for an international summit. Usually a vice minister of foreign affairs or finance.

To understand the dynamics of German involvement in the Plaza strategy, it is important to examine in greater detail the perspectives of both Pöhl and Stoltenberg. Pöhl was one of the more gregarious participants in the G-5 meetings during this period—an exception among the stereotypical tight-lipped central bankers in the group. But this did not detract from his shrewdness in handling such matters as exchange rates. He rarely used the same figure twice, for example, in illustrating ideas or discussing currency rates; in that way he kept his hands free and gave the impression that he was "a bit slippery."

Nobody could deny that through his competence and gravity, Pöhl enhanced the international standing of West Germany, and particularly of the Bundesbank. Pöhl drew on a diverse background; from economic and financial journalist, he became Vice Minister of Finance in Bonn. In 1977, he was named Vice President of the Bundesbank and was chosen to be its President by Chancellor Schmidt in 1979. In 1987, he was nominated to another eight-year term in that office by Helmut Kohl. According to officials in Bonn, it was Stoltenberg who recommended Pöhl for a second term, opposing the suggestion of some Christian Democratic Union (CDU) members that the Bundesbank President should, for a change, be a CDU member. It is no secret, however, that Schmidt would have preferred Wilfried Guth, Supervisory Board Chairman of the powerful Deutsche Bank, as Bundesbank President, and that he appointed Pöhl only after an embarrassing delay. Days after Pöhl took over as President, the deutsche mark dropped like a stone against the dollar—another embarrassment for Pöhl. He never forgot the humiliation of that "welcome" from the market.[2]

Obviously, in a country where the president of the central bank earns a higher salary than the head of state and enjoys virtually unchecked autonomy, the position is one of prestige and power. Even so, the Bundesbank president must maintain good relations with the federal government. The necessity of keeping lines open between Frankfurt (the Bundesbank) and Bonn (the Ministry of Finance) is illustrated by what happened when these lines clogged up. In February 1981, Pöhl tightened monetary policy by raising the Lombard rate from 9 percent to 12 percent. Despite persistent pressure from the Social Democratic Party (SPD) to ease monetary policy, Pöhl (an SPD member himself) held fast, and his relationship with Helmut Schmidt suffered as a result. Some Social Democrats argued afterward that the Bundesbank's tight monetary policy cost the SPD the election in 1983. Pöhl benefited from the experience, earning for himself a reputation as an inflation fighter. By 1985 the Bundesbank could rest assured that Bonn, occupied by a conservative government, would not meddle in affairs of monetary policy.

---

2. Jonathan Carr, *Financial Times*, 15 August 1986.

Stoltenberg, a longtime stalwart of the CDU's Protestant wing was, when he was 34 years old, named Minister of Technology by Konrad Adenauer, his political idol. He soon stood out as an expert on budget and finance matters in the Bundestag, the lower house of the West German parliament. His coolness and rationality led some to believe that he was much like Ludwig Erhard, father of the German "economic miracle." With a technocrat's temperament, he resembled Helmut Schmidt, another northerner, with whom he nurtured a mutually respectful friendship in spite of their different political allegiances. In certain respects he seems unpolitical and at times exhibits what one G-5 regular described as "German subtlety—that is to say, none." Stoltenberg has been the driving force of the Kohl government's fiscal conservatism, more than anyone in German politics. The Kohl-Stoltenberg policy of small government was the linchpin of the CDU-FDP (Free Democratic Party) coalition's economic program, and it resonated with the Reagan administration's emphasis on tax cuts and deregulation. Furthermore, by mobilizing restrictive government spending policies to the fullest, Stoltenberg succeeded in slashing the budget deficit, at least until 1986.

In a rare speech to an American audience, Stoltenberg took pride in the accomplishments achieved in his battle against the fiscal deficits. He asserted that the FRG had found the "right" fiscal policy, implying that other European countries had strayed considerably from that objective and noting that the West German budget deficit had been reduced from about 5 percent of GNP in 1981 to just over 2 percent in 1987, thereby creating the conditions for interest rate reductions and a positive climate for private investment.[3]

Given the strong West German commitment to price stability, realignment of currencies was necessary to avoid inflation. It is therefore puzzling that the Federal Republic did not initiate any strategy for realignment before the Plaza meeting, for example, at the Bonn Summit in May 1985. Kohl's lack of interest in international economic policy making and the reluctance of both the Bundesbank and the Ministry of Finance to discuss "their" issues at the summit provides a clue. Kohl and Reagan had another occasion to discuss currency issues when they met in Washington in October 1986—a critical juncture in currency diplomacy when the search for currency stability was under way. Again, they ignored the issue.

On the surface, relations between Bonn and Frankfurt were smooth, exemplifying the provisions of the Deutsche Bundesbank Act, which requires both the government and the Bundesbank "to commit to cooperation and mutual consultation."

---

3. Gerhard Stoltenberg, "The United States and Europe: Main Objectives for Economic Policies and International Cooperation," address at Georgetown University, 10 April 1987.

However, serious undercurrents ran beneath the surface. Beginning in the summer of 1986, the Ministry of Finance favored a reduction of the discount rate, whereas the Bundesbank insisted instead that government tax cuts should have gone much further, with, preferably, emphasis on a tax cut for business investment—a sentiment Pöhl expressed directly to Stoltenberg.

These tensions broke through the surface in late 1987, when Stoltenberg openly urged the Bundesbank to lower interest rates. Stoltenberg was under particularly heavy pressure from the farmers, who feared that competitiveness would be undermined if the deutsche mark appreciated further. In his home territory of Schleswig-Holstein, the CDU had already suffered losses in the local elections a few weeks before the stock market crash on Black Monday, mainly as a result of a local party scandal. This undoubtedly damaged Stoltenberg's image, since he was CDU Chairman in Schleswig-Holstein. For good reason Stoltenberg wanted a loosening of monetary policy rather than the relentless appreciation of the deutsche mark. But, as did earlier Finance Ministers in Bonn, Stoltenberg had to learn to live with the formidable bunch of professionals in Frankfurt.

Political Culture

However important the individual personalities and political viewpoints of Pöhl and Stoltenberg may be, macroeconomic policy making in West Germany is essentially conditioned by the cultural environment. In order to place into proper perspective the role of political culture as a structural determinant of policy, it is necessary to look into the institutional and political arrangements within the Federal Republic.

To understand current monetary policy in West Germany, one must go back to the interwar period, when the country suffered the devastating effects of hyperinflation as well as the total control of the national economy by the National Socialists. In reaction to that period, West German leaders incorporated the principles of price stability and a limited role for the state in economic life into West German law.

German economic policy in the postwar period has rested on three pillars: price stability, cautious countercyclical policy, and international competitiveness. Naturally there is diversity among the many domestic actors—the Bundesbank, the federal government, political parties, and other interest groups—that influence policy making; but across the spectrum of domestic political actors there is a broad consensus on these three principles.

These objectives shaped the institutional organization of postwar West Germany in several ways. First, the outcome of the effort to reduce the role of the state in economic life was a decentralized system of decision making.

Second, the primacy of price stability as an economic objective assured the Bundesbank virtual autonomy in the formulation of monetary policy. The lack of powerful institutional rivals due to the decentralization of federal power and the strength of the Bundesbank's own constituency, made up of the financial and banking communities, has given the banking community somewhat greater prestige than that of industry.

The federal government coexists alongside the state and local governments. The decentralized nature of the German government and its political interest groups is illustrated by the prevalence of coalition governments. Smooth transitions of power have taken place between coalition governments led by different parties—in 1969 the Social Democratic Party and the Free Democratic Party and in 1982 the Christian Democratic Union with the Free Democratic Party.

The Stability and Growth Act of 1967 was a watershed piece of legislation. It enlarged the range of action available to the federal government, allowing it to intervene in the area of anticyclical and discretionary fiscal policy. That the Keynesian act did nothing to mitigate the conflicts inherent in the power-sharing arrangement among principal actors is significant, for these conflicts would continue to surface and become more visible in times of crisis.

Three conflicts can be identified: between the banks and export industries over revaluation of the deutsche mark; between the Bundesbank and the federal government over the prudent level of public indebtedness; and between unions and business over justifiable wage and price levels.[4] The conflict between the financial and banking community and export industries intensified as the deutsche mark came under increasing pressure to revalue throughout the 1960s. Government support for deutsche mark revaluation in 1961 and 1969 reflected the Bundesbank's guidance on an anti-inflationary course and the relatively strong position of the bankers over the exporters. This German history may be contrasted to Japanese currency policy during the late 1960s and the early 1970s, when the politicians "against revaluation of the yen at any costs" prevailed (although Iichiro Hatoyama, Vice Minister of the Finance Ministry, was influenced by policy development in West Germany when he secretly ordered a study of the steps necessary to appreciate the yen, with a crawling-peg strategy).

The floating exchange rate system has complemented the Bundesbank's free reign over currency policy and strengthened its commitment to anti-inflationary monetary policy. One of its top officials admitted that the reason

---

4. Peter J. Katzenstein, *Policy and Politics in West Germany: The Growth of a Semi-Sovereign State* (Philadelphia: Temple University Press, 1987), 95–96. For my analysis of the institutional and political dynamics of macroeconomic policy making in West Germany, I owe much to this author's insights.

for the Bundesbank's love of floating exchange rates was that institution's preference for freedom of action.

The Bundesbank itself is a unique product of history—the traumatic history of Germany during the first half of the twentieth century. The incontestable importance of price stability held, regardless of age, social stratum, or political party. On 26 July 1957, the Deutsche Bundesbank Act was passed, which established the central bank as a federal corporation. In spite of its being required to support the federal government's general economic policy, the Bundesbank's autonomy in formulating monetary policy is fully guaranteed in the act.[5]

From its inception, the deutsche mark was purely a "paper currency"; that is, maintenance of the value of the currency is a direct function of control over the money supply, not of backing the currency with gold or foreign exchange. Engendered by a history of hyperinflation, German respect for the Bundesbank has helped to make this institution sacrosanct. The Bundesbank itself is instilled with a moral ethos. The nomination of the Bundesbank President is politically very important. As one official likes to put it, "People don't change the Bundesbank, the Bundesbank changes people."

As the postwar West German economy became integrated into that of the world and West Germany once again became a European power, a collision between domestic and international considerations was inevitable. The Central Bank Council of the Bundesbank is endowed with decision-making power and is skewed toward domestic considerations because of the preponderance of the *land** representatives. The Council has a Directorate of six officials appointed by the government, with a chairman as its head, and eleven members appointed by the Bundesrat [the upper house of the German parliament], each of whom heads one of the bank's *land* branches. The Council generally meets every two weeks and determines the Bundesbank's monetary and credit policies by simple majority vote. The Directorate is the central executive organ and as such is responsible for implementing the decisions made by the Council. Directors are nominated by the government and appointed by the President of the Federal Republic, but only after consultation with the Council.[6]

---

5. *The Deutsche Bundesbank: Its Monetary Policy Instruments and Functions,* Deutsche Bundesbank Special Series, no. 7 (June 1982), 5–6.

* *land*—The Federal Republic of Germany is composed of 11 states, or *laender* (*land* is singular): Baden-Würtemberg, Bavaria, Bremen, Hamburg, Hesse, Lower Saxony, North-Rhine Westphalia, Rhineland Palatinate, Saarland, Schleswig-Holstein, and Berlin. The system is a highly decentralized one in which the *laender* have considerable power relative to the federal government in Bonn. See Katzenstein, *Policy and Politics,* 15–17.

6. Ibid., 6–7.

Despite the domestic orientation of the Bundesbank, President Pöhl proved to be an effective diplomat by massaging this parochial contingent when its support was crucial and by otherwise steering an independent course around it. Pöhl relied on a virtuoso style and innate perceptiveness rather than bureaucratic experience to succeed in avoiding intransigent situations.

Helmut Schlesinger, Vice President of the Bundesbank, is usually associated with the "old school." Schlesinger commands respect among the West German banking community, being referred to as "the backbone of the inner core" for his unflagging devotion to price stability and conservatism—which in the words of one Ministry of Finance official was "perhaps even more than Bonn would have liked." Thus, Pöhl has had to contend not only with the weight carried by Schlesinger's opinion, but he also has had to appear not to be appeasing the Americans—so as not to alienate the "inner core" and lose all credibility. For this reason, for instance, Pöhl invited Schlesinger to his home for a discussion with Volcker in August 1986. He also requested that Stoltenberg include Schlesinger in other top-secret discussions on policy coordination. Previously such meetings had been restricted to Stoltenberg, Pöhl, and Tietmeyer. Schlesinger became a regular participant after the Louvre meeting.

Pöhl was thus forced to walk a diplomatic tightrope. When encountering international pressure for interest rate cuts, he would often indicate to other central bankers, especially to the Americans, that he had to deal with many problems on the inside and ask them to give him more time. In that way, Pöhl kept other central bankers guessing since they could not verify whether he actually favored a rate cut or whether he simply used the domesticist argument as an excuse.

An illustration of the domesticist conflict occurred in November 1987, after the stock market crash the previous month, when the verbal crossfire between Bonn and Washington heated up. US Treasury Secretary James A. Baker III renewed his criticism of West German monetary policy, claiming that interest rate increases engineered by Schlesinger had set off the crisis in the financial markets. Clearly the attack was meant to isolate the "inner core" veterans and make them look villainous. Instead, it created an uproar in West Germany and led to the mobilization of conservative ranks behind Schlesinger, which put Pöhl in a more delicate position.

Even as the switch to floating exchange rates enabled the Bundesbank to tighten its grip on monetary and currency policy, the central bank faced two new challenges to its control of monetary policy since the mid-1970s. These were, first, rapid increases in the budget deficit, and second, the growth in the position of the deutsche mark as the world's second reserve currency.

Fiscal Policy

The primary responsibility for the formulation of fiscal policy in the Federal Republic is left to the Ministry of Finance, which has gradually increased its leverage in this area since the 1950s.

Since the enactment of the Stability and Growth Act of 1967, the federal government has relied on fiscal policy to manage macroeconomic developments. Within the federal government, the Ministry of Finance has primary control over fiscal policy in the process of budget making. The Finance Minister consolidates spending proposals developed by mid-level bureaucrats throughout the government into general guidelines for the budget and then proposes a draft budget to the cabinet, where, together with the Chancellor, he exercises considerable influence.

This law has circumscribed the role of the Bundestag, which is restricted by law from introducing any change that will increase expenditures without a proposal for a matching increase in revenues. The same law allows the federal government to veto all changes in the budget that are the result of increased appropriations. Although the ruling coalition has no difficulty obtaining sufficient parliamentary support for its taxing and spending priorities, in practice its control over fiscal policy is undermined by the following two factors. First, since the 1970s, the coalition government has been so structured that the SPD has received control of the Ministry of Finance, while the FDP has staffed the Ministry of Economics, an arrangement that has weakened the federal government's ability to undertake comprehensive or drastic measures. Second, the federal government controls less than 50 percent of public investment, and only about 15 percent of the nation's total public spending and investment,[7] the remainder coming from *land* and local governments. The upper chamber of *land* governments can, in fact, veto a certain type of legislation that affects the territorial, financial, or administrative interests of its *land*. The strength of party politics at the local level further limits the ability of the federal government to pursue its own agenda.

With these constraints, the budgetary politics of West Germany, like those of Japan, are reactive in nature. Budgeting is influenced by abrupt, short-term changes in the nation's economic climate, such as those that proliferated during the economic crises of 1966–67, 1973–74, and 1979–80. The first crisis was followed by the introduction of a stronger emphasis on planning in budgeting, embodied in the Stabilization and Growth Act and subsequent laws of similar nature. The second crisis brought about a period of reduced

---

7. Katzenstein, *Policy and Politics*, 100–101.

management in the budgetary process. The third led to fundamental reductions in state intervention—deregulation, rejection of contracyclical fiscal policy, and privatization—and to reductions in public expenditures with a visible bias against social expenditures.[8]

As the 1980 election approached, the politics of budgeting hinged on two alternatives, reducing the budget deficit or cutting taxes. The Bundesbank favored the former prescription, while the FDP preferred the latter. The Kohl government accommodated both viewpoints, voiced by the two most independent institutional actors in German politics, by simultaneously pursuing both tax cuts and a reduction in the budget deficit.

Ideology

Without a doubt, ideology plays a role in German macroeconomic policy making. Since the mid-1970s, differences between the left wing of the SPD, along with the unions, which supported the welfare state with Keynesian deficit spending, and the right wing of the CDU-CSU as well as the FDP and business, which argued for improved investment opportunities and deregulation, grew sharper. In practice, however, the direct role of ideology is less pronounced, given an ingrained inclination toward an incrementalist approach and the party politics of coalition building.

Willy Brandt's newly elected SPD government, for example, found great difficulty in maneuvering between the two powerful and sophisticated economic ministers, Hans Friderichs of the FDP and Helmut Schmidt, who had succeeded Karl Schiller as Economics and Finance Minister in 1972. Brandt decided to separate the Economics and Finance Ministry into two independent ministries, as they had been previously, to maintain the SPD-FDP coalition, assigning Friderichs to the Ministry of Economics, while allowing Schmidt to keep the Finance post. Disputes over monetary policy followed when Friderichs emphasized the importance of continuing a highly restrictive monetary policy, and Schmidt argued for a more accommodative stance, which reflected concern within the SPD over negative effects on employment.

The dispute, it is reasonable to say, was "tactical rather than strategic and typical of later disputes within the coalition government" because successive SPD finance ministers—responsible for relations with the Bundesbank—worried about the tactical problems of coordinating the central bank's monetary policy with the government's fiscal policy, especially when they

---

8. Roland Sturm, "Budgetary Politics in the Federal Republic of Germany, *West European Politics* 8 (1985), 61.

perceived a need for reflation.[9] Schmidt aimed tactically at appeasement of the left wing of the SPD and, at the same time, a lessening of the burden on fiscal policy by transferring part of that burden onto monetary policy. Such maneuvering was necessary since mixed-party coalitions prohibited radical changes in policy. Besides that, the professional bureaucracy remained paramount in economic policy making and the Bundesbank emerged unscathed from the 1970s, its authority intact and unchallenged.

The Bundesbank, however, maintained its authority with sometimes painful effects. One instance, the stabilization crisis of 1966, induced by a highly restrictive monetary policy, helped push Chancellor Ludwig Erhard out of office. A second instance was in the early 1980s, as mentioned earlier, when Pöhl's drastic increases in interest rates contributed to Schmidt's fall from power. Katzenstein observes that "the Bundesbank's single-minded pursuit of monetary stability has been the most constant element in West Germany's economic policy to the chagrin of the CDU and the SPD alike."[10] Furthermore, the Bundesbank is bolstered by cultural support for its stabilization policies and for union wage restraint, both of which have supported each other.[11] Insofar as ideology matters in German economic decision making, the most important piece of ideology is the Bundesbank Standard—that manifestation of cultural, political, and psychological insecurity that acts as a social security blanket.

In sum, postwar German economic policy was shaped by two lessons: first, that the management of money is too important to be left to the politicians; and second, that national economic life is too important to be the exclusive domain of the federal government. The institutional and political arrangements that reflect these considerations have prevented implementation of policies that are either strongly Keynesian or strongly supply-side.[12]

In essence, general support for an incrementalist approach to macroeconomic policy—often appearing to foreigners as "German stubbornness"—reflects the systemic arrangement, where institutional competition ensures cross-checks and is founded on cultural inhibitions to drastic change. A US Treasury official who became accustomed to dealing with the Germans cautioned the Treasury's higher echelon not to aim for something spectacular: "You know, you can't propose to do something because you'll be imposing on someone else's *besitzstand,* which means, basically, acquired position,

---

9. K.H.F. Dyson, "The Politics of Economic Management in West Germany," *West European Politics* 4 (May 1981), 43.

10. Katzenstein, *Policy and Politics,* 97.

11. Dyson, "Politics of Economic Management," 54.

12. Katzenstein, *Policy and Politics,* 93.

accumulated benefits, prerogatives, and entitlements. Everybody's got their *besitzstand,* and you can move ahead as long as you don't diminish somebody else's, which vastly reduces your maneuvering room."[13]

In his analysis of the political dynamics of German economic policy making, Katzenstein concludes:

On balance, during the last thirty years, West Germany's semi-sovereign state has been a great asset in the conduct of economic policy. Whether it will continue to be an asset in the next thirty years is a question that is beginning to be asked by muffled voices and not only those of West Germany.[14]

The answer will depend on the role of the deutsche mark in the world economy and particularly its future within the EMS, as well as the crucial role of the Bundesbank as the nucleus of this system.

The European Monetary System (EMS)

Shortly after the conclusion of the Louvre Accord, Pöhl spoke to an American audience on his notion of the international monetary regime and its potential for stability. He emphasized that the European Monetary System had succeeded in establishing a zone of monetary stability in Europe. He attributed this success to the viability of the technical part of the system, intervention and the credit mechanism, and the broad convergence of economic policy objectives, headed by the priority given to price stability, for which he claimed, "Germany has been one of the front-runners."

It is certainly true that the unexpected resilience of the EMS throughout the 1980s would have been impossible without the full commitment of the Bundesbank. (Incidentally, Pöhl's first eight-year term coincided with the first eight years of the EMS.) It is fair to say that its success is also attributable to the Bonn government's painful task of "invariably agreeing to a revaluation of the deutsche mark at crucial realignment negotiations, despite considerable problems on the domestic policy front," in the words of a Bonn official, who added that "the German government never failed to encourage the Bundesbank to cooperate within the EMS."[15]

The Federal Republic's overriding interest rests logically with its European neighbors, with which it conducts more than half its foreign trade and has

---

13. Personal interview.

14. Katzenstein, *Policy and Politics,* 107.

15. Personal interview.

de jure (through the EMS) or de facto stable exchange rates. German bilateral trade with the United States accounts for only about 10 percent of total German trade and German bilateral trade with Japan, only about 3 percent. Recent volatility of the dollar, moreover, has induced German trading partners to search for a more stable international currency, which they have found in the deutsche mark. Even Great Britain—not a member of the EMS—has gradually delinked sterling from the dollar, with the pace accelerating during the period of the Plaza strategy and throughout 1987, so much that one British official asserted that the pound sterling had become completely uncoupled from the dollar.[16]

Based on the expectation that Great Britain would enter the EMS in the near future, Bundesbank officials became ever more confident of the EMS as a vehicle for its own currency strategy, for "you cannot tie your currency to a currency which, although it is the most important currency in the world, at the moment, does not really qualify as a standard."[17] Obviously, the deutsche mark had replaced the dollar as the currency standard in Europe.

It is, in fact, not an unreasonable claim that EMS discipline has helped some partners who, in the absence of a constraint imposed on them by membership in a "stability club," might not have had the same success. . . . in gain[ing] control over inflationary pressures at home and avoid[ing] the vicious circle of depreciation and inflation with which less disciplined countries. . . . have been confronted.[18]

After all, both France and Italy defected from the "snake" arrangement during the mid-1970s under the weight of domestic political pressure. The recent experience of the EMS has shown that these two countries are prepared to formulate domestic economic policies within the confines that EMS membership places on them.

The close identification of the EMS with the interests and policies of the Bundesbank acts as an incentive for smaller countries to join the EMS. The EMS provides a means not only for economic adjustment but also for avoidance of criticism for applying harsh adjustment measures, since the blame can be pinned on the "Bundesbank standard." Tying currencies to "a stable standard" leads to greater stability, and a consequent renewal of public confidence in monetary authorities. The era of high inflation in the

---

16. Personal interview.

17. "The EMS is now a deutsche mark zone because it sets the pace for price stability," confided one Bonn official to the author.

18. Karl Otto Pöhl, "The European Monetary System: A Model for a More Stable International Order?" Paul-Henri Spaak Lecture, Center for International Studies, Harvard University, 4 May 1987.

late 1970s and early 1980s, aggravated by the second oil shock, gave politicians and monetary authorities ample pretext to enter into this safety net.

This argument in favor of joining the EMS—to enhance the credibility commitment of monetary authorities to fight inflation—was used to support Britain's entry in the system. Along these lines, The *Economist* remarked somewhat scathingly:

[T]he biggest change will be the transfer of responsibility of Britain's monetary policy from the Bank of England to Germany's Bundesbank which, as the central bank keenest on sound money, sets the pace for others to follow. This would be a blessing: Tory governments may like appointing City gents as governors of the Bank, but Mr. Karl Otto Pöhl would do a better job.[19]

Entry into the "stability club" automatically poses a dilemma for a central banker's anti-inflation strategy. In countries where inflation is above average, there is an incentive for the central banker to use inflation as a tool of monetary policy. When the central bank resorts to inflation "surprises" in order

[T]o reduce unemployment, the public incorporates this information in their forecast of inflation. In the resulting equilibrium, the central banker does not succeed at surprising the public systematically (and thereby permanently increase employment) and the expected and actual rate of inflation is higher than the inflation rate that would prevail if the authorities could credibly precommit.[20]

On the other hand, if a restraint were imposed on the central bank's incentive to create inflation "surprises," the public would expect lower inflation, and the result would be a more cooperative picture overall. Joining the EMS, therefore, represents a way of changing the range of incentives that face the central banker.[21]

It is no secret that the Bundesbank dragged its heels when Schmidt first endorsed the creation of the system. Bundesbank officials feared that anti-inflationary policy could be compromised by the obligation to intervene. Not only did the Bundesbank persuade the Chancellor to reduce the number

---

19. *Economist,* 21 September 1985.

20. Greater detail on credibility as a motivation for membership in the EMS can be found in Francesco Giavazzi and Alberto Giovanni, "Limiting Exchange Rate Flexibility: The Experience and the Problem of the European Monetary System," March 1987, 10; processed.

21. Ibid.

of EMS participants, but it also reserved the right to suspend intervention in currency markets unilaterally if the Bank perceived a threat to its duty to safeguard the value of the deutsche mark. As one Bonn official remarked, "Inside the Bundesbank, there are still a lot of people who do not like the EMS." The same official explained further that there is sometimes within the Bundesbank a conflict between the decisions that would be made independent of EMS consideration and those based on West German obligations to the EMS. There is growing awareness of this problem.[22]

Ideally, the EMS represents the first step toward the ultimate goal of a European Economic and Monetary Union administered by a European central bank that would issue its own currency. Again, the biggest impediment to closer cooperation among the monetary authorities in EMS countries is the "bureaucratic empire" of the Bundesbank, to use the phrase of Helmut Schmidt, one of the founders of the EMS.[23] Recently, however, the German vision of the EMS has come under attack from other EMS members, especially after the major realignment of January 1987. In reality, European integration is still an ambitious objective for the future, which will require closer convergence of political and economic policies.

Two significant realignments took place within the EMS during the period from Plaza to Louvre. Unlike the smooth realignment of April 1986, which reflected "a trend toward easier monetary management in the EC,"[24] the second realignment in January 1987 came after "acrimonious talks" during 13 hours of negotiations.[25] Despite Stoltenberg's assertion that "on the basis of economic fundamentals [measured by real labor costs] there was no reason for realignment," the mechanism could no longer be supported by intervention alone. French officials precipitated the crisis by letting the franc drop through the floor, claiming that "it is a deutsche mark crisis, not a franc crisis." The Bundesbank was therefore compelled to join in the effort to maintain the value of the French currency. European central banks had already spent between $8 and $10 billion during the previous week, probably the largest concerted intervention in EMS history.

Finance Minister Stoltenberg's "own credibility may have suffered a knock by the rapidity with which Bonn submitted to the will of the markets. But, overall, West Germany has acted in accordance with the consistent 'stability-first' policy promulgated by the Bundesbank. . . . which seems if anything to have increased its influence over the Bonn government in recent

---

22. Personal interview.

23. Interview of Helmut Schmidt with the author.

24. Bank for International Settlements, *Annual Report,* Geneva, 1985–86.

25. *Financial Times,* 13 January 1987.

years," reported *Financial Times* journalist David Marsh.[26] Again, the realignment demonstrated the Bundesbank's tenacious adherence to doctrine whenever West Germany faces external pressure on the deutsche mark; it will respond by adjusting the currency rate upward instead of discouraging speculation by reducing domestic interest rates.

The January realignment did not allay all tensions, for almost immediately speculation that early reductions in European interest rates would occur provoked an increase in French bond and futures prices. Realignment should have obviated the need for any immediate reduction in German interest rates, but the continued weakness of the dollar produced fresh strains within the EMS. Although Stoltenberg had ruled out any cut in the discount rate until after the German elections on January 25, the Bundesbank announced a cut in the discount rate of one-half of one percentage point on January 22, while tightening monetary conditions to control the liquidity surge. This maneuver once again illustrated the power of the Bundesbank amid much criticism of its policies. One economist at Commerzbank in Frankfurt voiced a criticism shared by many in both the United States and Japan that the combination of measures looked half-hearted and contradictory.[27] The Bundesbank became the target of criticism within the EMS, accused of leading the economies of Europe into recession with its restrictive monetary policy.

Many critics assert that the EMS owes its success to a fair-weather phenomenon; that is, its infancy happened to coincide with a period of overvaluation of the dollar, since the system works best when the dollar is strong. When the dollar was overvalued, from March 1983 to July 1985, no realignment occurred in the EMS. The strong dollar enabled EMS currencies to maintain a "delicate balance of weakness" within the EMS since they were a less attractive option for speculation, reserves, or portfolios. The EMS held up rather well in that environment of improving competitiveness with the United States and moderate upward pressure on the deutsche mark. Subsequent dollar depreciation since 1985 has led to increased speculation in the deutsche mark, which has caused it to appreciate vis-à-vis other EMS currencies, and to strain EMS parity bands.

Suggestions for strengthening the EMS mechanism emerged after the realignment. Jacques Delors, President of the European Commission, and Mark Eyskens, Belgian Finance Minister, presented three possibilities: greater use of intramarginal intervention, greater coordination of interest rate policies, and possibly, direct intervention by the European Monetary

---

26. David Marsh, *Financial Times,* 13 January 1987.

27. *Washington Post,* 23 January 1987.

Cooperation Fund, which holds a considerable proportion of member states' reserves.[28]

The harshest criticism has come from France. Finance Minister Edouard Balladur later claimed that the January crisis could have been avoided, had a serious shortcoming of the EMS mechanism not prevented greater coordination of exchange market intervention and action on interest rates. He specifically advocated constructing a common strategy toward the dollar and the yen, reinforcing the cohesiveness of the system through greater coordination of economic policies and increasing coordination among central banks against speculative capital movements. Balladur's remarks implicitly criticized the Bundesbank for its reluctance to intervene and its failure to support the indicator system.[29]

French criticism, though, underscored a deeper concern about German monetary hegemony in Europe. A senior official of the French Ministry of Finance expressed his growing frustration with the perception of the EMS as the "D-mark zone."

Don't forget that the EMS is managed by Germany and France. Each time a major decision regarding the EMS is made, it is made together by Germany and France. European countries—France, Italy and probably the United Kingdom—we are not ready to accept—how can I say—the monetary leadership of Germany in Europe. We are not ready to accept the deutsche mark to be the European currency in the international zone system (EMS). It is perfectly true that Germany is a world economic power and Germany has a special responsibility, but as far as monetary questions are concerned, you can't consider that Germany was and is speaking for Europe as a whole.[30]

Just as the EMS factor was vital to the West German Plaza strategy, so was it to that of the French. The Germans sought to avoid the painful schism within the EMS that a free fall of the dollar might cause, while the French wanted to keep the West Germans from taking over the EMS. French political objectives in the Plaza strategy had special bearing on the "German question." The French recognized a superb opportunity to "press or push on German friends" in the initiation of the international policy coordination. As one French participant explained, "Germany was absolutely *the* determinant of our economic policy and yet it was sometimes difficult to work with them, especially German monetary authorities—the Bundesbank."[31]

---

28. *Financial Times,* 13 January 1987.

29. Edouard Balladur, "The EMS: Advance or Face Retreat," *Financial Times,* 17 June 1987.

30. Personal interview.

31. Personal interview.

Thus, the French had to devise some means of putting international pressure on Germany. The Plaza strategy served the purpose. "This international process was a good way for us to put pressure on Germany so that they would accept more growth, a more dynamic fiscal policy, reduction of interest rates, and more attention to exchange rates," remarked an architect of the French strategy.

The fact that West Germany placed such a high priority in their Plaza strategy on the protection of the EMS reveals the value of the EMS to West Germany. The EMS has served the interests of the Bundesbank by allowing it to slow deutsche mark revaluation, thus constituting what one European official called a form of "subtle mercantilism." The mercantilist benefit passes on to the West German export industries that are able to incorporate currency movements in decision making by taking advantage of delays in realignment. Moreover, the revaluation is actually less than the full difference in cost-effectiveness between the currencies involved. In other words, the EMS tends to revalue the deutsche mark in nominal terms and to depreciate the deutsche mark in real terms. This translates into a more moderate expansion in monetary policy than would have occurred without the EMS mechanism. West German support for the EMS, then, came out of a desire for greater monetary stability throughout Europe, at the sacrifice of marginally higher inflation at home.

Although West German officials wanted the realignment of the currencies—that is dollar depreciation—for managing the world economy and controlling inflation, a soft landing was critical to the West German Plaza strategy. The pace of realignment should be gradual so as to minimize its impact on the EMS. The EMS represents a means of solving the inherent conflict posed by export growth to West German strategy. Permanent export surpluses exercised a destabilizing effect on the value of the deutsche mark and, similarly, a destabilizing effect on European economic and political relations, by making the deutsche mark more attractive and subject to constant increases in value.[32] Although the subtle mercantilism embedded in the EMS sometimes alienated West Germany's trading partners, at the very least the EMS gave them some insurance against unilateral depreciation by guaranteeing mutual realignment when necessary.

Katzenstein suggests that the EMS was politically feasible in West Germany from a domestic standpoint because it offered something to everyone: the establishment of the EMS "seemed to meet long-standing demands of the dissatisfied unions for monetary expansion, curbed slightly

---

32. On these twin conflicts, see Wilhelm Hankel, "West Germany," in *Economic Foreign Policies of Industrial States*, ed. Wilfred L. Kohl (New York: Lexington Books, 1977), 120.

the power of the central bank, and promised to slow down the general upward drift of the deutsche mark, which had become a major problem for West Germany's export industry."[33]

Furthermore, the Bundesbank's anti-inflationary standard provides the basis for the rules of the game under a sphere of greater West German assertiveness. Now the EMS is regarded by some West Germans as an effective vehicle for the realization of greater West German leadership economically and politically, although others would rather use it as "a group in which we can hide." This version of leadership within the EMS, however, implies a regional rather than global orientation, a restriction with which many Germans seem content. One official, half-mockingly, confided, "We like to be a nation state. We like to be a middle power. Here in West Germany, there is a strong tendency to oppose growing up." West German participation in the EMS is quite compatible with German economic and political interests.

Conversely, participation in the EMS runs the risk of precluding a more important position for the Federal Republic in the international monetary system because Germans give higher priority to domestic and European matters than to wider international ones.[34] Nonetheless, it is fair to say that West Germany must take into account more fully the implication of its domestic economy for the EMS. To the extent that German consideration for safeguarding the EMS mechanism happens to be consistent with the broader global responsibility of the Federal Republic, the "DM-zone" is acceptable to the United States, Japan, and perhaps even France—although French officials would never admit it.

---

33. Katzenstein, *Policy and Politics,* 95.

34. See C. Fred Bergsten, "Economic Imbalances and World Politics," *Foreign Affairs* 65 (Spring 1987): 770–794.

■ *Tokyo Summit*

When representatives of the seven leading industrial countries met in Tokyo on 4–5 May 1986, only nine months after the G-5 had mapped out an initial strategy to realign currencies, the mood had changed dramatically.

The Plaza strategy had worked all too effectively in driving up the yen. From the Plaza meeting in September 1985 to the Tokyo Summit, the yen appreciated from 240 to 170 yen to the dollar. Already, the Japanese export sector was feeling the crunch, with small- and medium-sized firms affected the most. Japanese policymakers feared that a further rise in the yen would cause a slowing of the economy and perhaps a recession. Prime Minister Yasuhiro Nakasone, having endorsed the Plaza Agreement, found himself in hot water politically, and many speculated that his ability to reverse the direction of, or at least to stabilize, the yen at the summit would decide whether he would remain in office.

Meanwhile, the weaker dollar had failed to reduce the US trade deficit significantly. Protectionist pressure in the Congress had not subsided, and prospects for a firmer dollar remained bleak. Baker's noncommittal remarks about the dollar—constituting a de facto talk-down policy—sanctioned its continued fall, and did not foreshadow any shift in policy at the summit. With no renewed commitment from the US administration on exchange rates, the dollar's sharp drop before the summit signaled that Nakasone's political aggravations would increase.

Instead of responding directly to Nakasone's plea to stabilize the yen–dollar exchange rate, Baker struck out on a new initiative, unveiling a plan for policy coordination of which currency stabilization was only one component. Baker's proposal dominated the proceedings and was adopted as the main pillar of the Tokyo Declaration.

There were two innovations in the new cooperation strategy: the formation of a Group of Seven finance ministers that would meet frequently between summits, but at least once a year, and the use by the G-7 of economic indicators to assess the economic performance of the participants. As outlined in the communiqué by David C. Mulford, Assistant Secretary of the US Treasury, these indicators included GNP growth rates, inflation rates, interest rates, unemployment, fiscal deficit ratios, current account and trade balances, monetary growth rates, reserves, and currency rates.[1] The indicators would exercise a disciplining influence upon the seven finance ministers and central bank governors, in their conduct of "multilateral surveillance," and facilitate discussion of "appropriate remedial measures" whenever the indicators showed a substantial deviation.

In traditional summit spirit, the leaders' comments were positive but bland. West German Chancellor Helmut Kohl called the summit a "good success." British Prime Minister Margaret Thatcher said, "between us, we achieved our objectives. Mission accomplished. It was a valuable, constructive, and forward-looking summit." Even Paul A. Volcker, usually taciturn on these occasions, commented that "there's a lot to be happy about."[2]

The press, while welcoming the US administration's more assertive stance in international economic affairs, expressed varying degrees of confidence in the prospects for the new plan for increased coordination. "The President now accepts that he can no longer ride alone in the world economy. If he wants to cut taxes, he has agreed to take account of the objectives of other countries."[3] Perhaps the New York Times put best what was in most minds: "The new system, born of political compromise, will succeed or fail on the strength of the political discipline built into it."[4] The European press was in general more skeptical of the prospects for better economic management among the summit countries. The Economist noted that Baker's "propaganda victory" at Tokyo was essential in fighting protectionist pressures that could spark an international trade war. Such a trade war would be devastating for Japan, which is the reason, claimed the British weekly, that Nakasone "gritted his teeth and called the economic talks fruitful," even though he failed in his main aim of getting the summitteers to agree to stop the dollar from falling any further.[5]

Among US Treasury officials, Deputy Secretary Richard G. Darman was

---

1. The Venice Summit agreement, 10 June 1987, reduced the number of indicators to six, which, though not listed in the communiqué, were cited by Mulford as: economic growth, inflation, trade balances, government budgets, monetary conditions, and currency exchange rates; reported in the Washington Post, 11 June 1987. The current account balance was deleted from the list of variables agreed on in the Louvre Accord.

2. Paul A. Volcker, address to Columbia Business School, as quoted by Leonard Silk, New York Times, 7 May 1986.

3. Peter T. Kilborn, New York Times, 7 May 1986.

4. Peter T. Kilborn, New York Times, 8 May 1986.

5. Editorial, Economist, 10 May 1986.

the most positive. "You've got a procedure to assure that the countries, between summits, really do something." He also stressed the view that "even if we should not be able to implement this in the way we'd like, we are better off."[6] In contrast, Mulford expressed a more cautious view, admitting that the plan contained uncertainty. "It's not possible under the present system to force countries to make economic policy changes." Mulford seemed to think that the agreement relied on little more than "the . . . peer pressure that has marked policymaking for a while."[7]

Enhanced Surveillance

The enhanced surveillance strategy proposed by the United States and based on the use of economic indicators was largely the work of Baker and Darman. Certainly, the indicator idea was not new; it had been explored first in the early 1970s and had been used as a reference mechanism by the G-5 to review economic performance since the early 1980s.

The first use of indicators in international monetary relations took place from 1969 to 1973 within the European Community. Under the Barre Plan, a set of seven indicators was designated to gauge four objectives: growth, low unemployment, price stability, and external balance. The indicators acted as early warning signals that would prompt discussions and remedial measures by the appropriate arm of the European Commission, should one or more of the four rates deviate past some established level.

In 1972, the "Volcker" Plan, put forward in the Committee of 20 negotiations, included an indicator system whereby a country's deviation from an established norm level of international reserves would trigger application of "graduated pressures" on the offending country to impel it to take the necessary steps toward adjustment. European participants objected to the automaticity implied in the plan, which would "punish" both deficit and surplus countries; and although they wished to prevent excessive imbalances in the current account, they were unwilling to accept automatic interference in their own policies when they attributed the imbalances to the United States in the first place.

Thus, European opposition directly precluded the adoption of the "Volcker" Plan by the Committee of 20 as a means of reforming the international monetary system, although both the switch to floating, formally put into operation in 1973, and the first oil shock, contributed to a shift in the US position toward favoring floating rates and no intervention. Since the mid-

---

6. Personal interview.

7. Robert D. Hershey, *New York Times*, 7 May 1986.

1970s, various other indicator plans have been proposed.[8] The International Monetary Fund (IMF) has observed the need for enhanced multilateral surveillance and has supported the use of indicators. As stated in its articles, surveillance is one of its primary functions but has "so far been largely ineffective on major industrial countries."[9] In the August 1985 report of the Group of 24 Deputies, "The Functioning and Improvement of the International Monetary System," the use of indicators was recommended in conjunction with a "mechanism to trigger consultations among the concerned countries and the Fund . . . whenever the indicators available suggest excessive short-term movements or misalignments of major currencies."[10] More generally, the Fund sees itself as the primary institution around which the system of surveillance and indicators should be built up.

In 1982, the IMF became involved in G-5 meetings as far as the surveillance function was concerned. Based on the agreement made at the Versailles Summit, the Managing Director of the IMF would submit to the G-5 ministers and governors his assessment of the economic situation of each country and his suggestion on how to improve it.[11] Jacques de Larosière was the first Managing Director to attend a G-5 meeting in late 1982. The difficulty of the job was expressed by one top official at the IMF, "You mustn't be too technical but you must be clear. You must be a little bit thought-provoking. And you have to put the real major issues, options, and problems on the table." So delicate was this task that de Larosière used

---

8. For a description of early proposals for indicator systems, see John Williamson, "Target Zones and Indicators as Instruments for International Economic Policy Coordination," Report to the Group of 24, 9 September 1986; processed. See also *Targets and Indicators: A Blueprint for the International Coordination of Economic Policy*, POLICY ANALYSES IN INTERNATIONAL ECONOMICS 22 (Washington: Institute for International Economics, September 1987). In this study John Williamson and Marcus H. Miller put forward a proposal that combined indicators and targets. Their blueprint called for the G-7 to pursue two intermediate targets—a rate of growth of domestic demand and a real effective exchange rate. According to the plan, monetary and fiscal policies would be conducted according to three principles:
(1) World short-term interest rates would be adjusted if aggregate growth of nominal income threatened to diverge from the sum of growth targets of nominal demand for the participating countries.
(2) Short-term interest rates would be revised as a supplement to intervention in exchange markets to keep currencies within targets of 10 percent.
(3) National fiscal policies would be coordinated in terms of national growth targets for domestic demand.

9. "Summary of Recommendations of the Group of 24," *IMF Survey*, September 1985, 2.

10. Ibid.

11. Robert D. Putnam and Nicholas Bayne, *Hanging Together: The Seven-Power Summits* (Cambridge: Harvard University Press, 1984), 160.

to rehearse with his counselors at the IMF before each presentation to the G-5 ministers.

For indicators, the IMF used GNP and GDP, current account, prices (CPI), interest rates, and exchange rates, which were included with tables and comparisons, along with the Managing Director's analysis, in a paper that was sent ahead of the meeting. The discussion of the surveillance normally lasted an hour, with the first fifteen or twenty minutes devoted to the IMF presentation and the remaining time given to the ministers' comments.

Volcker and Pöhl had been involved in the evolution of the indicator mechanism. It remains unclear, however, to what extent Volcker threw his weight behind the Baker-Darman proposal. According to one report, "Volcker helped Baker put together a plan for economic coordination among the industrial countries that was adopted at the Tokyo Summit," since he "liked the Baker plan of trying to move the US, Japan, and Europe back toward some semblance of fixed exchange rates."[12] No doubt Baker felt encouraged by Volcker's approval after they had discussed the proposal during their weekly Thursday morning breakfast meeting. Nonetheless, it was principally Darman who infused new life into the indicator concept, trying to turn it into a sort of stability mechanism and buttressing it with the new G-7 process.

Baker and Darman secretly began to promote an indicator mechanism in April 1986. Baker consulted with Secretary of State George P. Shultz before he adopted it as an official policy recommendation. Shultz removed from Darman's original set of indicators what he considered a too interventionist device—a commodity price index. After having gained the approval of Shultz and White House Chief of Staff Donald T. Regan, Baker, and Darman presented the indicator idea to the British at the Interim Committee meeting of the IMF in April 1986. With British support, the American team also obtained French and Japanese backing in secret bilateral meetings around the time of the Organization for Economic Cooperation and Development meetings of April 17 in Paris. By the opening of the summit, the plan had been all but agreed on.[13]

This victory of the Baker-Darman team did not occur immediately or without effort; several serious problems came to the fore, which had to be dealt with first. One point of contention was foreshadowed in a statement before the April 1986 Interim Committee, in which Baker, alluding to the Tokyo Summit program, and acknowledging both the strengths and weaknesses of the current international monetary system, recommended that the

---

12. William Neikirk, *Volcker: Portrait of the Money Man* (New York: Congdon Press, 1987).

13. Hobart Rowen, *Washington Post,* 11 May 1986.

IMF Executive Board should implement the surveillance of economies, with abbreviated assessments to be publicized by the Managing Director. Furthermore, he suggested five qualities that should be looked for in a strengthened system: symmetry, breadth of policy, flexibility, political will, and automaticity.[14] On April 10, Darman stated more explicitly that a precondition for the stability of any system is "an effective mechanism" to guarantee "routine meeting and monitoring of the key countries . . . [using] standard indicators for systematic review, and a commitment to agree to adjust policy fundamentals."[15] Thus, the US administration was advocating a strong disciplinary mechanism for the new "system," paralleling its position in the early stages of international monetary negotiations held under the auspices of the Committee of 20.

As in 1972, the United States argued in 1986 from a deficit position. Both West Germany and Japan, the principal surplus countries, opposed the near-scientific verification process that Darman's "objective indicators" seemed to connote. In their eyes, the automaticity concept lacked credibility—"What would be the reaction of the US Congress if the G-5 would decide that the US deficit should be cut by $50 billion next year?" asked a top Bundesbank official. The Germans had already learned the lesson of indicators through their brief experience with the indicator mechanism in the EMS:

We had this discussion in the EMS at the end of the '70s. At that time, some thought we should have some automaticity of indicators. It was refused at that time, because we felt we should keep room for maneuvers in our monetary policy. In the EMS, those who were most in favor of indicators were those who diverged more from the equilibrium than others, Belgium, for example. And they never reacted, they never took any decision just because an indicator indicated they should move up interest rates.[16]

As a West German senior government official put it, "Since mankind [has] existed, people have used indicators—the sunrise is an indicator. Fishermen use indicators to find the fish. What is the purpose of statistics if you wouldn't have indicators?" But the problem is, he pointed out, that you must assume the political responsibility for using them:

---

14. James A. Baker III, statement to the IMF Interim Committee, Washington, 9–10 April 1986.

15. Richard G. Darman, comments at Evans-Novak Political Forum, Madison Hotel, Washington, 10 April 1986.

16. Personal interview.

In the EMS, we have an indicator mechanism. It was meant to be an alarm signal, but it doesn't really work as an alarm signal. It is just an intervention point. It does not trigger changes of economic policy of our country. Parliament is not summoned and told that the bell is ringing and let's change labor law. The same would be true with these indicators.[17]

Ultimately the offending word, *objective,* which had appeared in the original language of the Tokyo Declaration and seemed to connote automaticity, was dropped to accommodate the German and Japanese positions.

The discussions during the summit focused on two cases of wording in the Baker proposal, which had stated that the heads of state were to encourage finance ministers and central bankers to reach *agreement* on appropriate remedial measures whenever there were significant deviations from *intended objectives.* Some participants, including the Japanese, pointed out that *intended objectives* might trigger an automatic imposition of policy and that an *agreement* seemed to connote something compulsory. Their arguments prevailed, so the language was changed, from *intended objectives* and *agreement* to *intended course* and *make the best effort to reach an understanding,* respectively, to lessen the sense of obligation. "The thrust of the whole argument revolved around this one consideration. We're not going to allow indicators to meddle into the domestic politics and sovereignty," explained Vice Minister of Finance for International Affairs Tomomitsu Oba.[18]

The major objective of the American indicator strategy was to induce growth and to bolster domestic demand in West Germany and in Japan. US officials grew increasingly worried over slow growth in both countries, particularly in West Germany, and its troubling implications for external imbalances and the world economy. The US team bluntly suggested that the German growth target for the indicator mechanism should be 3.5 percent for 1986 and that strong action was needed to guarantee that this rate was reached. Growth rates, a core target of the indicator mechanism, have remained a contentious issue.

The exchange rate was also an explosive issue. In question was what weight should be given to the exchange rate, among all the indicators. West Germany and Japan insisted that the exchange rate be treated as a product of macroeconomic policies, not as a policy objective in itself. But Japanese and West German objections to US emphasis on exchange rates was only part of the general problem of deciding which indicator among all of them should be given highest priority. Each of the G-7 nations considered one indicator more important than the others, but they did not argue about priorities.

---

17. Personal interview.

18. Tomomitsu Oba, "Two focuses and accomplishments at the Tokyo Summit," *Kinyu Zaisei Ji jo* (Monetary and fiscal report), 26 May 1986.

For the United States, the political liability of the trade deficit determined that current accounts and exchange rates would be rated above other indicators. Baker emphasized repeatedly that "increased reliance will need to be placed on exchange rates," to adjust resulting imbalances.[19]

French officials also emphasized the importance of exchange rates, even recommending that the number of indicators be reduced from ten to two or three in order to focus attention on the variables through which international influences are directly transmitted, namely, the balance of payments, interest rates, and above all, exchange rates.[20] France's underlying goal in advocating an indicator strategy was to arrive at a target-zone system, which it had long supported. The kind of system envisaged was, briefly, one in which exchange would be managed on the basis of established ranges, within which deviations would be allowed. Intervention to support the ranges would be nearly automatic. Michel Camdessus, Governor of the Bank of France, made this clear when he spoke at the World Bank–IMF annual meeting in September 1986: "France has for several years been making serious proposals to its partners with a view to the adoption of a system of reference zones for exchange rates. It seems to me that the time has come to think seriously about this."[21]

On the other hand, West Germany and Japan maintained that consideration of fiscal deficits and interest rates should be given priority, in line with their argument that huge budget deficits and lofty interest rates in the United States were the main causes of the external imbalance. Baker's original draft had not even included interest rates as an indicator. When Toyoo Gyoten, Director of International Finance of the MOF (promoted to Vice Minister of Finance for International Affairs later in the summer of 1986) questioned Mulford in Tokyo about this apparent bit of political maneuvering, "He just grinned and agreed to putting it in," recalled Gyoten.[22]

In follow-up discussions at the deputy level—coordinated with the IMF, after de Larosière had met informally with the Executive Directors of the G-7 countries—the ten indicators adopted at Tokyo were classified into the following categories: (1) indicators of policy objectives, (2) indicators of performance, and (3) intermediate indicators. The levels of GNP and prices, for example, were designated macroeconomic policy objectives that each

19. Hobart Rowen, *Washington Post,* 4 June 1986.

20. Michel Camdessus, statement to the Joint World Bank–IMF Annual Meeting, 30 September 1986.

21. On the official French use of the term "reference zones" (*zones de référence*), see chap. 8.

22. Personal interview.

government sets for itself. Fiscal policy would be manipulated in support of policy objectives to achieve a desired level of performance.

The interest rate was categorized as an intermediate indicator since it is the product of primary indicators, such as fiscal policy and overall economic objectives. It is not surprising that the most difficult behind-the-scenes negotiations involved exchange rates. With French backing, the United States insisted that the exchange rate be classified as a policy objective. The US administration's original draft for discussing construction of an indicator mechanism after the Tokyo Summit specified precise exchange rate targets as indicators for each member country. Japan, West Germany, and Great Britain countered that because it is a residual of macroeconomic policy, the exchange rate should be treated as an intermediate indicator. Both West Germany and Japan had been prepared to stabilize exchange rates earlier than the United States and should have been willing to adjust monetary and fiscal policies at the margin to keep those rates stable. Their fear that the United States would exploit an indicator system to its own advantage—to slash the surpluses of Japan and West Germany and to manipulate exchange rates—prevented them from pursuing this approach during the spring and summer. Their inflexibility on this issue gave way as domestic political pressures forced US trading partners, Japan in particular, to step up efforts to stabilize bilateral exchange rates. By September, a vague consensus had emerged in favor of using the exchange rate as a policy objective. "It has evolved that way under the 'stop-high-yen-by-all-means political' pressure," explained a Japanese Ministry of Finance official.[23]

G-5 versus G-7

Richard G. Darman's idea to form a Group of Seven finance ministers, provoked suspicion and resistance from the rest of the G-5, who were reluctant to give up the secretive, intimate atmosphere that had formerly characterized G-5 meetings. To a considerable degree, this political debate obstructed the substantive discussion on indicators. To the "old pros" within the G-5—Pöhl, de Larosière, Volcker—and to their own bureaucratic deputies, Baker and Darman were inexperienced newcomers. For their part, Baker and Darman found the arcane format structurally weak because it precluded external scrutiny and was therefore virtually unchecked. One US administration official later described his encounter with the G-5 in the spring of 1985:

---

23. Personal interview.

Our first experience with the Group of Five was via the telephone—Regan's legacy—and it looked like a chaotic mess, with everybody having misunderstandings, no records, no nothing. . . . These guys would sit around and sort of read their public economic forecasts to each other for a good portion of the meeting. . . . [We decided] to either make this mechanism into something that's going to do serious work, or forget it. And we decided that we would use it.[24]

According to a senior State Department official, Shultz, a founding father of the Group of Five, recommended to Baker before the Plaza meeting that he use the G-5 as a vehicle for policy coordination.

The Group of Five was a precursor of the Group of Seven. In April 1973, the finance ministers George P. Shultz, Helmut Schmidt, and Valéry Giscard d'Estaing met in the White House library to discuss issues of international monetary policy. This meeting, which took place at the time of the Committee of 20 negotiations on international monetary reform, laid the foundations for what would be called the Group of Five after the addition of Great Britain, and the central purpose of the meeting was to discuss the international monetary crisis surrounding the breakdown of Bretton Woods. At the outset, finance ministers were present, along with a single official on the basis of the so-called "principal plus one" rule, and sometimes, the central bank governors. This meeting set a precedent for informality on the one hand, and maximum discretion on the other, both as a precaution against the protests of countries excluded and the "technical pettifoggery of bureaucrats" who preferred tightly held, high-level meetings.[25]

Two participants in the White House library meeting, Helmut Schmidt and Valéry Giscard d'Estaing, wished to pursue direct and informal contacts at a higher level when they became German Chancellor and President of France, respectively. The Helsinki Conference of July 1975, in which the leaders of the United States, Great Britain, France, and West Germany participated, provided the occasion for Giscard and Schmidt to press for a summit among those present and Japan as well. Giscard's insistence paid off and on 15–17 November 1975 France played host to the leaders of the four nations plus Italy and Japan at Rambouillet, where these six members of the present G-7 discussed a range of economic and political issues.[26]

In contrast to the G-7, the G-5 discussed an agenda more limited and more secret, a direct legacy of the series of meetings initiated in the White

---

24. Personal interview.

25. Putnam and Bayne, *Hanging Together: The Seven-Power Summits*, 53.

26. Ibid., 18.

House library. As they became more routine, G-5 meetings also became more comfortable and even less publicized. Baker and Darman set out to dismantle this structure and replace it with one more capable of achieving coordination of economic policy. Realizing the limitations of G-5 secretiveness, Baker had publicly supported "increased publicity for abbreviated assessments by the Managing Director [of the IMF] of countries' policies and performance."[27]

Baker and Darman deemed it necessary to tie the new group to a higher political authority to assure that agreements could be ratified at the level of heads of state. Otherwise, they argued, these finance ministers, constrained by the domestic bureaucracy, lacked the credibility necessary to negotiate international agreements. Furthermore, the link would increase the visibility of the group's activities, exerting more pressure on it to produce. "It is that kind of pressure to force the political system in the countries involved on a fairly routine basis to keep on attending to this, because, otherwise, it is very fragile," explained one US official. Actually, they were echoing a slightly earlier sentiment of Henry Kissinger, who had held that the gravity of world economic problems warranted the involvement and leadership of the heads of state.[28]

To achieve involvement, in late 1985 the US team floated the idea of forging a finance ministers' G-7 to parallel the G-7 summit. Promotion of the G-7 idea was fueled by Italian discontent at having been excluded from the Plaza and subsequent meetings of the G-5. Italy had resolved to participate in the Group of Five, and waged a full-scale diplomatic campaign to gain admittance. Prime Minister Bettino Craxi sent personal appeals to the other heads of state, urging their support.

The Italian issue was the first discussed at the London G-5 meeting in January 1986. Chancellor of the Exchequer Nigel Lawson, as host of the meeting, surprised some participants by abruptly stating, "Now we're going to talk about the Italian issue." But in fact, the heads of state, having failed to decide the issue themselves, were responsible for shunting the decision to this forum. "It was forced onto our agenda," said one of the deputies. Five days before the London G-5, Italian officials learned that a meeting would be held. Reagan had already given a favorable answer to Craxi. "Reagan had the Libya problem and he was being friendly with the Italians," was the explanation.[29]

In the US administration, the State Department had made it known to

---

27. James A. Baker III, statement to the IMF Interim Committee, Washington, 9–10 April 1986.

28. See Putnam and Bayne, *Hanging Together: The Seven-Power Summits*, 25–26.

29. Personal interview.

the Treasury that it would support the inclusion of Italy. Baker himself leaned toward it but was unsure of the position the White House would take on this issue at that time. From the Treasury's perspective, Canada and Italy would increase US leverage in getting other countries to go along with the indicator proposal and with the creation of a stronger political mechanism through which to coordinate economic policy.[30] When Baker arrived late in London, he had Darman telephone the White House to find out the most recent development. Baker had just learned that Reagan had given a more or less positive response to Craxi; he wanted to confirm that this was the final reply. The answer from the White House was positive and final. Baker supported Italy's inclusion at the London meeting. Lawson and German Finance Minister Gerhard Stoltenberg, on the other hand, insisted that the G-5 should remain intact. The French position was actually ambiguous. Mitterrand had already replied positively to Craxi's plea, which limited French Finance Minister Pierre Bérégovoy's maneuverability and forced him to state that it was a "problem of Elysée." Some members suspected the French Ministry of playing duplicitously, supporting the Italian position publicly while trying to block it in private.

The Japanese Ministry of Finance bureaucracy strongly opposed Italian inclusion. During the G-5 meeting, however, Takeshita personally expressed favor of the Italian position, to the surprise of Tomomitsu Oba. Takeshita was concerned that this issue, if left unresolved, would darken the Tokyo Summit and he therefore altered his position to bring about a definitive settlement of the matter. Takeshita was so struck by Baker's firm support of Italy, moreover, that he judged it safe to modify the official position.

Although an explicit settlement was not reached at the time, the group did come to a compromise: the issue of whether or not to establish a finance ministers' Group of Seven would be left to the heads of state and the existing G-5 would remain intact.

The original understanding of the difference between the two forums was, first, that the G-5 consisted of finance ministers, deputies, and central bank governors, while the G-7 would include only finance ministers and deputies; and second, that the G-5 would deal with intervention strategy, while the G-7 would conduct multilateral surveillance.

Italy, however, remained unsatisfied with membership only in this peripheral body and demanded that it be made a member of the core group of the world's most powerful industrial countries. Mounting tension erupted during the Tokyo Summit when, after the first day's discussion, the Italian delegation threatened its Japanese hosts that Craxi would not attend the

---

30. According to a Reagan administration official.

session on the following afternoon unless a consensus were reached on the G-7 issue that night.

The issue dominated the finance ministers' meeting that was held simultaneously with that of the heads of state on the morning of May 5. After heated debate, Canada relaxed its insistence on the abolition of the G-5 and, when Italy eventually followed suit, an agreement to form a finance ministers' G-7 was reached.

The respective roles of the G-5 and G-7 were also defined with regard to enhanced surveillance. Specific provisions for the G-7 included:

☐ an agreement to form a new Group of Seven finance ministers, including Italy and Canada, which will work together more closely and more frequently in the periods between the annual summit meetings

☐ a request to the seven finance ministers to review their individual economic objectives and forecasts collectively at least once a year, using the indicators . . . with a particular view to examining their mutual compatibility.[31]

On the existing G-5—though they refrained from using the expression "G-5" and instead referred to "the countries whose currencies constitute the Special Drawing Rights"—they:

[I]nvited the finance ministers and central bankers to conduct multilateral surveillance to make their best efforts to reach an understanding on appropriate remedial measures whenever there are significant deviations from an intended course and recommend that remedial efforts focus first and foremost on underlining policy fundamentals, while reaffirming the 1983 Williamsburg commitment to intervene in exchange markets when to do so would be helpful.[32]

Thus, although the G-7 issue appeared settled, there was still a hitch—the European Community's observer at the summit resisted the solution. From the start, the EC wanted to participate in the fledgling finance ministers' G-7 and made this known to the other countries. France was the only member to support the position of the EC, whose chairman that year happened to be a Frenchman, Jacques Delors. The EC dispatched Dutch Foreign Minister Hans van den Broek and Belgian Finance Minister Willy DeClercq to the meetings. They were adamant that the EC should be included in the new G-7, narrowing their position to admit no creation of a finance ministers' G-7 if the EC were rejected as a member. The United

---

31. Text of "Tokyo Economic Declaration" reprinted in the *New York Times,* 7 May 1986.

32. Ibid.

States and Japan strongly opposed the inclusion of the EC, reasoning that it would transform the G-7 into a G-15 and, furthermore, since the records of EC meetings were automatically transmitted to Portugal and Greece, it would compromise the security of the information considerably, precluding any discussions of highly sensitive currency issues. (The Germans did not come out expressly against the involvement of the EC commission.)[33]

Supported by Mitterrand, Delors again argued for EC admittance as the afternoon session drew to a close. US, German, and Japanese opposition remained firm. Nakasone, who presided over the meeting, closed the curtain by rejecting the EC proposal with a simple, "I *am* sorry."

This strong insistence by the EC stemmed from Belgian and Dutch concerns that their relative positions within the community would erode if Italy became a member of the finance ministers' G-7. Illustrating this concern, the Dutch Ambassador, Richard H. Fein, approached Japanese Ambassador to the United States, Nobuo Matsunaga, just before the Tokyo Summit, informing him that the Dutch did not object to the continuation of the G-5 but did oppose the creation of a G-7. It appeared to be a repetition of Dutch opposition to Italy's admittance to the G-7 Economic Summit in 1975 when France had proposed it to the other five heads of states.[34]

The new US approach surprised all of the capitals of the G-5 countries to some degree, upsetting the tightly knit financial elite—better known as the "currency mafia."[35] Finance ministry officials as well as central bank governors sensed an attempt to undermine their jurisdiction and independence. Many believed that it was part of a political publicity show. Thus, although Baker's proposal elicited an anxious response from most of the participants, nowhere was this more pronounced than in Japan, where *Baker shokku* [Baker's shock] became a uniquely Japanese phenomenon.

Shokku

As was noted in chapter 3, in Japan any new proposal by foreign governments, especially the United States, that aimed to influence Japanese economic policy in a significant way was perceived as *gaiatsu* (foreign

33. Oba, "Two focuses and accomplishments at the Tokyo Summit," 22.

34. Yoichi Funabashi, "Samitto No Shiso" (The politics of the G-7 Summit), *Asahi Shimbun*, 20 June 1980.

35. According to Oba's definition, the "currency mafia" consists of smaller and larger groups: the smaller "mafia" has only five members—all deputies of the finance ministers; the larger one includes the ministers and the central bank governors and deputies, for a total of 50–60. Interview with Tomomitsu Oba, *Ekonomisuto* (Economist), 22 July 1986.

pressure) and provoked an immediate assumption that Japan was being bashed or victimized.

The Japanese response surprised the US administration, since Baker's proposal was not particularly revolutionary—it had its roots in the work of the Committee of 20, of which Japan had been a member during the early 1970s. Furthermore, Baker and Darman had carefully presented their version to the other G-5 ministers and deputies during the preparatory stage in April. A senior US administration official later expressed dismay at the *shokku* experienced in Japan, "There was consultation here before the summit . . . [during the meeting of the Interim Committee] and the OECD meeting etc. . . . I don't think there was any feeling here of lack of consultation."[36]

The specifics of the US plan, especially the original draft that placed more emphasis on automaticity in policy coordination, made the others apprehensive, particularly the Japanese. Baker handed Takeshita his draft proposal when they met in Tokyo on May 3, just before the summit. Although Oba had informed Takeshita of its contents in late April, Mulford stressed to Oba that "besides the President and Baker, only Regan, Shultz, Darman, and myself know this," thereby suggesting that the Japanese were to consider the proposal carefully and at the highest level. Takeshita reported the proposal only to Nakasone, who was to have a meeting with Reagan a few hours later.

During that meeting, Reagan removed a paper from his pocket and began to read the outline of the plan, asking for Nakasone's endorsement. Nakasone responded that the "general direction" was good but that some aspects, the language in particular, were a problem and would need to be modified. Finally he summed up his reservations, saying, "We are all sovereign nations. Therefore, we should keep in mind that we should not interfere in the domestic affairs of the other countries."

The entire discussion shocked Foreign Minister Shintaro Abe, who had not been briefed on the proposal. The Foreign Ministry had been kept completely in the dark because the summit sherpa, Deputy Minister of Foreign Affairs Reishi Teshima, had not been informed. As the sherpa for the host country, he should have received the information on the proposal from the US sherpa, Allen Wallis, Under Secretary of State; Wallis, however, had been informed neither by Baker nor by Shultz.

On the following morning, in a cabinet-level meeting on economic measures, when Oba explained the plan to the ministers, Abe exploded, feeling that he had lost face. Worried over the disharmony caused by the

---

36. Personal interview.

incident, Nakasone phoned Takeshita after the meeting, "Abe is really mad. Will you do something about it?"

Takeshita conveyed his apology to Abe, explaining that "his mouth had been gagged by Baker-san," while Oba telephoned Masaharu Gotoda, Cabinet Secretary, and conveyed his apology. Deputy Minister for Foreign Affairs Shinichi Yanai and his sherpa, Teshima, placed protest calls to Vice Finance Minister Yamaguchi and to Oba, respectively. The Economic Planning Agency (EPA) also protested to the Ministry of Finance.

Other agencies, the Ministry of International Trade and Industry (MITI) in particular, and the Bank of Japan (BOJ), speculated that the new mechanism might interfere with their own jurisdiction. Throughout the day MITI desperately tried to obtain the proposal paper—they finally got an Italian version that night but found no one in the agency able to translate it—and the BOJ did not hesitate to communicate concern over the possible erosion of its independence over monetary policy to the Ministry of Finance.

Basically, the *shokku* had four causes. First was the deep fear among monetary authorities that an indicator system with a high degree of automaticity would force Japan to reduce its sizable trade surplus, and/or to revalue the yen further. They suspected, for good reason, that the system might evolve into a target-zone system that set the yen's value at a very high rate. Some even sensed that the indicator system itself was a target zone in disguise. Their apprehension caused them to resist by all means the more disciplined indicator system. "When you are in huge surplus like now, you would be in serious danger to value the yen at an unreasonably high rate in a target-zone system. And it would be political suicide to Nakasone and Takeshita," commented a well-placed Finance Ministry official at the time.

The second stemmed from the determination of the Ministry of Finance to monopolize currency management. MOF officials feared that the adoption of "enhanced surveillance" would lead to an increase in the number of determinants of currency values and dissemination of the relevant information—at the expense of their own monopoly on currency management. This fear was particularly strong within the Budget and Tax Bureaus. The Cabinet Bureau of the Ministry of Finance anxiously expressed its fears to Oba that, first, it would easily invite interference from other agencies, and second, that the Ministry's hands would eventually become tied by commitments to foreign countries. Oba had to placate the Bureau by replying, "It's not so different from the surveillance discussions in the past G-5. Not to worry." This fear was heightened when the Foreign Ministry tried to involve itself in currency management and diplomacy during the summit. The Ministry of Finance therefore kept a tight lid on its maneuvers to prevent further interference. The turf battle over control of currency waged between the Ministry of Finance and the Foreign Ministry intensified in the spring. One round of the fight was glimpsed when the Ministry of Finance barred the participation of Ambassador Matsunaga in the Baker-Takeshita meeting in Washington on 8 April 1986. Another took place shortly before this meeting, when the Foreign Ministry arranged with the US State Department for a Prime Minister's envoy to meet secretly with a White House official in San Francisco to discuss certain issues including exchange rate policy.

The suspicion of the other economic agencies, MITI especially, constituted the third cause of *shokku*. MITI officials feared the undermining of their power and influence if the Ministry of Finance were allowed to monopolize the management of a broad range of indicators. MITI unleashed a counter-offensive by successfully arranging a meeting of Michio Watanabe, MITI Minister, and another LDP "new leader" with Regan in Tokyo on May 7. During the meeting, Watanabe stressed that it would be desirable for the US administration to increase consultations with MITI to promote economic policy coordination. According to interpretations offered at the time, MITI's move was aimed more at the MOF than at the US administration.[37]

Finally, *shokku* was caused by straining the traditional, decision-making process of consensus building. The top-to-bottom style of decision making, exemplified in the Baker proposal, was very much alien, even upsetting, to the bottom-to-top Japanese ways. Yet G-5 politics, and especially Baker diplomacy, forced Japan to behave differently. Oba once remarked that only a *gaiatsu* shock could change the consensus-based Japanese style of decision making into one of majority rule.

The Politics of the G-7 Indicator System

The introduction of an indicator system by Baker and Darman was a political endeavor, motivated by political considerations and subject to political conflicts. In broad terms the conflict was between greater economic policy coordination and increasingly nominal national sovereignty in an age of economic interdependence. Policy coordination, to be effective, requires discipline and some degree of automaticity, so it challenges the state's traditional ordering of priorities and puts pressure on the decision-making processes that reflect them.

During this period of more vigorous attempts to coordinate economic policy, bureaucratic interests conflicted on three levels: the conflict between finance ministers (politicians) and their deputies (bureaucrats), the conflict

---

37. "Other agencies upset with MOF's one-man show," *Nihon Keizai Shimbun,* 8 May 1986.

between the finance ministry and foreign ministry, and the conflict between finance ministries and central banks. The conflict between finance ministers and their deputies became most visible in the United States, where the higher-ranking political appointee tried to introduce a brand new political position to the bureaucracy. Baker and Darman, especially, perceived the bureaucracy's resistance to the new mechanism and felt that their deputies were undercutting the new strategy to protect their own interests. As a result of the suspicions, Mulford suffered some undermining of his bargaining power and credibility with his counterparts in other countries. Oba later complained about US representation in the G-5 and G-5D meetings:

The G-5 had a long-standing rule that only three people were allowed to participate in the meetings: finance minister, his deputy, and central bank governor. So when Darman sat in the chair, there was no room for Mulford. He had to go to the adjacent room. It caused some problems for the deputies of the other countries. It was Mulford with whom we discussed in the G-5D meetings but he was not at the G-5. It was a matter of power balance in the Treasury, so it can't be helped. But it was a bit difficult for us.[38]

Oba's complaints were echoed by the other deputies who felt that Baker confided exclusively in Darman and that Mulford was not well informed. "When asked about Baker's intention, [Mulford] said, 'Well, I'm not sure' and that's the trouble to us . . . David was extremely good and he really felt that on the debt side he was a leading man but on this network of politics of exchange rates, relationships with Fed and the White House, Darman was the key and Mulford was on the outside. So Mulford was of no use among the deputies," a European deputy said.[39] Tietmeyer was so annoyed that he told his colleagues he would have Stoltenberg raise the problem directly with Baker.

The way that Baker and Darman treated Mulford was considered by the other deputies "a little uncivil."[40] At one point during the Plaza meeting, Darman, returning to the meeting room to find Mulford seated next to Baker, patted him on the shoulder as a motion to leave the room. At the London G-5, Mulford was not allowed into the meeting room. At this time, Baker requested of Lawson that Mulford be allowed to attend the meeting, but Lawson declined on the advice of his deputy, Geoffrey Littler. Again, at the Louvre, Mulford was made to wait by himself in an adjacent room,

38. Tomomitsu Oba, "The political economy of currency diplomacy," *Toyo Keizai* (Oriental Economist), 22 May 1987.

39. Personal interview.

40. Comment made by one deputy to the author.

although the French allowed him to attend the informal evening dinner session. Thus, Baker and Darman exploited every opportunity to present their political agenda directly to the other ministers. The fact that Baker sent "second class to us" not only damaged the egos of the other deputies, but also created a practical difficulty at the negotiating table. Also, underneath the rejection of Mulford as an equal by other deputies lay their fear of the possibility that their turf would be violated by outsiders. Both Tietmeyer and Oba expressed the concern that if the United States were allowed to send another official, their own governments would demand the right to send other representatives.[41]

Later, a senior US administration official said of the uneasiness of Baker and Darman about the G-5 deputies, "They think that the deputies felt that it [the negotiating process] should operate with the deputies and with the minimum necessary involvement of the finance ministers. The deputies' view was that finance ministers would only cause problems and that they could successfully handle the governments of the world on their own." It was known in the Treasury that Darman criticized the way Mulford "handled" the issues with his foreign counterparts. He felt that it was Mulford who succumbed to the pressures from other deputies to weaken the agreed-on indicator system. Darman was also frustrated by Mulford's inability during the preparatory stage to persuade the Germans to agree to the reference-range idea—the essence of the Louvre Accord. It was Darman's own breakthrough—accomplished in a secret meeting with Tietmeyer in Washington in January 1987—that reinforced his convictions.

In the same vein, Minister of Finance Kiichi Miyazawa also faced resistance from the MOF bureaucracy, especially with regard to his fiscal expansion strategy. To the dismay of Miyazawa during his very first briefing at the Finance Ministry, officials dismissed any need for a supplementary budget, citing the positive projections of Japanese economic performance. Unlike his predecessor, Takeshita, Miyazawa failed to show respect for the bureaucracy or willingness to depend on their recommendations. He had already established a set of policy initiatives based on his fiscal expansion strategy.

Takeshita could have exploited the Baker proposal to pressure the MOF bureaucracy during the Tokyo Summit as Miyazawa later tried to do, but Takeshita, the quintessential consensus builder, was mindful of possible repercussions on his relationship with Nakasone and the MOF. Any attempt to outmaneuver the bureaucracy would surely have alienated him from the MOF, which maintained its undeviating adherence to tight fiscal policy.

The second conflict, between finance ministry and foreign ministry,

---

41. Comment made by a deputy to the author.

manifested itself most clearly in Japan. The Foreign Ministry strengthened its hand when the issues were linked with the G-7 summit agendas, especially since Nakasone, who was keenly interested in summit diplomacy, committed himself fully to the agendas. This was clearly illustrated in the spring of 1987 when the Foreign Ministry became untraditionally involved in shaping a new fiscal stimulus package through skillful exploitation of *gaiatsu*. A linkage of the G-5 with the G-7 summit, however, might, in Oba's words, drive the Finance Ministry "underground again."[42]

Finally, the conflict between finance ministers and central banks continued to be pronounced throughout the Plaza process, as observed with regard to monetary policy coordination in chapter 2. Central bank opposition toward the indicator proposal was not an exception. Even within the United States, the initiator of the indicator proposal, there was some hesitancy in adopting an indicator "system." The Fed considered the more ambitious original version "too complicated and too mechanistic." "My view was that it . . . was going to fall . . . of its own weight," said a top official.[43] But even after significant modifications of the proposal, similar caution was expressed, "They didn't adopt a mechanism, they adopted an idea." In the case of the Bundesbank, the officials believed that they, too, should have room for maneuverability with regard to their monetary policy. Pöhl lambasted the indicator system publicly, complaining that it "robotized" the adjustment process.[44]

The creation of a finance ministers' G-7 will continue to affect power politics between and within the G-5 countries. This was already demonstrated visibly at the Louvre meeting when Italy walked out in protest. The prospect of Italy's surpassing France in terms of GNP after overtaking Great Britain will heighten the tension further. Britain's likely entry into the EMS in the future will affect G-7 politics by complicating bilateral relations between Great Britain and the United States at the very least. The insistence of countries like the Netherlands and Belgium on including the European Community in the finance ministers' G-7 will also continue to be a problem. It will be the responsibility of West Germany, as the predominant European power, to shape European strategy into some cohesive form. The likely result of an intensification of squabbles on the European continent would be a push toward the consolidation of a G-2 between the United States and Japan.

As the global economy becomes more profoundly interdependent, the

---

42. Interview with Tomomitsu Oba, *Ekonomisuto* (Economist) 22 July 1986.

43. Personal interview.

44. Karl Otto Pöhl, "You Can't Robotize Policymaking," *The International Economy* (Washington), October/November 1987: 20–26.

task will be to address the issue of national sovereignty and the conduct of national economic policy. One month after the Tokyo Summit, Baker said in a speech, "The Tokyo arrangements do not involve any ceding of sovereignty, nor should they." At the same time, he stressed, "but if the system is to work, the participants will of their own volition—to be sure—under the watchful eye of their peers—have to take external considerations into account in formulating their domestic economic policies. For the United States this only reflects the reality that the time is long past when the United States could, in setting domestic policies, relegate external considerations to an insignificant order of importance."[45]

The redirection of US economic policy reflected in this statement was welcomed by representatives of the other G-5 nations, who could recall their irritation at Regan's announcement in 1981 that the United States would refrain from intervening in foreign exchange markets. One high-ranking official of West Germany's Ministry of Finance remembered later that Bonn was forced to go along with the indicator mechanism because it was seen as a departure from previous policy and an opportunity not to be missed. "At least it would give us some discretionary edge [with which] to change US policy."[46]

On the down side, it could well be argued that the indicator mechanism was "a kind of international Gramm-Rudman-Hollings," in which the process overwhelmed policy and gave a shield with which politicians could deflect pressures to make the needed adjustments.[47] In this light it could be remembered that the United States eschewed those recommendations of the Versailles intervention study that had focused on the American fiscal deficits. It is unclear to what extent Baker's indicator plan was an attempt to impose on the White House and Congress the discipline to produce significant reductions in the budget deficit. In any case, the effort has been lost on both the administration and the Congress to the extent that the United States has not shown a willingness to accept the disciplinary effects. The other countries have continued to suspect that the United States would be able to push a disproportionate share of adjustment onto them.

---

45. James A. Baker III, remarks at the National Foreign Trade Council, 11 June 1986; processed.

46. Personal interview.

47. C. Fred Bergsten, "Crisis and Reform of the International Monetary System," Ernest Strurc Memorial Lecture, Johns Hopkins University (Washington), 13 November 1986.

◼ G-2–G-3

The Tokyo Summit failed to satisfy the expectations of Japanese export industries and politicians and posed a threat to the political stability of Nakasone. Just before the closing of the Tokyo meeting, the yen–dollar rate was registered above 165 in the Tokyo market—advancement of another postwar record of the high yen. The Japanese press condemned Nakasone's "failure to stop yen appreciation." Opposition parties and politicians representing factions against Nakasone, including Miyazawa, tried to exploit this unfavorable appraisal to oust Nakasone. Washington looked on, stunned by the sudden deterioration of Nakasone's support base, and wondered whether Baker had pushed currency realignment too far, too fast.

Aggressive Bilateralism

On 9 May 1986, appearing on a television interview program, Richard G. Darman was pressed to defend his and Baker's strategy:

Interviewer: Don't you feel any dismay at having killed the political future of Yasuhiro Nakasone?

Darman: I think he is an extraordinarily effective and courageous politician, and I certainly don't think that we have—

Interviewer: Well, you know the story in Japan is that he's through, because that summit did nothing to bring down the yen, and—

Darman: As I said, he has been a courageous leader in Japan, trying to point the way toward the Japanese economy of the future, which could be somewhat different from the one of the present. And any time one moves against the status quo, one has to encounter a degree of political resistance.[1]

---

1. "One on One," with John McLaughlin, 9 May 1986. Transcript available from Federal Information Systems, 620 National Press Building, Washington, DC 20045.

As the yen continued to climb in 1986, political pressure had been mounting visibly on the Nakasone cabinet by Japanese exporters, especially small- and medium-sized firms, who faced a substantial drop in the demand for their products. During February and early March 1986, the dollar had declined across the board. Initially, the market focused on the yen, which was buoyed by mounting monthly trade surpluses and the view that declining oil prices would benefit the Japanese economy particularly. The dollar, which had closed at 191.40 yen to the dollar at the end of January, declined steadily throughout early February falling under the psychologically important level of 180 yen to the dollar to reach 177.40 yen to the dollar— a seven-and-a-half-year low—by February 19. It then stalled after the Japanese Finance Ministry confirmed that it was developing plans to ease regulations on capital outflows, hoping thereby to increase the demand for dollars by Japanese institutional investors.[2]

On March 19, the yen reached 174.30 to the dollar—a postwar high, the previous having been 175.50 yen to the dollar in 1978. The Bank of Japan reacted by intervening in the New York market in the first attempt since the Plaza to brake the appreciation of the yen. Japanese monetary authorities had tried to persuade the Treasury beforehand to intervene with them in the market. The Japanese expected that Volcker's repeated cautions against a rapid decline of the dollar would have helped their argument, but the Treasury refused to act.

The yen's further advance in late March impelled Finance Minister Noboru Takeshita to telephone Baker and request a joint intervention to stabilize the currencies. Baker declined, explaining that opposition to such "reverse" intervention remained strong in the administration. Instead, the Treasury allowed the Bank of Japan (BOJ) to intervene in the New York market through its account at the New York Federal Reserve Bank and promised not to oppose this unilateral intervention publicly.

In fact, Japan's intervention received very little sympathy in Washington, where the Treasury's main concern was that protectionist forces in Congress would gain momentum as currency realignment stalled. "Japan's move would be politically counterproductive. It would be impossible for the US to begin to intervene at a given level, considering the kind of protectionist problems we have here," observed a Treasury Department official.[3]

The Treasury Department was also worried lest broader initiatives be jeopardized. Joint intervention with the Japanese might impede efforts at improving systemic coordination of economic policies through use of the economic indicator system around which Baker and Darman hoped to build

---

2. *Federal Reserve Bank of New York Quarterly Review* 11 (Summer 1986): 48.

3. Personal interview.

a consensus. One senior administration official later commented on the US approach, "We really said to the Japanese, 'Look, don't ask us to intervene today or tomorrow, at this rate or that rate. Let's improve the system. Let's improve economic policy coordination and then we will be able to get to the bottom of these issues.' "[4]

Meanwhile, there existed ideological resistance to "fixing" the exchange rate on the part of those who favored the floating exchange rate system. Within the administration, Under Secretary of State for Economic and Agriculture Affairs Allen W. Wallis was one of them. An economist from the University of Chicago flatly stated, on the day following BOJ intervention, "I doubt that Japan's intervention had much effect on the market. The market for foreign exchange is huge. Analysis and experience show that [by intervening in the market] governments really just throw their money away."[5] Some business interests continued to advocate a decline of the dollar. In a letter to the White House at this time, the Business Roundtable, a lobby representing blue-chip corporate America, urged further dollar decline.

The Japanese did not lessen the pressure on the Reagan administration. On April 8 Baker met with Takeshita in Washington. Evidently holding a rate of 180 yen to the dollar in his mind as a bottom line, Takeshita pushed Baker to "agree to currency stability." He then explained the irony that his first name, Noboru, means to appreciate, and that "As the yen has appreciated, so has my popularity sunk." His plea was a classic expression of *amae*—a Japanese cultural and psychological trait that means to whine for sympathy as a little brother would to a big brother. Baker replied, "I'm sure your popularity will rise again if you boost Japan's domestic consumption." This answer was much the same as it had been in March, when he had agreed to stability, but he refrained from making any commitment on yen–dollar exchange rates.

Takeshita, like Baker, had received acclaim for his role in the Plaza Agreement. But the ensuing appreciation of the yen had since forced the Finance Minister into a corner politically. Japan's small- and medium-sized industries, which depend upon exports and which also wield disproportionate political clout, started to point accusing fingers at Takeshita. For the first time in his long political career, he was not invited to a political campaign speech of one of his faction members whose constituency happened to be the Tajimi area of central Japan, known for its exports of porcelain.[6]

---

4. Personal interview.

5. *Asahi Shimbun,* 21 March 1986.

6. Yoichi Funabashi, "Tokyo Economic Summit Looms as Key Test for Japanese Politicians," *Washington Post,* 20 April 1986.

After Takeshita had failed to influence Baker, Nakasone launched a campaign to convince Reagan of the need to stabilize the yen–dollar rate at around 180, targeted at the upcoming Camp David meeting.

In late March, Nakasone secretly dispatched his personal envoy to San Francisco to explore the possibility of stabilizing currencies and meeting with Gaston Sigur, Assistant Secretary of State for East Asian Affairs, and Steve Danzansky, Director of the International Economy for the National Security Council. Danzansky was opposed, mentioning the political embarrassment Vice President George Bush had suffered as a result of his remarks on the imposition of an oil import fee to stabilize collapsing domestic oil prices and adding that an effort to stabilize currencies at the present level by joint intervention would invite similar criticism, this time from US export industries.

The aim of Nakasone's strategy was, in large measure, to circumvent the Treasury and appeal directly to the national security and foreign policy-making establishment, anticipating a more favorable response from the latter. On this matter, however, all branches of the administration stood firm.

Nevertheless, Nakasone was not dissuaded from reiterating the importance of stabilizing the yen–dollar rate at its current level during his meeting with Reagan on April 13. Predictably, Reagan answered that the exchange rate should be left to the natural forces of the market. The Japanese Prime Minister issued another plea after his return to Japan, where further appreciation of the yen caused pre-summit tremors. He sent his personal message to the US President, explaining that his mounting "political difficulties" were caused by the high yen.

It is inaccurate to say that the White House showed no concern for Nakasone's political situation, for during the summit meeting the President seemed sympathetic. The US administration came to Nakasone's rescue after the Japanese press reported on May 4 that President Reagan had repeatedly rejected Nakasone's requests for joint intervention. On May 5 the White House arranged a briefing by a senior State Department official, who denied the account, stating that Nakasone had never made such a request and that there was no confrontational atmosphere on the currency issue.[7]

In May, the yen continued its relentless drive upward in the foreign exchange markets in the absence of any announcement of specific measures being undertaken by monetary authorities. Statements by US officials that there was "no change in intervention policy" fueled the yen's climb to 161.25 on May 9 and 159.99 on May 12, some 38.5 percent above its low a year earlier. In his testimony to the Senate Finance Committee on May 13,

---

7. *Asahi Shimbun,* 5 May 1986.

Baker made a personal attempt to rescue Nakasone by assuring the market that the dollar had more than fully offset its earlier appreciation against the yen.

The market instantaneously responded to what it interpreted as a gesture to help Nakasone, and pressure on the yen abated temporarily. At that time, the Treasury left open to speculation whether or not the move was politically motivated. Although it was suspected in some quarters that Baker's testimony had nothing to do with Japanese politics, it was, in fact, intended to help Nakasone, even though it was short of the joint intervention desired by the Japanese. Even Beryl Sprinkel, a staunch laissez-faire monetarist, began arguing for some scheme to prop up Nakasone politically. Later a senior US administration official admitted that it was a rescue attempt:

It was right after the Tokyo summit that Nakasone had his problems. He was politically dead . . . about ten days after the summit. That was when we really gave the help that counted. We have that well documented.[8]

By "documentation" the official was perhaps referring to the personal thank-you letter that Nakasone sent to the President and to Ambassador Matsunaga's special telephone call to Baker in appreciation of his testimony. In September, further evidence was given in the secret meeting between Baker and Miyazawa in San Francisco, where Baker reminded Miyazawa of the help Nakasone had received from the US administration before his election, adding that he hoped to find the same kind of support reciprocated by the Japanese before the American midterm elections.

In the meantime, Baker's much trumpeted economic indicator strategy was being sabotaged by other countries. Baker's repeated clarion calls to Tokyo and Bonn to stimulate their domestic economies went unanswered. Clearly, coordination of monetary policies had not progressed since March. Even normally discreet officials of the Federal Reserve Board openly expressed frustration with their counterparts in Japan and West Germany, urging them to cut their discount rates. No positive reply was heard throughout the summer.

Sometime in August, Baker adopted a more aggressive posture toward Japan and West Germany to prompt the policy coordination that would keep his indicator plan from crumbling. Baker circumvented the more pluralistic G-5 and G-7 approaches in favor of "aggressive bilateralism," through which he hoped to shore up the process of policy coordination by making bilateral deals first with Japan and then West Germany.[9]

---

8. Personal interview.

9. The expression "aggressive bilateralism" was coined by *New York Times* columnist Leonard Silk. See Leonard Silk, "The U.S. and the World Economy," *Foreign Affairs* 65 (Spring 1986): 458–476.

The Japan Card

On September 6, Baker held a meeting with Miyazawa in San Francisco. Mulford and Gyoten, who had attended a Working Party 3 (WP-3) meeting of the Organization for Economic Cooperation and Development (OECD) in Paris, flew in together. Baker had initiated the contact that finally resulted in this meeting on the advice of Secretary of State George P. Shultz.

Baker had called on US Ambassador to Japan Mike Mansfield to arrange private meetings, first with Miyazawa, then with Nakasone for September 1. In the course of planning, however, the arrangements were somehow leaked to the Ministry of Finance and the Foreign Ministry. Finance Ministry officialdom was stunned to learn that Miyazawa had kept plans for the meeting secret. The Foreign Ministry requested that a meeting between Baker and Foreign Minister Tadashi Kuranari be arranged, claiming that, according to their US sources, Baker wanted to see Kuranari as well. The Ministry of Finance remained unimpressed. In the end, the leak caused Baker and Mansfield to cancel the meeting proposed for September 1.

In a second attempt, Baker asked Mansfield to reschedule the meeting, this time in the United States. According to a Japanese source, he even offered to fly to Hawaii if that would facilitate the arrangements, but all agreed on San Francisco. In a message to Miyazawa, the US administration stressed confidentiality, implying that besides Baker and Mansfield, only Reagan, Regan, and Shultz had been informed of the meeting. Under extreme pressure to preserve secrecy, Miyazawa at first planned to go alone, but eventually allowed Gyoten to accompany him. Throughout the meeting, Baker and Miyazawa did not use interpreters or take notes, nor did they hold a mutual press conference afterward.

During the two-and-a-half-hour meeting, Baker expressed concern over the prospects for both the Japanese and American economies. He argued that Japan should demonstrate its determination to stimulate domestic demand. In addition, he stressed the importance of tax reform, explaining the historic tax reform legislation that the US Congress had just drafted. With regard to Japan's tax reform efforts, Baker expressed concern over the planned introduction of a new sales tax and questioned whether it was meant to provide an incentive to Japan's export sector. While acknowledging that the new Japanese tax system was meant to be revenue neutral, he hoped that the Japanese government would institute tax reductions to stimulate its economy more vigorously.

Although Baker stopped short of advocating specific fiscal policies, he did make it clear that he expected Japan to lower the discount rate, citing as an example the two occasions since July when the Federal Reserve had lowered its rate. In response, Miyazawa projected GNP growth of a little more than 3 percent in the Japanese economy for fiscal 1986, stimulated by the supplementary budget that he planned to introduce and to which he had strong personal commitment. Furthermore, he asserted that the new sales tax was not aimed at export promotion, nor would the tax rate be too high, pointing out that most commodities and products in Japan were already subject to a sales tax. Miyazawa did not need to be convinced of the need for fiscal stimulus measures, for he had already advocated them. As Finance Minister, he would push even harder, as he told Baker without hesitation.

Baker persisted in trying to extract a belated quid pro quo for the "help" that the US administration had extended to Nakasone before the Japanese general election in July. "Since we helped you the last time, it's your turn to help our election. We are going to have a midterm election. I want you to help us now," Baker is said to have commented.[10] The "help" to which Baker referred was his own testimony to the Senate Finance Committee on May 13.

Miyazawa was equally insistent upon the need for stabilization of the yen–dollar rate. Before he left for San Francisco, he met Nakasone for a discussion of the issue. Besides urging Miyazawa to tell Baker to make serious cuts in the US budget deficit, Nakasone directed Miyazawa to stabilize the yen–dollar rate at around 170—a mission Nakasone himself had not been able to accomplish.[11] Miyazawa was under pressure. He argued that further yen appreciation would dampen domestic demand in Japan, while dollar depreciation would work to restrict capital flows from Japan to the United States.

At the end of the discussion, Miyazawa proposed that they should work out the next steps toward enhanced policy coordination on the basis of the fiscal, monetary, and currency fronts. Miyazawa and Baker then directed Gyoten and Mulford to draft a paper with that objective.

During the meetings of the G-5 and G-7 held on the fringes of the September meeting of the International Monetary Fund (IMF), Baker's frustration came to the surface when his policies—fiscal policy and "talk down"—came under attack. Another finance minister observed of an emotional Baker, "I am not sure why Baker became so irritated, arguing the same things again and again. We're all politicians. And politicians are accustomed to being criticized. But he's a lawyer and tends to be adversarial. That's perhaps why he doesn't seem to put up with it." Another bemused participant expressed, "It is not the currency market which is volatile. My goodness, it is Baker who is!"[12]

---

10. Interview of Japanese officials with the author.

11. Interview of Yasuhiro Nakasone with the author.

12. Interviews of participants with the author.

Clearly the euphoric atmosphere in Washington, created by the 1985 Plaza Agreement and heightened after the May Tokyo Summit, was dissipating. After one year, the US trade deficit had not narrowed in response to depreciation of the dollar; and policy coordination, pledged by the G-5 at the Tokyo Summit in May, existed on paper only. During the Summit, Clayton Yeutter, US Trade Representative (USTR), sent a memo to Baker prepared by a USTR economist that cautioned the administration not to expect a "quick change of the trade deficit figure too soon because most of the other indices have not reflected the appropriate trade weighting and have left out some countries that really matter in trade."[13] Baker, appearing on "This Week with David Brinkley" on September 28, was asked by Sam Donaldson why he had failed to persuade Japan and West Germany to lower their discount rates. He replied, "Well, you can say [that] you failed, and so forth. . . . The fact of the matter is, they have not reduced their interest rates here over the near term. But that doesn't mean that we're not going to continue to talk and discuss and meet on these issues."[14]

In a statement before the Interim Committee of the IMF on September 28, Baker cautioned that policy coordination required more vigorous responses from the others:

The success of [indicator] arrangements will depend on the willingness of each country to take external considerations more heavily into account in formulating domestic economic policies. . . . If together we cannot, or will not, use these arrangements effectively to support and guide our efforts to promote higher growth, smaller imbalances, and greater exchange rate stability, then we will have to consider—and pressures will grow for— other, less flexible arrangements.[15]

This was an unambiguous warning to US trading partners who were avoiding more stimulative economic policies. "Other, less flexible arrangements," was interpreted, correctly, as a euphemism for more rigid target zones and an assertion of US resolve to push the dollar down if necessary.

It was against this climate of heightened tensions and growing public criticism that Baker and Miyazawa met in the Secretary's office at the US Treasury on September 26, just a few hours before the G-5 would convene in the third floor conference room. This time Miyazawa arrived in Washington

---

13. Interview of a US administration official with the author.

14. ABC News, "This Week with David Brinkley," 28 September 1987. Transcript available from RLS Reporting Associates, 733 15th Street, NW, Suite 440, Washington, DC 20005.

15. James A. Baker III, statement to the IMF Interim Committee, Washington, 28 September 1987.

with a stronger hand. The government of Japan had announced a supplementary budget of 3.6 trillion yen ($23.2 billion) one week earlier. The purpose of the stimulus package was twofold: first, to offset the deflationary impact of the yen's appreciation against the dollar during the past year; and second, to meet foreign demands for more expansionary policies that would boost imports and reduce Japan's trade surplus.

This new stimulus package exceeded that of October 1985 by more than $3 billion, making it the largest that Tokyo had adopted so far. A substantial portion of it—as much as $6.5 billion—was expected to be financed through a new issue of construction bonds, which was seen as a retreat of some sort from Nakasone's commitment to reduce government borrowing. The Japanese government optimistically forecast 4 percent real growth in fiscal 1986—the target that Nakasone and Takeshita had promised repeatedly in support of the new package—while the Nomura Research Institute was predicting that the package would add a mere 0.6 percent to real growth, raising the total to only about 2.5 percent for 1986.[16]

Although Baker praised the Japanese initiative as "a step in the right direction," some members of the Treasury Department voiced skepticism about the real impact of the package, given the failure to reduce the interest rate in Japan.

The other major subject discussed by Miyazawa and Baker was the exchange rate. When Miyazawa was ushered into the Secretary's office on September 26, Baker said, "Let's remember the exchange rate now," and proceeded to lead Miyazawa over to the data machine. The screen read 154.20, meaning that the yen–dollar rate had stabilized roughly between 152 and 154 since their last meeting in San Francisco. This development encouraged both sides toward tacit agreement to stabilize the currencies and to move forward on the policy coordination efforts initiated in San Francisco, which included currency stabilization measures, although Miyazawa felt that the yen was still a little too high.

The Baker-Miyazawa Deal

The joint communiqué negotiated after the September 26 meeting and announced by Baker and Miyazawa on October 31 listed a number of economic measures that both governments were taking and planned to take in the future. Its real importance, however, lay in the US administration's public commitment to currency stability. Miyazawa had argued during the meeting that exchange rate instability could jeopardize stable economic

---

16. *Japan Economic Institute Report*, no. 35B (Washington), 26 September 1986, 2.

growth, and Gyoten had pushed to incorporate a statement of this kind in the communiqué. In addition, both finance ministers agreed that "action by the key industrial countries was critical at this time to promoting world economic growth, reducing imbalances, and resolving international debt problems." In this connection, each outlined actions for strengthening coordination policy.

For Japan, this included: first, the government's decision to submit a supplementary budget to the Diet to "provide a substantial stimulus" to the Japanese economy; second, the government's intention to implement as soon as possible a tax reform plan including reductions in the marginal tax rates for both personal and corporate income to stimulate investment and business activity; and third, the Bank of Japan's decision— effective October 31—to reduce its discount rate from 3.5 percent to 3 percent.

The measures agreed to by the United States were: a full commitment to significant and steady reductions in the US budget deficit, consistent with the Gramm-Rudman-Hollings amendment; enactment of a tax reform plan; and resistance to protectionist pressures.

Up to this point, it would seem that Baker had won the round, since he promised nothing new; he conceded, however, on the exchange rate issue. The communiqué stated that they "shared the view that exchange rate instability can jeopardize stable economic growth" and that they "expressed their mutual understanding that with the actions and commitments mentioned above, the exchange rate realignment achieved between the yen and the dollar since the Plaza Agreement is now broadly consistent with the present underlying fundamentals." No specific measures were cited as a way of maintaining exchange rate stability, although they "reaffirmed their willingness to cooperate on exchange market issues," a signal of willingness to intervene in the event that the market took a malevolent direction.[17] It was at the request of Gyoten that this veiled warning was included in the communiqué.

Finally, they "called on other major industrial countries to join in these efforts to promote global growth, reduce imbalances and promote open markets." This part was inserted on the insistence of Mulford and was obviously directed at West Germany, in particular. "Read the last sentence. That means the US and Japan lead first and call the others to follow us. It's the beginning of a G-2 (Group of Two)," said a well-placed Treasury official shortly after the announcement was made. The United States had informed the other major industrial countries of this addition only a few hours

---

17. For the text of the Baker-Miyazawa communiqué, see *Treasury News* (Washington: US Department of the Treasury), 31 October 1986, 1–2.

previously. The same official confided, "Are you asking if they were frustrated? Sure they were."[18]

In fact, the communiqué did appear to document the birth of a G-2. The Europeans, especially the Germans, were wary. An editorial comment in the *Financial Times* titled "The Isolation of Europe" deplored that "when they [the Europeans, notably Germans] refused to join in a coordinated adjustment, the other two currency blocks evidently felt quite comfortable at leaving them out."[19]

In Washington, also, there was speculation on a new G-2. Felix Rohatyn, senior partner at Lazard Frères & Company, stated that it reflected the "special relationship between Japan and the United States that spells the end of the US–British special relationship. After all, you can only dance with one partner at a time." He further explained:

This country is obviously drawn to those countries on the rim—Japan, Korea, Taiwan, Malaysia, and don't forget China. . . . And I think the new special relationship with Japan will be the linchpin of the Pacific relationship. Meanwhile, the Atlantic Alliance is somewhat undermined by the unwillingness of the West Germans to carry [a fair share] of the load, and by the economic weakness of Great Britain.[20]

The "Baker-Miyazawa Accord" proved not to be carved in stone. This became apparent as the New Year approached, when the yen came under pressure to move higher and the US administration allowed it to do so despite its commitment to currency stabilization. As a matter of fact, one senior Treasury official admitted his less than enthusiastic endorsement of the communiqué. In a briefing to reporters after its announcement, he made clear his view that "the current yen rate was at the low end of its recent trading range against the dollar." He also warned that "it doesn't mean that any particular rate is appropriate. . . . There is no commitment for any particular action regarding an exchange rate." Specifically, he asserted that "there's been no change in intervention policy in the United States." This served as confirmation that the Treasury thought that the yen should be appreciated further for the level to be called optimal, although neither side admitted that it had struck a deal on a reference rate or range at the time.

When the yen weakened, as the announcement day drew nearer, dropping from 153–154 to 161–163, the Treasury became suspicious. Mulford questioned Gyoten by telephone, asking whether "Japan did something to

---

18. Personal interview.

19. *Financial Times*, 1 November 1986.

20. Quoted in Hobart Rowen, *Washington Post*, 9 November 1986.

change the exchange rate" and even posed a veiled threat that if "Japan would do something" the communiqué should not be announced at the scheduled time. Gyoten argued that it was not the business of the Ministry of Finance and held that it was the right moment to announce the communiqué. Miyazawa was angry to learn of Mulford's remark and told Gyoten to convey to Mulford that he would have to resign his post if the United States canceled the announcement, since a cancellation would probably spell political problems for Japan. Gyoten informed Mulford diplomatically that Miyazawa was upset and recommended strongly that the announcement be made.

It was against this background that the communiqué was altered to include the word *broadly*, at Mulford's insistence. The communiqué then read "realignment . . . is now broadly consistent with the present underlying fundamentals," obviously a retreat from full commitment to support of the existing bilateral exchange rate. Later, a senior Treasury official explained how he had analyzed the situation:

We negotiated for weeks and weeks; and throughout that whole time the rate was mainly 153–154 and a few days before we announced, it went to 161. . . . At that time [September 26], the rate was about 154 and the agreement on the desirability of doing something was very clear in that meeting.[21]

Why did the rate change so abruptly just before the announcement? The same official's suspicion that the Ministry of Finance had leaked information to Japanese money men in order to rig the yen–dollar rate was shared by other Treasury officials, as were his ill feelings toward Miyazawa.[22] "Miyazawa made a mistake at that point because he forgot where the currency had been when he was negotiating . . . and he seemed to imply that it wasn't going to go back at all. When the sharp move came, he was in very bad shape. He came back here, you know, very fast," the official added sarcastically, referring to Miyazawa's hurried visit to Washington in January 1987, when he realized that Baker had not, in fact, helped him to stop a further appreciation of the yen.

Even though Baker, in the words of his aide, "recognized [that] Miyazawa had domestic political problems and needed to play up the current rate more than the September rate," Treasury officials, particularly Mulford, felt somewhat cheated by Miyazawa's maneuver in Japan.[23] Certainly Miyazawa

---

21. Personal interview.

22. A well-placed Treasury official recalled, "We assumed that the Finance Ministry had leaked its own views to the banking system." Personal interview.

23. Personal interview.

emphasized the strong commitment of the US administration to stabilize the currency around 160 for domestic consumption, considering it politically imperative for him to do so. As mentioned earlier, before Miyazawa left for San Francisco, Nakasone impressed upon him the need to obtain assurance from Baker that the rate would be stabilized at about 170. A senior Treasury official later commented, "It was clear to me that 170 was an important level to them. But, in my view, it was in the nature of a pipe dream. Gyoten maybe talked about 170, but there was no way we were going to entertain any kind of operation to produce a 170 rate."[24] Miyazawa was under enormous pressure to stay close to that level. In fact, they did not agree to any definite rate or range. As US officials pointed out, "there was a moral commitment that both agreed the rate should not exceed boundaries." Of course, "there was a verbal discussion [on the rate and the range] and the United States was committed to helping," but "it was implicit" and "there was no signed document."

For their part, the Japanese feared that the United States could easily cheat on the commitment by "talking down" the dollar. In the San Francisco meeting, Miyazawa reminded Baker that the public statements had made it difficult to defend exchange rates and were adding to market uncertainty. Though he expressed it subtly, Miyazawa was directly requesting that the United States be less vocal.

Aside from the weak mechanism for stabilizing exchange rates, the "Accord" was a vulnerable product, because it was a package deal, a quid pro quo bargain of fiscal stimulus from Japan for currency stability. Therefore, if the United States should consider Japan's fiscal stimulus measures inadequate in support of the US side of the deal, the Accord would be in danger of crumbling. And it did.

Following the EMS realignment in January 1987, Reagan administration officials started to talk down the dollar. Currency markets were thrown into turmoil once again, and the dollar fell precipitously. The US administration's displeasure hinged, in part, on Japan's unfulfilled promise to stimulate its economy, although West German resistance served as a target as well. A prominent Treasury official said of the effect on the US commitment:

You always have to keep in the back of your mind that within that agreement was also a commitment to stimulate the domestic economy. It became fully apparent that the supplementary budget introduced in late September and finally implemented was taking away more than it was giving. There was less commitment on Baker's part as the budget was not playing the role he had expected.[25]

---

24. Personal interview.

25. Personal interview.

Although the October communiqué had produced a quieting effect on the markets throughout November and the first half of December 1986, several developments worked to reverse the market's optimism about the dollar. Many market participants were becoming convinced that US domestic demand was slowing and that any signs of strength would prove temporary, reflecting shifts in the timing of transactions before new tax laws took effect at the beginning of the year. The prospects for 1987 were increasingly viewed as dependent upon a turnaround in the US trade position. The loss of a majority in the Senate by the Republicans in the November election was interpreted as complicating the administration's efforts to resist protectionist legislation or calls for a lower dollar. Political uncertainties intensified after revelations that some US officials had participated in the controversial Iran-Contra arms deal. On December 31, preliminary US trade statistics for the month of November were released showing a massive deficit of $19.2 billion. In the light of this deterioration in the US trade position, the market interpreted statements made by US officials as consistent with the view that the United States welcomed a lower dollar.

Meanwhile, just as the deutsche mark moved upward as the market sentiment toward the dollar turned bearish in early January, tensions within the EMS heightened and intervention to preserve existing parities increased. EMS currencies were caught up in a speculative whirlwind. The EMS exchange rate structure was maintained by the intervention until the weekend of January 10, when a meeting of the finance ministers of the EMS resulted in a realignment.

The selling of dollars against yen also accelerated. Miyazawa and Sumita made it known to the markets that the Japanese central bank would intervene to prevent the dollar from depreciating further, to use Miyazawa's expression, "regardless of the cost." On January 13, after the dollar had dropped to below 158 yen to the dollar, Japanese exporters rushed to sell dollars and Japanese investment houses and pension funds flooded the market with forward sales to hedge their dollar exposures. The dollar declined more than 1 percent against the yen in heavy trading that day. On the following day, the *New York Times* reported that an unidentified US administration official wanted the dollar to decline further, unleashing a rash of dollar sales against both the yen and the deutsche mark. The dollar fell more than 3 percent against both currencies within a few hours of extremely nervous trading.[26]

On January 19 the dollar dropped to a postwar low of 149.98 against the yen. In stark contrast to the near frantic intervention efforts of the Bank of Japan, the US monetary authorities stayed noticeably away from the market.

---

26. Peter T. Kilborn, *New York Times,* 14 January 1987.

In near-desperation, Miyazawa rushed to a snow-covered Washington on January 21.

Washington's immediate reaction to the announcement of Miyazawa's visit was negative. "It happened very fast. I think we did discuss here whether it [his visit] was really desirable or not but before we even discussed it very much, he left," recalled a Treasury official. "Why did he come?" another Treasury official asked after Miyazawa had arrived. "He [Miyazawa] could've phoned Baker."[27] The highly publicized visit was regarded as potentially embarrassing to Baker, who might possibly have been accused of reneging on the pledge in the joint communiqué to stabilize the currencies.

Miyazawa made it known that the visit was a gamble. At that time he was under heavy pressure from industry and politicians. He could not blame his predecessor for the new problems any longer. The fact that he had made such a fanfare of the joint communiqué in late October and unmistakably implied that 160 was the agreed-upon stability point exacerbated his present position. With the new session of the Diet, moreover, he faced the enormous task, as Finance Minister, of enacting the fiscal 1987 budget and the new tax reform bill—both explosive issues politically. In order to get them passed, it was imperative for him, first and foremost, to stop the appreciation of the yen. Just before he flew to Washington, the opposition parties sent letters to him demanding that he tell Baker to keep his promise to do something about the yen–dollar rate.

The Japanese Finance Minister also had to prove his accountability to Nakasone. Partly to test Miyazawa as a potential successor, Nakasone had assigned the portfolio to him the previous summer. The political and psychological burdens were all the more grave since he was one of those who had criticized the ineffectiveness of the yen diplomacy of the Nakasone government. Before his departure, Miyazawa telephoned Nakasone and asked his views of the trip. Nakasone's reply was "you have to go." Then he lectured, "You always have to speak to Washington when you want to manage a good relationship with Americans. You have to think of the domestic politics and the Diet. Therefore, you have to be visible in speaking up to Washington. You have to go."[28]

After the January 21 meeting in the Treasury Department conference room, both Baker and Miyazawa made an announcement stating "their continued support for the understandings and agreements contained in their joint announcement of October 31, 1986." In other words, it was a reaffirmation of the October communiqué.

By the time of Miyazawa's trip to Washington, the yen had appreciated

---

27. Personal interview at the time.

28. Interview of Nakasone with the author.

from its rate at the time of the October communiqué. In this latest statement, however, they repeated that "the yen–dollar exchange rate has been broadly consistent with underlying fundamentals," choosing merely to add that "there were recent instances of temporary instability in exchange markets." There was no hint at a new defense line rate or range. That the United States admitted some temporary instances of instability did not automatically mean that the administration considered the markets disorderly, which would have obliged the Treasury to intervene in the market. In fact, the agreement that the exchange rate was "broadly consistent with underlying fundamentals" if anything legitimized the US policy of nonintervention.

This time Miyazawa's new bottom line was 150 yen, and he used every argument in support of it: the negative effect on economic growth in Japan, Japanese investment abroad, and the need to build up the confidence of the Japanese business community. But again Baker refused to commit himself to defense of any specific rate automatically, although he assured Miyazawa that he was just as interested in a more stable currency relationship as Miyazawa was and would make every effort to stabilize it. Baker's commitment was essentially the same as the one he had made in October. "The same type. In neither of the two bilateral agreements was there a specific amount of intervention that was committed to," explained one US official.

On January 28, one week later, "US authorities intervened in the yen in a manner consistent with the joint statement [announced on January 21]."[29] In a coordinated move with the Japanese monetary authorities, the Foreign Exchange Trading Desk purchased $50 million against the sale of yen. Although the amount of the intervention was marginal, it was the first "reverse" intervention—action on the part of the US monetary authorities to defend the floor of the dollar—since the United States had committed itself to a ceiling of the dollar at the Plaza meeting. "[Because of the] commitment, we didn't agree on the specific time that we would [intervene]. We felt that it was important to give a little signal in the marketplace even though you don't say anything. They know who is trading," recalled an official at the Treasury.[30]

But behind this temporary mending of the fences between Baker and Miyazawa, one serious problem grew—the problem of credibility. One administration official said:

The other thing I suppose we accomplished at the meeting was that we impressed upon him [Miyazawa] why the markets were behaving this way. Essentially, it was the markets' perception of the loss of credibility of Japan. So shortly after doing a supplementary [budget], which turned

---

29. *Federal Reserve Bulletin*, no. 73 (Washington), May 1987, 333.

30. Personal interview.

out not to have a lot in it, they took back even more in the '87 budget that they had given with the other hand. . . . I don't know why they did that. . . . It must have been the Ministry of Finance experts who over-whelmed Miyazawa. They must have pulled the wool over his eyes.[31]

Despite the good impressions Baker and Darman had of Miyazawa from the outset, there were some doubts in the Treasury about his ability to deliver. "In San Francisco," recalled a Treasury official, "Miyazawa took the basic line that the supplementary [budget] was under his control. That he would not be able to have an impact on the '87 budget. . . . Once we had discovered that the supplementary was not as stimulative as it should have been, his explanation was that we would have to wait until the '87 budget because that was when he would have an opportunity for impact with the budget." Another Treasury official admitted that he was confused when he heard that Miyazawa could do something on the supplementary budget but not much on the fiscal 1987 budget. "Why can he do something earlier and not later?"

"In terms of his political relationship with Baker, [it is] his believability [that] is now at stake. Because, now, he is fully responsible," voiced a Treasury official, shortly after the Washington G-5 meeting in April 1987.[32]

The credibility gap was reciprocated on the other side of the Pacific. Just as the Treasury entertained suspicions about the credibility of Miyazawa, the Ministry of Finance gradually grew skeptical of Baker's credibility. One Finance Ministry official complained, "He did not deliver the promise he made in October. His reliability is questioned here." The Japanese, as well as the Germans, resented the talk-down tactics of the US administration. In early 1987, when the US press reported the apparent talk-down policies of unnamed officials, they felt that they had been completely ignored. Baker's denial of being the "source" and his subsequent effort to minimize the effect did not help. Nonetheless there were positive effects from this yen–dollar diplomacy. The massive intervention of the Bank of Japan in early 1987 could have met some resistance from the US authorities but for the October communiqué. And eventually, the result was a coordinated inter-vention with the United States. On the US side, Baker used this Japan card to the fullest—maximizing an effort to pressure West Germany and leading the way to the Louvre.

"German Stubbornness"

Why did the US administration play the Japan card? What motivations and expectations lay behind the use of this strategy? Was this G-2 strategic or

---

31. Personal interview.

32. Personal interview.

tactical? How did the Japanese play to the card in response? How did the Germans react? After all, to what extent, and in what ways did it affect policy coordination? What did it signify for the future?

Washington and Tokyo each has its own conception of the G-2, based on different perspectives and political considerations. As was seen in chapter 1, Takeshita cherished the goal of promoting his own international recognition through a G-2 dialogue with Baker. Ministry of Finance officials wanted a G-2 meeting, leaving the Europeans out. "These Europeans would be quick to jump on us and say to do this or to do that whenever they would join in the meeting, handily forgetting that they can't deliver that much," said an MOF official later. Beneath the comment, though, lay the fear that the Europeans would demand a disproportionately higher yen against the European currencies in any realignment with the dollar.

On the US side, there were various justifications for a G-2 policy. The existence of the EMS, along with the independent power of the Bundesbank, American policymakers reasoned, would complicate efforts if they dealt first with the Europeans. They felt that the Japanese would be much easier to handle. Furthermore, ad hoc contact of finance ministers on a G-2 basis could bypass the cautious, cliquish central bankers and accelerate the pace of coordination. A Bank of Japan official confided that he suspected that the G-2 policy coordination strategy of the Baker Treasury, particularly in the summer of "aggressive bilateralism," was an attempt to circumvent the BOJ.

Generally speaking, the G-2 strategy of the Baker Treasury aimed to elicit more cooperative responses to policy coordination initiatives from West Germany by force of the joint pressure exerted by the United States and Japan. The strategic aim of the Treasury lay in forging a tripartite understanding among the United States, Japan, and West Germany. A senior official of the Treasury explained the development of the strategy they had employed in the autumn of 1986:

Germans were not very cooperative. When you analyze the currency levels, you could make the argument that the yen had appreciated through its previous nominal high and that it had moved to new ground. You could make no such argument at the time for the deutsche mark. The D-mark was still trading at that time above 2. . . . There was an enormous psychological barrier in Germany about that 2 rate. Their previous high was 1.69. The Japanese high was 175. It was now trading at 152. So, there was a real justification for showing a preference. . . . There was clearly a more constructive attitude among the Japanese about negotiating than there was within the Germans. So we thought we should move in that direction.

The actual agreement [the October joint communiqué] demonstrated in a very clear way what happens if you decide you want to step out of the coordination process and stonewall. The United States will work with whoever is available and extend that to bilateral contacts. There was a very salutary lesson to the others and it brought people back around together.[33]

It is true that the Plaza meeting was made possible by the direct dialogue between Baker and Takeshita in June 1985 and that the G-2 initiative of the United States and Japan preceded the initiatives of the Europeans, including West Germany. Intensive bilateral talks between the United States and West Germany followed, especially on the deputy level. Hans Tietmeyer, Vice Minister of the Ministry of Finance in West Germany, played a key role in preparations for both the Plaza meeting and the Louvre meeting. Unfortunately for Tietmeyer, however, Baker preferred to approach his counterpart in Tokyo (Takeshita, during the Plaza preparation, and Miyazawa, prior to the Louvre) rather than his counterpart in Bonn. It may not be accurate, though, to assume that the United States followed a premeditated course in placing greater emphasis on its relationship with Japan and thereby formulating a solid G-2 strategy.

In fact, the United States had earlier tried to pursue a G-3 strategy—as a more vigorous follow-up to the Tokyo Summit agreement to coordinate international economic policy on a trilateral basis. One Treasury official remarked, "Originally, you have to remember that it was not just a bilateral US–Japan agreement. It was an effort to get a US–Japan–Germany agreement and the German authorities were unwilling to carry on the discussions. Between September and December they were unwilling to enter into any talks about the need to stimulate their economy in exchange for exchange rate stability."

Volcker's secret meeting with Pöhl at his home in Frankfurt in mid-August 1986 was just one example of the US' direct bilateral contacts between the United States and West Germany. Other contacts at the deputy level were attempted, but all failed to produce an agreement. The crossfire between Baker and Stoltenberg in the September G-5 and G-7 meetings drove the two sides farther apart.

From the German point of view, the United States was still too naive to understand West Germany's special situation. Contrary to the forecast projected by the United States, both Bonn and Frankfurt were confident of a "very favorable economic outlook for Germany," to quote a top Bundesbank official, thus dismissing the US charge that West Germany did not make enough effort to stimulate its economy.

German resistance contrasted to the Japanese "cooperation" and was characterized unkindly in some quarters as German stubbornness. Hobart

---

33. Personal interview.

Rowen, in his *Washington Post* column, described the Germans as "maddeningly self-content."[34] It is, however, far-fetched to attribute German lack of cooperation to mere stubbornness. The Germans had ample reason to resist. First and foremost, as pointed out repeatedly by the German officials themselves, was the difference between the trade structures of Japan and West Germany. Only about 10 percent of German exports go to the United States, whereas roughly 37 percent of Japanese exports are destined for the American market. The European Community provides West Germany with its largest export market, within which France is its largest trading partner.[35] The appreciation of the deutsche mark against the dollar, although substantial, did not affect the competitiveness of exporters in West Germany to the same degree that it did those in Japan. Bonn showed some resiliency in withstanding US pressure to stabilize the deutsche mark in return for some stimulus policy, even though domestic political pressure was mixed. Exporters favored an economic stimulus while others, such as the banking community, objected to US pressure to reflate. This is in contrast to the traditional one-directional pressure exercised on the Japanese government by powerful interests to stop the further appreciation of the yen, which has become modified in recent years. Second, West Germany always had to consider the ramifications of its policies on the EMS mechanism. At least until September 1986, the EMS countries opposed US talk-down offensives.

On 21 September 1986, European finance ministers met in Gleneagles, Scotland, in an avowed effort to "stand up and speak with one voice toward the United States."[36] Initiated by the Germans, this meeting was considered their victory. In return for the endorsement of the German position by the other Europeans, German monetary authorities agreed to take a more flexible stand on intramarginal intervention to support EMS parities. During the last week in September and the first week in October, the Bundesbank purchased "more than a billion dollars" in what was the largest "reverse" intervention undertaken by the Germans since the Plaza.[37]

The Baker-Miyazawa communiqué of 31 October 1986 added a new complication for Europe, which France and West Germany discussed. The French, who had argued at Gleneagles for long-term currency stability, in contrast to the German focus on stability for the time being, urged the

---

34. Hobart Rowen, "Germany: Maddeningly Self-Content," *Washington Post,* 7 May 1987.

35. Organization for Economic Cooperation and Development, *Statistics of Foreign Trade,* Series A, 1985–1986; International Monetary Fund, *Direction of Trade Statistics Yearbook 1986,* Washington.

36. *New York Times,* 22 September 1986.

37. Figure provided to the author by a Bundesbank official.

Germans to stimulate their economy in exchange for currency stability from the United States. "We considered [that], from the French perspective, we would be headed on a dangerous course," said a French official later. But the Germans, at least at this stage, were not persuaded. Bundesbank officials did not accept the French premise that the central banks should use monetary policy to stabilize exchange rates, and interpreted the Gleneagles Accord as such. Furthermore, the Germans argued that the United States had not yet really decided on a dollar strategy: "I felt that there were still different views on that between Baker and Volcker. Volcker thought the dollar declined enough, but Baker, not," a German official offered as one of the reasons for German reluctance at this time.

Third, West Germany felt that the appreciation of the yen against the dollar should proceed differentially from that of the deutsche mark. This was the consensus of the European countries. They all regarded the equal appreciation of the nondollar currencies against the dollar as "unfair" because, they reasoned, Japanese trade surpluses and their aggressive intrusion into European markets caused the imbalance in the first place.

Fourth, and closely related to the previous point, Bonn expressed its frustration on the spillover effects of the US–Japan trade disputes on currencies—believing that they had led to the appreciation of the yen and, subsequently, to that of the deutsche mark. Stoltenberg commented that the imbalance problem was essentially a US–Japanese one and, somewhat pejoratively, remarked that the much-celebrated G-2 should be the right place to solve it.[38] The central question could be put: Why do we have to share a disproportionate burden and cost to correct the US imbalance, since the real problem lies in the Pacific, not the Atlantic? This opinion further substantiated German reluctance.

Fifth, there was a deeply rooted fear among the German leaders that the original strategy of the United States—to build a G-3—might erode or diminish the maneuverability or leverage that West Germany now enjoyed. Extracted from the European context, the size and dynamism of the German economy would be substantially less compared to those of the United States and Japan. This might naturally put constraints on the use of German economic power. The fact that West Germany had evolved into a truly European power placed Bonn in a dilemma: West Germany had found that enhanced power within the European framework enabled it to be projected as a European power on the global screen, but at the same time, potentially growing German power is circumscribed if it is restricted to Europe.

Despite US aggressive bilateralism, which played off West Germany against Japan, the West Germans and the Japanese did attempt, albeit

---

38. Press conference after a meeting of the IMF Interim Committee, 10 April 1987.

sporadically, to explore a mutually defensive stance vis-à-vis the United States. During the rapid decline of the dollar in April 1986, before the Tokyo Summit, the Bundesbank and the Bank of Japan intervened in the currency market hand in hand "perhaps intending to stabilize the currencies and send the message to the U.S. that Baker's indicator proposals should not be welcome."[39]

Another episode that illustrates German–Japanese dialogue occurred after the Interim Committee meeting of 28 September 1986. According to a Japanese official, Stoltenberg met Miyazawa in Washington and proposed that both should intervene in the market "on a single day basis" if disorderly market conditions prevailed on the following day to induce speculators to buy deutsche marks. Unexpectedly quiet trading on the next day obviated the need for intervention by the two countries. Cooperation of the two in a joint intervention was also recognized after the Louvre meeting, when the Bundesbank sold yen against dollars and the Bank of Japan sold deutsche marks against the dollar, as described in chapter 8.

On the whole, however, the cross-relationship between Japan and West Germany was never very strong, and neither side pursued the possibility of fortifying it. It is fair to say that Pöhl and Sumita kept in constant contact and exchanged views throughout the period whenever they met at BIS and IMF World Bank meetings. The same does not hold true for the relationships of the finance ministers. There was no significant joint effort to increase pressure on the United States to reduce the budget deficit.

This lack of any cross-relationship forced Bonn to respond to the bilateral call from Washington and, eventually, to bilateral arrangements similar to those concluded between Baker and Miyazawa. The Baker-Stoltenberg meeting on 14 December 1986 in Kiel, Stoltenberg's hometown in northern Germany, came about as a result of consistent pressure applied by Washington. They discussed a wide range of topics, including the delicate political situations of both countries. Baker stressed the importance of steady growth in West Germany and the merits of drastic tax cuts. Stoltenberg, not committing himself to any specific measures, explained the political implications of German tax reform and the tax cut. He reacted positively to Baker's concerns, which heartened his American guests. They exchanged frank views on reference ranges, setting forth "what's possible for both of us," to quote one German official. They discussed also the future course of policy coordination, agreeing to the general framework—the German pledge to stimulate domestic demand in return for a US commitment to stabilize currencies.

---

39. "Japan and West Germany move to build coalition to stabilize the currencies," *Nihon Keizai Shimbun*, 9 May 1986.

The Kiel meeting, however slight its immediate effects were, represented a watershed in US–German accommodation, particularly on the reference range issue, laying the groundwork for the Louvre Accord. One US official stated:

I think until that time, Mulford had been dealing with Tietmeyer on the target-range system that we were trying to get developed through the deputies. Tietmeyer had been very resistant. We discussed the substance of it in outline at the luncheon. . . . There was enough of a discussion of it that, I think, Tietmeyer could see Stoltenberg in our presence was much more flexible than Tietmeyer had been.[40]

One by-product of the Kiel meeting was a secret mission made by Tietmeyer to see Darman in Washington during the following month. They followed up the discussion about the reference-range idea, tax strategy, and monetary policy. Again, none of the divergent views on any of the issues was settled. Nonetheless, the meeting helped them to communicate with one another more effectively. "If we hadn't had the conversation . . . they would not have [had] confidence that we were not necessarily committing [ourselves] to a rigid target zone," recalled a senior US administration official later.[41] The Germans surely sensed that the Americans had become more accommodating; both the Kiel meeting and Tietmeyer's subsequent visit to Washington were "decisive factors in making the American side show greater understanding and flexibility."[42] The aggressive bilateralism of the Baker Treasury had at last yielded a framework for G-3 policy coordination.

Toward a Tripartite Regime?

Throughout the period under consideration, from the Plaza to the Louvre, France and Great Britain were forced to play secondary roles. Both were challenged by Italy's ongoing campaign to be a part of the core of five. Their monetary policy actions were regarded as residuals of the Bundesbank's EMS policy, and intervention by each was regarded as a mere ripple in the ocean. To be sure, Lawson displayed formidable intellect and sophistication, and both Bérégovoy and Balladur exuded mature statesmanship. Nevertheless, the once important role that each had had occasion to play in the arena of international currency diplomacy—Great Britain in the 1940s and France in the 1970s—appeared to have disappeared.

---

40. Personal interview.

41. Personal interview.

42. Remark made by an official in Bonn to the author.

It may be misleading, however, to argue that France and Great Britain were reduced to the status of marginal players. Both influenced to a considerable extent the nature of economic policy coordination by the positive or negative commitments they made. It is certainly true to say that their ability to influence US strategy or the US–Japanese arrangements was limited by the political and economic resources they had at their disposal. It is equally valid to note that each, on certain occasions, affected the intra-European arrangements, thereby helping to determine the consequences of policy coordination.

The French, in particular, exploited the opportunity to bargain with the Germans, which contributed, to some extent, to the shaping of the Louvre Accord. From the very beginning the French considered the Plaza strategy "the opportunity, the first in the last ten years, to make some progress in a very pragmatic way to build a more stable and organized international monetary system."[43] They stuck to this goal. A lone advocate of target zones, France favored target zones of an "ideal type," which made the range idea of the United States appear more moderate, as will be seen in the next chapter. Efforts made by France to analyze the political commitment requisite to building a target-zone system induced the United States to take a more ambitious approach to reformation of the international monetary system. This is particularly evident in Richard Darman's formulation of a target-zone strategy. As noted in chapter 5, another French objective of the Plaza strategy was to create a pressure-building device out of G-5 policy coordination directed at German growth. French insistence on the need for an economic stimulus in West Germany was yet another example of the convergence of US and French interests, which resulted in increased pressure by both on West Germany in late 1986.

Balladur, less than three weeks after the Baker-Miyazawa agreement of October 1986, announced that his country would like to accept the invitation to "join" the arrangement—stimulus in exchange for currency stability—and would urge its partners in the European Monetary System to do the same.[44] The French position doubtless pleased Washington, where one Treasury official remarked after the Louvre that "our only ally is now France," and added, half grinning, "strange bedfellows, huh?" Thus, the French card was also in the hand of the Treasury.

Compared to the clear-cut strategy of the French, the actions of Great Britain were ambiguous. With regard to monetary policy, Lawson, an ideologue of the free market, dominated the planning. From the start he

43. Comment by a French Ministry of Finance official to the author.

44. C. Fred Bergsten, "Economic Imbalances and Politics," *Foreign Affairs* 65 (Spring 1987): 770–794.

was discomfited by the concept of managing economic policies and did not, in fact, commit himself wholeheartedly to the Plaza intervention strategy. He showed some irritation with the "abrupt U-turn of the American posture at Plaza," observed one European official. He grappled, moreover, with reconciling international developments in the sphere of monetary policy with domestic monetarist policies that had been ideologically espoused by the Thatcher government. Finally, Great Britain's position as an oil producer complicated its policy making.

The uncertainty of Britain's entry into the EMS further clouded Lawson's strategy. As a Tory loyalist, he was mindful of the political rhetoric of "splendid isolation," yet he continually found his options narrowed as long as sterling diplomacy was kept separate from the EMS. The pound sterling was becoming uncoupled from the dollar and was linked increasingly to the deutsche mark, as was admitted by a senior British official.[45] Lawson's advocacy of a "managed float" strategy was interpreted as a warming-up exercise for participation in the EMS. There was a change in Britain's stance. A French participant said,

I believe that intellectually and ideologically, Mr. Lawson was perhaps most reluctant in the group toward this approach [reference range]. He tended to be more skeptical. Yet there was a change in Great Britain in favor of more concerted management of exchange rate fluctuations and it developed up to the Louvre Agreement. In fact, they were anxious for stability between pound sterling and European currencies.[46]

Both France and Great Britain must have realized that US strategy was based essentially on the trilateral arrangements among the United States, Japan, and West Germany. After aggressive bilateral diplomacy of Washington with both Tokyo and Bonn, consultation with Paris and London was a formality. At the Plaza, there was a debate over French obligations to intervene to the same extent as the Germans. The German argument, that European intervention should be treated collectively through the EMS mechanism, prevailed, and the French were spared much of the intervention. The British, however, intervened massively during the three-month period after the Louvre. British intervention took place on a scale second only to Japan, with Italy third. "We were mopping up the dollar in big way," claimed a British official.[47] Neither Baker, nor Takeshita, nor, later Miyazawa, cared much about French and British contributions to the intervention to bring down the dollar or, later, to support the currency at the Louvre.

---

45. Personal interview.

46. Personal interview.

47. Personal interview.

During the period from the Plaza to the Louvre, the economic balance of power clearly shifted, concentrating gradually on the three principal players: Japan, the United States, and West Germany. This is not to claim that France and Great Britain were reduced to marginal players, for they did contribute substantially to the Plaza strategy, with respect to both monetary policy initiatives and the reference-range concept. Furthermore, movement toward a tripartite monetary regime has been constrained by the excessive manipulation of the G-2 strategy by the United States, the inability of Japan to exploit its newly acquired financial power, and the reluctance of West Germany to pursue more thorough monetary integration within the EMS.

Louvre

"Let's call a spade a spade, gentlemen," French Finance Minister Edouard Balladur said, raising the curtain.

Champagne Florens Louis was already poured in the 19 glasses on the dinner table at the Palais du Louvre. The finance ministers and central bank governors of the Group of Five chatted over Turbot Soufflé Cardinale and the Puligny Montrachet 1982 brought from the wine cellar of the French Ministry.

It was shortly after 7:30 in the evening of 21 February 1987. The discussion over dinner and the meeting the next day produced the Louvre Accord—the most serious attempt to implement systemic currency stabilization among the Group of Five after more than a decade of unchartered floating exchange rates.

Plaza II

Nigel Lawson, British Chancellor of the Exchequer, summed up the meeting in two words: "Plaza Two. . . . I see this meeting as the lineal descendent of the Plaza meeting. . . . Then we all agreed that the dollar should fall, now we all agree we need stability."[1]

In the Louvre Accord, as it came to be known, the finance ministers and central bank governors declared that their currencies were "within ranges broadly consistent with underlying economic fundamentals." While stopping short of endorsing target zones openly, the policymakers indicated that they were ready to intervene to help stabilize exchange rates at "around current levels." According to Lawson, they "had full discussions on circumstances under which [they] would intervene jointly."[2] West Germany and Japan agreed to stimulate demand at home, and the United States renewed its pledge to cut its swollen budget deficit.

Although the Louvre meeting had been planned for Sunday, February 22,

1. *New York Times,* 23 February 1987.

2. Ibid.

as a meeting of the G-7, the principal deals were made by the G-5 ministers and central bank governors, who met on Saturday, February 21, in the Louvre's Salon de Familia and, subsequently, in the dining room of the French Ministry of Economics and Finance.

The Louvre meeting was the product of the efforts of James A. Baker III, US Secretary of the Treasury, to win from Kiichi Miyazawa, Japanese Finance Minister, and Gerhard Stoltenberg, West German Finance Minister, substantive stimulus measures in return for a US agreement to stabilize the dollar. Specifically, the Baker-Miyazawa Accord of 31 October 1986, a pledge to keep the dollar at the prevailing level, set in motion the stimulus-for-stabilization machinery. A meeting between Baker and Stoltenberg in Kiel in December 1986 was also an attempt to push the process in this direction.

Baker had originally explored the possibility of meeting with the other G-5 ministers in December 1986, but his efforts were frustrated by the failure of the G-5 deputies to agree even on an agenda. During his January talks with Baker, Miyazawa expressed his readiness for a G-5 meeting the following week, on January 27, which Baker thought was too early. Wanting to hold the meeting as soon as possible, he then offered February 7 as a tentative date, which Baker again agreed with reservations. Finally, the meeting was scheduled for February 21.

Certainly Miyazawa and Baker's reaffirmation of the currency stability pledge made during the January visit to Washington might help to form the basis of a G-5 pact. The near-desperate manner of his trip made him look weak at home. In Japan, unfriendly press reports having described his visit as a "mercy for grace trip," he needed to prove to the public that his bilateral deal with Baker was valuable. He had learned how risky bilateral diplomacy with the United States could be, realizing that Baker had used it as a tactical maneuver to pressure West Germany. He sensed that the bilateral deal by itself ran the risk of being violated, and he concluded that the United States–Japan deal must be promptly transformed into a formal agreement of the G-5 and G-7. Baker, however, warned Miyazawa not to rush the meeting, advising instead that any accord be "precooked" for guaranteed success. In particular, he wanted advance assurances from the Germans on an expansion package. When Miyazawa volunteered to cut Japan's discount rate by one-half a percentage point as a "token" of their January discussion, he was urged to save the "souvenir" for the G-5 meeting to maximize the impact of the action.

After a series of telephone contacts at the G-5 deputy level, the deputies gathered at a preparatory meeting hosted by Daniel Lebegue, Director of the French Ministry of Finance, in Zurich on January 29, just after the German elections of January 25. Because the Louvre meeting was to be held at the G-7 level, the deputies met again with the addition of those representing the Italian and Canadian deputies in Rome on February 4, during the Venice Summit sherpa meetings.

Although the G-5 deputies still failed to come up with an agreement on a package deal, they managed to draft the communiqué during a meeting in Zurich. "It was actually quite an important meeting," said a European deputy, "because it was in this meeting in which the conceptual consensus on the need to stabilize the currencies near the prevailing levels was finally made."[3]

The G-5 deputies tried again to hammer out their differences in Paris before the Louvre meeting, but in the end two substantial issues remained unresolved: how to compromise on a reference range concept to stabilize currencies and how to coordinate fiscal policies. They disagreed, furthermore, on the language to describe the reference-range principle in the communiqué—whether *levels* or *range* should be used. The draft forwarded to the ministers, therefore, had parentheses inserted—"around the present (levels, range)"—signifying that the issue had not been resolved.

In the face of the impasse, especially on German resistance to a new commitment on tax cuts, Baker nearly canceled the meeting. A senior Treasury official later explained:

The Secretary actually did come to the decision that we should not have the meeting. Then the thing that prevailed was one or two shreds of possibility for some progress for Japan and Germany. Plus the very weighty argument that in an incremental process, if you didn't have a meeting, you had to calculate the costs of that process.[4]

An intensive debate followed at the top echelon of the Treasury Department as to whether the meeting should be canceled. Assistant Secretary of the Treasury for International Affairs, David C. Mulford, astute observer of market sentiment, argued that it should *not* be canceled. "Does the market want substance or stability?" he asked. In his view, the market was searching for stability. "If you don't have a meeting, you would have a lot of negative press stuff, market stuff, and you have to try to estimate what the market wants," he argued.[5]

The precipitous decline of the dollar since early 1987 had made foreign investors in the United States more anxious. The joint communiqué announced by Baker and Miyazawa in January and subsequent US coordinated intervention to stop further dollar decline reflected the concern of the US

---

3. Personal interview.

4. Personal interview.

5. Personal interview with a senior US administration official.

Treasury over continuing decline of foreign capital inflows into the United States. "Baker was now aware that a continual appreciation of the yen was making investment decisions difficult and a period of stability would help these prospects."[6] Concern over capital inflows was intensified as the Louvre meeting came closer.

Baker may have thought that the cancellation of the G-5 meeting could give him additional leverage vis-à-vis Japan and West Germany. Already having strengthened his hand by talking down the dollar in early January, another push might have worked. By the last week of January, however, he must have sensed the dangers of brinkmanship diplomacy. Precipitated by a run on the dollar following the Treasury's talk-down policies, the interest rate had already started to rise and was not arrested by Volcker. Furthermore, the dollar had to be stabilized before the Treasury auction in February. The necessity of financing the US current account deficit had finally trapped Baker and forced him to go to the Louvre.

By early February the perception of the need to stabilize currencies was shared by Japan and West Germany. In the case of West Germany, the realignment of the EMS in early January and its aftermath posed another obstacle to further revaluation of the deutsche mark. After the unspectacular results of the January general elections in Germany and in anticipation of the election in the *laender* the Bonn government became "more anxious to stabilize currencies."[7]

Finally, only a few days before the Louvre meeting, Baker elicited promises from Japan and West Germany that they would take additional measures to stimulate their economies. In a long telephone conversation, Stoltenberg assured Baker that the German government could promise an increase in the tax-reduction package scheduled to take effect in 1988. Around the same time, the Japanese told the Americans that the Liberal Democratic Party (LDP) would be prepared to propose fiscal stimulus measures after the fiscal 1987 budget had been passed.

In a last-minute telephone conversation Balladur confirmed the agreed aspects of the currency stability package with both Baker and Stoltenberg. By the time of the G-5 meeting, "there was broad agreement between the United States and France," according to a French participant; on the question of reference ranges, the French "did not need to convince James Baker. He was already convinced." On the morning of February 21, Baker confirmed commitments he had made in bilateral meetings with Miyazawa and Stoltenberg.

In a G-5 meeting on the afternoon of February 21 finance ministers and

---

6. Comment by an official of the US Treasury Department.

7. Interview of a French participant with the author.

central bank governors addressed three main issues: the use of economic indicators to help gauge the need for policy changes within the G-5, the drafting of the communiqué, and the clarification of the role of the G-5.

Italy protested the fact that the G-5 was meeting on the day before the G-7 meeting, threatening not to attend the G-7 meeting. As a result, the G-5 ministers and governors felt compelled to define the nature and function of the G-5 once again. It took about an hour for them to decide that they would maintain the G-5 mechanism despite Italy's objection.

Although Volcker complained that the discussion of the Italian issue was a waste of time,[8] the French took it very seriously. At the dinner table, Balladur excused himself, explaining that he had an appointment with Giovanni Goria, Italian Finance Minister. Then Balladur, Lebegue, and Jacques de Larosière, Governor of the Bank of France and former Managing Director of the International Monetary Fund, met with Goria at his hotel where they urged him to attend the G-7 meeting on the following day. Goria said he regretted that he could not attend because he had received instructions from the Prime Minister's office not to do so. After the meeting, Goria wrote a note to Balladur saying that he would leave Paris at six o'clock in the morning. Balladur reported his departure to the other participants in the morning.

The final drafting of the communiqué proceeded on the basis of the draft written by the deputies. In the communiqué, the participants recognized that the trade and current account imbalances of larger countries posed serious economic and political risks. Therefore, "the reduction of the large unsustainable trade imbalance is a matter of high priority and . . . achievement of more balanced global growth should play a central role in bringing about such a reduction."

Next, they made pledges to fight against protectionism and to cope with the developing countries' debt issues. After elaborating the pledges of each country to pursue policy coordination, they agreed to additional refinements in the use of economic indicators for multilateral surveillance. Accordingly, they adopted a set of seven "key variables": growth, inflation, current account and trade balances, budget performance, monetary conditions, and exchange rates. The deputies were to elaborate on the mechanics of surveillance by the Venice Economic Summit.

Finally, they agreed that exchange rate adjustments made since the Plaza Agreement would continue to contribute to the reduction of external imbalances and that currencies were "within ranges broadly consistent with underlying economic fundamentals, given the policy commitments."

Concern over the potential for substantial exchange rate shifts between

---

8. Peter T. Kilborn, "Can the Big Seven Learn to Waltz?" *New York Times,* 31 May 1987.

their currencies, which could damage growth and adjustment prospects, led the Louvre participants to agree on closer cooperation to foster stability of exchange rates around present levels. There were two points, however, on which the participants' views diverged, replaying the dispute among the deputies. The French and Americans preferred the word *range* to *levels*, while the Japanese, Germans, and British had the reverse preference. Apparently the objection of West Germany, Japan, and Great Britain to the term *range* derives from their hesitance to accept the ideology of the reference mechanism. "The word *range* sounds somewhat systematic," explained one deputy who opposed using the term. West Germany and Great Britain were particularly sensitive to the way the French presented the reference range idea. The fact that the use of the word *margin* by Balladur at the dinner table prompted heated counterarguments from West Germany and Great Britain illustrates their objection to any association with a target zone. Neither West Germany nor Great Britain was inclined to allow the French to declare the acceptance of a target zone from the balcony of the Louvre Palace. By adamantly insisting on the use of the word *levels*, the German side eventually prevailed.

The Japanese were, furthermore, reluctant to specify any range that would include a higher yen. For this reason, they preferred the word *levels*, which would give them greater flexibility. "You don't need to define [the] *level* because it's the present one. On *range*, you have to clarify what it really means," explained a Japanese participant later.

Miyazawa then raised the question of using the word *present*. He sought the opinion of Lawson, who had often arbitrated questions of English usage during communiqué drafting. Miyazawa said that *present* connoted too specific a time frame, and he wanted to give a more ambiguous impression. Lawson then proposed using *current*, which Miyazawa accepted. To most of the participants, "it was not a substantive issue at all."[9] This little language exercise was, in fact, a way of manipulating the translation for Japanese domestic consumption. To Miyazawa *present* connoted the exchange rate on the spot, which he deemed excessively high for the yen, while *current* implied a somewhat broader span of time, which could make the potentially uncomfortable specification of the exchange rate more nebulous. On this point, Miyazawa carried the day.[10]

---

9. Comment by a French official to the author.

10. The Japanese delegation translated *current* into *tomenno*, which connotes a broader time frame, instead of the more on-the-spot *genzaino*, the usual translation of *present*.

"Around the Current Levels"

A Japanese participant at the Louvre revealed in the fall of 1987 that he had sensed that the phrase "around the current levels" had been a sort of trap when Balladur began discussing specific figures at the dinner table, proposing to the participants that after they had committed themselves to the language in the announcement, they should address the ranges to be used. The French, who were eager to adopt target zones, may have previously received the tacit support of the United States for this. The suspicion of the Japanese participant deepened with each course.

Since the language itself had been the focal point of the deputies for some time before the Louvre, it would be farfetched to conceive of the French move as a trap, however. The French simply took advantage of the situation to advance their own political cause. Strangely enough, American and French officials found they shared nearly the same position on the reference range principle.

Balladur's proposition was as follows. First, the exchange rates of the previous day, Friday, February 20, (153.50 yen to the dollar, and 1.8250 deutsche marks to the dollar in round numbers) would serve as the baseline rates. Second, the currencies would be allowed to float within 5 percent on either side of this base. Third, monetary authorities would begin consulting on intervention when rates first deviated by 2.5 percent in either direction from the base.

Under the Balladur proposal, the 5 percent range would put the yen between 146.19 and 161.17 (based on the IMF formula), and the deutsche mark between 1.7380 and 1.9262. The threshold for consultation would be 149.75 yen and 1.7804 deutsche marks, respectively, on the low side, and 157.33 yen and 1.8706 deutsche marks on the high side.

According to German participants, Baker at first seemed to support the French proposal. His opinion appeared to change, however, once both Stoltenberg and Pöhl had expressed unyielding opposition to the use of specific figures. Said Pöhl, "Let's leave everything open and wait and see how the market responds." One participant recalled that Baker turned cautious at this point, saying that he agreed with the Germans. "Don't let us be too precise," Baker is reported to have said. Lawson argued a similar line. "We can't have a system in which we set up a target for the market to aim at."[11]

Miyazawa, the one most vehemently opposed to specific figures, was reticent during the discussion. One participant recalled that the Japanese were primarily spectators in the meeting. Miyazawa's silence must have

---

11. Comment by a French participant to the author.

disquieted Balladur, who realized that Miyazawa's reluctance to support the reference range would threaten his chances to draw the meeting to a successful conclusion. Balladur asked Miyazawa what he was ready to do and urged him to break his silence. Miyazawa refused to accept a baseline of 153.50 yen to the dollar, which would have made the intervention point start beyond 149.75—an unacceptable point since it was above 150. "The 150 rate is very important politically in Japan. What we need now is currency stability and Japanese industry will get assured if they are given stability—even 150 is very high," said Miyazawa. He proposed that intervention begin, instead, at just below 150 yen to the dollar.

When the Japanese finance minister then proposed that the yen–dollar range should be established at between 150 and 170, Balladur promptly asserted that the yen should be revalued by at least 5 percent more. Other Europeans agreed. Following the crossfire between the Japanese and the others, the discussion returned to intervention strategy and specific ranges. Each of the players expressed his views, some of which were recalled as follows by one of the participants:

[Stoltenberg] tended to leave the discussion of actual rates and intervention up to Pöhl. He opposed Balladur's rigid system because it might lead to target zones.

[Lawson] also spoke against setting clear ranges, echoing the general chorus around the table opposed to Balladur.

[Baker] wanted ranges and I think he simply accepted that a specified range was going to be helpful. When it came to the substantive discussions, Paul Volcker took over. When it came to the modalities of how you do it, Volcker was actually more involved.

[Volcker] was genuinely agreeing with the concept of an area in which you would operate. But, you see, he had the problem, also, that he was not prepared to commit himself to intervention. I suspect that Baker and Volcker, who were quiet in much of the discussion, were waiting to see how it was coming out to see if it was acceptable, and [they] weren't going to force the pace.[12]

The discussion got stuck on Balladur's proposition again and again. Eventually somebody asked, "Can someone explain to me what we are really talking about?" Jacques de Larosière spoke on behalf of Balladur, the Chairman. He "interpreted what everybody was saying and put shape to it," in the manner of a "perfect Cartesian expositor," said one admiring participant.[13] As if still donning his Managing Director's hat, de Larosière

---

12. Personal interview.

13. Personal interview.

clarified the arguments already presented. He said that they had determined to operate from the current rates—153.50 yen and 1.8250 deutsche marks— and that cross-rates would be used at the outset for the purpose of establishing the framework but not after that. As for the rules, they had decided to place margins on either side of the central rate, wherein intervention was not necessary but might be used for tactical reasons. Outside those margins were bands within which intervention was expected to take place. Intervention would not be regulated according to any strict rules; countries would never be obliged to intervene at all, nor would the magnitudes of intervention be specified. "We don't always have to intervene, but basically, if we're in either of those bands, we're trying to get the rates back towards the center." De Larosière's performance, considered brilliant by some, smelled "too French" to others.

Here entered Richard G. Darman. The US Deputy Secretary of the Treasury put forward his own interpretation of the general thrust of the discussion. He stressed consultation and cooperation over automaticity. In his view, each country would undertake to keep rates within a range of plus or minus 2.5 percent; a divergence beyond plus or minus 2.5 percent would signal the desirability of intervention. Cooperative efforts would be expected to intensify up to plus or minus 5 percent, beyond which the only obligation was consultation on policy adjustment and realignment.[14]

While de Larosière had basically used his interpretive powers to clarify the proposition already on the table, Darman's exposition seemed to "be fishing for something," recalled one European participant. Darman thought that de Larosière's interpretation was too rigid to accommodate everyone politically and that it was necessary to persuade the Japanese that the real targets were plus or minus 2.5 percent. At the same time, it was equally necessary to persuade the French and—more important—himself, that the plus or minus 5 percent range was now legitimized. This had to be managed carefully, however, so as not to make the Germans think that it was a whole new system or one that was too constraining. Darman's exercise, then, was motivated essentially by political considerations: by rewording, he sought to make the propositions more palatable to everyone.

The Germans continued to resist. Pöhl refused to talk about specific figures, making this quite clear to the others. Although he said that he would go along with de Larosière's exposition, which had actually been made partly in percentage and partly in numerical terms, he insisted that he would not be tied to this formulation, adding that he accepted it as a good working basis for the operation, but that the operation had to be settled by the central bankers day by day on the spot, and that he was not

---

14. Personal interview.

going to be bound. Gradually "people realized that what Pöhl was saying verbally seemed quite different from the others, but in fact, was not really different in substance."[15]

The explanations of de Larosière and Darman did not budge Miyazawa. His bottom line was 150—the number he had tried hard to defend in his talks with Baker in January. Miyazawa emphasized once again his political difficulties back home, which made a ceiling as high as 145 and a floor as low as 160–165 unacceptable. The others, however, were not willing to accept his numbers. The West German position was that exchange rate arrangements should reflect the market sentiment and that establishing an exchange rate baseline arbitrarily would distort the market. Although a month earlier Baker had promised to defend the yen–dollar rate at about 150, he now chipped in to suggest a ceiling of 140 yen, a level above even the 5 percent band.

In the final hour of the Louvre dinner, de Larosière and Darman worked together to give final shape to a joint proposal. Two specified midpoint rates were agreed: 1.8250 deutsche marks to the dollar and 153.50 yen to the dollar; plus or minus 2.5 percent was determined as a first line of defense for mutual intervention on a voluntary basis, while at 5 percent consultation on policy adjustment was to be obligatory; between these limits of 2.5 percent to 5 percent, intervention efforts were expected to intensify. All the agreements were to be kept strictly confidential and were provisional until the Washington G-5 meeting in April.

Then Balladur intervened. He said that it was all entirely acceptable with one exception. He wanted a discussion of the position of the franc in this arrangement, proposing that they establish the central rate of the French franc against the dollar in terms of the level of the deutsche mark against the dollar. Lawson then said that as far as the pound sterling was concerned, he reckoned that it was a bit weaker than it ought to have been because of declining oil prices, and therefore, he wanted to operate within a slightly skewed range—that is, with the sterling's midpoint a bit above where it was. He carefully refrained from defining exactly where that point was and nobody objected. Lawson was trying to do exactly what Miyazawa had attempted to do without success—to move the midpoint from previously agreed levels, except that Lawson wanted the midpoint higher and Miyazawa wanted it lower. As one participant put it, Miyazawa "couldn't find a way to reconcile the use of 'around the current levels' with asymmetry: He was unlucky. Nigel Lawson got away with it." The reason was quite simple. "Sterling wasn't their main interest. The midpoint of deutsche mark–dollar

---

15. Interview of a participant with the author.

and yen–dollar, that was all Jim Baker was interested in; it was all Miyazawa was interested in," said a European deputy.[16]

The Politics of Intervention

The ministers and governors did not stop after resolving the range issues, but delved into the modalities of intervention in a manner similar to that at the Plaza. The United States proposed establishing a "war chest" of $4 billion to last until the next G-5 meeting. "Americans were starting to get itchy about how much they were to commit themselves to spend," recalled a European participant. Miyazawa favored massive intervention. The Europeans argued once again that the scale did not matter but the impact on the markets did. Miyazawa was reminded by a European that markets functioned like a black hole in the cosmos and sucked in everything—all the intervention reserves. Agreement on a total amount of $4 billion was reached relatively smoothly, with again the assignment of roughly a third of the amount of intervention each to the United States, Japan, and Europe. The intervention period was to last until the next G-5 meeting in early April.

The discussion then focused on the amount of intervention needed to defend the floor of the dollar. Miyazawa alone expressed concern over the need to defend the dollar ceiling. He tried not to commit himself to defend the ceiling because he felt that it was too high. The other participants took note, deciding to discuss whether to move the ceiling of the yen–dollar rate in the near future, but the precipitous appreciation of the yen after mid-March obviated further discussion.

During the first five weeks after the Louvre meetings, however, the dollar remained relatively stable against the yen and strengthened against the deutsche mark and other European currencies. Evidently, the communiqué's statements gave confidence to the exchange markets, putting upward pressure on the dollar and the pound, currencies with relatively high interest rates. In February and early March, the dollar rose against the deutsche mark, and sterling rose against all major currencies.

On March 11, the dollar reached 1.8745 deutsche marks, prompting US monetary authorities to sell $30 million against marks, since the upper "margin" of 1.8706 deutsche marks to the dollar had been agreed on at the Louvre. It was the first demonstration of the US monetary authorities' commitment to defense of the range. Currency dealers believed the intervention to have been much larger than it actually was and saw it as a signal

---

16. Personal interview.

that major central banks would, as the Louvre Accord provided, now intervene to maintain the dollar at its current level. Feeling protected from a higher dollar, the market—which had expected the dollar to decline in the long run anyway—backed off from dollar bidding.[17]

After mid-March, trade problems weakened the confidence of investors in the dollar, and it began to fall. The market perceived Japan to be making too little progress in reducing its trade surplus, with the government entangled in tax reform debate, and its pledges in Paris to boost domestic demand appearing to have stalled. On March 23, the dollar moved below the 150 yen threshold, activating stop-loss orders and triggering heavy dollar sales by Japanese investment houses, insurance companies, and corporations. American sanctions against $300 million worth of Japanese products for the violation of a semiconductor agreement on March 27 fueled protectionist fears in the United States, putting further pressure on the dollar.

Trade issues, especially protectionism, were the main cause of the market's nervousness over the dollar. US retaliation against the Japanese for their market restriction on semiconductors was followed on April 29 by the passage in the House of the Gephardt amendment to the pending trade bill, which restricted imports from countries defined as having "excessive trade surpluses" with the United States. This caused a massive sale of dollars in world currency markets.

In Japan, defense of the 150 yen was a political imperative. Under strong pressure from the Ministry of Finance, the Bank of Japan bought dollars in record amounts throughout the spring of 1987. Japan does not release precise intervention data, but estimates are that during the first quarter of 1987, the BOJ conducted market operations totalling $16 billion. US monetary authorities also took note of the dollar's dip to under 150 yen. Between March 23 and April 6, the New York Federal Reserve Bank's open market desk bought dollars against yen daily, for a total of about $3 billion. The operations were coordinated with the BOJ and several European central banks. By the end of March, the dollar had settled at around 147 yen.

Market participants then began to look anxiously toward the April G-7 meeting in Washington, to be held on the periphery of the semiannual World Bank–International Monetary Fund (IMF) meetings, for signs that the finance ministers were committed to exchange rate stability.

At the Washington meeting, Miyazawa was again isolated. By that time, the yen had appreciated 7 percent above the baseline (thus, outside of the 5 percent range), in spite of the mutual intervention described above. For a while, he attempted to win agreement to get the yen–dollar rate back to the Louvre baseline, but he again faced European opposition. The European

---

17. *Federal Reserve Bank of New York Quarterly Review* 12 (Spring 1987): 6.

representatives claimed that the yen deserved to appreciate more than the deutsche mark. Besides that, they cautioned that they "would lose all credibility with the markets if they tried to do that and spend a huge amount of money in getting the yen back, getting nowhere themselves."[18]

Miyazawa was forced to accept Baker's suggestion to rebase the yen against the dollar at the previous night's level. The yen–dollar rate on April 6 was 146, with a 2.5 percent margin of 142.43–149.65 and a 5 percent band of 139.04–153.30. Miyazawa was thus assured by the others that 150 was still broadly within the range.

In the meeting, Baker expressed concern about the fall of the dollar "more alarmingly than ever before in the whole series of G-5 meetings."[19] At the same time, he blamed the West Germans for their lack of intervention after the Louvre, adding that the United States should not carry a disproportionate share of the burden, since US monetary authorities were not in a position to hold huge amounts of yen and deutsche marks to sell in intervention operations.[20] He also proposed that Europeans commit themselves to intervention to defend the yen–dollar range, and intervention volume was raised to $15 billion, with one-third still allotted to each of the three poles, which was to continue until the "war chest" was empty.

In the end the G-7 reaffirmed their commitment to stabilize the dollar, and Japan pledged to propose an "urgent" stimulus package of 5 trillion yen ($34 billion) later in April. At that point, however, the Japanese package was only a proposal by the LDP. West Germany offered no stimulus measures, for Stoltenberg asserted that West Germany had reached "the limit of its growth potential."[21] The United States made its familiar pledge to work to reduce its budget deficit.

Baker called the meeting "quite successful" and the proposed Japanese package "quite meaningful."[22] To the markets, however, the April G-7 meeting appeared to yield no new substantive policy initiatives. Coupled with the discouragingly small improvement in the February trade figures, announced April 14, sentiment toward the dollar remained bearish. The G-7 communiqué "was conspicuous for omitting any specific, significant actions to support the dollar," said James S. Vick, Vice President and Senior Corporate Trader at Manufacturers Hanover Trust Company. By this omis-

---

18. Comment by a European participant to the author.

19. Interview of participants with the author.

20. Nonetheless, there were some instances when US monetary authorities held deutsche marks in the portfolio. For instance, according to one currency specialist, Beryl Sprinkel gave permission to have $2–3 billion in reserves in 1983.

21. *Wall Street Journal*, 9 April 1987.

22. *New York Times*, 9 April 1987.

sion, the countries "seemed to be accepting the current level of the dollar and the downward direction," he said.[23] He was right. At the April meeting the G-7 only approved the new rate "around the most current levels," without adjusting macroeconomic policies.

Two days after the meeting, the dollar fell to 144.20 yen. As it continued to fall in the following days, the United States conducted market operations in coordination with operations by the BOJ and European central banks. On three of the nine business days between April 7 and April 17, the US desk purchased $532 million against the yen.

American officials began right after the meeting to step up their public warnings about the dangers of the falling dollar. Volcker, who had been in the past worried about a dollar free fall, cautioned a Senate banking subcommittee on April 7 that "further sizable depreciation of the dollar could well be counterproductive." He added that "what we need now, instead of more depreciation, is action here and abroad to carry through on those other methods needed to support growth and adjustment—specifically action to reduce the budget deficit here and to provide stimulus abroad."[24] The deep concern over the possible free fall of the dollar was now fully shared by Volcker and Baker.

As the dollar continued to drop throughout April, Baker now tried to "talk it up." In a speech to the Japan Society on April 15, he warned of the dangers of the dollar's fall:

Let me make one point clear: A further decline of the dollar against the other main non-dollar currencies could very well be counterproductive to our goal of higher growth in those countries. Thus, we fully intend to continue to cooperate closely to foster stability of exchange rates.[25]

By the last week in April, the dollar again came under strong selling pressure, as Japan appeared unlikely to pass an expansionary budget and US–Japan trade negotiations faltered.

Under these conditions, the dollar fell below 140 yen, dipping to a 40-year low of 137.25 on April 27. Against European currencies, the dollar declined below 1.8 deutsche marks, at one point trading as low as 1.7710 deutsche marks. From February through the end of April, the dollar had declined 3 7/8 percent on a trade-weighted basis against all G-10 currencies.[26]

---

23. *Wall Street Journal,* 10 April 1987.

24. *New York Times,* 8 April 1987.

25. James A. Baker III, remarks at the Annual Dinner of the Japan Society, New York, 15 April 1987.

26. *Federal Reserve Bank of New York Quarterly Review* 12 (Spring 1987): 7.

During the same period, total US intervention equaled $4.0636 billion of purchases, and $30 million of sales. According to the New York Federal Reserve Bank, the Bank of Japan, Bundesbank, and other European central banks bought dollars in "extraordinary" amounts during the period in support of agreements made in Paris in February and at the Washington G-7 in April.[27] While the scale of intervention following the Plaza meeting had been less than half of the agreed amount, intervention after the Louvre exceeded it.

Despite such heavy operations, the Japanese were troubled with what they perceived to be only lukewarm efforts by US monetary authorities to uphold the dollar. In late April in Washington, Prime Minister Yasuhiro Nakasone hinted to Reagan and Baker that he was dissatisfied with US currency stabilization efforts. Baker shot back that the United States intervention had exceeded $5 billion since January, an unusually large amount by US standards.

Some MOF officials were also unhappy that West Germany intervened even less than France, Great Britain, and Italy—only $750 million during the three-month period following the Paris talks.[28] The Bundesbank intervened little because it feared that massive intervention to prop up the dollar would swell West Germany's currency reserves and create excessive liquidity. Unlike the yen, the deutsche mark ended April at nearly the same level as during the Paris meetings.

When West Germany did attempt to intervene, it found itself with insufficient yen in its foreign reserves to sell in the currency market. In the past, German operations usually involved the buying or selling of dollars, its main reserve currency. The Bundesbank therefore agreed to sell special drawing rights (SDRs) to the Bank of Japan (BOJ) in return for yen, which it then sold in the currency market. This transaction between the BOJ and the Bundesbank was agreed on at the Bank of International Settlements (BIS) meeting in Basel on April 13 as a part of the swap-line pact in which the BOJ offered to provide yen as a "war chest" to the European central banks.[29] German comments suggested it was they who initiated the transaction. "We intervened because our Japanese friends [in the BOJ] thought it useful that we enter the market," a Bundesbank official said later. "We offered them a plan."[30]

To the Japanese, the intervention demonstrated the good intentions of

---

27. Ibid.

28. The figure of $750 million was provided to the author by an official of the Bundesbank in mid-June 1987.

29. *Asahi Shimbun,* 28 April 1987.

30. Personal interview.

the West Germans and awakened them to the notion that other countries besides the United States and Japan might contribute to currency stabilization. The BOJ later reciprocated by selling deutsche marks in the Tokyo market in tandem with the Federal Reserve Board when the West German currency was under upward pressure in late April.[31]

It should be noted that not all central bank intervention was motivated to defend the Louvre Accord. Some European countries, in particular, took advantage of the relative strength of their currencies against the deutsche mark, the dollar, or both, to replenish official reserves by buying dollars.[32] Later in June, a Bundesbank official commented on this dollar "buying spree." "They like to buy dollars in order to increase their reserves. It's voluntary. The British bought more than $10 billion. The Japanese $15 billion. Even Sweden bought $3 billion. France and Italy, too. They love it."[33] In 1987, central banks reportedly bought about $140 billion of dollar assets.[34]

Fiscal Policy in Motion

The ministers and central bank governors at the Louvre had keenly realized that any further decline of the dollar would be counterproductive. To stabilize currencies, as well as to correct external imbalances, they finally declared that fiscal policy coordination was urgently needed. The agreement of the Bonn government to a tax cut did not produce any noticeable effect on growth in West Germany, and the US administration failed to cut the budget deficit substantially. However, the Louvre Accord at last propelled changes in Japanese fiscal policy to boost domestic demand.

When there had been little real improvement in the US trade deficit by early 1987, newspaper articles criticizing Treasury Secretary Baker began to appear. The sharply lower dollar was supposed to turn the trade numbers around, but the numbers were not improving. The stock and bond markets registered sharp declines. The once overwhelming confidence in Baker, both at home and abroad, began to wane.

Having attacked the trade deficit with exchange rate adjustments for a year and a half, Baker now pressed harder the demand side of the trade equation. West Germany and Japan must expand internally to absorb more

---

31. *Asahi Shimbun,* 27 April 1987.

32. *Federal Reserve Bank of New York Quarterly Review* 12 (Spring 1987): 8.

33. Personal interview.

34. Pierre Lanquetin, President of the Swiss National Bank, statement reprinted in the *Journal of Commerce,* 22 February 1988.

of the world's exports, he said. Their surpluses were unsustainable. In testimony at a congressional hearing in late January, Baker appeared to be losing patience with America's trading partners. "All we're asking," Baker said, "is that the other major industrial countries of the world do whatever they can, both fiscal and monetary, to permit their economies to grow as much as they can, consistent with the gains that the world has made against inflation."[35]

American disappointment with Japan's and West Germany's fiscal measures intensified by early 1987. In late December 1986 a senior Treasury official stated that the US administration was disappointed with what it considered a lack of effort by Japan and West Germany to spur their internal economies, referring specifically to the "lack of growth element" in the Japanese budget.[36] This official, like another, hinted that unless the two countries stimulated their economies, the dollar would have to fall further, destabilizing the already volatile markets.

Japan

The Treasury Secretary was particularly upset with Japan's FY 1987 budget that raised government spending a minuscule $77 million to $338.1 billion (160 yen = $1), a 0.02 percent increase in nominal terms over FY 1986 and the smallest spending increase in 32 years. Miyazawa was well aware the budget would be sharply criticized in the United States, but it had been drawn up in the summer of 1986 just before his appointment as Finance Minister, and he was obligated to support it.

Miyazawa instead attempted to push another supplementary budget through the Diet, which was no easy task. First, he had to be extremely cautious not to invite unwittingly the opposition parties to exploit the situation by demanding a total revision of the original 1987 budget. The opposition parties might argue that since the supplementary budget was proposed so early in the budget season, there was still time to fashion a completely new budget. Second, he faced formidable opposition in the Ministry of Finance, which was doggedly trying to reduce the budget deficit, and from Nakasone himself, who had built much of his economic platform on fiscal consolidation—a contingency plan to redress the budget deficit hemorrhage. Miyazawa could expect little help from the Keidanren, Japan's premier business lobby, because the Nakasone-MOF alliance had co-opted

---

35. James A. Baker III, statement to the Joint Economic Committee, US Congress, 30 January 1987.

36. *Asahi Shimbun,* 23 December 1986, evening edition.

many of its most important senior members. In the fall of 1986, Miyazawa had managed to push through the Diet a supplementary budget, totalling 3.6 trillion yen. The resistance was more formidable this time.

Baker was disappointed not only with the meager Japanese budget—the first supplementary budget had provided little stimulus to the economy—but also with important aspects of the Nakasone Cabinet's tax reform plan. The tax plan, representing the first major overhaul of the Japanese tax code in 16 years, won approval from the LDP's Tax System Commission in October 1986. The package included tax cuts for both individuals and corporations. The number of taxable income brackets would be reduced from the current 15 to 6 in two years, and marginal rates in all brackets would be lowered in two steps. To recover revenue lost from the tax cuts, the Tax System Commission approved a 5 percent sales tax that would include service transactions and take effect 1 January 1988.

The Japanese government stressed that the tax reform package would add vitality to the economy, but the US administration was skeptical. The administration was particularly upset with the sales tax provision, which it felt would retard the domestic economy and limit consumption, which needed to be promoted, at a time when the high yen was already slowing growth in the export sector. To many in the administration, the sales tax appeared to offset the stimulus achieved from the income tax cuts, rendering the total package a wash. According to a well-placed Treasury official, the Treasury's internal projection for the net positive growth from the tax proposal was a scant 0.1 percent of GNP, a figure the official called "pathetic."[37] He warned that under the current conditions in Japan, the yen might have to appreciate further.

At the Louvre meeting, Miyazawa noted the strong resistance to the sales tax among the opposition parties as well as some LDP members and suggested that the sales tax provision might not even pass in the Diet in the spring. One participant in the meeting said he hoped it would not pass and asked Miyazawa what would happen if it did not. In that case, Miyazawa responded, the government would be forced to issue government bonds to compensate for the loss of revenue. Another participant commented that that would be better, prompting Miyazawa to chide his colleagues for making "unfinance minister-like comments."

Miyazawa, a Keynesian, did not try to hide his own criticism of the austere Japanese budget and fiscal policies of the Nakasone-MOF alliance generally. Indeed, Miyazawa enlisted foreign pressure in an alliance with domestic expansionists to advance his stimulative policies. In the face of heavy criticism when the yen began to appreciate steeply a month after the

---

37. *Asahi Shimbun*, 23 December 1986.

Accord, he managed to make a commitment of a 5 trillion yen fiscal package at the Washington G-5 meeting in April. Although the package was not approved until late spring, it originated to a certain degree, in Japan's Louvre Accord pledge that a "comprehensive economic program will be prepared after the approval of the 1987 budget by the Diet, so as to stimulate domestic demand, with the prevailing economic situation duly taken into account." It was later increased to 6 trillion yen at the Venice Summit.

West Germany

In Germany, the tax issue was tangled in the coalition politics of the CDU-CSU and FDP alliance. In June 1985, the Kohl government had enacted tax legislation to reduce personal income taxes by 10.9 billion deutsche marks in 1986 and 8.5 billion deutsche marks in 1988, and had outlined a plan to enact a 44 billion deutsche mark tax cut in 1990. Because the Kohl government wanted to cut back the revenue loss from 44 billion deutsche marks to 25 billion deutsche marks, it proposed to raise 19 billion deutsche marks by closing tax loopholes, raising some consumer taxes, and cutting state subsidies.

As the general election of 25 January 1987 approached, the tax issue became a serious stumbling block in the coalition bargaining. Until they were agreed, the Germans could offer no major stimulus packages to boost demand. As one German official put it later, "We need a majority before we commit to other countries. We don't want to commit ourselves like Nakasone or Miyazawa and find ourselves unable to deliver."[38]

The FDP, buoyed by pressure from the United States for more drastic tax cuts, lobbied heavily for further reforms—specifically a tax reduction on top earners (then at 56 percent) and small businesses, the bastion of FDP support. Otto Lambsdorff, a former Economics Minister and economic spokesman for the FDP, called for sizable cuts that would take effect in 1987. In addition, doubting the Kohl government's forecast of 2.5 percent GNP growth for 1987, the FDP urged more stimulative policies. (Later a Bonn official expressed bafflement at the FDP's criticism of the forecast: "I should point out that in the German government, it is the Ministry of Economics, headed by the FDP Chairman Martin Bangemann, that is responsible for economic forecasting.") To compensate for its recommended cuts, it drew up a list of 21 billion deutsche marks' worth of subsidies that could be abolished.

The Christian Democrats were split over who should benefit from tax

---

38. Personal interview.

cuts. The party's "social wing," which had resisted a cut for the top bracket, called instead for more tax exemptions. Fearful that supporting a cut in the top tax rate would weaken their support among working-class voters, shown to be waning in the January 25 election, Norbert Blum, the CDU's Labor Minister, and Heiner Geissler, its General Secretary, voiced public opposition to cutting the top rate. More conservative Christian Democrats resisted tax reduction because they felt it would swell government deficits and lead to higher inflation. Finance Minister Stoltenberg had for a long time tied his support of tax reform to balancing the budget. The CSU, the CDU's Bavarian sister party, distrusted tax reform that threatened to eliminate farm subsidies.

To enact tax reform, the government needed majority support not only in the Bundestag [the lower house of parliament], but also in the Bundesrat [the upper house]. The Bundesrat would be likely to obstruct tax reduction regardless of the party in control because tax cuts signify a loss of revenue for the *laender*. In five *laender*, the SPD, which opposed tax cuts for top earners, held the majority of elected seats.[39] In the regions where the CDU held power, the southern high-tech belt around Stuttgart and Baden-Württemberg, there was strong resistance to the elimination of subsidies that would accompany tax reform. Because of the sensitivity of the issue, the Kohl government wanted to delay any decision on how to raise revenue to pay for the cuts until after the elections in five *laender* in the summer of 1987.

The January 25 Bundestag elections strengthened the hand of the FDP in its drive to enact tax cuts and tax reform. While the CDU-CSU maintained their control, their voting share dropped from 48.8 percent to 44.3 percent in 1983, while the FDP's share of votes rose from 7.0 percent to 9.1 percent. Consequently, the FDP and others in favor of an early tax cut and tax reform found themselves with new leverage in postelection intragovernment bargaining. This was the background of West German tax politics in January 1987. At the Louvre, four weeks after the election, Stoltenberg agreed to "frontload" 5.2 billion deutsche marks of the 1990 tax cut to 1988. A few days later, the coalition agreed to a comprehensive tax reform package scheduled to take effect in 1990.

The tax cut measures proved to be too modest. The West German economy grew by a disappointing 1.7 percent in 1987, according to the Organization for Economic Cooperation and Development (OECD). The October stock market crash precipitated support for stimulus policies, while political storm clouds were gathering around increases in the budget deficit. The slow pace

---

39. By the end of 1986, Bavaria, Baden-Württemberg, Rhineland-Palatinate, Lower Saxony, and Schleswig-Holstein were basically controlled by the CDU, while the SPD controlled the other *laender*, alone or in coalition.

and incremental nature of fiscal policy formation in West Germany continued to frustrate the United States and the others. At the Louvre, when Stoltenberg had tried to assure them that the West German economy would start to gather speed in April—"after slower growth in the winter due to cold weather"—he was instantly pelted with critical questions by Baker and Lawson. Concern about the weakness of growth in the economy contributed to the precariousness of the whole policy coordination effort after the Louvre.

Beyond the Louvre Accord

By the time of the Louvre meeting, the realization was growing among the Americans and the French that their interests and objectives had come more into line. A Treasury official went so far as to describe the situation as a "French–American alliance." True, Baker and Darman did not discuss their reference range concept in explicit terms. They took care not to give the impression that they were trying to sell the target zone idea.

Baker remained noncommittal whenever target zones were mentioned by the French in all of the G-5 meetings, from the Plaza to the Louvre. To a French proposal for target zones offered at the Plaza, for example, Baker simply pronounced the idea "unrealistic." When Balladur mentioned the subject during the September 1986 G-5 meeting, he reiterated his opposition. Even at the Louvre, when the Americans were "fishing for something," they played their cards carefully, listening rather than speaking up. They avoided molding the product in ideological terms even though they had been quietly investigating currency stability plans based on the range principle since April 1985, several months before the Plaza meeting.

The Washington G-5 meeting in April 1985, the first such session that Baker and Darman attended as full participants, was a learning process that would influence the US Plaza strategy. One participant recalled how the US strategy was born:

These guys are all hypocritical . . . Here are all of these people totally opposed to targets. Of course except for the French. And they want to pick up exact numbers. I mean very specific—decimal points! So I recognized right away the obvious—that the thing to do was not to argue this issue on the level of ideology but just come up with a practical operating system that had a different character and keep on saying that we didn't have any target zone system—we could say that later.[40]

Darman particularly was drawn to a target zone concept from the outset. When he was invited to a small luncheon meeting in May 1985 at the

---

40. Interview of US Treasury official with the author.

Institute for International Economics in Washington, bastion of target zoners such as C. Fred Bergsten and John Williamson, he surprised the other participants with his keen interest in target zones. In Darman's opinion, however, their concept of target zone was too narrow. "I really think that you have a better chance of getting it if it is tied to a broader political mechanism and tied to a broader range of policy variables. Don't peg it all on exchange rates," he said. He even suggested that they were not ambitious enough. "I think you can get them faster if you start there than if you start where you are."

He knew that American supply-siders would be favorably disposed to a new move if they interpreted it as a step toward a gold standard and he hoped that, if the liberals like the Institute specialists would also be inclined to a target-zone currency stabilization mechanism, the Treasury would have a sufficient base of support, on both the right and the left, to back it. Darman kept his ambitions quiet, and the United States remained officially opposed to target zones.

The French were first to sense a subtle shift in the US stance. A French participant at the Louvre recalled an episode during the IMF–World Bank meetings in Seoul, two weeks after the Plaza, that suggested American sympathy for limited currency ranges. During a discussion among the G-5, French Finance Minister Pierre Bérégovoy passed a note to Baker, who was sitting next to him, which said, "the Plaza looks like it was an agreement for a reference zone." Baker read the note and scribbled a reply. "Reference zone, no. Reference range, yes." The French were heartened to know that the United States was leaning toward some kind of range system and dared to push their position further, although the French had to guess what Baker really meant by making a distinction between zone and range.[41]

French Director of the Treasury Daniel Lebegue had elaborated a target-zone system in late 1985, anticipating that it could influence American policy planners. In the proposal entitled "Reforming the International Monetary System," he stressed first that the primary aim of the French proposal was to restore exchange rates to their rightful eminence in economic policy decision making. He recognized the recent change of atmosphere with regard to currency stabilization: "The idea is less provocative today than it was a few months ago."

---

41. Later a Reagan administration official explained Baker's intention in the following way. "The word 'target zone' had sort of developed a bad name as far as the Germans, the British, and the Japanese were concerned, and as far as some elements of the United States were concerned. There are all sorts of variations of target-zone proposals. Some are too rigid. And it was the rigid target-zone proposals that most people opposed.... If you didn't use the term you might be able to convince people that very, very flexible and broad—if you want to use that term—ranges should be something different from zones. And you could generate more support."

Lebegue suggested that the policy of "frank discussions" on the "right level" for exchange rates within the EMS should also be followed by the larger countries. He proposed a gradualist approach toward exchange rate stability among the "biggest countries." First, in the most preliminary stage as soon as exchange rates deviated significantly from set ranges, the situation would be analyzed. The ranges should be kept confidential initially and made public only at some later date. Next, more restrictive measures designed to ensure adherence to the reference zones would come into play. After a gradual process lasting as long as necessary it would be desirable to institutionalize the mechanism. The aim here was not to create an overly rigid system; it was always possible to modify the set, he argued.

Lebegue proposed a tentative reference zone of 5–10 percent on either side of a central value, within which "in all likelihood, a good many theoretical computations would produce exchange rate values. . . . A sound dose of empiricism ought also to preside over the fixing of the initial zones."[42] He insisted further that the main problem was not whether monetary authorities could effectively guide or counteract movements of the market. "[T]hat is not the main problem. The lesson of the last few years is that the markets cannot function properly without points by which to take their bearings, and that is what the reference zones would provide." He also identified volatile markets and high interest rates as destabilizing forces that could be controlled through "improved concertation" around the reference zone.[43]

On the occasion of a private international monetary conference in February 1986, Lebegue had exchanged views with Charles Dallara, Deputy Assistant Secretary of the Treasury.[44] Treasury officialdom had opposed target zones and Dallara had been known to the French as a "hard liner." To Lebegue's surprise, Dallara seemed receptive to the French idea, but he became convinced that the French should be prepared to accept a more pragmatic version of a target-zone system.

Incidentally, the conference yielded an interesting by-product. Jean Michel Charpin, the Director of the Centre d'Etudes Prospectives et d'Informations Internationales, the institution that cohosted the conference, suggested to Lebegue that the French replace the term target zone (*zone de cible*), which

---

42. Daniel Lebegue, "Reforming the International Monetary System," *Economie Prospective Internationale* (Paris: Centre d'Etudes Prospectives et d' Informations Internationales), 24 November 1985.

43. Ibid.

44. According to a participant at the conference on the International Monetary System, 6-8 February 1986 (Paris: Centre d' Etudes Prospectives et d' Informations Internationales and the Institute for International Economics).

in French has a militaristic connotation and sounded too harsh. Soon after, the French Finance Ministry, at Lebegue's suggestion, decided to abandon *zone de cible* and replace it with the less combative expression, *zone de référence*. Again at the Louvre, "we were very careful not to use provocative language," confided a French participant.

With the support of Dallara and the Treasury staff, Darman concluded that an adjustable target zone, one that still relies on the fundamentals, not intervention, as a first step was sensible and possible. In a private memo to Baker, Darman sounded out his proposal for a band on the order of 10–15 percent on either side of the central value, stating that the numbers were not analytically derived. The Darman memo, which was drafted in April 1985, also included an indicator mechanism, policy coordination, and intervention strategy—in short, the essence of the new policy initiatives of the Baker Treasury from the Plaza to the Louvre.

In the United States, Beryl Sprinkel, Chairman of the Council of Economic Advisors (CEA), suspected that the Plaza strategy had somehow evolved into a target-zone system, which Baker directly denied. As was seen in discussing US domestic politics in Chapter 3, Secretary of State George P. Shultz did not support the intervention strategy nor any idea of fixing the exchange rate. Baker and Darman never openly endorsed currency zones, ranges, or any other such system. The suspicion grew that the indicator system put forward at the Tokyo Summit was a target-zone system in disguise. Baker's growing prestige after the Plaza meeting and Tokyo Summit, enhanced by Volcker's support for him, virtually silenced the more ideological "floaters."

Like Baker, Volcker has not endorsed a target-zone system, especially since he became Chairman of the Federal Reserve Board, but "he has never been a big fan of floating exchange rates," a close friend confirmed. Volcker's philosophy on the international monetary regime was most lucidly articulated in his memorable lecture in England on 9 November 1978, several days after the announcement of the Carter administration's dollar-rescue package. In the lecture, Volcker, then President of the Federal Reserve Bank of New York, basically supported the "practical choice to work ahead within the broad framework of a floating system," although he stressed that "freely floating exchange rates, instead of delivering on the promise of more autonomy for domestic monetary or other policies, can greatly complicate domestic economic management."[45]

In his view, "a floating rate offers two enormous advantages in a world

---

45. Paul A. Volcker "The Political Economy of the Dollar," The Fred Hirsch Lectures, sponsored by the Fred Hirsch Memorial Committee, Warwick University (Coventry, England), 9 November 1978. Reprinted in the *Federal Reserve Board of New York Quarterly Review* 3 (Winter 1978–79): 1–12.

of uncertainty, and where more than one sovereignty is involved, it requires neither explicit international agreement nor a closely defined commitment to defend." For large countries, these advantages are likely to remain decisive. He cautioned, however, that "they do not negate the fact that, at some point, left to themselves the swings in market rates can become so large as to damage the growth and stability of countries with both depreciating and appreciating currencies." Nonetheless, he hesitated to espouse a new currency system. Instead, his approach was:

more in the nature of quiet mutual contingency planning. Clearer understanding of a few leading nations among themselves about what extremes of fluctuation are mutually tolerable, and which should be strongly resisted, would seem to me to enhance the prospect for effective domestic policy making, as well as lay a base for more stability in international markets.

After all, we have the example before us of even the largest country, the United States, finding that it had to care when it found its domestic policy undercut by extreme exchange rate movements—a lesson long ago learned in the United Kingdom. At the same time, a sense that extreme fluctuations will be resisted and reversed could help stabilize market expectations, and thus reduce the risk of those extreme fluctuations developing in the first place.[46]

Darman may well have interpreted Volcker's expression "quiet mutual contingency planning," and explicitly, his argument for "tolerating" some fluctuations while "resisting" others, as a suggestion for target zones, without actually calling it as such. Baker and Darman counted on Volcker's sharpened practical sense and aligned themselves with him for the creation of the reference range mechanism. Of course, a position in explicit support of target zones might have incited their numerous opponents within the administration and bureaucracy. At the Federal Reserve Board there was suspicion over a target-zone system on the grounds that it might be vulnerable to the "increased possibility of politicians' interference."[47] Later in 1987, after the stock market crash, opponents immediately jumped on Baker and demanded that the Louvre Accord be scrapped.[48] Sprinkel tried to exploit the situation to undercut the Louvre Accord when on November 19, as the Chairman of the Economic Policy Committee of the OECD, he included in the prestatement of the conclusion of the discussions to be released to the press that "the difficulty arises when the attempt is made to maintain

---

46. Ibid.

47. Comment by a senior official of the Federal Reserve Board to the author.

48. For an example, see William Niskanen, "A Lower Dollar vs. Recession," *New York Times,* 27 October 1987.

exchange rate levels not consistent with the fundamentals over a certain period of time," and criticized an attempt to "fix" the exchange rates. His maneuvers were promptly challenged by Takao Akabane, Vice Minister of Japan's Economic Planning Agency, who argued that to release Sprinkel's prestatement would give the impression to the public that the EPC would endorse an attempt to dump the Louvre Accord. Sprinkel backed off.[49]

Internationally, the mission was even more difficult. The West Germans and the Japanese were becoming ever more nervous about what they interpreted as a quite ambiguous American policy. And again, after the United States showed an interest in using the exchange rate as a key variable in a set of economic indicators, they tended to believe that the indicator system was a target-zone system "in sheep's clothing." This fear was particularly strong among Japanese officials. Nonetheless, they wanted to stabilize currencies, hoping above all to stop further appreciation of the yen. By the time of the Louvre, they had nearly capitulated to support of a range mechanism or any mechanism if it would brake the yen. Here ideological hostility to target zones was not primary. In West Germany, resistance to a target-zone system was strongest in the Bundesbank, where officials doubted its practicality and effectiveness. They did not believe that the government should have the power to interfere in monetary policy making by setting exchange rates. Bundesbank officials owed more allegiance to the market mechanism than to the politicians.

The preliminary search for a new international monetary regime was explored and attempted consciously and conceptually by Lebegue, Darman, and Volcker in the Plaza strategy. Their interests and perspectives were quite different, however. Lebegue's ideas were representative of mainstream French orthodoxy on target zones. Darman's strategy reflected the political necessity of the United States as a debtor nation to stabilize the dollar: together their ideas were the pillars of the policy coordination strategy. Volcker's pragmatism dictated the need for some "quiet mutual contingency planning." An intellectual confluence of these views helped to shape the Louvre Accord. Certainly economic forces in early 1987—a rapid fall of the dollar and rising interest rates—decisively pushed Baker into a currency stabilization arrangement and forced him to share Volcker's concern about the future of the dollar. Thus, the Louvre Accord was the product of ad hoc political imperatives and, above all, the political needs of the United States. Because of its ad hoc nature, the Louvre Accord had inherent weaknesses.

---

49. Interview of a member of the Japanese delegation with the author.

Conceptual Framework

An appraisal of the conceptual framework of the range system agreed upon at the Louvre yields seven key aspects. One, the ranges have not been announced. Two, the selection of the central values for the cross-rates was based on the exchange rate of the day before the meeting—153.50 yen to the dollar and 1.8250 deutsche marks to the dollar. Three is the width of the margin and band. Four, the margins and bands were designated in terms of nominal bilateral rates against the dollar rather than real effective exchange rates. Five, the arrangements were provisional—"until further notice." Six, intervention was on a consultative basis rather than an obligatory basis. Seven, the relation between the rebasing of the range and prespecified policy was not clearly defined.[50]

Confidentiality and Credibility

The discussions at the Louvre, particularly the Saturday G-5 meeting, were the most secretive since the Plaza meeting of September 1985. Japanese Finance Minister Kiichi Miyazawa appealed to his colleagues to maintain the confidentiality of the meeting, warning of politically embarrassing repercussions should its contents be leaked.

The ministers and central bank governors were careful not to release the numbers discussed in the meeting. Certainly they considered the explosive potential of the information. They feared the immediate reaction of the markets, which might prove too rigorous a test of the fragile commitments. Their concern was justified, given that the nature of the initial endeavor was to search for a new type of mechanism. The fact that it has been kept confidential indicates the experimental cast of the exercise and the conditional nature of the participants' commitments.

Confidentiality, coupled with the highly informal manner of the political consensus building over the working dinner meeting, contributed to the proliferation of interpretations of the agreement in the member countries. Both US and French officials believed that, once the system had been established for some time, the details could be published as part of a gradual process of institutionalization. Lawson, during the IMF–World Bank meetings in September 1987, divulged the nature of the arrangements, which surprised both the West Germans and the Japanese, leading them to suspect

---

50. On the policy implications of target zones, see John Williamson and Marcus H. Miller, *Targets and Indicators: A Blueprint for the International Coordination of Economic Policy*, POLICY ANALYSES IN INTERNATIONAL ECONOMICS 22 (Washington: Institute for International Economics, September 1987).

that Lawson was laying the groundwork for entry into the EMS, as well as serving as the mouthpiece for Baker.[51] But confidentiality had a drawback. "Remember, it was only dinner conversation," was the comment of one participant trying to play down the intensity of the agreement. Another participant said, "If there should be an agreement resulting from the dinner conversation, it must be Darman's concluding summary. At least nobody challenged it. But, if asked whether it was actually agreed or not, nobody forced the decision." Still others maintained that they had achieved a consensus on the conceptual framework as well as the actual ranges.

The divergent views on the intensity of the commitment were expressed in a Washington G-5 meeting in the fall of 1987. At that time Lawson suggested that if and when the time came to adjust a currency's value, the movement of its central rate should be confined within the existing ranges. This appears to have been an effort to formalize the range mechanism. The West Germans, however, did not support the idea of institutionalizing the Louvre system to that degree.[52] A West German participant recalled, "I was much astonished to hear that at the meeting." He complained that "Lawson gave the wrong impression that the whole process focused too much on the exchange rate."

Baseline

It is debatable whether it was optimal to position the baseline of the ranges on the spot exchange rate. It could legitimately be argued that the prevailing exchange rates did not represent any kind of fundamental equilibrium rates, given the enormity of the external imbalance between the United States and its trading partners. Therefore, any meaningful currency realignment was precluded. In fact, some economists did argue that the incorrect selection of the central rate was destined to undermine the Louvre Accord.

Another crucial point, however, is whether it would have been politically acceptable to establish a baseline of the dollar below the one agreed at the Louvre. The Japanese, particularly, would not have committed themselves to a higher level for the yen, and the West Germans would have vetoed it as well. Besides that, the ad hoc process deterred them from exploring more ambitious "equilibrium exchange rates." To avoid interminable discussion, they had no choice but to pick up the current level.

If in the future member countries expected that rebasing would be determined by the spot exchange rate, they would have an incentive to

---

51. *Financial Times*, 2 October 1987.

52. Ibid.

manipulate exchange rates before the next G-5 session in the hope of positioning their currencies more favorably in relation to the others. Doubts about the true intentions of the US administration were heard in other capitals when the officials started to talk down the dollar in early January. The Treasury's inquiry into the "rigging" of the yen–dollar rate by the Japanese Ministry of Finance before the Baker-Miyazawa Accord had illustrated the concern that the baseline rate could be manipulated. The crucial question involves US commitment to the baseline and range. The prospect of a unilateral move by the US administration to depreciate the dollar and hence to redraw the baseline whenever it finds it necessary unsettles its trading partners. When the United States once again allowed the dollar to decline after the October stock market crash, one exasperated senior official of the Japanese Ministry of Finance commented, "This is not a rebasement. It's a debasement. The United States, as a debtor nation, simply wants to keep debasing the dollar as long as the debtor status lasts." It was a telling comment. The fact that, at the Louvre, the United States had been compelled to negotiate a currency stability pact does not necessarily preclude the further debasing of its currency. In fact, the unilateral devaluation of the dollar after the October crash deepened anxiety among US trading partners over the sincerity of its commitment to the Louvre Accord. The United States continues to face a dilemma between the necessity of stabilizing the dollar and the intensified temptation to depreciate it.

Margins and Bands

Another important point is the width of the margin and band. Certainly a plus or minus 5 percent band cannot be called narrow when compared to the arrangements of Bretton Woods and EMS. It will be recalled, however, that Balladur's—and hence de Larosière's and Darman's—range of 2.5 and 5 percent, respectively, for margin and band was just half the range that Lebegue had proposed in his paper. It was also narrower than Darman's suggestion to Baker in his memo (5 percent and 7.5 percent). These narrower figures had already been aired among the G-5 deputies when Lebegue at one point put them on the table, although there was no substantive discussion of them. A narrower margin and band would more closely resemble a fixed exchange rate system. Certainly it matched the French position and strategy perfectly. A French participant later admitted that Balladur used the narrow range for this reason. It was an unmistakable political maneuver to make the new arrangement look like a target zone à la French. By dinnertime the French had become confident that they could sell the reference-range idea. It would have made a perfect finish for them if a narrower range were accepted.

Such an arrangement is less than resilient and likely to lose its credibility, for in general, the narrower the band, the more often realignment will be needed. Certainly the authors of the Accord realized the slim probability that the rates could be maintained within such a narrow range. They knew that the ranges would have to be rebased in the future, again confidentially. Had a disciplinary component been built into the accord, they would not have agreed to such narrow ranges. Related to the same point, they agreed that the arrangement would be effective only until the next G-5 meeting, less than two months away, a period during which they expected that the narrower range could hold. In other words, the narrowness of range also reflected the temporary nature of the agreement.

Another reason for the narrow band was political. As an American participant explained, the Japanese would have found wider ranges unacceptable because, given a central base of 153.50, a wider band would have raised the upper limit of the yen. Miyazawa's dogged insistence on 150 was politically motivated. Facing pressure in Japan to halt the rising yen, Miyazawa's overriding objective was to defend what one Japanese official called the "150 yen maginot line." He feared that a wider range would force Japan to accept a much higher yen for the margin and band. The narrow margins and bands proved ineffective, however, in the absence of significant policy adjustment.

Nominal Bilateral Exchange Rates

The thought of defining exchange rate relations in terms of the real exchange rate was explored at the deputy level in preparation for the Louvre meeting. It was also mentioned by a French participant at the working dinner but was promptly dismissed as "impractical." "From the standpoint of practitioners, exchange rates must be defined only in nominal terms. We were not to trace the past performance but to search for some practical guidelines for the present and the future actions," a participant explained.

Cross-rates were set in a "comprehensive way"—that is, with the dollar's bilateral exchange rates with all four currencies, although the mechanism rested essentially on two rates: the yen and the deutsche mark.

Provisional Arrangements

The participants basically agreed to continue the ranges until the next G-5 meeting—"on a six-week basis"—partly because they wanted to evaluate how pledges by Japan and West Germany on fiscal policy would be implemented before they deemed the ranges appropriate. Baker received the full support of the others when he emphasized the provisional nature of the Accord.

Since the Plaza meeting, policy coordination had been fashioned step by step, on an ad hoc basis. Most hoped that the process would become institutionalized, but with caution. As a first step they were content enough to agree to develop the institutional arrangements gradually, based on the range concept, however embryonic. Moreover, given the strong resistance of West Germany to a more rigid range mechanism, the only politically feasible choice was for provisional arrangement.

Nonobligatory Intervention

The Japanese, with huge foreign reserves and an inclination toward non-sterilization, preferred a more binding intervention commitment, while the Germans abhorred tying their hands to a compulsory mechanism. German cautiousness was based on the Bundesbank's fear of compromising its control over monetary policy and also on its resistance to intramarginal intervention within the EMS. Pöhl repeatedly stressed that intervention should not be obligatory and, with Volcker's support, his argument prevailed.

Interaction Mechanism or "Consultation"

Of all the weaknesses inherent in the Louvre mechanism, the failure to create interaction between realignment and domestic fiscal and monetary policy adjustment was the most crucial. The participants at the Louvre had assigned the deputies to flesh out the indicator mechanism further by the Venice Summit. Thanks largely to the resistance of Japan and West Germany, however, the indicator system was not implemented to the point where it would link exchange rate realignments to macroeconomic policy adjustment. There was still a perception that the United States had an incentive to talk down the dollar, which created a disincentive to stronger commitment to macroeconomic policy adjustment for the others. A senior US administration official explained that the reason they had to rebase the yen–dollar range in the spring of 1987 was the "market's judgment that Japan couldn't deliver on the fundamentals and had lost its credibility."[53] Shortly after the Washington meeting in April 1987, a high-ranking official of the Japanese Ministry of Finance ruefully commented that he could not comprehend how prospects for Japan to improve on the fundamentals could have changed in

---

53. Personal interview.

just over a month, particularly since Japan's fiscal stimulus package was likely to be a meaningful one. "When I learned that the yen–dollar rate had been rebased in Washington, I was so shocked that I almost fell from my chair. Miyazawa must have been electrified more than at the Louvre."[54]

Although it was reported later that year that Baker demanded the rebasing of the deutsche mark–dollar rate in his meeting with top West German monetary officials in Frankfurt on 19 October 1987, it was not rebased at the time. The de facto rebasing came in December 1987 when the G-7 ministers announced jointly that further dollar depreciation would be counterproductive. (On this point, a West German official emphasized that the December "rebasing" should be regarded as an "accepted present rate" *not* a rebasing. "All in all, that's what we have to accept. But it does not mean that it's an agreement."[55])

The ad hoc nature of the arrangement permitted the unilateral action on the part of the United States to rebase and served to undermine the mechanism. At the Louvre, they had agreed that they would consult on policy adjustments when the exchange rates reached the 5 percent band, but they had failed to specify any practical measures for how to do it. Later Balladur pointed out that "the Louvre Accord was a good agreement but it was never implemented fully. Who implemented what, how, how much, was not fully explored nor decided."[56]

Besides the conceptual difficulties, there was an important political problem: who won, and at whose expense? Although the French tried to keep a low profile, there was no denying that the Louvre represented a huge political boost to Balladur, Prime Minister Jacques Chirac's right-hand man. Of course, although nobody said that what they had produced looked like a target zone, the French have not missed any opportunity to portray it as such. The other participants, especially West Germany and Great Britain have been much alarmed at this perception and refused to recognize the arrangement as a new system. Furthermore, "We did not want France to declare a diplomatic triumph," said a European participant.[57]

When asked the reason for the "failure" of the Louvre Accord, a Federal Reserve Board official replied, "Baker did not have enough on the table." He was referring to the failure of fiscal policy coordination and Baker's inability to deliver any promise on what the President and the US Congress would do. The inability to coordinate fiscal policies had cast a dark shadow over the Plaza strategy from the start. The same was true at the Louvre.

---

54. Personal interview.

55. Personal interview.

56. Personal interview.

57. Personal interview.

Although Japan finally set in motion its fiscal policy adjustments, the United States and West Germany did not follow. Baker's pledge to reduce the US budget deficit did not bring forth any new fiscal policy initiative. Nervousness in the bond market caused prices to plummet two months after the Louvre. By autumn, Japanese institutional investors were scared away, their willingness to purchase Treasury bonds having declined, and stock markets plunged. The intensified concern over the US budget deficit thus strained monetary policy once again.

Equally important was the failure of the Louvre Accord to provide the accompanying monetary policy to defend the range mechanism. In the communiqué only Japan stated that its central bank would reduce its discount rate. West Germany simply pledged that "monetary policy will be directed at improving the condition for sustained economic growth while maintaining price stability." US monetary policy would "be consistent with economic expansion at a sustainable noninflationary pace"—a familiar refrain for inaction and nondirection. "Look at the Louvre communiqué, you'll never find 'coordination of monetary policy.' Never!" claimed one European central banker. "There is no indication whatsoever that they intend to coordinate monetary policies in order to obtain the relative stability in exchange rates that they declare is the objective."[58] An official of the Federal Reserve Board echoed that analysis, "We did not commit ourselves to any change of monetary policy at the Louvre. We started to think of defending the dollar seriously in the April–May crisis period, but not at the Louvre."[59]

At the Louvre meeting, Pöhl insisted even more emphatically than he had at the Plaza that the monetary policy operation, particularly the tactical ranges of intervention for day-to-day consultation, should be left to the central banks. De Larosière and even Lawson supported Pöhl. Baker's position was that US trading partners should keep interest rates low in relation to the US interest rate and the central banks should be encouraged to defend the agreed range by cooperative monetary policies and joint interventions. Volcker kept conspicuously quiet during the conversation. Volcker "obviously did not want to undermine the American position."[60]

At the Louvre, as in previous G-5 meetings, central bankers refrained from discussing how they would use monetary policy to support the commitments made. Accordingly, they did not elaborate on how to employ monetary policy, when needed, to maintain rates within the agreed ranges. It was left to the ad hoc manipulation of short-term interest rates by US

---

58. Personal interview.

59. Personal interview.

60. Comment by a participant to the author.

and Japanese monetary authorities in late April, partly to facilitate the May auction of Treasury bonds to Japanese investors. It was a short-lived operation, however. The Bank of Japan neutralized its actions, taking steps to raise interest rates after the Federal Reserve Board increased its discount rate in September 1987. The Bundesbank, ever fearful of a potential inflationary surge as a result of the intervention undertaken after the Louvre meeting, had already tightened monetary policy. The lack of monetary policy coordination to enforce the range mechanism made the Louvre Accord vulnerable to the markets' assault, which eventually culminated in the October crash. Later, a Reagan administration official attacked the Bundesbank's monetary policy:

[w]hat happened was that the Germans used it [monetary policy] for a while and then they started raising the interest rates, which was counterproductive to defending the ranges unless the United States raised its rates to keep the differential. The United States and Japan, in the aftermath of the Louvre, coordinated their monetary policies quite successfully. But the Bundesbank decided for domestic reasons to start to raise interest rates. And we needed to let them know that it was contrary to the spirit of the Louvre—that the United States was not going to follow their action because to do so would risk the possibility of recession in the United States.[61]

Before the G-7 announcement in December 1987, Balladur had insisted that currency stabilization depended on stronger, coordinated implementation of monetary policy, but the Group of Seven was unable to find an acceptable proposal for how to do this. The Louvre range agreement fell victim to the inaction both on fiscal and monetary policy coordination.

---

61. Personal interview.

◼ Lessons

By late 1987, the once trumpeted international policy coordination of the Plaza strategy was under heavy criticism in the G-5 countries. The stock market crash in October had exposed underlying weaknesses in the structure of the policy coordination process. Overwhelmed by the stock market meltdown, the Reagan administration held down interest rates and let the dollar fall once again, in apparent disregard of the spirit of the Louvre Accord. "So shocked was the US administration over the crisis, it did not give a damn about the Louvre for two weeks after the crash," commented one G-5 regular.[1] Martin Feldstein, former Chairman of the Council of Economic Advisors (CEA), declared that America should "explicitly but amicably abandon the policy of international policy coordination."[2]

For others, however, the crash served as convincing evidence of the need for policy coordination to deal with the roots of the crisis—unsustainable external imbalances among nations and excessive exchange rate volatility. The *Wall Street Journal* proposed that "international financial leaders start thinking of trying to forge out of this crisis a more permanent exchange-rate regime."[3]

Some participants have drawn lessons about policy coordination from the experience of the Plaza strategy. James A. Baker III, US Secretary of the Treasury said:

There is room for progress in economic policy coordination among the major industrialized countries and it takes constant care, attention and

---

1. Personal interview.

2. *Wall Street Journal,* 9 November 1987.

3. Editorial, *Wall Street Journal,* 20 October 1987. See also *Resolving the Global Economic Crisis: After Wall Street. A Statement by 33 Economists from 13 Countries,* Special Report 6 (Washington: Institute for International Economics, December 1987).

work . . . and the fact that you might not succeed, every time, in achieving optimum macroeconomic policy moves doesn't mean that you should stop trying to get those . . . The lesson is, keep after it [policy coordination]. Keep doing it.[4]

The lesson learned by Noboru Takeshita, Japanese Finance Minister at the Plaza meeting, was that "it's now clear you can't correct external imbalances just with currency adjustment. That's number one. Number two, you can't do that just with Japan's efforts. The United States has to deliver what it has promised."[5] To Paul Volcker, former Chairman of the Federal Reserve Board, the lesson was simple: "There was a lot of talk, but few actions."[6]

Some policymakers admitted candidly that they had to take their cue from the market. "The impact of market judgment is more powerful than many political leaders and economists had imagined," said David C. Mulford, Assistant Secretary for International Affairs of the US Treasury. The market, long sensing the inadequacy of policy coordination since the Plaza, passed its own judgment on Black Monday. According to Mulford, the market's message was clear:

Economic policy coordination among the major trading nations must continue to be strengthened and the needed adjustment within and among nations accelerated. World attention is now more clearly focused than ever before on the coordination process that emerged from the Plaza Agreement, the Tokyo Summit, and the Louvre Accord.[7]

Despite considerable sentiment in favor of greater policy coordination, the path leading to this goal is fraught with impediments. Already the Plaza process has witnessed how easily monetary policy can "uncoordinate." The indicator mechanism and the reference ranges of the Louvre Accord have undergone stringent tests. It remains to be seen how viable both mechanisms will prove in the future.

The immediate players—finance ministers and central bank governors—come and go. Thus, the future US administration may again be tempted to resort to a unilateral approach to the "world problem," just as Nixon, Carter, and Reagan have done at the outset of their respective administrations.[8]

---

4. Interview of James A. Baker III with the author.

5. Interview of Noboru Takeshita with the author.

6. Interview of Paul A. Volcker with the author.

7. David C. Mulford, remarks at the Asia/Pacific Capital Markets Conference, San Francisco, 17 November 1987.

8. C. Fred Bergsten, "America's Unilateralism," in C. Fred Bergsten, Etienne Davignon, and Isamu Miyazaki, *Conditions for Partnership in International Economic Management,* The Triangle Papers 32 (New York: Trilateral Commission, 1986), 3–5.

The increasingly ominous position of the United States as the world's largest debtor nation may strain the delicately spun arrangements resulting from the Plaza to Louvre period. Nationalistic and anti-American feelings that have been growing in both Japan and West Germany, partly in response to US protectionism, may retard or even halt the nascent process. Another collapse of financial markets, or global recession, could hurl the G-5 countries into turmoil, making accomplishments so far resemble the achievements of Sisyphus. Despite these obstacles to coordination, it remains an imperative.

The world economy has changed radically since the early 1970s, when the Bretton Woods system collapsed—so radically that no country, however great it may be, can afford to ignore the reverberating consequences of its domestic policies on the world economy, and hence, on its own vital interests. Each country must, therefore, be more dedicated to coordinating policies to ensure its economic security and the welfare of its citizens. Economic policy coordination for economic security must be on a par with issues of national security on the political agenda. The gap remaining between the reality of the "changed world economy"[9] on one hand and the myth of insulated sovereignty on the other must be narrowed further so that politicians, and the public as well, are forced to reconsider policies that may not be compatible and consistent with international responsibilities. Economic policy coordination among the most advanced industrial powers is a painful necessity with which each country must cope—painful because policymakers will no longer be able to apply the "one country capitalism" formula, nor will they be able to blame "externalities." Simply pointing an accusing finger at unpredictable markets will not suffice. It is imperative for countries to "develop a set of quite robust rules for national good behavior and the achievement of global objectives."[10]

Economic policy coordination initiated at the Plaza meeting should be studied critically as a possible model of success or failure for future policy coordination strategies. After all, the Plaza strategy was the first major venture to reform international economic policy making among the industrial countries since Bretton Woods fell apart, except for the brief experience of the 1978 Bonn Summit policy agreements. It was also the first critical response to the anarchy of the "nonsystem" of floating exchange rates, and represented a search for greater stability in the international monetary system.[11] Furthermore, it was an effort to enhance international surveillance

---

9. Peter F. Drucker, "The Changed World Economy," *Foreign Affairs* 64 (Spring 1986): 768–791.

10. Stephen Marris, "Managing the World Economy: Economics, Institutions, and Politics," Professor Dr. Gaston Eyskens Lecture, Katholiecke Universiteit (Leuven, Belgium), November 1986, 8–30.

11. On the word *nonsystem*, see John Williamson, "The Benefits and Costs of an

of national economic policies by combining into one framework the Group of Seven summit and the Group of Five—bringing together heads of state, finance ministers and central bank governors—thereby infusing the political will and weight of the highest authorities into the economic policy coordination mechanism. Inevitably, the process of increasing coordination will have to build upon the experience and the lessons from the latter half of the 1980s, particularly the G-5 strategy from the Plaza meeting of September 1985 to the Louvre meeting of February 1987.

It is certainly true that achievements during this period did not satisfy the expectations of the enthusiasts of more vigorous policy coordination. The critics of the Plaza strategy have cited numerous shortcomings, of which five are primary. The most frequently heard criticism is that so-called policy coordination is "just PR." In this view, the Plaza strategy does not represent a departure from previous efforts, and, in fact, there is nothing new in the G-5, which has existed since the early 1970s. To say that the Plaza turned a new leaf in policy coordination would be misleading at best, for it contained no innovation and no substance. The second criticism is that the sole purpose of the Plaza strategy was to "buy time." According to this view, its only success has been to stave off protectionist forces in the US Congress, with no achievements beyond that. The third criticism is that the Plaza strategy was basically an attempt by the US administration to cover up the failure of the Reagan miracle. International coordination was used to gloss over the administration's failures and distribute the blame for external imbalances among the G-5. The fourth is that "the road to hell is paved with good intentions." In other words, although the ministers and governors acted in good faith, the Plaza strategy actually made matters worse than they would otherwise have been because bad policies were made. Finally, some critics assert that the Plaza meeting itself was a "nonevent." There was simply no need for it: the dollar had already started to depreciate so there was no need to push it. If anything, intervention was counterproductive.

The view that the G-5 Plaza strategy was a publicity stunt is substantiated to some extent by the actions of the players themselves. The politicians tended to play up policy announcements, while career bureaucrats in the ministry of finance and central banks felt uncomfortable under the focus of public gaze and therefore objected to the publicization of policy making. Some would be insulted to hear that the Plaza G-5 had changed anything because they had been involved in G-5 policy coordination for a considerable time. Karl Otto Pöhl, President of the German Bundesbank, emphasized

International Monetary Nonsystem," in *Reflections on Jamaica,* by Edward M. Bernstein et al., Essays in International Finance, no. 115, Princeton University, April 1976.

this point: "Effective economic and monetary cooperation also occurs independent of the major well-established institutions, and did so long before the meeting at the Plaza Hotel in New York in 1985 became, as it were, synonymous with cooperation."[12] Pöhl did not hide his almost nostalgic longing for the "good old days" of the secretive "Library Group"—a forerunner of the current G-5—that was initiated in the White House Library by George P. Shultz, Helmut Schmidt, and Valéry Giscard d'Estaing in 1973. Pöhl remarked, "in retrospect, it seems to me that the informal character of those meetings . . . was highly conducive to the frank exchange of views within the group—and thus to the effectiveness of its work." Paul Volcker shared his colleague's uneasiness over the publicity and the over-expectations generated whenever the G-5 met. In congressional testimony given on 19 February 1987, just before the Louvre meeting, Volcker explained:

I don't like the feeling that we have to have emergency meetings. . . . I don't like to see those meetings become quite the event that they some-times have become recently. . . . I think that's a great mistake to feel that you can't meet without having a series of specific decisions.[13]

The same feeling is most strongly pronounced among the deputies of the finance ministers, who were previously accustomed to "running the house" themselves. Instead, during the Plaza to Louvre period, Baker and Darman took the lead in transforming the G-5 into a politically charged forum. But this is not to argue that the exercise was "just PR." In fact, the criticism of publicity during the period from Plaza to Louvre is overturned if the usefulness of its role is recognized. Publicity can be used to help achieve goals. In this case, public announcements gave strong cues to the markets and also helped to assure US citizens that the administration was indeed "doing something" about the trade problem.

The issue goes even deeper than PR; it is a question of competing political motivations within institutional arrangements. Whenever an attempt is made to change the political rules and shuffle institutional processes, the concern is who will win and who will lose from the redistribution of authority. Publicity heightens the awareness of change and may increase tensions within and among institutions. Furthermore, one must not lose sight of the political and economic objectives that motivated the process in

---

12. Karl Otto Pöhl, "You Can't Robotize Policymaking," *The International Economy* (Washington), October/November 1987: 20–26.

13. Paul A. Volcker, testimony before the US Senate Banking Committee, 19 February 1987.

the first place, despite the fact that the emphasis on publicity seems to have overshadowed the substance and to have created a dynamic of its own.

During this period all the G-5 governments shared an interest in combatting protectionist forces in the US Congress and, therefore, in "buying time." There is no denying that the containment of ubiquitous protectionist pressures, which were exacerbated by the overvalued dollar and the burgeoning US trade deficit, was the principal motivation for the intervention strategy initiated at the Plaza. Maintaining free trade should, therefore, be regarded not as a mere tactic to buy time, but as an objective in itself. Agreement on the need to alleviate trade problems, futhermore, led to greater cooperation on monetary policy. From this point of view, it was, to a large extent, a successful campaign. But it has evolved into much more: monetary policy coordination, an indicator mechanism, and a reference range approach.

Baker, of course, was interested in buying time because of the approaching election. A former senior administration official commented:

Jim Baker is a brilliant politician, and a politician is concerned only about reelection, not about policies. Jim Baker bought time to get by the next set of congressional elections. He really bought time until this Spring [of 1987]. That's what the Plaza Accord was all about.[14]

Baker's domestic political priorities notwithstanding, there is considerable evidence to suggest that the Plaza exercise was more than a strategy to buy time. At least from the US perspective, it was a strategy to combat protectionism in the Congress (short-term strategy), to maintain world economic growth by stimulating domestic demand in Japan and West Germany (medium-term strategy), and to ease the burden of debt service of the United States depreciating the dollar (long-term strategy).

Another, more forceful, criticism of the policy coordination process emphasizes the Reagan administration's ever present malaise—the budget deficit, a problem that continues to plague the G-5. According to this view, policy coordination was not the solution to this primary problem, but the G-5 countries "covered up" the issue to make it appear that there were other problems to be tackled.

The critics argue further that all participants, the US administration included, knew that US policies or "nonpolicies" were at the root of the enormous international imbalances. Nevertheless, the United States continued to urge West Germany and Japan to stimulate their economies to solve what was essentially a US problem. With the realization that the imbalances

---

14. Personal interview.

were generated by the United States in the first place, Baker's "aggressive bilateralism," used to pressure both West Germany and Japan, bred discontent and resentment in those countries. On the other hand, although policy coordination could have been approached differently, the process did yield positive results. After all, the US budget deficit was reduced by $70 billion in fiscal 1987. Given Reagan's intransigence on the budget and fiscal policy, the dollar depreciation policy was not so much a cover-up as it was a pragmatic response, and perhaps the only available tool to those who sought to redress the imbalance problem. It is evident from Baker and Darman's efforts that they viewed dollar depreciation as only a first step toward policy reform.

Closely related to the foregoing criticism is the one charging that the intentions of the participants, however good they may have been, were translated into inadequate policies. Criticisms of the validity and effectiveness of the Plaza strategy from this point of view encompass a range of questions involving monetary policy, fiscal policy, and exchange rate policy. Whether or not the participants chose the right combination of policies to achieve their legitimate goals is a question for further analysis. It must be noted, however, that decision making can happen only through a political process, both domestic and international. How this process is formed will determine the way specific policies are decided and consequently, how "the right combination of policies" can be chosen.

Finally, the view that the Plaza G-5 was in effect a nonevent attacks a crucial premise held by the proponents of policy coordination. The nonevent theory does not end at the Plaza, but applies to the Louvre as well. It can be argued that "if there wouldn't have been a need for a Plaza Agreement, perhaps there wouldn't be a need for a Louvre Agreement," as one European central banker contended.[15] Asserting that policy coordination was irrelevant, Martin Feldstein said, "I don't think anything much happened at the Plaza. So I guess from my perspective, the whole thing has been a mistake."[16] In an article for *Foreign Affairs,* he elaborated his views:

Although much has been said and written about that G-5 meeting, I believe that its significance in reducing the dollar has been greatly exaggerated. There is no doubt that it did initiate a temporary turning point in Japanese monetary policy; the Japanese government increased domestic interest rates with the aim of raising the value of the yen in an attempt to forestall support for anti-Japanese protectionist legislation that was then heating up in the Congress. But for West Germany and the other G-5

---

15. Personal interview.

16. Interview of Martin Feldstein with the author.

countries, the Plaza meeting was essentially a non-event, and even the change in Japanese monetary policy was soon abandoned.[17]

This view was expressed also by some of the G-5 officials. One high-ranking German official was just as frank:

To interpret the Plaza as a technical device, one could say in fact finance ministers and central banks already had the Plaza strategy. The dollar was coming down gradually. There was no need for the Plaza Agreement—for a staged theater.[18]

Another European official used the metaphor of a cowboy—a logical one whenever the tough guy at the top of the Treasury—a Connally or a Baker—happens to come from Texas:

A cowboy would not take his gun and shoot without any need because he knows it would cause a stampede.... The cattle were already moving in the right direction. Then Baker summoned the cowboys at the hotel and shot off his gun (and also some Japanese fireworks).[19]

It is arguable whether the Plaza action was necessary to keep "the cattle moving in the right direction." But without the coordination of exchange rate policy to manage currency realignment, a "stampede" might have ensued. At least some of the participants, central bankers, for the most part, endorsed the package at the Plaza with the feeling that, because the dollar was already on its way down, the announcement of calculated intervention might preempt a dangerous free fall or even obviate the need for intervention since the markets would be sure to respond to the announcement. Pöhl's suggestion at the Plaza that the participants be prepared to intervene in the opposite direction should the dollar decline too rapidly or too far reflected this sentiment. Their desire to make the decline of the dollar "manageable" and "orderly" was exemplified in both the secret nonpaper and the public announcement of the Plaza. Most of the participants, including a habitually critical Bundesbank official, now regard the dollar decline during the period as having been steady and smooth.

Some critics, such as Feldstein, enjoy forecasting the direction of the market with the strength of hindsight. But a senior US administration official asked whether these critics could have predicted the movement of

---

17. Martin Feldstein, "Correcting the Trade Deficit," *Foreign Affairs* 65 (Spring 1987): 799.

18. Personal interview.

19. Personal interview.

the dollar as it developed during the summer of 1985. There was a rebound of the dollar in midsummer, and even after the Plaza meeting, upward pressure on the dollar frequently canceled the effects of mutual intervention and did not subside easily, as was described in chapter 1.

In sum, it is fair to say that all these criticisms of the Plaza strategy involved a grain of truth, but none have been completely substantiated. The Plaza strategy was not simply a cosmetic operation, although it was an attempt to exploit what a senior Treasury official called "the financial market and the media market" to maximize the impact of the announcements. It was not just an attempt to buy time, even though time was needed to combat the protectionist forces in Congress and, possibly, to prevent a world recession that the lack of growth and domestic demand in G-5 countries might have caused.

The Plaza strategy was in part a way for the US administration to avoid an embarrassing declaration of the failure of Reaganomics. The Baker-Darman team did, however, acknowledge the gravity of the budget deficit and openly pledged to reduce it. Given the decline in US dominance over the world economic system, moreover, it was completely logical and necessary for the United States to ask its trading partners to share the burden of adjustment. It was therefore also indispensable for them to search for a new political process that would promote greater coordination.

Finally, policy coordination can be achieved only when there is a confluence of politics and markets. No matter how powerful the markets may be, they are unable by themselves to determine outcomes.

The Criteria of Policy Coordination

Any critical assessment of policy coordination must consider the broader historical and political context of growing economic interdependence, the search for a new international monetary regime after the experience of floating exchange rates, and the structural changes resulting from the erosion of American hegemony. Given the need for the major economic powers to continue to coordinate policy, moreover, the obvious question then becomes *what* should the objectives of policy coordination be and *how* can these objectives be accomplished? Before getting the details, however, it is necessary to clarify the concept of policy coordination. What constitutes policy coordination? How does policy coordination differ from policy cooperation? From consultation? From convergence?

According to Henry Wallich, a former governor of the Federal Reserve Board, "cooperation" covers a spectrum of arrangements, of which consultation lies at one end and coordination at the other. Consultation involves a lesser degree of commitment, usually signifying a mere exchange of information, whereas coordination requires greater commitment on the part of governments, occurring usually in situations in which policymakers are more sensitive to international pressures and the implications of their policies. Convergence describes the process whereby the policies and/or performance of countries become more similar. It should be noted that effective coordination of policies may or may not lead to convergence.[20]

Criteria for evaluating the Plaza strategy can be drawn from two aspects of coordination: substance and process. The substance of policy coordination should be appraised according to three criteria: (1) whether it promoted noninflationary growth and sustainable current balances, (2) whether it opened and liberalized world trade, and (3) whether it strengthened alliance management. With respect to the substance of policy coordination, it can be said that the Plaza strategy did not overcome three delays: the delay in cutting the US budget deficit, Japan's delay in opening markets, and West Germany and Japan's delay in stimulating domestic demand. Since mid-1987, however, partial rectification of these delays has been realized. The US budget deficit was reduced by $70 billion in 1987; Japan's domestic economy began to expand and imports of manufactured goods began to increase at a rapid pace, causing a noticeable reduction of the external imbalance. It is, however, still too early to tell whether the external imbalance of the United States has shrunk enough to reach a sustainable level. With regard to the liberalization of the world trading system, it should be pointed out that the Plaza strategy successfully contained US protectionist forces. It is hoped that Japan's new horizon of "growth from within" and as an "importing superpower" has advanced efforts to revitalize the world trading system. The slow pace of domestic demand expansion in West Germany and the lack of strong initiatives to promote a more open trading system continue to be a deterrent. Alliance management between the United States and its trading partners has been maintained regardless of some strains of the economic policy adjustments.

The process of the Plaza strategy can be analyzed according to four criteria: (1) whether it contributed to a broad consensus on analytical issues or a more practical approach to coping with the issues (ideology), (2) whether policy coordination exercised a systematic effect on markets, bringing about more effective management of them (markets), (3) whether it strengthened understanding among legitimate domestic groups that are involved in or have an interest in the process of international coordination and increased sensitivity to foster transnational cooperation among institutions and interest

---

20. Michael Artis and Sylvia Ostry, *International Economic Policy Coordination*, Chatham House Papers, no. 30 (London: Royal Institute for International Affairs, 1986), 21.

groups (politics), and (4) the extent to which the coordination process developed into a credible regime (system).[21]

Ideology: Analytical Impact

The importance of consensus on analytical issues varies according to economic circumstances and the ambitiousness of cooperation. Since the early 1980s, new interpretations of theory have proliferated, as evidenced by the advent of conservative governments that adhere to supply-side and monetarist policies, partly in response to unprecedented economic conditions, such as inflation with economic stagnation and interest rate volatility.

The erosion of Keynesianism and the lack of universal acceptance of rival theories have made dialogue among the policy planners more difficult on a theoretical basis. The most acute disagreement originating from theoretical divergence arose over interpretations of the determinants of the exchange rate. The encompassing nature of the dispute convinced scholars of international economy of the caliber of Richard Cooper that "until the analytical or theoretical framework of determining exchange rates is somehow put into place and a new theoretical consensus reestablished, it will be impossible to determine what exchange rates should be or how they can possibly be achieved." Cooper went so far as to say that "the current disarray among economists about positive propositions is the single most important, and in fact, the decisive barrier to effective policy coordination."[22]

Agreement on exchange rate policy alone is not a sufficient condition for convergence of economic policies or performance. Domestic monetary and fiscal policies will have extranational effects. Domestic economic policymaking has not been immune to dispute. For example, monetarists argue that demand management, calling upon both fiscal and monetary policy, will not have a noticeable effect on real variables, such as employment and income, on a medium- or long-term basis. Some go as far as to say that they do not have any effect on these variables even in the short run. Accordingly, what the government ought to do is to abandon discretionary fiscal policies and to aim exclusively at price stability.

This narrow form of monetarism has not lived up to the expectations of its proponents. Central bankers, after some trial and error, have concluded that strict adherence to a fixed money-supply target alone will not reduce

---

21. The author is indebted to C. Randall Henning for his insights in developing criteria for the analysis of the process of international economic policy coordination.

22. Richard Cooper (1985), quoted in Robert Gilpin, *The Political Economy of International Relations* (Princeton, NJ: Princeton University Press, 1987), 161.

inflationary expectations or inflation itself. They have come to realize also that money-supply targets, if not accompanied by exchange rate stability, will not achieve the basic objectives of growth and price stability, especially under the present circumstances, in which the demand for money has become more variable and less predictable.

In contrast to the emerging consensus on monetary policy, or more accurately, a consensus on what monetary policy should not be, positions on fiscal policy remain divergent. Three schools of thought that figure in the current political debate on fiscal policy in each of the three countries studied here can be categorized as Keynesian fiscal policy, neutral fiscal policy, and anti-Keynesian fiscal policy. Certainly this divergence of views on fiscal policy is wide enough to make macroeconomic policy coordination difficult to achieve even if it were intended.[23]

The extent to which differences in the analytical or the ideological framework block cooperation should not be overestimated, however. Differences in economic beliefs often mask conflicts of interest and often vanish when the conflicts of interest are accommodated.

It is also possible that differences in economic beliefs can mask conflicts of interest and contribute to cooperation at the same time. For example, divergent theoretical positions did not prevent most non-American G-5 policymakers from concluding that the US budget deficit was the root of the problem. International consensus is neither a necessary nor a sufficient condition for international coordination. In fact, the consensus on the need to reduce the US budget deficit was an insufficient condition for coordination. The question of consensus aside, ideology can be a crucial determinant of the course of policy coordination, as manifested in exchange rate and fiscal policy making in the United States.

Markets: Systematic Effects

Among the variables available for policy coordination, the exchange rate perhaps reflects most visibly the appraisal by the international markets of the economic fundamentals. Policy coordination presupposes management of market forces. Thus, the idea that policy coordination is the antithesis of the freely floating exchange rate mechanism is tested first and foremost by the stability and sustainability of currency relations in the markets. Paul Volcker pointed out the delicate relationship between the market and policy:

---

23. On the differing views of monetary and fiscal policies, see Marris, "Managing the World Economy," 47–52.

[i]f . . . markets come to believe exchange rate stability is not itself a significant policy objective, we should not be surprised that snowballing cumulative movements can develop that appear widely out of keeping with current balance-of-payments prospects or domestic price movements. At that point, freely floating exchange rates, instead of delivering on the promise of money autonomy for domestic monetary or other policies, can greatly complicate domestic economic management.[24]

In order to ensure the desired effect on the markets and manage the movement of the market, fiscal policy, monetary policy, and exchange rate policy must be interconnected and coordinated effectively.

It can be argued that the scope and magnitude of international policy coordination is limited in practice because of its subordination to national policy making. From the point of view of the individual country, the effect of its policies on its own economy is usually perceived to be greater than the potential effect on the economies of other countries; therefore, policymakers will consider what is advantageous to the national economy before considering the needs of the international economy.[25]

It is possible, however, that the growing interdependence of national economies magnifies the cross effects of policies among countries and the feedback to its own economy. Japanese Ministry of Finance theoretician Haruhiko Kuroda, for example, upholds the value of policy coordination by emphasizing the cross effects of policies.[26]

Recognition of the impact that the policies of one country will have on the economies of others is required to produce overall positive-sum results. Perhaps the most effective way of reducing the US trade deficit, for example, would be to induce a recession in the United States; likewise, unleashing high inflation might provoke reductions of the budget deficit. Obviously, whether or not these actions would be beneficial to the United States in the long run is not the only issue, for it is certain that such policies would have negative repercussions on the world economy.

Although shifts in economic power among nations have been expressed in terms similar to those used to describe the military balance, international economic policy making has more room for maneuverability than does

---

24. Paul A. Volcker, "The Political Economy of the Dollar," the Fred Hirsch Lectures, sponsored by the Fred Hirsch Memorial Committee, Warwick University (Coventry, England), 9 November 1978, reprinted in *Federal Reserve Bank of New York Quarterly Review* 3 (Winter 1978–79): 7.

25. See F. E. Kydland and E. C. Prescott, "Rules Rather than Discretion: The Inconsistency of Optimal Plans," *Journal of Political Economy* 85 (1977): 473–491.

26. Haruhiko Kuroda, "Keizai Kyocho Seisaku No Kanosei Ni Tsuite" (On the possibility of policy coordination), *Financial Review* (Tokyo: Financial and Monetary Research Institute, Ministry of Finance), March 1987.

military-strategic policy making, which is based essentially on zero-sum calculations. The innumerable economic interests and channels that combine countries into an integrated world economy increase the possibility for positive-sum results.

To summarize, it is crucial that international coordination of monetary policy, fiscal policy, or exchange rate policy should have a predictable effect on the course of national economies and must be consistent across policies so as to produce overall positive-sum effects.

Politics: Linkage, Pressures, and Coalition Building

Member countries are required to "strengthen legitimate domestic interests in the process of international cooperation and simultaneously strengthen international dimensions in the domestic political process."[27] This sort of delicate diplomacy requires the deft management of the players. Any political incentive that would advance this objective must be exploited fully. Any attempt to coordinate economic policies requires incentives strong enough to override the incentives for any one state to act unilaterally. Likewise, disincentives need to be strong enough to make the costs of defection appear higher than the benefits from coordination.

Mobilizing domestic support for international cooperation, creating controlled and timely pressure for policy change, and building international coalitions for policy coordination are critical tasks. The framers of the Plaza strategy were well aware of the need for linkage and pressure building. "If the system is to work, the participants will of their own volition take external consideration into account in formulating their domestic economic policies," emphasized Baker.[28] The extent to which any single country can coordinate its economic policy with others depends of course on its ability or willingness to assess the implications of its domestic economic policy on them. The indicator mechanism was in fact designed to facilitate this process and institutionalize it.

One means of pursuing policy coordination is through coalition building across national borders. It is sometimes true that a government can make its domestic program more palatable to the domestic body politic if it is part of a grander, internationally coordinated effort. Furthermore, governments have historically used outward-looking initiatives to divert public attention away from domestic politics. This holds both for considerations

27. Marris, "Managing the World Economy," 106.

28. James A. Baker III, remarks before the National Foreign Trade Council, 11 June 1986.

of a political and economic nature. For example, the Tripartite Monetary Agreement of 26 September 1936 was used by the French Popular Front to divert attention from devaluation of the French franc. By emphasizing international monetary stabilization, the Popular Front government "cloak[ed] its failure at achieving economic recovery and maintaining confidence in the franc."[29]

System: Confidence, Mechanism, and Regime

Policy coordination must be based on a working process that is institutionalized, and one that is considered credible by its participants. Furthermore, the initial ad hoc arrangement should be encouraged to develop gradually into an international regime.

Harvard University Professor Robert D. Putnam defines economic policy coordination as:

[T]he process by which national policies are adjusted to reduce the adverse consequences (or reinforce the positive consequences) that the policies of one or more states have on the welfare of other states, so that the national policies differ from those policies that would have been expected from purely national or autarkic policymaking.[30]

This type of cooperation contradicts the basic tenets of the neorealist school, which characterizes the international arena as a Hobbesian state of anarchy, wherein each state seeks to enhance its own power and prestige: "Public goods are under-supplied, public bads are over-supplied, and free-riders abound."[31] Under these assumptions, policy planners are under constant pressure to renege or cheat on their commitments. In theory, voluntary defection from commitment can be distinguished from involuntary, although it is sometimes difficult to discern the difference in practice. Variations of both kinds of defection occur in the international political economy "depending on the visibility and solemnity of the commitment, its verifiability, the frequency of dealing among the contracting parties, the value that they

---

29. Charles P. Kindleberger, *A Financial History of Western Europe* (London: Allen and Unwin, 1984), 397.

30. Robert D. Putnam, "Domestic Politics, International Economics, and Western Summitry, 1975–1986, or International Cooperation and the Logic of Two-Level Games," paper presented at the Annual Meeting of the American Political Science Association, Washington, 28–31 August 1986.

31. Bruno S. Frey, *International Political Economics* (New York: Basil Blackwell, 1984), chap. 7.

attribute to those other deals, and the number of other players."[32] Mutual confidence is essential to any credible process. The likelihood and nature of defection depends first on the nature of the membership and the degree of confidence among members; second, on the constraints that institutional structures place on the effective implementation of mechanisms; third, on the arrangements for burden sharing; and fourth, on how serious and binding each member judges the arrangements to be.

In order to deter defection, it is imperative to devise some mechanism to cover "the costs of negotiation . . . and also those of policing any agreement which is arrived at."[33] Costs are incurred through the process of negotiation and are typically distributed disproportionately as a result of unequal intercountry relationships and intracountry institutional relationships. Externalities resulting from decisions on economic policy create strong incentives for individual countries to "ride on the back" of others and to cheat on negotiated positions. Free riders or cheap riders can benefit from spillovers from other countries' policies without sharing the burden of implementing similar actions.

One rather primitive form of regulation is through peer pressure, taking advantage of the fact that states have an interest in maintaining a certain reputation. Peer pressure works best where the participants consist of a relatively small number of actors that share common interests. In general, consensus among players is more easily obtained in a small group also because the majority can more effectively pressure the minority—which may consist solely of a single actor.

The G-5 has evolved into a forum in which peer pressure is an important component. In the G-5, the small number of actors ensures that no one can escape from being directly and personally lambasted by the others, which increases pressure on each member country. On the other hand, institutional structures within each country may impede coordination efforts by increasing the likelihood of defection. Thus, any credible mechanism must combine balanced burden sharing with a genuine commitment from members.

To be durable and effective, the positive effects that may accrue from an ad hoc process of coordination must be accumulated and transformed into a permanent structure. Regulation of coordinated agreements takes a different form in a "nonsystem," such as that created by the floating exchange rate agreement, than in a formal system, such as the Bretton Woods regime of fixed exchange rates. The erosion of "law and order," apparent in the international monetary system since the demise of Bretton Woods and in the international trading system with the frequent disputes and exceptions

---

32. Putnam, "Domestic Politics," 15.

33. Artis and Ostry, *International Economic Policy Coordination*.

under the General Agreement on Tarriffs and Trade (GATT), has multiplied the incentives to cheat. Two examples are the "dirty float" of the late 1970s and the "Voluntary" Restraint Agreements of the 1980s.

The process by which the G-5 and G-7 operate is a substitute for a formal rule-binding regime. The costs are usually higher, when, as in this case, the players must continuously manage the process of policy coordination, than when the rules are clarifed and enforced by a permanent policing system that discouraged cheating.

Only a successful effort to build a solid international economic regime will enable effective coordination of policy in the long run. Coordination based on *process* can only succeed if it is accompanied by vision, and developed in the direction of creating a structure for such a regime. Of course, to be stable, any new regime should reflect the shifting balance of economic and political power.

From Plaza to Louvre: A Critical Appraisal

With the above criteria in mind, I shall examine Plaza strategy's potential and limitations as a model for policy coordination.

Ideology: Analytical Framework

Viewpoints diverged most noticeably around fiscal and exchange rate policies. While the Plaza meeting signaled a shift away from the hands-off policy that had characterized the Reagan administration's earlier position toward markets, it did almost nothing to lift the stalemate on fiscal policy. Differing assessments of the effects of fiscal policy were often heard throughout the entire Plaza strategy period.

Masaru Yoshitomi, a leading Japanese economist, argued that:

[A]s far as the fiscal policies are concerned, only US action can effectively influence its own current account deficit: even joint expansionary fiscal action by Japan and Germany has little effect on the US external account. This asymmetry stems from the sheer size of the US economy, the high import elasticity of US income, and the different composition of imports by commodity and region between the United States and Japan [and West Germany].[34]

---

34. Masaru Yoshitomi, "Growth Gaps, Exchange Rates and Asymmetry: Is it Possible to Unwind Current-Account Imbalances Without Fiscal Expansion in Japan?" in *Japan and the United States Today: Exchange Rates, Macroeconomic Policies, and Financial Market Innovations*, ed. Hugh T. Patrick and Ryuichiro Tachi (New York: Center on Japanese Economy and Business, Columbia University Graduate School of Business, 1986), 24.

Obviously, Yoshitomi's analysis, which is substantially the same as that of the Ministry of Finance, is at odds with that of the US Treasury Department.

The conflicting theoretical frameworks underlying fiscal policies—Keynesian, neutral, anti-Keynesian—among countries and among institutions within each country considerably handicapped adjustment efforts.

The rather hasty manner in which the Plaza was convened did not allow the participants time enough to explore the theoretical and analytical dimensions of the actions they advocated. Many aspects of the intervention scheme were discussed by the deputies during the weeks that led to the Plaza meeting, but the role of monetary policy in relation to exchange rate policy was not fully analyzed. At no time, for example, did they discuss whether the intervention should be sterilized or nonsterilized. In addition, no analysis was made of the potential impact of dollar depreciation on capital inflows into the United States. Quantitative targets of reducing imbalances were not even discussed. Baker had only believed that the decline of the dollar would reduce the US trade deficit quickly, albeit with some delay as a result of the J-curve effect.

The problem of differences in analytical framework was intimately linked with the ideological position of each country. The influence of ideology in economic policy coordination should not be underrated. It took almost five years for the United States to be emancipated—at least to some degree—from the confines of Reaganomics. Perhaps one of the reasons Baker did not select an economist for the post of Under Secretary of the Treasury after Beryl Sprinkel's departure was his aversion to ideological disputes, although certainly he wanted to prevent rivalry with his deputy, Richard G. Darman.

The United States deliberately camouflaged its shift in policy at the Plaza. There was no mention of intervention in the Plaza announcement. Since intervention might be interpreted as a radical departure from former policy, the Agreement read: "they stand ready to cooperate more closely to encourage this [some further orderly appreciation of the main nondollar currencies] when to do so would be helpful." The key phrase here was "cooperate more closely," which became synonymous with joint intervention.

The difficulty in describing what was actually conceived at the Louvre comes from the lack of qualifying language used in the communiqué and hence to the extent that ideology was defused. By avoiding ideologically charged code-words the participants were able to find common ground. The G-5 participants at the Louvre meeting, for example, avoided the expression "target zone," and even "reference zone," because all of them understood that any association with a particular ideological framework would endanger the prospect of reaching a consensus. As noted in the previous chapter, even French target zone diehards were careful not to adopt an ideological tone in the conversations at the Louvre.

Thus, despite the departure that it represented, the Louvre Accord was carefully left "unnamed." David C. Mulford testified to the Congress that the administration had "*refrained* from establishing a system of target zones," although he did not say that it *opposed* establishing target zones.[35] One US administration official explained, "I thought we could codify a system by the time of the Louvre—I very much hoped that we could. I was disappointed that we didn't. . . . We could have brought the system to an agreed, not just a behavioral change, but a rhetorical change that people wouldn't be ashamed of, that people would say, look, here's the new system and we're proud of it."[36]

Fiscal policy also was a highly charged ideological issue. Throughout the period, both Japan and West Germany persistently resisted US attempts to exact concrete commitments on fiscal stimulus. Both countries tactfully alluded to the "nightmare" of their experience with the "locomotive" strategy of the late 1970s to legitimize their resistance to changing their fiscal policies. They also exploited the Reagan administration's own rhetoric against Democratic "pump-priming" fiscal policies to counter US pressure.

The challenge of defusing ideology was demonstrated by the remarks of an official from the Japanese Ministry of International Trade and Industry (MITI) in a meeting of the Organization for Economic Cooperation and Development (OECD) in April 1987. When asked about the apparent contradiction between the Japanese government's announcement of boosting domestic demand while pledging to continue fiscal consolidation, Hajime Tamura answered, "We're not going to wave the flag of fiscal consolidation, nor are we going to drop it, either. No. We're not going to make it half-mast because that would mean death. All we will do is just to wrap it around the pole for a while."[37]

One of the achievements of the Plaza strategy was to forge consensus despite the existence of ideological obstacles. By decodifying phrases identified with particular ideologies into more neutral ones, the participants were able to negotiate on a pragmatic level.

Markets: Systematic Effects

Two months after the stock market crash of October 1987, a White House official confessed that he had realized now that "the performance of policy

---

35. David C. Mulford, testimony before the Subcommittee on International Finance and Monetary Policy, US Senate Committee on Banking, Housing, and Urban Affairs, 26 March 1987.

36. Personal interview.

37. Interview of Hajime Tamura with the author.

coordination is rated by the market every moment. We face opinion polls by the markets every day. Now the markets are expecting too much." Policy coordination was an effort of the policymakers to manage the markets, whether through the exchange rate, the interest rate, or unemployment. Although most of the participants regard the decline of the dollar since the Plaza meeting as "basically smooth and orderly," until, at least, the Louvre meeting, it is still too early to conclude that the markets are managed better now than they were three years ago.

The most violent reactions in the currency market occurred whenever it sensed a stall or a lack of coordination in policy adjustment efforts. This happened in January and February 1986, because of the discrepancy between monetary and exchange rate policy attributed to a disagreement between Baker and Volcker; in May and June 1986, because of uncoordinated monetary policies; in January and February 1987, because of the resistance of West Germany to stimulation of its economy and the US unilateral "talk down" policy; and finally, in November and December 1987, because of the market crash and the perceived abandonment of the Louvre Accord.

In fact, the fragility of policy coordination became apparent almost as soon as the Plaza strategy was initiated. The blitz of joint intervention masked inaction on fiscal policy, for one thing. The strategy served as an excuse to forestall action on fiscal policy adjustment, particularly in Japan. Ministry of Finance officials anticipated that the intervention strategy would deflect foreign and domestic pressure for a fiscal stimulus package by making the exchange rate relationship more acceptable to foreigners. For them, it was a choice of the lesser evil. Furthermore, the impact of exchange rate realignment could be limited by the inaction or noncoordination of other policies. In the United States, the sense of urgency to reduce the budget deficit was somewhat dissipated by currency realignment. In effect, immobility of fiscal policy sabotaged the Plaza Agreement.

Politics: Linkage, Pressures, Coalition Building

The conscious effort to incorporate international considerations into the domestic political process and build a domestic constituency for international cooperation took various forms during the period of the Plaza strategy. The most important linkage was the joint effort to combat protectionist pressures, especially those in the US Congress, by the member countries.

Linkage

Deep concern over protectionism in the Congress was transmitted by Baker to the other G-5 ministers. In fact, Baker and Darman had at first considered holding the Plaza meeting just before Labor Day to coincide with the return of Congress. They had wanted to maximize the impact of policy coordination to head off protectionist forces in the United States. The date of the Plaza meeting was set in such a way as to send a clear message to the Congress, and to a great extent, it was a successful strategy.

Formulators of monetary policy were forced to be acutely sensitive to political considerations throughout the Plaza–Louvre period. As part of the coordination process, the politicians basically got from the central bank governors what they wanted—lower interest rates. Politicians are seldom reluctant to coordinate policy internationally when the circumstances warrant it. In this respect, the analysis of the Plaza strategy as a cover for failures of Reaganomics is more plausible to the extent that the argument is amended to recognize the political incentives it had for the other participants.

In the United States, the Plaza strategy can be said to have provided the Reagan administration with a convenient smoke screen. Instead of admitting that faulty US policies had created the high dollar, the administration was able to project a positive, strong image by spearheading an initiative to correct economic imbalances. Noticeably missing in the Plaza announcement was direct mention of dollar depreciation, for that would have implied weakness in the international position of the United States. Instead, policy coordination was to achieve "further orderly appreciation of the main nondollar currencies against the dollar," thereby implying that adjustment was required by the nondollar currencies. As one Treasury official later affirmed, "no country ever likes to say that their currency will depreciate. That's a direct talking down. A government does not make statements that imply weakness. A government always refers to the other countries that need appreciation."[38] In Japan, the Ministry of Finance bureaucracy sought a yen–dollar realignment through intervention, first out of fear that the lopsided currency relationship would inevitably lead to an explosion of protectionist forces in the United States, and second, out of hope that currency alignment could deflect US pressure for Japan to pursue expansionist fiscal policies. West German officials wanted to engineer a "soft landing" of the dollar to maintain EMS parities. The French saw in policy coordination an opportunity to advance their target zone concept and, more importantly, to enhance growth prospects in Germany through international pressure. Thus, "cover-up" tactics have benefited all participants.

---

38. Personal interview.

From the point of view of America's trading partners, the first term of the Reagan administration served as an example of "belligerent noncooperation" in economic policy making. When, finally, the United States made overtures signaling its willingness to cooperate, the alleged abandonment of its unilateralist leanings was insufficient to lure trading partners to the bargaining table. Given its past record, the administration had to offer them some sort of political collateral to ensure that reciprocal and symmetrical gains, or at least some advantage would result from coordination. The trading partners had cause to believe, in fact, that "coordination" was an attempt to reassert American strength by tipping the scales, and producing one-sided gains for the United States.

Such considerations were at the core of the dispute over the indicator system, since it appeared that the mechanism would help that country in a deficit position, namely, the United States, while placing the burden of adjustment on the surplus countries, namely, West Germany and Japan. German policymakers, however, reconsidered the indicator proposal in the light of the possibility that through this mechanism concerted pressure could be applied to US policymakers, to deter them from future unilateralism, at the very least. A Ministry of Finance official in Bonn confided that the "discretionary edge" was Bonn's bottom line in endorsing the indicator system concept. Thus, the potential value of the indicator mechanism lay in its ability to divide the adjustment burden more equitably among both deficit and surplus countries.

The crucial question is, was the potential value of international coordination realized? More specifically, to what extent did foreign pressure tilt US domestic policy making—especially fiscal policy making—toward consideration of international implications?

US policymakers thought foreign pressure had a marginal effect; as one explained, "[foreign pressure] is not all that consequential to the United States ... although we ... thought that ... such pressure would not be a bad thing."[39]

With respect to fiscal policy—reducing the budget deficit substantially— Baker failed to strengthen the international perspective in the domestic political process. Senator Bob Packwood (R-OR) could not recall any direct pressure from Baker to cut the budget deficit out of the external considerations, although he praised Baker's efforts overall.[40] On the contrary, Baker tried impatiently to use the indicator mechanism to strengthen domestic

---

39. Interview of US administration official with the author.

40. Personal interview.

interests in the international forum—for example, to call for more growth in Japan and West Germany to take up the slack in the United States. Eventually the administration acknowledged the reality of the painfully slow pace of change in the fiscal policy of its trading partners. One senior administration official drew an instructive lesson:

We could yell and scream all day and all night about the importance of changing the U.S. savings rate and in our culture that isn't going to change fast. The public savings rate can change but the private savings rate is not going to change fast in the U.S., just the way it's not going to change all that fast in Japan. And it's not going to change all that fast in Germany. The Germans are not going to stop worrying about inflation overnight. These things are deeply set.[41]

Coalition Building

Compared to the 1978 Bonn Summit "locomotive" strategy, cross-country coalition building in support of fiscal expansionism between the United States and both Japan and West Germany was quite limited during the Plaza strategy.[42] Various institutions and interest groups in West Germany and Japan had an incentive to build a coalition with the Baker Treasury: for example, to press for more far-reaching changes in fiscal policy. For example, Hajime Tamura's meeting with Baker on the fringes of the OECD ministerial meeting in April 1987 was a deliberate effort on the part of MITI—traditionally fiscal expansionist—to build pressure against the Ministry of Finance (MOF). An informal alliance of interests between Baker and Tamura reinforced the position of each, specificially giving domestic credibility to Tamura's argument for fiscal stimulus measures—that is, the 6 trillion yen stimulus package in the spring.

Another example of cross-national coalition building occurred when the US Treasury and the Federal Reserve Board urged the Bank of Japan to lower the discount rate in late July 1986 in conjunction with a Fed rate cut. The MOF temporarily refused to give intervention reserves to the central bank to force it to cut the discount rate. In doing so, they anticipated that the markets would drive the yen higher and force the BOJ, which was prevented from intervening, to lower the rate.

This kind of coalition building did not have its counterpart between

---

41. Personal interview.

42. On the transnational coalition building in the Bonn Summit of 1978, see Robert D. Putnam and C. Randall Henning, *The Bonn Summit of 1978: How Does International Economic Policy Coordination Actually Work?* Brookings Discussion Papers in International Economics, no. 53 (Washington: Brookings Institution, October 1986).

Japanese and West German interests. The asymmetry is a result not only of the negative experience of the Bonn Summit, but also because Bonn and Tokyo calculated that concerted pressure on Washington would only invite retaliation by Washington toward each of their governments. Nakasone's explanation to Reagan at the 1987 Venice Summit as to why its allies were unable to force the United States to cut its budget deficit (see the introduction) indicates the unwillingness of America's trading partners to pressure it; in general. In all, coalition strategy during the Plaza–Louvre period was used sporadically and did not produce durable alliances of nations.

System: Confidence, Mechanism, Regime

David C. Mulford, Assistant Secretary of the Treasury for International Affairs, reviewed policy coordination in the following manner:

Economic policy coordination among the major industrial nations has been a growing force in the international arena since the Plaza Accord in 1985. It was given a formal framework at the Tokyo Summit last year, and following a year of discussions and negotiations, was reaffirmed as a working process at the Venice Summit in June. All seven summit countries have agreed to the new arrangements for economic policy coordination, including the use of economic indicators and regular consultations on our respective economic policies and on exchange rates.[43]

In the Treasury's view, the indicator mechanism and the Louvre Accord were both components of the "working process" of economic policy coordination. Implicitly underlying the Plaza strategy was the assumption of some of its framers—the Americans first and foremost—that it was an attempt to institutionalize the process of policy coordination with regard to both macroeconomic and exchange rate policies. Yet the so-called "process" proved rife with miscommunication, misunderstanding, mistrust, and voluntary or involuntary defection. To assess the efficacy of the process, the criteria for the system should be looked at from the perspective of confidence, mechanism, and regime.

Confidence

Inability or unwillingness to defend the pledged range of exchange rates, "talk-down" and "talk-up" tactics, and the ad hoc nature of intervention policies often strained the process of confidence building.

---

43. David Mulford, "US-Japan Relations: The View from the Treasury," address at the Japan Society, New York, 16 July 1987.

During most of the period, the Reagan administration's talk-down tactics had pernicious effects on the other countries, especially Japan and West Germany. Typical of the approach were Baker's public remarks on the desirability of a further decline of the dollar in the spring of 1986 and a senior official's hints in early 1987 that the dollar would depreciate further. Baker later admitted that he had deliberately "talked down" at least until the spring of 1986.[44] Later a senior administration official criticized Baker's talk-down manipulation while referring to the October crash:

Where he got in trouble was by going public with the use of that [dollar devaluation] lever. Because it helped get the market out of control, the market said, "wait a minute. If he is using it as a lever and we believe it won't work, there is no bottom. If he *isn't* using it as a lever, and he just actually wants the dollar to go down, then there is no stability. And if he isn't clear whether it is one or the other of those, then he doesn't understand his own system and his own business and we'll have a problem of confidence, which should make the dollar go down."[45]

The unilateralist nature of talk-down politics drew objections from Japan and West Germany. Neither was consulted in advance of the US administration's informal sanction of dollar depreciation. Both Miyazawa and Stoltenberg had occasion to caution Baker on the powerful effects of public announcements. Miyazawa was particularly hard hit by Baker's remarks, which seemed to contradict all his assurances to the Japanese public that he and Baker had agreed to stabilize currencies at prevailing rates in late October 1986. Serious doubts about the solemnity of the administration's "moral" commitments to stabilize currencies were not restricted to Japan, but echoed throughout Europe as well.

On the other hand, US monetary authorities had ample reason to question Japan's commitment, as was described in chapter 7. The yen's abrupt drop to 162–163 yen to the dollar just before the October communiqué deepened the Treasury's suspicion that it had been manipulated by the Ministry of Finance and resurrected memories of the MOF's "dirty-float" practices to keep the yen from rising during the mid-1970s. The Treasury Department was also disturbed about Japan's attempt to portray the communiqué agreement as a definitive commitment from the United States to defend the yen–dollar level at 160 and objected to Japanese talk-up-the-dollar campaigns.

---

44. Baker told the Joint Economic Committee on 30 January 1987. "The last time we were talking down the dollar was when I testified up here in the cycle of testimony at this time last year. And if you'll go back and check the record, you'll see that we have not said for over a year that we would not be displeased to see a further orderly, gentle decline of the dollar. So I'd like to put those remarks to rest."

45. Personal interview.

Furthermore, both the 1986 supplementary budget and the increase in government expenditure for fiscal 1987 proved on closer examination to contain little substance. As a consequence, Mulford warned Japan that "the unfortunate result is a decline in Japan's credibility in the outside world and a rise in 'Japan bashing' behavior even by the sympathetic observers who have concluded perhaps that continued threats and pressures are the only way to get needed results."[46]

Bilateral deals, represented by the October joint communiqué and its reaffirmation in January, lacked the degree of discipline necessary for maintaining a stable yen–dollar relation. This shortcoming as well as the manipulative objectives of aggressive bilateralism, once perceived, dashed all illusions of a potential G-2 economic condominium and prompted Miyazawa to play on the G-5 level.

In fact, even after the Louvre Accord had dissipated some of the suspicion and misunderstanding between the countries by clarifying the working rules, the G-5 decision to change the rules six weeks later left Japanese officials to question the capability of the agreement to stand up against market forces. During the April G-5 meeting, the central yen–dollar rate was rebased, notwithstanding the argument of Miyazawa, who insisted that the reference ranges agreed upon at the Louvre should be defended. The rebasing, in effect, simply ratified what had already transpired in the markets. Miyazawa was then forced to "pay" for the rebasing with more fiscal stimulus.

Mechanism

The Plaza strategy introduced into the coordination process an element of mechanism building. At the Plaza meeting, the efforts of the finance ministers to coopt central bankers into the coordination process created a channel for mutual consultation. At the Tokyo Summit in May 1986 the G-7 finance ministers' forum was created to combine the political will and authority of the highest political offices with policy coordination. The reference-range concept at the Louvre was adopted to stabilize currencies "around the current levels."

The process of building a mechanism was not a smooth one because of obstacles in its way. First there were the problems of membership in the club. Here, international politics were involved. Second, domestic political and institutional resistance to the creation of a new mechanism was strong. Next, the assignment of the burden of adjustment and its incorporation in

---

46. David C. Mulford, "US-Japan Relations."

the mechanism posed thorny problems. Finally, the countries had varying degrees of commitment to the adopted mechanism.

Membership

The G-5 Plaza strategy from the beginning was propelled by the political dynamics of inclusion and exclusion from the club. Manipulations of the Group of Two (the United States and Japan), the Group of Three (the United States, Japan, and West Germany), and even the Group of One (the United States alone) affected the behavior of the actors during the process of policy coordination. In such close-knit clubs, nobody wants to be left out. The United States still tends to act as if it alone can determine the rules of the game—for example, with solo discount rate cuts during the summer of 1986 and unilateral depreciation of the dollar—although since the adoption of the Plaza strategy, this unilateral approach has been less prominent.

The Baker Treasury pursued a G-2 strategy in order to induce West Germany to go along. It was received warmly in Japan, where it satisfied a nascent yearning for a greater presence in the international arena. Eventually, as a result of indirect pressure exerted on West Germany by the G-2, the deal that was agreed on first by the G-2—a stimulus package in exchange for currency stability—served as the basis for the Louvre Accord.

On the other hand, political regrouping had negative effects as well. The G-2, in fact, was shortly perceived as the Japan card, held exclusively by the Americans and used to make demands on the Japanese in apparent contradiction to Baker's commitment to stabilize currencies in October.

At the same time, rivalry and even mistrust between Japan and West Germany developed under the strain of aggressive bilateralism. The perception of American–Japanese collusion deterred West Germany from coordinating policies. (Stoltenberg remarked that the much-celebrated G-2 was the right place to correct imbalances, as was described in chapter 7). It caused the European demands for differential appreciation of the yen in relation to European currencies to become more vociferous.

German reluctance to challenge the formation of a G-2 was also rooted in geopolitical considerations. West Germany is strengthened by its leadership position within the European Community, but if taken out of this setting, its bargaining position is much weaker.

Since mid-1986, the G-5 has focused on the problem of the Asian Newly Industrializing Countries (NICs). In the Louvre Accord and in subsequent announcements, the NICs were targeted as the villains for resisting the adjustment of external imbalances. Frustrated with the slow pace of adjustment, G-5 members needed to find an external scapegoat, although certainly the NICs did represent a challenge to the club.

The G-5 appears to be an appropriate forum through which to promote policy adjustments. It is composed of two institutions that compete over certain aspects of monetary policy, however, particularly the currency in each country—the finance ministry and the central bank.

Differences in political and institutional arrangements between countries complicate coordination of policy (see chapters 3–5). Japan and West Germany have not hidden their skepticism about the ability of the US administration to deliver, specifically its pledge to reduce the budget deficit, because it was understood that budget legislation was the domain of the Congress, not the executive branch. It is for this reason that the Gramm-Rudman-Hollings Amendment provoked a positive response from the others, since it appeared that progress would be made on the US budget.

From the point of view of the relationship between the Federal Reserve Board and the executive branch—the White House and the leadership of the Treasury—the Plaza strategy can be seen as an effort on the part of the executive branch to link the central bank's monetary policy more closely with its policy coordination initiatives, as was illustrated clearly in the nonpaper adopted at the Plaza (see chapter 1). Paradoxically, though, the appearance of mutual agreement prevented the administration from applying the old American political practice of using the Federal Reserve Board as a scapegoat.[47] The Reagan administration's "Fed-bashing," almost a routine practice during the first term, disappeared in the second term. Asked about the new administration's relation with the Federal Reserve Board, Baker responded:

[I]t ought to be a two-way street. If the Fed has a right to criticize fiscal policy, the Administration, after having made every effort to work privately and cooperatively, should, if it disagrees, have a corresponding right to criticize monetary policy. And it should not automatically be characterized as Fed-bashing.[48]

This departure from Fed-bashing was a sort of truce between Baker and Volcker. Baker recognized that Volcker's support of the Plaza strategy was necessary to its success.

---

47. On a political theory of "Fed as scapegoat," see Edward J. Kane, "Politics and Fed Policy Making: The More Things Change the More they Remain the Same," in *Central Bankers, Bureaucratic Incentives, and Monetary Policy*, ed. E. Froedge Toma and M. Toma (The Netherlands: Martinus Nijhoff, Kluwer Academic Publishers, 1987), chap. 10.

48. Tom Redburn, "U.S. Moves to Slow Rise of the Dollar," *Los Angeles Times*, 16 February 1985.

In West Germany, decentralized decision-making bodies and the undisputed independence of the Bundesbank add another deterrent to policy coordination. Although reluctance to subordinate its monetary policies to external consideration is not restricted to the German central bank, the Bundesbank has asserted the independence of its monetary policy most strongly. Nonetheless, officials in both Bonn and Frankfurt demonstrated their commitment to keep the EMS functioning smoothly—if necessary, by responding to member countries' pressure for deutsche mark realignment and interest rate reduction.

In Japan, structurally weak leadership—the bottom-to-top decision-making system, supremacy of domesticists over internationalists, Liberal Democratic Party (LDP) faction politics, institutionalized bureaucratic turf battles, and the ineffectiveness of the Prime Minister's office—has been preeminent in slowing the pace of policy coordination. Yet, a combination of factors (foreign pressure, lobbying by MITI and Gaimusho (Ministry of Foreign Affairs), Miyazawa's political agenda, and Nakasone's summit strategy) enabled Japan to come up with a 6 trillion yen stimulus package.

Burden Sharing

The most critical aspect of the mechanism building process has been conflict over how to divide the burden of adjustment between the surplus and deficit countries. The core of the problem with indicators was this very issue. As it had with the "Volcker" Plan in the early 1970s, the United States tried, in its most recent approach at the Tokyo Summit, to employ the indicator mechanism to shift the adjustment burden from deficit to surplus countries—contrary to the Bretton Woods system. The argument that "if you force the deficit countries to share the major burden, the deflationary bias is embedded in the system," was once again mobilized by the United States.

Intervention strategy was also the source of considerable contention, largely due to mutual distrust between the United States and West Germany over burden sharing. Each considered the intervention of the other inadequate. German officials insisted that dollar depreciation had begun, not with the Plaza, but in early 1985 and that the Bundesbank had already undertaken a disproportionate share of the burden. The United States and Japan both considered the Plaza Agreement the starting point of adjustment. Neither the United States nor Japan was convinced by West Germany's argument that intervention by EMS countries was inherently different because of the unique function of the Bundesbank in keeping exchange rates stable within the EMS. What some referred to as burden sharing, however, is a misnomer, since monetary authorities can in some cases make a profit from intervention.

A European G-5 regular commented, "What the hell do you mean by burden sharing? If this operation works, we all make money off it." And this was the case when some non-US central banks had to intervene by selling dollars as part of the intervention strategy after the Plaza meeting. Intervention, therefore, was not necessarily of the zero-sum nature that some have suggested. In sum, burden sharing, the key to the viability of any mechanism for policy coordination, has not occurred.

Commitment

The Plaza strategy produced two important international agreements: the nonpaper at the Plaza meeting and the reference range strategy at the Louvre meeting. In both cases, however, the intensity of the commitment among members varied. The United States openly considered them full agreements, while West Germany was less forthcoming. Chapters 1 and 8 noted the difficulty of referring to these as international agreements, given the informality and unregulated manner in which they were negotiated. German officials asserted that they would not tie themselves to any set of obligations, while Japanese authorities believed the same commitments to be more binding. The Germans attached greater importance to "signaling" the market and market developments than to the amount of the intervention strategy at the Plaza or the Louvre. Some participants even questioned the legitimacy of the nonpaper at the Plaza. As one Japanese later admitted, because of the German opposition he personally was uncertain how binding the intervention agreement really was (see chapter 1). As mentioned earlier, a lack of formality also characterized the arrangements of the Louvre Accord. In this respect, the Plaza strategy did not differ substantially from the ad hoc process of former G-5 agreements. As Tomomitsu Oba said, "It was highly difficult to build a give-and-take relationship on a time differential basis in an environment of no institutional memory because, not only would you not 'take' in return for giving, but once you would give, you might end up giving more the next time."[49] The rules of operation are loose enough to allow all participants to interpret them liberally and with discretion. Furthermore, the confidentiality of the arrangements makes verification nearly impossible, so individual credibility becomes suspect. At the same time, the markets are left guessing.

---

49. Tomomitsu Oba, "Political economy of currency diplomacy," *Toyo Keizai* (Oriental Economist), 22 May 1987, 12.

Central to the analysis of the Plaza strategy are its implications for international regime building. The most crucial question is whether the Louvre Accord will evolve into a new international monetary regime or whether it will collapse of its own weight. The unprecedented situation of the world's largest economy having the world's largest debt will force the United States to be more sensitive to the stability of the dollar in the years ahead, given its dependence on heavy injections of foreign capital.

Monetary and even fiscal policy making will be more sensitive to exchange rate considerations. The failure of the floating exchange rate nonsystem and the unexpected durability of the EMS will encourage efforts to buttress the Louvre Accord. Furthermore, many erstwhile worshippers of floating exchange rates in official circles have subtly shifted their positions. One of them, a governor of the Federal Reserve Board, confided that he shifted his position to that of a "dirty, dirty floater," sounding as if he still harbored guilt for his switch from a "pure floater."[50]

The idea of a strategy in two stages—first, to reduce imbalances, then to build a regime—has gradually gained support among Plaza strategy participants. Nigel Lawson's surprise conversion to the managed-float philosophy, whatever its motivation, was most dramatic. But more subtle changes in position were already under way among the monetary authorities in the G-5. One of the Japanese participants stated that there might be no alternative but to pursue a flexible and movable reference range system, on a trial and error basis, for a certain period of time.[51]

Even a usually skeptical West German official wondered about the possibility that the G-5 would inadvertently create a new system. "We are in a preparatory phase for a new system. I'm not sure. No, I am absolutely not willing to talk about a new system, but I'm not sure." The official referred to the meaning of the G-7 announcement on 23 December 1987 as the third stage, agreeing that the dollar should not fall further (after its soft landing at the Plaza and the reference range of the Louvre).[52]

With the emergence of Japan as a world banker and investor, and the gradual erosion of the Japanese monetary authorities' discretionary power over the exchange rate (due to liberalization of the capital market), it will be increasingly in Japan's interest to promote management and stability of the global monetary system.

Certainly, the Louvre Accord is fragile, as was elaborated in the previous

---

50. Interview with the author.

51. Personal interview.

52. Personal interview.

chapter. The failure to link currency realignment (via the reference range à la Louvre) to domestic fiscal and monetary policy adjustment was the most crucial area of its weakness. Besides that, US unilateralism did not completely give way to coordination. The temptation of US administrations to depreciate the dollar unilaterally has proven not to wither away during the period examined and is likely to remain in the future. It is too early, however, to declare, as some do, that the Louvre Accord is already dead. The process of which the Louvre Accord was a part is still evolving and will continue to exist simply because the G-5 countries do not have an alternative means to tackle the imbalance and currency instability problems. The gradual institutionalization of the currency stability mechanism which led to the Louvre Accord should be regarded as a useful learning process.

The Herculean task of institutionalizing the process of reform into a structural monetary regime, in which the rules of the game are stipulated clearly and observed regularly, remains to be achieved. It may be naive and unrealistic to envisage some kind of supranational policing system capable of enforcing the rules effectively, but as C. Fred Bergsten has pointed out, "No international system is worthy of the name unless it has consequential impact on national policies and tilts them in the direction of greater international compatibility—and thus sustainability."[53] Although the Plaza strategy has given impetus to regime building, in essence the exercise remains an ad hoc process of adjustment. On this point, it should be remembered that the inability to bring about an effective linkage between rebasing (realignment) of reference range and the macroeconomic policy adjustment strained the provisions of the Louvre Accord. The US effort to invigorate the indicator mechanism did not produce any concrete results and instead, helped, to a considerable degree, to undermine the Louvre Accord.

The United States introduced the indicator concept originally with the expectation that it would evolve into a more automatic system. The reform was therefore one of *process* as opposed to *structure*. The Treasury officials who promoted the idea agreed that the mechanism would require time to develop fully. The other participants in the G-5 also realized that its potential to evolve into a regime capable of handling international adjustment problems would depend on the political will of each government.

Strong resistance to the indicator mechanism among the G-5—from Japan, West Germany, and Great Britain, in particular—has remained constant throughout the period. Central bankers and representatives from economic agencies in each country have expressed legitimate concerns over the

---

53. C. Fred Bergsten, "Economic Imbalances and World Politics," *Foreign Affairs* 65 (Spring 1987): 770–794.

uncertainty of their jurisdictions and the potential erosion of their influence under an indicator system. Unlikely to recede in the foreseeable future is the issue of national sovereignty, which will erupt whenever a government is directed to change the course of its economy on the basis of economic indicators. In sum, political and institutional constraints have so far prevented the emergence of a viable indicator system.

Historical Perspective

The Plaza strategy emerged as a response to the anarchy produced by the "nonsystem" of floating exchange rates and to a growing recognition of economic interdependence. International coordination of economic policies was undertaken with the serious intention of managing the system. Coordination was meant to be the foundation on which an alternative system would be built.

Heightened economic sensibilities caused by increasing interdependence among countries tend to create, first, the politicization and domesticization of international economic policies—demonstrated by the mutual intervention agreed at the Plaza; second, the propensity to negotiate nearly all new policy initiatives—the Baker-Miyazawa Deal, for example; third, the inclination to manipulate policies with the use of "brinkmanship diplomacy"—Baker's near decision to cancel the Louvre meeting; and fourth, the temptation to exploit international agreement by threatening noncompliance—the US threat to nullify the Louvre Accord by letting the dollar fall in response to inadequate domestic stimulus in West Germany.[54]

As the linkage among trade policy, monetary policy, fiscal policy, and exchange rate policy has become stronger with each more sensitive to the others, greater policy coordination is required across a spectrum of issues. Economic interdependence among the G-5 has also been increased as the world financial and information revolutions have spawned deregulation of industries and liberalization of markets. The break-up of AT&T (1982), the privatization of NTT (1986), the liberalization of Japan's capital market (since 1980), London's "Big Bang" (1987), and the creation of 24-hour currency markets have accelerated the pace of interdependence and intensified the sensitivities of economies on an unprecedented scale. The Yen–Dollar Accord, which facilitated the steady flow of capital from Japan to the United States through the liberalization of the Japanese capital market,

---

54. With regard to the gradual increase in the power element involved in the process of economic interdependence, see Yoichi Funabashi, *Keizai Anzen Hosho Ron* (The theory of economic security) (Tokyo: Toyo Keizai Shimpo Sha, 1978).

contributed to the longevity of the supply-side strategy of attracting capital inflows and thereby further enmeshed the economies of the United States and Japan. Under these circumstances, the governments simply cannot afford to ignore the feed-back effects of their policies.

The "nonsystem" of floating exchange rates since 1973 has demonstrated that countries do not behave according to the predictions of the proponents of floating rates. There is almost unanimous consent that floating has caused excessive swings in exchange rates and the accumulation of unsustainable external imbalances that restrict the freedom of governments to shape and implement macroeconomic policy. The so-called "nonsystem" has further undermined international policy cooperation and contributed to a destabilization of the global trading system by unleashing protectionist forces with every swing of the exchange rate. In sum, to repeat the indictment by Michael Artis and Sylvia Ostry of the system of floating exchange rates, "it has implied a retrogression" because "opportunities for mutually beneficial policy readjustment have been and are being missed."[55] Although the alternative has thus been explored, and found wanting, the path to a new regime as discussed above, has been blocked by ideological, political, and economic constraints.

Finally, the strengthening of interdependence has accompanied the erosion of American leadership. The creation of the G-7 summit in 1975 was an acknowledgment of the need for collective leadership in international economic issues because of a perception of declining US hegemony. However, the strong dollar of the early 1980s created the illusion that "the United States is back," strengthened by Reagan's military build-up and supply-side economics. But by early 1985 this illusion had been dispelled when policymakers of the G-5 countries recognized the implications of the overvalued dollar and US deficits, and American leadership, once again, was thrown into question.

The most explicit expression of the limits of the US power was actually made by Treasury Secretary James A. Baker III in late 1986. Although it went almost unnoticed, Baker defined the new leadership role of the United States as follows:

Our leadership has taken a form different from that of recent historical experience. The recent model has been one of national dominance in an international economic system—as represented by the United States in the aftermath of World War II, or by Britain in the latter half of the 19th century. Our new leadership is more in the manner of an architect and builder, patiently and tenaciously pursuing a vision of economic growth

---

55. Artis and Ostry, *International Economic Policy Coordination,* p. 53.

and prosperity—trying to persuade others what may be accomplished while contributing our fair share.[56]

To exemplify this "new leadership . . . in the manner of an architect and builder," Baker cited six "headways": the Plaza Agreement in September 1985; coordinated discount rate reductions by the G-5 in March 1986; the second round of discount rate cuts by the G-5 absent Germany in April 1986; the indicator mechanism agreed on at the Tokyo Summit; the first multilateral surveillance exercise by the G-7 finance ministers in September 1986; and the Baker-Miyazawa communiqué in October 1986. And of course Baker later added what he called "another milestone"—the Louvre Accord.

This new concept of leadership will challenge the next administration, should nationalism or isolationism find its way into political initiatives. Yet, as the world's largest debtor the United States will become increasingly dependent on foreign capital inflows for its economic well-being, and the vision of reduced leadership—"a form different from the national dominance model"—will prove to be the inevitable alternative for the United States. The renewed, visible, erosion of US hegemony thus calls for enhanced coordination of policies, which will doubtless take place in the foreseeable future.

Conclusion

The G-5 Plaza strategy continues to be an evolving process, one of trial and error. The gradualistic process-building approach is not enough. Instead of achieving the consensual agreement of the G-5, policy coordination has in most instances depended on a series of deals within the context of the G-2 or the G-3. The possibility of backsliding, overcommitting, or reneging has continually threatened the credibility of these deals, in some instances removing incentives to further cooperation. The inherent anarchy of the "nonsystem" could overwhelm the ad hoc approach of the Plaza strategy.

In order to avoid this, the G-5—particularly Japan, the United States, and West Germany—must accelerate efforts to build a more credible and effective international monetary regime. Building consensus on the conceptual frame-work of policy coordination, to which the Plaza strategy contributed, should continue to be encouraged through pragmatic approaches, such as Volcker's "quiet mutual contingency planning." In order to manage the markets in a more systematic fashion, the G-5 countries should commit themselves fully

---

56. James A. Baker III, remarks before the Chicago Economic Club, 11 December 1986.

to policy coordination. On this point, the US talk-down policy contributed negatively to the otherwise more effective management of the markets.

The Plaza strategy failed to make binding the implementation of pledged policy changes. In this sense, it compares unfavorably with policy coordination launched by the Bonn Summit in 1978. The Plaza process did not create a process for confidence, mechanism, and regime building. These weaknesses have contributed to the vulnerability of the Louvre Accord.

The Louvre Accord can, however, be used as the starting point of an incremental experiment. A more strenuous effort to connect rebasement— or realignment—with monetary and fiscal policy coordination should be made. The effects of aggressive bilateralism have already highlighted the limits and danger of process diplomacy that is not accompanied by structural change. Without more clarity and guidelines, the process will surely lose momentum. Any structural change manifested in a new economic regime, moreover, must realistically give a larger share of the responsibility to Japan and West Germany and, perhaps, the EMS.

The indicator system initiated at the Tokyo Summit would ideally have assumed the politically painful task of adjusting macroeconomic policies. It is certainly beneficial and necessary for G-5 and G-7 to work toward an ideal type of multilateral surveillance mechanism. Yet no one should be deceived into thinking that the indicator system by itself, however sophisticated it may be, will replace political bargaining among nations. The G-7 indicator exercise should be made public to sensitize the domestic body politic in each country to the growth of interdependence in the global economy.

Specifically, increased awareness and understanding by various groups and institutions in different countries is necessary to increase opportunities for cross-border coalition building. Two strategic aspects of the coalition building merit special attention. The first is the need to exploit the G-7 summit, making it the highest vehicle of policy coordination. The second is the need to heighten the awareness of the constraints of domestic political and institutional arrangements to the policy coordination. The G-5 and G-7 countries have not fully exploited the new linkage between the G-5, the G-7, and the heads of state. It was designed to give the coordination process the necessary political authority as well as to create "a direct link between the formation of domestic policies and the international coordination process."[57] This linkage should be used and fully connected and tested so that the heads of state are able to transform the G-7 summit into

---

57. James A. Baker III remarks before the Joint World Bank–IMF Annual Meeting (Washington), 30 September 1987.

the highest headquarters for policy coordination—including fiscal policy adjustments, which is the most politically difficult task.

The ability to determine the obstacles to international policy coordination posed by particular institutional arrangements requires careful scrutiny of the domestic politics of each country involved. The checks-and-balances system of American politics and the role of the Congress in the formulation of fiscal, monetary, and trade policies, will continue to complicate efforts at coordination of policies among countries. It is advisable for the United States to seek domestic reinforcement through process reforms. Although the increased attention of the Congress to interest and exchange rate implications for the domestic economy will not automatically facilitate coordination, Congress should reorganize its present hydra-type jurisdiction over trade issues. Powerful committees in both houses—for example, the Senate Finance Committee, and the House Ways and Means Committee—should be assigned a greater role in international economic policy making. Only a full partnership between the executive and legislative branches will provide the means for constructive policy coordination. Summit meetings between the two branches to discuss macroeconomic policy adjustments—such as that which took place after the October stock market crash—should be encouraged before the annual G-7 summit meeting. The administration should be obliged to report the impact of exchange rates and the federal budget on the domestic and world economies. Public testimony by the Managing Director of the International Monetary Fund should also be encouraged.[58]

In Japan, structurally weak leadership will remain an obstacle to international policy coordination. Bureaucratic intransigence and the lack of strong initiatives from political circles will leave to market forces the task of rectifying imbalances and will therefore constitute a destabilizing force in international economic peacekeeping. It will require an enormous amount of intellectual and political energy to explore the possibility of political and institutional rearrangement or reform.

Fundamentally, this enormous task will only be accomplished by allowing the emerging economic and social transformations under way in Japan to be reflected in the political and electoral system. The policy recommendations presented in the Maekawa Reports address the new course Japan must take in the interest of its own survival and international economic peacekeeping, but this must be accompanied by political and institutional rearrangements. Japan should take advantage of the G-7 summit linkage with the G-5 and the G-7 to enhance the Prime Minister's authority to circumscribe the resistance from the bottom and to force the domesticists in the Kasumigaseki

---

58. Marris, "Managing the World Economy," 110–111.

bureaucracy to consider international repercussions in setting domestic policy. Simultaneously the Prime Minister should play a greater role in formulating international economic policy, thereby strengthening the leadership potential of the premiership.

On the level of political parties, the chairman of the Policy Research Council of the West German Liberal Democratic Party should become more fully engaged in international economic policy making. The unique viewpoint of the chairman, who controls the committees of sector "policy tribes," could strengthen the link between domestic policies and cooperation on the international level.

West Germany should also take a hard look at its policy-making system. The Bundesbank's monetary policy should have greater sensitivity to the need to manage and enliven the EMS. At the same time, the United States should be prepared to accept the EMS fully and redefine the role of the dollar with and within the EMS. It should be remembered, furthermore, that France had considerable influence in West Germany's rate cut in early 1987. Persistent support for target zones from the French in particular has provided a conceptual alternative to the floating exchange rate system. In very broad terms, the less ideological and nationalistic climate in France can continue to contribute much on the intellectual frontier. Baker's "French card" proved to be more effective when France took the initiative in pressuring West Germany to coordinate policies than when Baker simply blamed the Germans for doing nothing.

Political parties should also be enrolled in the coordination process. To keep Bonn and Frankfurt more accountable to their international responsibilities, the Free Democratic Party (FDP), one of the two most independent institutional actors in the German political system—the other, of course, being the Bundesbank—should have greater influence in the German effort at policy coordination. Only with its decisive views could "German stubbornness" be mellowed from within.

Finally, there is a need for greater coalition building across national borders. Forging coalitions across countries and between counterpart institutions requires imagination and a keen political sense to determine who, actually and potentially, shares interests most acutely. The FDP should play a bigger role in building coalitions on various levels. The Japanese MITI and the Ministry of Foreign Affairs could also form cross-agency coalitions if necessary. The G-7 economic summit should be exploited as a means for achieving this kind of coalition building among various agencies. Nevertheless, transnational coalition building to facilitate the policy coordination process is still minimal. In this sense, the G-5 countries have underutilized their greatest political asset—democratic and pluralist political institutions.

Chronology

	Forum	Event
1985		
17 January	G-5	Commitment to undertake coordinated intervention as necessary; Washington
25 February		Dollar peaks at 263.65 yen in New York market
26 February		Dollar peaks at 3.4770 deutsche marks in New York market
11 April		George P. Shultz speech; Princeton
2-4 May		Bonn Summit
19 June		Mulford-Oba bilateral talks
21 June		Baker-Takeshita exploratory talks
22 June	G-10	Publishes G-10 Report
22 July		EMS realignment
23 July	OECD Working Party 3	Mulford-Oba discuss monetary policy, trade policy, countering congressional protectionism; Paris
21 August		Mulford-Oba discuss monetary policy and US tax reform; Hawaii
15 September	G-5	Deputies negotiate Plaza Agreement; London
20–21 September	EC ministerial conference	Secret discussion among French, German, and British finance ministers and central bankers; Luxembourg
22 September	G-5	Plaza Agreement; New York

	Forum	Event
23 September		Reagan trade policy speech
1985		
6 October	G-5	IMF-World Bank Meeting; Seoul, South Korea
late October		BOJ raises the short-term interest rate (two-month bill rate) from 6.43% (September rate) to 8.12% (mid-December rate)
13 November	G-5	Deputies follow up on the Plaza meeting; Paris
12 December		Gramm-Rudman-Hollings signed into law by President Reagan
1986		
18–19 January	G-5	London; "satisfied with the progress"
30 January		Japanese interest rate cut from 5% to 4.5%
10 February	Bank for International Settlements	Volcker-Pöhl; agree to lower interest rates; Basel
24 February	Federal Reserve Board	"Palace coup": Volcker out-voted by governors on unilateral discount rate cut
6 March		West Germany lowers discount rate from 4% to 3.5%; France, from 8.5% to 8.25%
7 March		Japan lowers discount rate from 4.5% to 4%; United States, from 7.5% to 7%
16 March		French general elections
7 April		EMS realignment

	Forum	Event
8 April		Baker-Takeshita meeting; Washington
21 April		US–Japan coordinated discount-rate cut: Japan, from 4% to 3.5%; United States, from 7% to 6.5%
4–5 May		Tokyo Summit
30 May	G-5	Deputies follow up on indicator plan
6 July		LDP victory in Japanese elections; Miyazawa becomes Finance Minister, replacing Takeshita (who becomes General Secretary of the LDP)
10 July		Fed lowers discount rate from 6.5% to 6%
21 August		Fed lowers discount rate from 6% to 5.5%
1986		
21 September		European finance ministers united front against US talk-down policy; Gleneagles, Scotland
26 September	G-5	Washington
27 September	G-7	Washington
29–30 September		IMF–World Bank Joint Meeting; Washington
31 October		Baker-Miyazawa Accord; Japan lowers discount rate from 3.5% to 3%
4 November		US midterm elections; Democrats gain control of Senate
14 December		Baker-Stoltenberg meeting; Kiel, West Germany

	Forum	Event
1987		
12 January		EMS realignment
21 January		Baker-Miyazawa meeting: issue joint statement; Washington
23 January		Bundesbank lowers discount rate from 3.5% to 3%
25 January		West German elections
28 January		First US intervention to defend floor of dollar
29 January	G-5	Deputies meet in Zurich
4 February	G-7	Deputies' preparatory meeting for Venice Summit; Rome
20 February		Japan announces discount rate cut from 3% to 2.5%
21–22 February	G-5, G-7	Louvre Accord, Italy boycotts G-7 meeting; Paris
7 April	G-5	Yen–dollar range rebased; Washington
8 April	G-7	Washington
9–10 June		Venice Summit
4 September		Fed raises discount rate from 5.5% to 6%
26 September	G-7	Statement issued
19 October		Stock market crash
23 December		G-7 statement issued

List of Acronyms

BIS	Bank for International Settlements
BOJ	Bank of Japan (Japan)
CDU	Christian Democratic Union (West Germany)
CSU	Christian Social Union (West Germany)
CEA	Council of Economic Advisors (United States)
EPA	Economic Planning Agency (Japan)
EPC	Economic Policy Council (United States)
EMS	European Monetary System
FOMC	Federal Open Market Committee (of the US Federal Reserve Board)
FDP	Free Democratic Party (West Germany)
GAO	General Accounting Office (United States)
GATT	General Agreement on Tariffs and Trade
JETRO	Japan External Trade Organization
LDP	Liberal Democratic Party (Japan)
MOSS	Market Oriented Sector Selective Talks
MOF	Ministry of Finance (Japan)
MFA	Ministry of Foreign Affairs (Japan)
MITI	Ministry of International Trade and Industry (Japan)
NAM	National Association of Manufacturers (United States)
OECD	Organization for Economic Cooperation and Development
SPD	Social Democratic Party (West Germany)
USTR	United States Trade Representative
WP-3	Working Party 3 of the OECD

Individuals Interviewed by the Author

The United States

Wayne D. Angell, Governor, Board of Governors of the Federal Reserve System

Stephen H. Axilrod, Staff Director for Monetary and Financial Planning, Board of Governors of the Federal Reserve System

Norman A. Bailey, former Special Assistant to the President for National Security Affairs and Senior Director of International Economic Affairs

James A. Baker III, Secretary of the Treasury

E. Gerald Corrigan, President, Federal Reserve Bank of New York

Sam Y. Cross, Executive Vice President, Federal Reserve Bank of New York

Charles H. Dallara, Senior Deputy Assistant Secretary for International Economic Policy, Department of the Treasury

Stephen I. Danzansky, Senior Director, National Security Council

Michael R. Darby, Assistant Secretary for Economic Policy, Department of the Treasury

Richard G. Darman, Deputy Secretary of the Treasury

Thomas C. Dawson, Deputy Assistant to the President and Executive Assistant to the Chief of Staff to the President

Joseph B. Eichenberger, Assistant Financial Attaché, Embassy of the United States, West Germany

Robert C. Fauver, Director, Office of Industrial Nations and Global Analysis, Department of the Treasury

Martin Feldstein, former Chairman, Council of Economic Advisors

James Frierson, Chief of Staff, Office of the United States Trade Representative

Robert L. Harlow, Economist, Office of Industrial Nations and Global Analyses, Office of the Assistant Secretary for International Affairs, Department of the Treasury

John K. Hartzell, Financial Attaché, Embassy of the United States, West Germany

George R. Hoguet, former Principal Deputy Assistant Secretary for International Affairs, Department of the Treasury

Manuel H. Johnson, Jr., Vice Chairman, Board of Governors of the Federal Reserve System

Alfred H. Kingon, Cabinet Secretary and Assistant to the President

Marc E. Leland, former Assistant Secretary for International Affairs, Department of Treasury

Preston Martin, Vice Chairman, Board of Governors of the Federal Reserve System

Douglas W. McMinn, Assistant Secretary for Economic and Business Affairs, Department of State

Tim McNamar, former Deputy Secretary of the Treasury

Lee L. Morgan, Chairman of the Board (Retired), Caterpillar Tractor

David C. Mulford, Assistant Secretary for International Affairs, Department of the Treasury

William Niskanen, former Acting Chairman, Council of Economic Advisors

Bob Packwood, US Senator

Alexis Rieffel, Technical Director to the US Executive Director, International Monetary Fund

Steven M. Roberts, Assistant to the Chairman, Board of Governors of the Federal Reserve System

Gaston J. Sigur, Assistant Secretary for East Asian and Pacific Affairs, Department of State

Anthony Solomon, Chairman, S.G. Warburg (USA) Inc.

Beryl Sprinkel, Chairman, Council of Economic Advisors

Dennis Thomas, Assistant to the President

Edwin C. Truman, Director, Board of Governors of the Federal Reserve System

Paul A. Volcker, Chairman, Board of Governors of the Federal Reserve System

Allen W. Wallis, Under Secretary for Economic and Agricultural Affairs, Department of State

David Walters, Chief Economist, Office of the US Trade Representative

Robert B. Zoellick, Counselor to the Secretary and Executive Secretary of the Treasury

Japan

Shintaro Abe, Minister of Foreign Affairs; Chairman of the General Council, Liberal Democratic Party

Shoichi Akazawa, Chairman, Japan External Trade Organization

Shinji Fukukawa, Vice Minister of International Trade and Industry

Masaharu Gotoda, Minister of State, Chief Cabinet Secretary

Toyoo Gyoten, Vice Minister for International Affairs, Ministry of Finance

Kazutoshi Hasegawa, Private Secretary to the Prime Minister

Shigeru Hatakeyama, Director of the Research and Planning Division, Minister's Secretariat, Ministry of Finance

Takashi Hosomi, Chairman, Overseas Economic Cooperation Fund

Masayoshi Ito, Chairman of the Policy Research Council, Liberal Democratic Party

Yoshiaki Kaneko, Director of the Short-term Capital Division, International Finance Bureau, Ministry of Finance

Akira Kanno, Executive Director, Bank of Japan

Takehiko Kondo, Special Assistant to the Vice Minister of Finance for International Affairs, Ministry of Finance

Goro Koyama, Director and Counselor, the Mitsui Bank Limited

Isao Kubota, Special Assistant to the Vice Minister for International Affairs, Ministry of Finance

Michihiko Kunihiro, Director General, Councillor's Office on External Affairs, Cabinet Secretary

Haruhiko Kuroda, Counselor of the Minister's Secretariat, Ministry of Finance

Nobuo Matsunaga, Ambassador to the United States

Haruo Maekawa, Chairman of the Board of Directors, Kokusai Denshin Denwa Co., Ltd; former Governor of the Bank of Japan

Kiichi Miyazawa, Chairman of the General Council, Liberal Democratic Party; Minister of Finance

Yashushi Mieno, Senior Deputy Governor, Bank of Japan

Akio Morita, Chairman, Sony Corporation

Atsushi Nagano, Personal Secretary to the Minister of Finance

Yasuhiro Nakasone, Prime Minister

Akira Nishigaki, Director General of the Budget Bureau, Ministry of Finance

Atsuo Nishihara, Counselor, Embassy of Japan, West Germany

Tomomitsu Oba, Vice Minister for International Affairs, Ministry of Finance

Shijuro Ogata, Deputy Governor for International Relations, Bank of Japan

Takeshi Ohta, Deputy Governor for International Relations, Bank of Japan

Yoshiyuki Okuma, Chief of the Foreign Exchange Division/Foreign Department, Bank of Japan

Eisuke Sakakibara, Director of the First Fund Planning and Operation Division/ Finance Bureau, Ministry of Finance

Shigemitsu Sugisaki, Director of the Research Division, Tax Bureau, Ministry of Finance

Satoshi Sumita, Governor of the Bank of Japan

Noboru Takeshita, Minister of Finance; Secretary General of the Liberal Democratic Party

Yo Takeuchi, Chief Representative of the Japan Center for International Finance, Washington

Hajime Tamura, Minister of International Trade and Industry

Masaaki Tsuchida, Private Secretary to the Prime Minister

Makoto Utsumi, Minister, Embassy of Japan, the United States; Director General of the International Finance Bureau, Ministry of Finance

Koji Watanabe, Director General of the Economic Affairs Bureau, Ministry of Foreign Affairs

Michio Watanabe, Minister of International Trade and Industry

Ken Yagi, Special Officer for Research and Planning, International Finance Bureau, Ministry of Finance

Mitsuhide Yamaguchi, Vice Minister of Finance

Izumi Yamashita, Chief Represenative in Frankfurt, Bank of Japan

Yoshihiko Yoshino, Vice Minister of Finance

Western Europe

Edouard Balladur, French Minister of Finance

Nicholas Bayne, United Kingdom Permanent Representative to the Organization for Economic Cooperation and Development

Alain Benon, Cabinet Secretary to the French Minister of Finance

Jonathan C. Carr, Chief Correspondent to Bonn, *The Economist*

Jacques de Larosière, Governor, Bank of France

Lamberto Dini, Deputy Governor, Bank of Italy

Karlheinz von den Driesch, Assistant to the West German Minister of Finance

Leonhard Gleske, Director, German Bundesbank

Wolfgang Glomb, Assistant to the Vice Minister of Finance, West Germany

Georg Grimm, Director General for Economic and Financial Policy, West German Chancellor's Office

Guenter Grosche, Executive Director for West Germany, International Monetary Fund

Gerd Hausler, Head of the President's Office, German Bundesbank

Norbert Kloten, Member of the Council, German Bundesbank

Daniel Lebegue, Director of the Treasury, French Ministry of Finance

Geoffrey Littler, Second Permanent Secretary, H.M. Treasury, the United Kingdom

Anthony D. Loehnis, Overseas Director, Bank of England

Christian Merle, Assistant to the Director of the Treasury, French Ministry of Finance

Bernhard Molitor, Director of Economic Policy, West German Ministry of Economics

Hélène Ploix, Executive Director for France, International Monetary Fund

Karl Otto Pöhl, President, German Bundesbank

Wolfgang Rieke, Department Head of the International Division, German Bundesbank

Rudiger Von Rosen, Executive Vice Chairman, Federation of the German Stock Exchange

Helmut Schmidt, Former Chancellor of West Germany

Helmut Schlesinger, Vice Chairman and Deputy President, German Bundesbank

Horst Schulmann, Deputy Managing Director, The Institute of International Finance

Theo Sommer, Editor-in-Chief, *Die Zeit*

Gerhard Stoltenberg, West German Minister of Finance

Hans Tietmeyer, West German Vice Minister of Finance

Jean-Claude Trichet, Director of the Treasury, French Ministry of Finance

Norbert Walter, Senior Economist, Deutsche Bank

Documents

1. Announcement by G-5 Ministers and Governors

January 17, 1985

The Ministers of Finance and Central Bank Governors of France, Germany, Japan, the United Kingdom, and the United States announced today that they had met to discuss a range of international economic and financial issues. The meeting, part of a regular series of consultations among these countries on economic and financial matters of mutual interest, also involved IMF Managing Director de Larosière for a discussion of the economic policies and prospects of the major industrial countries.

The Ministers and Governors, noting the recent developments in the exchange markets, expressed their commitment to work toward greater exchange market stability. Toward this end, the Ministers and Governors:

- Reaffirmed their commitment to pursue monetary and fiscal policies that promote a convergence of economic performance at non-inflationary, steady growth;

- Stressed the importance of removing structural rigidities in their economies to achieving the objectives of non-inflationary, steady growth and exchange market stability, and expressed their intent to intensify efforts in this area; and

- In light of recent developments in foreign exchange markets, reaffirmed their commitment made at the Williamsburg Summit to undertake coordinated intervention in the markets as necesssary.

The Ministers and Governors believe that this approach will provide a solid framework for sustaining recovery, reducing inflation, increasing employment, and achieving greater exchange rate stability.

2. Announcement of the Ministers of Finance and Central Bank Governors of France, Germany, Japan, the United Kingdom, and the United States

September 22, 1985

1. Ministers of Finance and Central Bank Governors of France, the Federal Republic of Germany, Japan, the United Kingdom, and the United States met today, September 22, 1985, in the context of their agreement to conduct mutual surveillance and as part of their preparations for wider international discussions at the forthcoming meetings in Seoul, Korea. They reviewed economic developments and policies in each of their countries and assessed their implications for economic prospects, external balances, and exchange rates.

2. At the Bonn Economic Summit in May 1985 the Heads of State or Government of seven major industrial countries and the President of the Commission of the European Communities issued an Economic Declaration Towards Sustained Growth and Higher Employment. In that Declaration the participants agreed that:

> The best contribution we can make to a lasting new prosperity in which all nations can share is unremittingly to pursue, individually in our own countries and cooperatively together, policies conducive to sustained growth and higher employment.

3. The Ministers and Governors were of the view that significant progress has been made in their efforts to promote a convergence of favorable economic performance among their countries on a path of steady noninflationary growth. Furthermore, they concluded that their countries are restoring the vitality and responsiveness of their economies. As a result of these developments, they are confident that a firm basis has been established for a sustained, more balanced expansion among their countries. This sustained growth will benefit other industrial countries and will help ensure expanding export markets for developing countries, thereby contributing importantly to the resolution of problems of heavily indebted developing countries.

4. They believe that this convergence of favorable economic performance has been influenced increasingly by policy initiatives undertaken by their countries. Moreover, each of their countries is committed to the implementation of further policy measures which will reinforce favorable convergence and strengthen the sustainability of the current expansion.

5. Ministers and Governors were of the view that recent shifts in fundamental economic conditions among their countries, together with policy commitments for the future, have not been reflected fully in exchange markets.

Recent Economic Developments and Policy Changes

6. Ministers and Governors expect that real growth in aggregate for their countries will be about 3 percent this year, compared to negative growth of −0.7 percent in 1982. Although this figure is down slightly from 1984, growth will be more balanced than at any time in the last four years. After the particularly rapid U.S. growth of 1983–84, there is now increased evidence of internal growth in the other countries. In particular, private investment has picked up strength. The current expansion is occurring in a context of fiscal consolidation; it is not dependent on shortlived fiscal stimulus. As a result of the changes in the components of growth, real growth in their countries can be expected to remain strong as U.S. growth moderates.

7. The current sustained expansion is occurring within a framework of declining inflation, a phenomenon that is unprecedented in the past three decades. Inflation rates are at their lowest in nearly 20 years, and they show no signs of reviving.

8. There has been a significant fall in interest rates in recent years. Apart from welcome domestic effects, this has been particularly helpful in easing the burden of debt repayments for developing countries.

9. This successful performance is the direct result of the importance given to macroeconomic policies which have reduced inflation and inflationary expectations, to continued vigilance over government spending, to greater emphasis on market forces and competition, and to prudent monetary policies.

10. These positive economic developments notwithstanding, there are large imbalances in external positions which pose potential problems, and which reflect a wide range of factors. Among these are: the deterioration in its external position which the U.S. experienced from its period of very rapid relative growth; the particularly large impact on the U.S. current account of the economic difficulties and the adjustment efforts of some major developing countries; the difficulty of trade access in some markets; and the appreciation of the U.S. dollar. The interaction of these factors—relative growth rates, the debt problems of developing countries, and exchange rate developments—has contributed to large, potentially destabilizing external imbalances among major industrial countries. In particular, the United States has a large and growing current account deficit, and Japan, and to a lesser extent Germany, large and growing current account surpluses.

11. The U.S. current account deficit, together with other factors, is now contributing to protectionist pressures which, if not resisted, could lead to mutually destructive retaliation with serious damage to the world economy: world trade would shrink, real growth rates could even turn negative, unemployment would rise still higher, and debt-burdened developing countries would be unable to secure the export earnings they vitally need.

Policy Intentions

12. The Finance Ministers and Governors affirmed that each of their countries remains firmly committed to its international responsibilities and obligations as

leading industrial nations. They also share special responsibilities to ensure the mutual consistency of their individual policies. The Ministers agreed that establishing more widely strong, noninflationary domestic growth and open markets will be a key factor in ensuring that the current expansion continues in a more balanced fashion, and they committed themselves to policies toward that end. In countries where the budget deficit is too high, further measures to reduce the deficit substantially are urgently required.

13. Ministers and Governors agreed that it was essential that protectionist pressures be resisted.

14. Ministers recognized the importance of providing access to their markets for LDC exports as those countries continue their essential adjustment efforts, and saw this as an important additional reason to avoid protectionist policies. They welcomed the GATT preparatory meeting scheduled for late September and expressed their hope that it will reach a broad consensus on subject matter and modalities for a new GATT round.

15. In this context, they recalled and reaffirmed the statement in the Bonn Economic Declaration on the debt situation.

> Sustained growth in world trade, lower interest rates, open markets and continued financing in amounts and on terms appropriate to each individual case are essential to enable developing countries to achieve sound growth and overcome their economic and financial difficulties.

16. The Ministers agreed that they would monitor progress in achieving a sustained noninflationary expansion and intensify their individual and cooperative efforts to accomplish this objective. To that end, they affirmed the statements of policy intentions by each of their countries, which are attached.

Conclusions

17. The Ministers of Finance and Central Bank Governors agreed that recent economic developments and policy changes, when combined with the specific policy intentions described in the attached statements, provide a sound basis for continued and a more balanced expansion with low inflation. They agreed on the importance of these improvements for redressing the large and growing external imbalances that have developed. In that connection, they noted that further market opening measures will be important to resisting protectionism.

18. The Ministers and Governors agreed that exchange rates should play a role in adjusting external imbalances. In order to do this, exchange rates should better reflect fundamental economic conditions than has been the case. They believe that agreed policy actions must be implemented and reinforced to improve the fundamentals further, and that in view of the present and prospective changes in fundamentals, some further orderly appreciation of the main non-dollar currencies against the dollar is desirable. They stand ready to cooperate more closely to encourage this when to do so would be helpful.

The *French Government* intends to pursue its policy aimed at reducing inflation, moderating income growth, and achieving continued improvements in external accounts. It will further intensify its efforts to speed up structural adjustment and modernization and thus lay the basis for job creating growth.

Therefore, it is determined:

1. To pursue vigorously disinflation.

2. To secure the attainment of monetary aggregates growth targets, consistent with decelerating inflation.

3. To curb public expenditures progressively so as to lower the tax burden while reducing the government borrowing requirement.

4. To foster the investment recovery allowed for by the improved financial situation in the business sector.

5. To take further steps towards liberalization and modernization of financial markets, to increase competition in the financial sector so as to reduce financial intermediation costs, and give a greater role to interest rates in monetary control.

6. To foster job creation through the implementation of an innovative and active policy in the field of education and training and by promoting constructive discussions between social partners on work organization.

7. To resist protectionism.

The *Government of the Federal Republic of Germany,* noting that the German economy is already embarked on a course of steady economic recovery based increasingly on internally generated growth, will continue to implement policies to sustain and extend the progress achieved in strengthening the underlying conditions for continuing, vigorous, job-creating growth in the context of stable prices and low interest rates.

In particular, the Government of the Federal Republic of Germany will implement policies with the following explicit intentions.

1. The priority objective of fiscal policy is to encourage private initiative and productive investments and maintain price stability.

2. Toward this end, the Federal Government will continue to reduce progressively the share of the public sector in the economy through maintaining firm expenditure control. The tax cuts due to take effect in 1986 and 1988 form part of the ongoing process of tax reform and reduction which the Federal Government will continue in a medium-term framework.

3. The Federal Government will continue to remove rigidities inhibiting the efficient functioning of markets. It will keep under review policies, regulations, and practices affecting labor markets in order to enhance the positive impact of economic growth on employment. The Federal Government and the Deutsche Bundesbank will provide the framework for the continuing evolution of deep, efficient money and capital markets.

4. The fiscal policy of the Federal Government and the monetary policy of

the Deutsche Bundesbank will continue to ensure a stable environment conducive to the expansion of domestic demand on a durable basis.

5. The Federal Government will continue to resist protectionism.

The *Government of Japan,* noting that the Japanese economy is in an autonomous expansion phase mainly supported by domestic private demand increase, will continue to institute policies intended to ensure sustainable noninflationary growth; provide full access to domestic markets for foreign goods; and internationalize the yen and liberalize domestic capital markets.

In particular, the Government of Japan will implement policies with the following explicit intentions.

1. Resistance of protectionism and steady implementation of the Action Program announced on July 30 for the further opening up of Japan's domestic market to foreign goods and services.

2. Full utilization of private sector vitality through the implementation of vigorous deregulation measures.

3. Flexible management of monetary policy with due attention to the yen rate.

4. Intensified implemention of financial market liberalization and internationalization of the yen, so that the yen fully reflects the underlying strength of the Japanese economy.

5. Fiscal policy will continue to focus on the twin goals of reducing the central government deficit and providing a pro-growth environment for the private sector. Within that framework, local governments may be favorably allowed to make additional investments in this FY 1985, taking into account the individual circumstances of the region.

6. Efforts to stimulate domestic demand will focus on increasing private consumption and investment through measures to enlarge consumer and mortgage credit markets.

The *United Kingdom Government,* noting that the British economy has been experiencing steady growth of output and domestic demand over the past four years, will continue to pursue policies designed to reduce inflation; to promote sustained growth of output and employment; to reduce the size of the public sector; to encourage a more competitive, innovative, market orientated private sector; to reduce regulation and increase incentives throughout the economy; and to maintain open trading and capital markets free of foreign exchange controls:

In particular, the United Kingdom Government intends:

1. To operate monetary policy to achieve further progress towards price stability and to provide a financial environment for growing output and employment; and to buttress monetary policy with a prudent fiscal policy.

2. To continue to reduce public expenditure as a share of GDP and to

transfer further substantial parts of public sector industry to private ownership.

3. To reduce the burden of taxation in order to improve incentives and to increase the efficient use of resources in the economy.

4. To take additional measures to improve the effective working of the labour market, including the reform of Wages Councils and improvements in youth training; and implement proposals to liberalize and strengthen competition within financial markets.

5. To resist protectionism.

The *United States Government* is firmly committed to policies designed to: ensure steady noninflationary growth; maximize the role of markets and private sector participation in the economy; reduce the size and role of the government sector; and maintain open markets.

In order to achieve these objectives, the United States Government will:

1. Continue efforts to reduce government expenditures as a share of GNP in order to reduce the fiscal deficit and to free up resources for the private sector.

2. Implement fully the deficit reduction package for fiscal year 1986. This package passed by Congress and approved by the President will not only reduce by over 1 percent of GNP the budget for FY 1986, but lay the basis for further significant reductions in the deficit in subsequent years.

3. Implement revenue-neutral tax reform which will encourage savings, create new work incentives, and increase the efficiency of the economy, thereby fostering noninflationary growth.

4. Conduct monetary policy to provide a financial environment conducive to sustainable growth and continued progress toward price stability.

5. Resist protectionist measures.

3. Tokyo Economic Declaration

May 6, 1986

1. We, the Heads of State or Government of seven major industrialized countries and the representatives of the European Community, meeting in Tokyo for the twelfth Economic Summit, have reviewed developments in the world economy since our meeting in Bonn a year ago, and have reaffirmed our continuing determination to work together to sustain and improve the prosperity and well-being of the peoples of our own countries, to support the developing countries in their efforts to promote their economic growth and prosperity, and to improve the functioning of the world monetary and trading systems.

2. Developments since our last meeting reflect the effectiveness of the policies to which we have committed ourselves at successive Economic Summits in recent years. The economies of the industrialized countries are now in their fourth year of expansion. In all our countries, the rate of inflation has been declining. With the continuing pursuit of prudent fiscal and monetary policies, this has permitted a substantial lowering of interest rates. There has been a significant shift in the pattern of exchange rates which better reflects fundamental economic conditions. For the industrialized countries, and indeed for the world economy, the recent decline in oil prices will help to sustain non-inflationary growth and to increase the volume of world trade, despite the difficulties which it creates for certain oil-producing countries. Overall, these developments offer brighter prospects for, and enhance confidence in, the future of the world economy.

3. However, the world economy still faces a number of difficult challenges which could impair sustainability of growth. Among these are high unemployment, large domestic and external imbalances, uncertainty about the future behaviour of exchange rates, persistent protectionist pressures, continuing difficulties of many developing countries and severe debt problems for some, and uncertainty about medium-term prospects for the levels of energy prices. If large imbalances and other distortions are allowed to persist for too long, they will present an increasing threat to world economic growth and to the open multilateral trading system. We cannot afford to relax our efforts. In formulating our policies, we need to look to the medium and longer term, and to have regard to the interrelated and structural character of current problems.

4. We stress the need to implement effective structural adjustment policies in all countries across the whole range of economic activities to promote growth; employment and the integration of domestic economies into the world economy. Such policies include technological innovation, adaptation of industrial structure, and expansion of trade and foreign direct investment.

5. In each of our own countries, it remains essential to maintain a firm control of public spending within an appropriate medium-term framework of fiscal and monetary policies. In some of our countries there continue to be excessive fiscal deficits which the governments concerned are resolved progressively to reduce.

6. Since our last meeting we have had some success in the creation of new jobs to meet additions to the labour force, but unemployment remains excessively high in many of our countries. Non-inflationary growth remains the biggest single contributor to the limitation and reduction of unemployment, but it needs to be reinforced by policies which encourage job creation, particularly in new and high-technology industries, and in small businesses.

7. At the same time, it is important that there should be close and continuous coordination of economic policy among the seven Summit countries. We welcome the recent examples of improved coordination among the Group of Five Finance Ministers and Central Bankers, which have helped to change the pattern of exchange rates and to lower interest rates on an orderly and non-inflationary basis. We agree, however, that additional measures should be taken to ensure that procedures for effective coordination of international economic policy are strengthened further. To this end, the Heads of State or Government:

■ agree to form a new Group of Seven Finance Ministers, including Italy and Canada, which will work together more closely and more frequently in the periods between the annual Summit meetings;

■ request the seven Finance Ministers to review their individual economic objectives and forecasts collectively at least once a year, using the indicators specified below, with a particular view to examining their mutual compatibility;

With the representatives of the European Community:

■ state that the purposes of improved coordination should explicitly include promoting non-inflationary economic growth, strengthening market-oriented incentives for employment and productive investment, opening the international trading and investment system, and fostering greater stability in exchange rates;

■ reaffirm the undertaking at the 1982 Versailles Summit to cooperate with the IMF in strengthening multilateral surveillance, particularly among the countries whose currencies constitute the SDR, and request that, in conducting such surveillance and in conjunction with the Managing Director of the IMF, their individual economic forecasts should be reviewed, taking into account indicators such as GNP growth rates, inflation rates, interest rates, unemployment rates, fiscal deficit ratios, current account and trade balances, monetary growth rates, reserves, and exchange rates;

■ invite the Finance Ministers and Central Bankers in conducting multilateral surveillance to make their best efforts to reach an understanding on appropriate remedial measures whenever there are significant deviations from an intended course; and recommend that remedial efforts focus first and foremost on underlying policy fundamentals, while reaffirming the 1983 Williamsburg commitment to intervene in exchange markets when to do so would be helpful.

The Heads of State or Government:

■ request the Group of Five Finance Ministers to include Canada and Italy in

their meetings whenever the management or the improvement of the international monetary system and related economic policy measures are to be
discussed and dealt with;

- invite Finance Ministers to report progress at the next Economic Summit
meeting.

These improvements in coordination should be accompanied by similar efforts
within the Group of Ten.

8. The pursuit of these policies by the industrialized countries will help the
developing countries in so far as it strengthens the world economy, creates
conditions for lower interest rates, generates the possibility of increased financial
flows to the developing countries, promotes transfer of technology, and improves
access to the markets of the industrialized countries. At the same time, developing
countries, particularly debtor countries, can fit themselves to play a fuller part
in the world economy by adopting effective structural adjustment policies,
coupled with measures to mobilize domestic savings, to encourage the repatriation of capital, to improve the environment for foreign investment, and to
promote more open trading policies. In this connection, noting in particular the
difficult situation facing those countries highly dependent on exports of primary
commodities, we agree to continue to support their efforts for further processing
of their products and for diversifying their economies, and to take account of
their export needs in formulating our own trade and domestic policies.

9. Private financial flows will continue to play a major part in providing for
their development needs. We reaffirm our willingness to maintain and, where
appropriate, expand official fincancial flows, both bilateral and multilateral, to
developing countries. In this connection, we attach great importance to an early
and substantial eighth replenishment of the International Development Association (IDA) and to a general capital increase of the World Bank when
appropriate. We look for progress in activating the Multilateral Investment
Guarantee Agency.

10. We reaffirm the continued importance of the case-by-case approach to
international debt problems. We welcome the progress made in developing the
cooperative debt strategy, in particular building on the United States initiative.
The role of the international financial institutions, including the multilateral
development banks, will continue to be central, and we welcome moves for
closer cooperation among these institutions, and particularly between the IMF
and the World Bank. Sound adjustment programmes will also need resumed
commercial bank lending, flexibility in rescheduling debt, and appropriate access
to export credits.

11. We welcome the improvement which has occurred in the food situation in
Africa. Nonetheless a number of African countries continue to need emergency
aid, and we stand ready to assist. More generally, we continue to recognize the
high priority to be given to meeting the needs of Africa. Measures identified in
the Report on Aid to Africa adopted and forwarded to us by our Foreign Ministers
should be steadily implemented. Assistance should focus in particular on the
medium- and long-term economic development of these countries. In this
connection we attach great importance to continued cooperation through the

Special Facility for Sub-Saharan African countries, early implementation of the newly established Structural Adjustment Facility of the IMF and the use of the IDA. We intend to participate actively in the forthcoming United Nations Special Session on Africa to lay the foundation for the region's long-term development.

12. The open multilateral trading system is one of the keys to the efficiency and expansion of the world economy. We reaffirm our commitment to halting and reversing protectionism, and to reducing and dismantling trade restrictions. We support the strengthening of the system and functioning of the GATT, its adaptation to new developments in world trade and to the international economic environment, and the bringing of new issues under international discipline. The New Round should, *inter alia,* address the issues of trade in services and trade related aspects of intellectual property rights and foreign direct investment. Further liberalization of trade is, we believe, of no less importance for the developing countries than for ourselves, and we are fully committed to the preparatory process in the GATT with a view to the early launching of the New Round of multilateral trade negotiations. We shall work at the September Ministerial meeting to make decisive progress in this direction.

13. We note with concern that a situation of global structural surplus now exists for some important agricultural products, arising partly from technological improvements, partly from changes in the world market situation, and partly from long-standing policies of domestic subsidy and protection of agriculture in all our countries. This harms the economies of certain developing countries and is likely to aggravate the risk of wider protectionist pressures. This is a problem which we all share and can be dealt with only in cooperation with each other. We all recognize the importance of agriculture to the well-being of rural communities, but we are agreed that, when there are surpluses, action is needed to redirect policies and adjust structure of agricultural production in the light of world demand. We recognize the importance of understanding these issues and express our determination to give full support to the work of the OECD in this field.

14. Bearing in mind that the recent oil price decline owes much to the cooperative energy policies which we have pursued during the past decade, we recognize the need for continuity of policies for achieving long-term energy market stability and security of supply. We note that the current oil market situation enables countries which wish to do so to increase stock levels.

15. We reaffirm the importance of science and technology for the dynamic growth of the world economy and take note, with appreciation, of the final report of the Working Group on Technology, Growth, and Employment. We welcome the progress made by the United States Manned Space Programme and the progress made by the autonomous work of the European Space Agency (ESA). We stress the importance for genuine partnership and appropriate exchange of information, experience, and technologies among the participating states. We also note with satisfaction the results of the Symposium on Neuro-science and Ethics, hosted by the Federal Republic of Germany and we appreciate the decision of the Canadian Government to host the next meeting.

16. We reaffirm our responsibility, shared with other governments, to preserve

the natural environment, and continue to attach importance to international cooperation in the effective prevention and control of pollution and natural resources management. In this regard, we take note of the work of the environmental experts on the improvement and harmonization of the techniques and practices of environmental measurement, and ask them to report as soon as possible. We also recognize the need to strengthen cooperation with developing countries in the area of the environment.

17. We have agreed to meet again in 1987 and have accepted the invitation of the President of the Council of the Italian Government to meet in Italy.

4. Statement of the Group of Seven Finance Ministers

September 27, 1986

1. The Finance Ministers of seven major industrialized countries met today to conduct the first exercise of multilateral surveillance pursuant to the Tokyo Economic Declaration of their Heads of State or Government of May 6, 1986. The Managing Director of the International Monetary Fund also participated in this meeting.

2. The Ministers reviewed recent economic developments and their economic objectives and forecasts collectively, using a range of economic indicators, with a particular view to examining their mutual compatibility and to considering the need for remedial measures.

3. The Ministers noted that progress had been made in promoting steady, non-inflationary growth in their countries.

4. There is broad agreement among the Ministers on the economic outlook in their countries: Prospects for further growth in 1987 are generally favorable, and more jobs will be created, although the level of unemployment will remain high in some countries. Inflation is likely to remain low. Interest rates have fallen with particular beneficial effects for indebted developing countries.

5. However, the Ministers noted that the present scale of some current account imbalances cannot be sustained. The exchange rate changes since last year are making an important contribution towards redressing these imbalances, and their full effects will increasingly come through in the period ahead.

6. The Ministers agreed that cooperative efforts need to be intensified in order to reduce the imbalances in the context of an open, growing world economy. They noted, in this connection, that economic growth in surplus countries was improving, but such growth will need to be sustained—and in some cases increased. Countries with major deficits must follow policies which will foster significant reductions in their external deficits, and they committed themselves, among other things, to make further progress in reducing their budget deficits in order to free resources to the external sector. These actions should help stabilize exchange rates, and all are necessary so that imbalances can be reduced sufficiently without further significant exchange rate adjustment.

7. In the circumstances, the Ministers agreed that the policies of all countries during the period immediately ahead would be formulated with the following objectives in mind:

■ To continue to follow sound monetary policies supporting non-inflationary growth and contributing to international adjustment in order to help maintain the conditions for business confidence and for lower interest rates.

■ To continue the process of removing structural rigidities in order to increase the long-term production potential of their economies.

■ To continue efforts to resist protectionist pressures.

8. The Ministers agreed that the major industrial countries bear a special responsibility to foster an open, growing world economy which is particularly important for the resolution of the international debt problem.

9. In order to fulfill their responsibilities in the context of thorough implementation of the Tokyo Economic Declaration used to achieve the objectives set out above, they agreed to the close and continuous coordination of economic policy during the period ahead.

5. Baker-Miyazawa Joint Communiqué

October 31, 1986

U.S. Secretary of the Treasury, James A. Baker III and Japanese Finance Minister Kiichi Miyazawa today announced that, as part of the ongoing dialogue between the United States and Japan on economic, trade, and financial issues, they have reached agreement on cooperative action and understandings regarding a number of economic issues of mutual concern.

Both Ministers stressed the importance of continuing cooperative action by Japan and the United States to address global economic problems. They agreed that action by the key industrial countries is critical at this time to promoting world economic growth, reducing imbalances, and resolving international debt problems.

In this connection, Minister Miyazawa outlined the following actions being taken by Japan to help fulfill its responsibilities in the world economy:

- The Government of Japan (GOJ) has decided today to submit to the Diet a supplementary budget in order to implement the 3.6 trillion yen package announced in September, designed to provide a substantial stimulus to the Japanese economy. This stimulus will be achieved through additional investments in key areas such as public works, housing, and construction. The GOJ will monitor progress in implementing expeditiously the stimulus package to assure that its expected impact on growth is realized.

- The GOJ intends to put in place, as soon as possible after Diet approval, a tax reform plan, including reductions in the marginal tax rates for both personal and corporate income. In this connection it was noted that on October 28 the Government Tax Council recommended, following its interim report, reducing the effective tax rate for corporations to below 50 percent and reducing the highest marginal tax rate on personal income. Such cuts in tax rates will increase investment and give incentive for more business activities. More generally, the tax reform will provide a system which better reflects taxpayers' choice, unleashing the growth potential of the Japanese economy. The structure and implementation of tax reform would provide additional stimulus to the Japanese economy while providing for needed financing to continue the process of fiscal consolidation.

- The Bank of Japan has decided today to reduce its discount rate from 3.5 percent to 3 percent, effective November 1, 1986.

Secretary Baker welcomed the actions and plans of Japan to stimulate growth and to reduce imbalances. He stated that, for its part, the United States:

- Remains fully committed to significant and steady reductions in the U.S. budget deficit, consistent with the Gramm-Rudman-Hollings Act;

- Has just enacted an historic tax reform which will provide additional incentives to invest and to work and will promote growth in the U.S. economy; and

■ Has continued to resist protectionist pressures and work towards free and fair trade.

Minister Miyazawa expressed his appreciation for U.S. policies in these areas, noting that they complement Japan's economic policy actions.

Minister Miyazawa and Secretary Baker agreed that these actions will contribute significantly to promoting growth in Japan, the United States, and the rest of the world, as well as to reducing global trade imbalances. In this connection, they shared the view that exchange rate instability can jeopardize stable economic growth. They expressed their mutual understanding that with the actions and commitments mentioned above, the exchange rate realignment achieved between the yen and the dollar since the Plaza Agreement is now broadly consistent with the present underlying fundamentals and reaffirmed their willingness to cooperate on exchange market issues.

Secretary Baker and Minister Miyazawa expressed their common view that these cooperative actions represent important steps in fulfilling their commitments from the Tokyo Summit, and the September meeting of the Group of Seven Finance Ministers in Washington, to pursue close and continuous coordination of economic policy. They agreed to stay in close touch on these matters, and called on other major industrial countries to join in these efforts to promote global growth, reduce imbalances, and promote open markets.

6. Baker-Miyazawa Joint Communiqué

January 21, 1987

Japanese Minister of Finance, Kiichi Miyazawa and U.S. Secretary of Treasury, James A. Baker, III met today to discuss economic, trade, and financial issues of mutual interests to their countries.

Both ministers stated their continued support for the understandings and agreements contained in their joint announcement of Oct. 31, 1986. In this connection, they agreed to continue cooperative efforts to stimulate growth and to reduce external imbalances.

Secretary Baker and Minister Miyazawa agreed that developments in exchange markets warrant monitoring. The ministers expressed their view that during most of the period since Oct. 31, 1986, the yen/dollar exchange rate has been broadly consistent with underlying fundamentals, although there were recent instances of temporary instability in exchange market. Accordingly, the ministers reaffirmed their willingness to cooperate on exchange market issue.

Both ministers agreed that in order to promote global growth, reduce imbalances and promote open market, closer coordination of economic policies among all major industrial countries is critical. Towards this end, they agreed to intensify consultations with other major industrial countries.

7. G-6 Communiqué

February 22, 1987

1. Ministers of Finance and Central Bank Governors of six major industrialized countries met today in Paris to conduct multilateral surveillance of their economies in the framework of the Tokyo Economic Declaration of May 6, 1986 pursuant to which the group of seven Finance Ministers was formed. The Ministers and Governors, using a range of economic indicators, reviewed current economic developments and prospects. The Managing Director of the IMF participated in the discussions.

2. The Ministers and Governors were of the view that further progress had been made since the Tokyo Summit in their efforts to achieve a sustainable, non-inflationary expansion. Their national economies are now in the fifth year of expansion, and the prospects are for continued growth this year, although the level of unemployment remains unacceptably high in some countries. A high degree of price stability has been attained, and there have been substantial reductions in interest rates. Exchange rate adjustments have occurred which will contribute importantly in the period ahead to the restoration of a more sustainable pattern of current accounts.

3. Progress is being made in reducing budget deficits in deficit countries, and fundamental tax reforms are being introduced to improve incentives, increase the efficiency of economies, and enhance the prospects of higher growth. Other important structural reforms are also being carried forward, including deregulation of business to increase efficiency and privatization of government enterprises to strengthen reliance on private entrepreneurs and market forces.

4. These positive developments notwithstanding, the Ministers and Governors recognize that the large trade and current account imbalances of some countries pose serious economic and political risks. They agreed that the reduction of the large unsustainable trade imbalances is a matter of high priority, and that the achievement of more balanced global growth should play a central role in bringing about such a reduction.

5. The Ministers and Governors reaffirmed their concern over continuing pressures for protectionism. They agreed that efforts to deal with economic problems by erecting trade barriers were self-defeating and pledged to intensify their efforts to resist protectionism and reaffirmed their strong support for the new round of trade negotiations. They welcomed the progress made in the preparatory work for the new GATT round and the recent positive conclusions of discussions between the United States and the European Community on bilateral trade issues.

6. The Ministers and Governors recognized that the major industrial countries have a special responsibility to follow policies which foster an open, growing world economy in order to support the efforts of developing countries, especially

debtor countries, to restore steady growth and viable balance of payments positions. They noted that the progress achieved by many debtor countries toward these ends have not solved all the problems and stressed the importance of all participants in the strengthened debt strategy reinforcing their cooperative efforts.

7. The Ministers and Governors agreed to intensify their economic policy coordination efforts in order to promote more balanced global growth and to reduce existing imbalances. Surplus countries committed themselves to follow policies designed to strengthen domestic demand and to reduce their external surpluses while maintaining price stability. Deficit countries committed themselves to follow policies designed to encourage steady, low-inflation growth while reducing their domestic imbalances and external deficits. To this end, each country has agreed to the following undertakings.

The Government of *Canada's* policy is designed to sustain the current economic expansion through its fifth year and beyond. In the budget for 1987/88, the Government has cut the fiscal deficit for the third consecutive year and remains committed to further progressive reduction. Canada will propose shortly an extensive reform of its tax system. It will continue with its policies of regulatory reform, privatization, and liberalization of domestic markets. It will vigorously pursue trade liberalization bilaterally with the United States and multilaterally within the Uruguay round. Monetary policies will continue to aim at the reduction of inflation and be consistent with orderly exchange markets.

The Government of *France* will reduce the central government budget deficit by 1 percent of GNP from 1986 to 1988 and in the same period will implement a tax cut program of the same order of magnitude (1 percent of GNP) with substantial tax rate cuts for corporations and individuals. It will pursue in 1987 its privatization program (with a projected $6 to $7 billion sale of assets) and reinforce the liberalization of the French economy, especially of labor and financial markets.

The Government of the *Federal Republic of Germany* will pursue policies to diminish further the share of public expenditures in the economy and to reduce the tax burden for individuals and corporations with a comprehensive tax reform aimed at reinforcing the incentives for private sector activity and investment. In addition, the Government will propose to increase the size of the tax reductions already enacted for 1988. The Federal Government will emphasize policies that enhance market forces in order to foster structural adjustment and innovation. Short-term interest rates, although already at a very low level in international comparison, have further dropped substantially during the last few weeks. Monetary policy will be directed at improving the conditions for sustained economic growth while maintaining price stability.

The Government of *Japan* will follow monetary and fiscal policies which will help to expand domestic demand and thereby contribute to reducing the external surplus. The comprehensive tax reform, now before the Diet, will give additional stimulus to the vitality of the Japanese economy. Every effort will be made to get the 1987 budget approved by the Diet so that its early implementation be ensured. A comprehensive economic program will be prepared after the approval of the 1987 budget by the Diet, so as to stimulate domestic demand, with the prevailing economic situation duly taken into account. The Bank of Japan announced that it will reduce its discount rate by one half percent on February 23.

The *United Kingdom* Government will maintain conditions for continuing the steady growth of GDP of the past five years and will continue to work to reduce inflation by following a prudent monetary policy. On external account the aim will be broad balance over the medium term. The share of public expenditure in the economy will continue to fall and the burden of taxation will be reduced, while public sector borrowing is maintained at low level. These and other measures to strengthen the supply performance of the economy, such as the privatization programme, will reinforce improvement over recent years in the growth of productivity.

The *United States* Government will pursue policies with a view to reducing the fiscal 1988 deficit to 2.3% of GNP from its estimated level of 3.9% in fiscal 1987. For this purpose, the growth in government expenditures will be held to less than 1 percent in fiscal 1988 as part of the continuing program to reduce the share of government in GNP from its current level of 23 percent. The United States will introduce a wide range of policies to improve its competitiveness and to enhance the strength and flexibility of its economy. Monetary policy will be consistent with economic expansion at a sustainable non-inflationary pace.

8. The Ministers and Governors noted that a number of newly industrialized economies were playing an increasingly important role in world trade. These economies have achieved strong growth based significantly on their access to open, growing export markets. Recently, some have accumulated trade surpluses which have contributed importantly to the present unsustainable pattern of global imbalances, thus increasing protectionist pressures. The Ministers and Governors considered that it is important that the newly industrialized developing economies should assume greater responsibility for preserving an open world trading system by reducing trade barriers and pursuing policies that allow their currencies to reflect more fully underlying economic fundamentals.

9. The Ministers and Governors also agreed to additional refinements in the use of economic indicators for the multilateral surveillance arrangements approved in the Tokyo Economic Declaration. As part of these refinements, they will:

■ periodically review medium-term economic objectives and projections involving domestic and external variables. The medium-term objectives and projections are to be mutually consistent and will serve as a basis for assessing national policies and performance;

■ regularly examine, using performance indicators, whether current economic developments and trends are consistent with the medium-term objectives and projections and consider the need for remedial action.

Initially, the objectives and projections will involve the following key variables: growth, inflation, current accounts/trade balances, budget performance, monetary conditions, and exchange rates.

10. The Ministers and Governors agreed that the substantial exchange rate changes since the Plaza Agreement will increasingly contribute to reducing

external imbalances and have now brought their currencies within ranges broadly consistent with underlying economic fundamentals, given the policy commitments summarized in this statement. Further substantial exchange rate shifts among their currencies could damage growth and adjustment prospects in their countries. In current circumstances, therefore, they agreed to cooperate closely to foster stability of exchange rates around current levels.

8. Statement of the Group of Seven

April 8, 1987

1. The Finance Ministers and Central Bank Governors of seven major industrial countries met today. They continued the process of multilateral surveillance of their economies pursuant to the arrangements for strengthened economic policy coordination agreed at the 1986 Tokyo Summit of their Heads of State or Government. The Managing Director of the International Monetary Fund also participated in the meeting.

2. The Ministers and Governors reaffirmed the commitment to the cooperative approach agreed at the recent Paris meeting, and noted the progress achieved in implementing the undertakings embodied in the Louvre Agreement. They agreed, however, that further actions will be essential to resist rising protectionist pressures, sustain global economic expansion, and reduce trade imbalances. In this connection they welcomed the proposals just announced by the governing Liberal Democratic Party in Japan for extraordinary and urgent measures to stimulate Japan's economy through early implementation of a large supplementary budget exceeding those of previous years, as well as unprecedented front-end loading of public works expenditures. The Government of Japan reaffirmed its intention to further open up its domestic markets to foreign goods and services.

3. The Ministers and Governors reaffirmed the view that around current levels their currencies are within ranges broadly consistent with economic fundamentals and the basic policy intentions outlined at the Louvre meeting. In that connection they welcomed the strong implementation of the Louvre agreement. They concluded that present and prospective progress in implementing the policy undertakings at the Louvre and in this statement provided a basis for continuing close cooperation to foster the stability of exchange rates.

9. Venezia Economic Declaration

June 10, 1987

Introduction

1. We, the Heads of State or Government of the seven major industrialized countries and the representatives of the European Community, have met in Venice from 8 to 10 June 1987, to review the progress that our countries have made, individually and collectively, in carrying out the policies to which we committed ourselves at earlier Summits. We remain determined to pursue these policies for growth, stability, employment, and prosperity for our own countries and for the world economy.

2. We can look back on a number of positive developments since we met a year ago. Growth is continuing into its fifth consecutive year, albeit at lower rates. Average inflation rates have come down. Interest rates have generally declined. Changes have occurred in relationships among leading currencies which over time will contribute to a more sustainable pattern of current account positions and have brought exchange rates within ranges broadly consistent with economic fundamentals. In volume terms the adjustment of trade flows is under way, although in nominal terms imbalances so far remain too large.

Macroeconomic policies and exchange rates

3. Since Tokyo, the Summit countries have intensified their economic policy coordination with a view to ensuring internal consistency of domestic policies and their international compatibility. This is essential to achieving stronger and sustained global growth, reduced external imbalances, and more stable exchange rate relationships. Given the policy agreements reached at the Louvre and in Washington, further substantial shifts in exchange rates could prove counterproductive to efforts to increase growth and facilitate adjustment. We reaffirm our commitment to the swift and full implementation of those agreements.

4. We now need to overcome the problems that nevertheless remain in some of our countries: external imbalances that are still large; persistently high unemployment; large public sector deficits; and high levels of real interest rates. There are also continuing trade restrictions and increased protectionist pressures, persistent weakness of many primary commodity markets, and reduced prospects for developing countries to grow, find the markets they need and service their foreign debt.

5. The correction of external imbalances will be a long and difficult process. Exchange rate changes alone will not solve the problem of correcting these imbalances while sustaining growth. Surplus countries will design their policies to strengthen domestic demand and reduce external surpluses while maintaining price stability. Deficit countries, while following policies designed to encourage steady low-inflation growth, will reduce their fiscal and external imbalances.

6. We call on other industrial countries to participate in the effort to sustain economic activity worldwide. We also call on newly industrialized economies with rapid growth and large external surpluses to assume greater responsibility for preserving an open world trading system by reducing trade barriers and pursuing policies that allow their currencies more fully to reflect underlying fundamentals.

7. Among the Summit countries, budgetary discipline remains an important medium-term objective and the reduction of existing public sector imbalances a necessity for a number of them. Those Summit countries which have made significant progress in fiscal consolidation and have large external surpluses remain committed to following fiscal and monetary policies designed to strengthen domestic growth, within a framework of medium-term fiscal objectives. Monetary policy should also support non-inflationary growth and foster stability of exchange rates. In view of the outlook for low inflation in many countries, a further market-led decline of interest rates would be helpful.

Structural policies

8. We also agree on the need for effective structural policies especially for creating jobs. To this end we shall:

- promote deregulation in order to speed up industrial adjustment;
- reduce major imbalances between agricultural supply and demand;
- facilitate job creating investment;
- improve the functioning of labour markets;
- promote the further opening of internal markets;
- encourage the elimination of capital market imperfections and restrictions and the improvement of the functioning of international financial markets.

Multilateral surveillance and policy coordination

9. We warmly welcome the progress achieved by the Group of Seven Finance Ministers in developing and implementing strengthened arrangements for multilateral surveillance and economic coordination as called for in Tokyo last year. The new process of coordination, involving the use of economic indicators, will enhance efforts to achieve more consistent and mutually compatible policies by our countries.

10. The Heads of State or Government reaffirm the important policy commitments and undertakings adopted at the Louvre and Washington meetings of the Group of Seven, including those relating to exchange rates. They agree that, if in the future world economic growth is insufficient, additional actions will be required to achieve their common objectives. Accordingly, they call on their Finance Ministers to develop, if necessary, additional appropriate policy measures for this purpose and to continue to cooperate closely to foster stability of exchange rates.

11. The coordination of economic policies is an ongoing process which will

evolve and become more effective over time. The Heads of State or Government endorse the understandings reached by the Group of Seven Finance Ministers to strengthen, with the assistance of the International Monetary Fund (IMF), the surveillance of their economies using economic indicators including exchange rates, in particular by:

■ the commitment by each country to develop medium-term objectives and projections for its economy, and for the group to develop objectives and projections, that are mutually consistent both individually and collectively; and

■ the use of performance indicators to review and assess current economic trends and to determine whether there are significant deviations from an intended course that require consideration of remedial actions.

12. The Heads of State or Government consider these measures important steps towards promoting sustained non-inflationary global growth and greater currency stability. They call upon the Group of Seven Finance Ministers and Central Bank Governors to:

■ intensify their coordination efforts with a view to achieving prompt and effective implementation of the agreed policy undertakings and commitments;

■ monitor economic developments closely in cooperation with the Managing Director of the IMF; and

■ consider further improvements as appropriate to make the coordination process more effective.

Trade

13. We note rising protectionist pressures with grave concern. The Uruguay Round can play an important role in maintaining and strengthening the multilateral trading system, and achieving increased liberalization of trade for the benefit of all countries. Recognizing the interrelationship among growth, trade, and development, it is essential to improve the multilateral system based on the principles and rules of the General Agreement on Tariffs and Trade (GATT) and bring about a wider coverage of world trade under agreed, effective, and enforceable multilateral discipline. Protectionist actions would be counterproductive, would increase the risk of further exchange rate instability, and would exacerbate the problems of development and indebtedness.

14. We endorse fully the commitment to adopt appropriate measures in compliance with the principles of stand-still and rollback which have been reaffirmed in the Ministerial Declaration on the Uruguay Round. It is important to establish in the GATT a multilateral framework of principles and rules for trade in services, trade-related investment measures and intellectual property rights. This extension of the multilateral trading system would also be beneficial to developing countries in fostering growth and enhancing trade, investment and technology transfers.

15. Basing ourselves on the Ministerial Declaration on the Uruguay Round and on the principles of the GATT, we call on all Contracting Parties to negotiate

comprehensively, in good faith and with due despatch, with a view to ensuring mutual advantage and increased benefits to all participants. Canada, Japan, the United States and the European Community will table a wide range of substantive proposals in Geneva over the coming months. Progress in the Uruguay Round will be kept under close political review. In this context the launching, the conduct, and the implementation of the outcome of the negotiations should be treated as parts of a single undertaking; however, agreements reached at an early stage might be implemented on a provisional or definitive basis by agreement prior to the formal conclusion of the negotiations, and should be taken into account in assessing the overall balance of the negotiations.

16. A strong, credible, working GATT is essential to the well-being of all trading countries and is the best bulwark against mounting bilateral protectionist pressures. The functioning of the GATT should be improved through enhancing its role in maintaining an open multilateral system and its ability to manage disputes; and through ensuring better coordination between the GATT and the IMF and the World Bank. We consider that it would be useful to have, as appropriate, in the course of the negotiations, a meeting of the Trade Negotiating Committee at the Ministerial level.

Agriculture

17. At Tokyo we recognized the serious nature of the agricultural problem. We agreed that the structure of agricultural production needed to be adjusted in the light of world demand, and expressed our determination to give full support to the work of the OECD in this field. In doing so, we all recognized the importance of agriculture to the well-being of our rural communities. In the past year, we have actively pursued the approach outlined at Tokyo, and we take satisfaction from the agreement in the Ministerial Declaration adopted in Punta del Este on the objectives for the negotiations on agriculture in the Uruguay Round.

18. We reaffirm our commitment to the important agreement on agriculture set out in the OECD Ministerial communiqué of May 13, 1987; in particular, the statement of the scope and urgency of the problem which require that a concerted reform of agricultural policies be implemented in a balanced and flexible manner; the assessment of the grave implications, for developed and developing countries alike, of the growing imbalances in supply of and demand for the main agricultural products; the acknowledgment of shared responsibility for the problems as well as for their equitable, effective and durable resolution; the principles of reform and the action required. The long-term objective is to allow market signals to influence the orientation of agricultural production, by way of a progressive and concerted reduction of agricultural support, as well as by all other appropriate means, giving consideration to social and other concerns, such as food security, environmental protection, and overall employment.

19. We underscore our commitment to work in concert to achieve the necessary adjustments of agricultural policies, both at home and through comprehensive negotiations in the Uruguay Round. In this as in other fields, we will table comprehensive proposals for negotiations in the coming months to be conducted in accordance with the mandate in the Ministerial Declaration, and we intend to review at our next meeting the progress achieved and the tasks that remain.

20. In the meantime, in order to create a climate of greater confidence which would enhance the prospect for rapid progress in the Uruguay Round as a whole and as a step towards the long-term result to be expected from those negotiations, we have agreed, and call upon other countries to agree, to refrain from actions which, by further stimulating production of agricultural commodities in surplus, increasing protection or destabilizing world markets, would worsen the negotiating climate and, more generally, damage trade relations.

Developing countries and debt

21. We attach particular importance to fostering stable economic progress in developing countries, with all their diverse situations and needs. The problems of many heavily indebted developing countries are a cause of economic and political concern and can be a threat to political stability in countries with democratic regimes. We salute the courageous efforts of many of these countries to achieve economic growth and stability.

22. We underline the continuing importance of official development assistance and welcome the increased efforts of some of our countries in this respect. We recall the target already established by international organizations (0,7%) for the future level of official development assistance and we take note that overall financial flows are important to development. We strongly support the activities of international financial institutions, including those regional development banks which foster policy reforms by borrowers and finance their programmes of structural adjustment. In particular:

- we support the central role of the IMF through its advice and financing and encourage closer cooperation between the IMF and the World Bank, especially in their structural adjustment lending;

- we note with satisfaction the contribution made by the Eighth replenishment of the International Development Association (IDA);

- we support a general capital increase of the World Bank when justified by increased demand for quality lending, by its expanded role in the debt strategy and by the necessity to maintain the financial stability of the institution;

- in the light of the different contributions of our countries to official development assistance, we welcome the recent initiative of the Japanese government in bringing forward a new scheme which will increase the provision of resources from Japan to developing countries.

23. For the major middle-income debtors, we continue to support the present growth-oriented case-by-case strategy. Three elements are needed to strengthen the growth prospects of debtor countries: the adoption of comprehensive macroeconomic and structural reforms by debtor countries themselves; the enhancement of lending by international financial institutions, in particular the World Bank; and adequate commercial bank lending in support of debtor country reforms. We shall play our part by helping to sustain growth and expand trade. A number of debt agreements have allowed some resumption of growth, correction of imbalances, and significant progress in restoring the creditworthi-

ness of some countries. But some still lack adequate policies for structural adjustment and growth designed to encourage the efficient use of domestic savings, the repatriation of flight capital, increased flows of foreign direct investment, and in particular reforms of financial markets.

24. There is equally a need for timely and effective mobilization of lending by commercial banks. In this context, we support efforts by commercial banks and debtor countries to develop a "menu" of alternative negotiating procedures and financing techniques for providing continuing support to debtor countries.

25. Measures should be taken, particularly by debtor countries, to facilitate non-debt-creating capital flows, especially direct investment. In this connection, the Multilateral Investment Guarantee Agency (MIGA) should begin to serve its objectives as soon as possible. It is important to maintain flexibility on the part of export credit agencies in promptly resuming or increasing cover for countries that are implementing comprehensive adjustment programmes.

26. We recognize the problems of developing countries whose economies are solely or predominantly dependent on exports of primary commodities the prices of which are persistently depressed. It is important that the functioning of commodity markets should be improved, for example, through better information and greater transparency. Further diversification of these economies should be encouraged, with the help of the international financial institutions, through policies to support their efforts for improved processing of their products, to expand opportunities through market access liberalization, and to strengthen the international environment for structural change.

27. We recognize that the problems of some of the poorest countries, primarily in sub-Saharan Africa, are uniquely difficult and need special treatment. These countries are characterized by such features as acute poverty, limited resources to invest in their own development, unmanageable debt burdens, heavy reliance on one or two commodities, and the fact that their debt is owed for the most part to governments of industrialized countries themselves or to international financial institutions. For those of the poorest countries that are undertaking adjustment effort, consideration should be given to the possibility of applying lower interest rates to their existing debt, and agreement should be reached, especially in the Paris Club, on longer repayment and grace periods to ease the debt service burden. We welcome the various proposals made in this area by some of us and also the proposal by the Managing Director of the IMF for a significant increase in the resources of the Structural Adjustment Facility over the three years from January 1, 1988. We urge a conclusion on discussions on these proposals within this year.

28. We note that UNCTAD VII provides an opportunity for a discussion with developing countries with a view to arriving at a common perception of the major problems and policy issues in the world economy.

Environment

29. Further to our previous commitment to preserve a healthy environment and to pass it on to future generations, we welcome the report by the environment

experts on the improvement and harmonization of techniques and practices of environmental measurement. Accordingly, we encourage the United Nations Environment Programme (UNEP) to institute a forum for information exchange and consultation in cooperation with the International Organization for Standardization (ISO) and the International Council of Scientific Union (ICSU), assisted by other interested international organizations and countries, so that continuing progress in this important field can be ensured. The priority environmental problems identified by the environment experts in their report should receive full attention.

30. We underline our own responsibility to encourage efforts to tackle effectively environmental problems of worldwide impact such as stratospheric ozone depletion, climate change, acid rains, endangered species, hazardous substances, air and water pollution, and destruction of tropical forests. We also intend to examine further enviromental issues such as stringent environmental standards as an incentive for innovation and for the development of clean, cost-effective and low-resource technology as well as promotion of international trade in low-pollution products, low-polluting industrial plants and other environmental protection technologies.

31. We welcome the important progress achieved since Tokyo, particularly in the International Atomic Energy Agency, in enhancing effective international cooperation, with regard to safety in the management of nuclear energy.

Other issues

32. We welcome the initiative of the Human Frontier Science Programme presented by Japan, which is aimed at promoting, through international cooperation, basic research on biological functions. We are grateful for the informal opportunities our scientists have had to take part in some of the discussions of the feasibility study undertaken by Japan. We note that this study will be continued and we would be pleased to be kept informed about its progress.

33. We welcome the positive contribution made by the Conference of High Level Experts on the future role of education in our society, held in Kyoto in January 1987.

34. We shall continue to review the ethical implications of developments in the life sciences. Following the Conferences sponsored by Summit governments—by Japan in 1984, by France in 1985, by the Federal Republic of Germany in 1986, and by Canada in 1987—we welcome the Italian government's offer to host the next bioethics Conference in Italy in April 1988.

Next Economic Summit

35. We have agreed to meet again next year and have accepted the invitation of the Canadian Prime Minister to meet in Canada.

* * * * *

10. Statement of the Group of Seven

September 26, 1987

1. The Finance Ministers and Central Bank Governors of seven major industrial countries met today. The Managing Director of the IMF also participated in the meeting. This continues the economic policy coordination process agreed by their Heads of State or Government at the 1986 Tokyo Summit and strengthened at the 1987 Venice Summit meetings. The Ministers and Governors are convinced that this process, including the use of economic indicators, provides an important and effective means of promoting a healthy and prosperous world economy and stable monetary system.

2. The Ministers and Governors reviewed together the events, policy developments, and evolution of foreign exchange markets since the Louvre Agreement and the April G-7 meeting in Washington. They were pleased with the exchange rate stability which has been achieved and which has benefitted their policies and performance.

3. In the Louvre Agreement the Ministers and Governors set out the policies which they intended individually to pursue, and undertook to monitor them together and as necessary intensify or adapt them. They note that some important decisions have been taken in individual countries which were envisaged in the February statement, and that generally the evolution of policies has been along the lines intended.

4. Some important favorable results are beginning to be seen. The substantial reduction in fiscal 1987 in the United States federal budget deficit is a very positive step, as is the continued determination in resisting protectionist pressures, and they particularly welcomed the announcement today by the President of the United States of his decision to sign legislation which will reinforce progress in reducing the budget deficit. The major program of additional expenditures and income tax cuts in Japan is being rapidly implemented. In Germany the reductions in income taxes from January 1988 will be greater than previously planned and the legislation for them has already been enacted. There have been reductions in external imbalances in real terms, although they remain high. Growth in domestic demand in surplus countries is picking up, but it is important that it improves further in some countries.

5. The Ministers and Governors note that the large trade surpluses of some newly industrialized economies continue to be an important factor contributing to external imbalances. They repeat their view expressed on earlier occasions that these economies should reflect their growing importance and responsibilities by reducing trade barriers and pursuing policies that allow their currencies to reflect more fully underlying economic fundamentals.

6. The Ministers and Governors commit themselves to take further appropriate actions as necessary to achieve the agreed goals set forth in the Louvre Agreement. They will particularly intensify their efforts to liberalize markets, implement tax reforms and pursue other structural changes to strengthen the vitality of their

economies, to foster a high rate of sustained non-inflationary growth and to reduce external imbalances. They reaffirmed their determination to fight protectionism, and to promote an open world trading system.

7. The Ministers and Governors reaffirmed their intentions to carry forward their economic policy coordination efforts. During the coming year the developments of their economies will be monitored closely under the strengthened surveillance arrangements outlined in the Venice Summit. In light of the progress achieved to date in laying the basis for a reduction of imbalances, and the prospects for further progress, Ministers and Governors reaffirmed that currencies are within ranges broadly consistent with underlying economic fundamentals. They recommitted themselves to continue to cooperate closely to foster the stability of exchange rates around current levels.

11. Statement of the Group of Seven

December 22, 1987

1. The Finance Ministers and Central Bank Governors of seven major industrial countries have conducted close consultations in recent weeks on their economic policies and prospects in light of developments in financial markets. They reaffirmed their conviction that the basic objectives and economic policy directions agreed in the Louvre Accord remain valid and provide for a positive development of the world economy. They will continue to carry forward their economic policy coordination efforts in 1988 under the arrangements endorsed at the Venice Summit.

2. The Ministers and Governors reemphasized their view that the major external imbalances in the world economy must be corrected. The policies which have been implemented this year are gradually showing the intended effects. In particular, the balance between domestic demand and output in the United States and in Japan and the Federal Republic of Germany has shifted in a direction which promotes external adjustment and in volume terms their trade imbalances are diminishing. The greater stability of exchange rates achieved for much of the past year, following the earlier substantial exchange rate changes, contributed to this adjustment. The marked exchange rate changes over the past few weeks, however, stress the need to strengthen underlying economic fundamentals and to continue policy cooperation.

3. Developments in stock markets since mid October may have some adverse effect on prospects for economic growth for the industrialized countries as a group. The Ministers and Governors believe, however, that with sound economic policies and effective coordination the rate of growth should be substantial. To this end they agreed that appropriate policies for strengthening non-inflationary growth in their countries are necessary.

4. Accordingly, the Ministers and Governors agreed to intensify their economic policy coordination efforts. Their common efforts are directed towards reducing external imbalances. In particular, the United States has secured Congressional action to implement the agreement between the President and the bipartisan Congressional Leadership on a two-year package of additional budget savings that will reinforce progress in reducing the budget deficit. Japan has implemented a major stimulus program to strengthen domestic demand and will see to it that in the FY 1988 budget the expenditure for general public works will not be less than that for the FY 1987 budget including the July supplemental. The Federal Republic of Germany will accelerate progress towards the increased, more balanced economic growth, and substainable external positions necessary for greater exchange rate stability.

Annex:
Policy Intentions and Undertakings

The *Government of Canada*'s fiscal strategy has succeeded in achieving a drop in the rate of growth of its spending and substantial, on-going declines in the budget deficit. Marked progress has been made in slowing the growth of debt, and towards the medium-term objective of stabilizing the debt-to-GDP ratio. Fiscal restraint has been accompanied by impressive growth of domestic demand, output and employment. Major structural initiatives directed at enhancing competitiveness and the underlying potential of the economy have been undertaken, particularly tax reform and the negotiation of a free trade agreement with the United States. Monetary policy remains geared to non-inflationary growth in a climate of orderly exchange markets.

The *Government of France* has fully met its commitment to reduce its fiscal deficit and tax burden. The fiscal deficit will be reduced by 0.8% of GNP from 1986 to 1988. Over the same period of time, tax cuts will amount to 1.3% of GNP. A further reduction of 45 billion french francs in the fiscal deficit and an additional 45 billion french francs in tax cuts are scheduled in a 1989–1991 three year program which constitutes the long term strategy of the government and will be implemented in the yearly budgets. The privatization program decided upon in early 1987 is being carried out, and its initial objectives have even been surpassed. The full implementation of the program will be resumed as soon as market conditions permit.

The French Government will continue to pursue its adjustment and liberalization policies. New measures to sustain household savings, develop financial markets and improve the competitiveness of firms have been taken. Additional steps will be taken in the same direction in 1988.

The *Government of the Federal Republic of Germany* has increased the amount of the tax reductions for 1988 and beyond to about 14 billion DM, and will not seek to offset the budget revenue losses arising from recent developments. In addition, the necessary decisions have been taken for the structural tax reform with a further net tax reduction of 20 billion DM from 1990 onward.

In order to strengthen private and public investment, the Federal Government will provide special loans for the next 3 years of about 21 billion DM under preferential conditions. Moreover, it will accelerate investment in telecommunication infrastructure and take initiatives for further deregulation of markets.

The Bundesbank has reduced short-term interest rates substantially during the last few weeks. Monetary policy will budget savings to reduce the U.S. budget deficit. This agreement provides for total budget savings, through a combination of spending restraint and increased taxes, in fiscal 1988 and 1989 of approximately $76 billion.

The budget agreement is part of an ongoing process of deficit reduction provided for under the revised Gramm-Rudman-Hollings legislation. It will reinforce the progress already achieved in reducing the deficit (including a fiscal 1987 cut of $73 billion or 1.9 percent of GNP) that has brought the deficit down to 3.4 percent of GNP from a peak of 6.3 percent.

The Administration will also continue to oppose steadfastly protectionist trade measures, while working for legislation authorizing negotiations to foster a more open and fair system for the international exchange of goods, services, and investment.

294

SPECIAL REPORTS

FORTHCOMING